ROME AND THE ROMANS

ROME, SHOWING TOMB OF HADRIAN

ROME AND THE ROMANS

A Survey and Interpretation

BY

GRANT SHOWERMAN, Ph.D.

PROFESSOR OF CLASSICS IN THE UNIVERSITY OF WISCONSIN, MADISON, WISCONSIN
DIRECTOR OF THE SUMMER SESSION, THE AMERICAN ACADEMY IN ROME
HONORARY DOCTOR OF THE UNIVERSITY OF PADUA
CAVALIERE DELLA CORONA D'ITALIA

NEW YORK
COOPER SQUARE PUBLISHERS, INC.
1969

TO

ZILPHA VERNON SHOWERMAN

Nec ferat ulla dies ut commutemur in aevo

AUSONIUS, *Epigram* XL

Originally Published and Copyright, 1931
By The Macmillan Company
Published By Cooper Square Publishers, Inc.
59 Fourth Avenue, New York, N. Y. 10003
Standard Book Number 8154-0315-1
Library of Congress Catalog Card No. 75-100609

Printed in the United States of America

TO THE READER

The following survey and interpretation of a great ancient civilization is meant especially for students of the literature and history of Rome. It is not, however, a textbook only. *Rome and the Romans* is addressed to all readers desiring acquaintance with the people whose character and institutions are at the foundations of our modern culture. Its purpose is humanistic. It aims to assemble, not all facts, but significant facts; to present information which will add not only to knowledge but to the meaning of life; to make learning readable and reasonable.

CONTENTS

PART I. ROME AND ITS MEANING

PART II. THE ROMAN

PART III. LIVING ROME

PART IV. GREATER ROME

ACKNOWLEDGMENTS

The author expresses his indebtedness and thanks to the Ullman and Henry *Latin Books* for many illustrations; to Professor Rostovtzeff for the use of two from his *Rome;* to Mr. James Loeb for approval of numerous quotations from the *Loeb Classical Library;* to Charles Scribner's Sons for permission to quote Professor Abbott's translation of two Latin inscriptions; to Professors Harold Bennett and W. H. Page of the University of Wisconsin for criticism of the chapters on the Senator and the Roman Law; and to Director Gorham Phillips Stevens of the American Academy in Rome for counsel and aid. The author desires to express special obligation to Professor B. L. Ullman, his editor. To the many works in the field of Roman life and letters to which he has resorted for information or confirmation, and to the commercial photographs employed in illustration, the reader will find reference in the appropriate places.

MAPS AND ILLUSTRATIONS

xiii

SALVE MAGNA PARENS SATURNIA TELLUS

Virgil, *Georgics* II, 173

PRIMA URBES INTER DIVOM DOMUS AUREA ROMA

Ausonius, *Ordo Urbium Nobilium* I

PART I
ROME AND ITS MEANING

ROME AND THE ROMANS

ETERNAL ROME

As far back as the time of Virgil, whose birth took place two thousand years ago, men spoke of Rome as the Eternal City. The world still uses the phrase, and the person is rarely met who does not know that it means the city of Rome.

"The Eternal City" is not only an attractive phrase, but a truthful one. There has never been a time since its founding when Rome was not a living city, and since the Roman State first spread beyond the bounds of Italy there has never been a time when Rome was not important to the world. Nor does its importance wane to-day. Rome in the twentieth century is a living, growing, vigorous, ambitious capital, the capital of a great nation as well as the capital of a world-wide church.

A city which has endured for upwards of three thousand years, which for over two thousand years has been a prominent figure in the affairs of men, and which for twenty centuries has been called Eternal, is not like other cities. We owe it to our intelligence as citizens of the modern world to understand the Meaning of Rome.

I

ITALY TO–DAY

The most direct way of beginning the study of Rome's meaning is to see the land of Italy and the city of Rome as they are to-day. We shall be in a great company if we do this. One million strangers entered Italy in 1925 from every quarter of the world, and among them were hundreds of thousands from the Americas.

The distance from Chicago to New York is about nine hundred miles; from New York to a French port, such as Cherbourg, the distance is about three thousand miles; and from Cherbourg through Paris, Dijon, Modane, Turin, Genoa, and Pisa to Rome, about nine hundred and fifty miles. The distance from Chicago to Rome is thus about five thousand miles. As both cities are approximately 42° north latitude, Rome is directly east of Chicago. We think of Italy and Rome as southern because of their warmth and because in English literature we read of them as in the south.

The route from any part of America to Italy is marked by much that is related to Italian lands. There are Italian-Americans in almost every city, and many public buildings, including the great State Capitols, owe their character to Italian or ancient Roman architecture. The same is even more true in France, where there are also actual ruins of ancient Roman times. Between Paris and Dijon, for example, are the remains of Alesia, high on a hill, the last refuge of Vercingetorix from Caesar. A great statue of the Gallic leader is visible from the train.

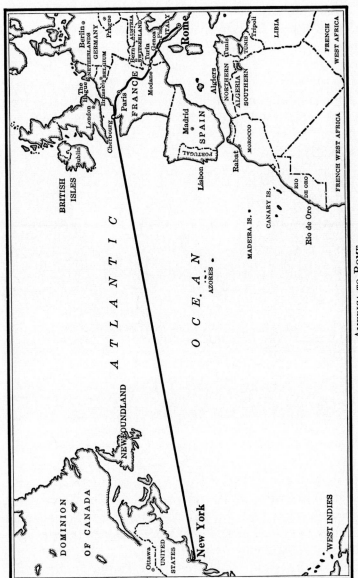

AMERICA TO ROME

The Kingdom of Italy, of which Rome has been the capital since July 2, 1871, and into which one descends pleasantly by electric train through the eight-mile tunnel of the Mont Cenis route at Modane, consists principally of the mainland of Italy and the islands of Sicily and Sardinia. Its area, 119,000 square miles, is about that of Nevada, about two

THE NATIONAL CAPITOL AT WASHINGTON

The dome owes its character to St. Paul's in London, which derives from St. Peter's in Rome, which in turn derives from ancient Rome.

and one half times that of New York, and more than twice that of Wisconsin. Sicily and Sardinia are each about ten thousand square miles, the size of Vermont. The Apennines form the great backbone of the peninsula, yet Italy is agricultural, and rich in grains, fruits, oil, and wine — "the garden of the world," in Byron's well-known phrase. The Piave, the Brenta, the Adige, the Po, the Arno, the Tiber, and the Volturno are the principal streams; there are beautiful lakes in the neighborhood of Rome and on the northern border; and there are fine harbors at Genoa, Spezia, Naples, Messina, Palermo, Taranto, Bari, Ancona, Venice, and Trieste. Italy has extensive colonial possessions in Africa, including Tripolitania.

The government of Italy is a constitutional monarchy. The reigning sovereign is Victor Emmanuel III, who succeeded Humbert in 1900, who in 1878 succeeded Victor Emmanuel II of Savoy and Sardinia, the first king of Italy. The Kingdom of Italy came into being in 1860, when Sicily and South Italy, conquered by Giuseppe Garibaldi, were annexed to the kingdom of Victor Emmanuel in the north of Italy. In 1870, the States of the Church, occupying Central Italy and Rome and thus dividing North from South, were also annexed, and the temporal dominion of the Church restricted to the Vatican quarter of Rome, which on February 11, 1929, became the Vatican State. In 1918, as a result of the World War, the Austrian portions of Italy south of the Alps about Trieste and Trent, and the port of Zara on the east shore of the Adriatic, were added. Italy now has a population of about forty millions.

The active conduct of government in Italy is in the hands of the cabinet or council, whose head is president of the council, or prime minister. The prime minister since 1922 is Benito Mussolini. The law-making bodies are the chamber of deputies, about five hundred representatives chosen by vote of the people, and the senate, composed of an unrestricted number appointed for life because of distinction in various important callings. The kingdom is divided into ninety-two provinces, including the new provinces in Trent and the Trieste region, and the province of Zara. Italy proper contains seventy-nine, the remainder, except

Zara, being in Sicily and Sardinia. All are under the
jurisdiction of an equal number of prefects and provincial
councils, each with its seat in the provincial capital. The
provinces, or counties, are further divided, the smallest unit
being the commune. There are more than eight thousand
communes, each likewise with a council and under the
authority of a *sindaco*. Since October, 1922, when the
Fascisti under their organizer Mussolini took over authority,
the working of the Italian constitution has been of necessity
irregular, but is gradually approaching the normal. The
Fascisti rose to prominence in 1919 as a much-needed protest against the laxities and disloyalties that followed the
war.

Besides the provinces, there are other divisions of Italy
whose names are much used. Every reader is familiar with
Tuscany, Lombardy, Piedmont, Venetia, the Marches,
Romagna, Umbria, and Calabria. These, and as many
more, represent the old-time dukedoms and principalities
whose union made possible the present kingdom. Many of
them, like Campania, Calabria, and Umbria, were known
by the same names in the times of Caesar, Cicero, and Virgil.
The Italian language as variously spoken in them results in
the many dialects of Italy. The Piedmontese find it difficult to talk with the Neapolitans, the Calabrians with the
Venetians; though the language written and spoken in
Florence is the standard and is universal with educated men.

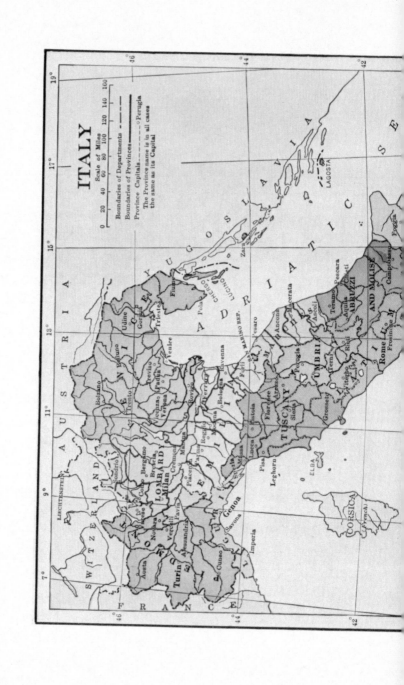

ITALY

Scale of Miles
0   20   40   60   80   100   120   140   160

Boundaries of Departments ------
Boundaries of Provinces ————
Province Capitals ——— o Perugia
The Province name is in all cases
the same as its Capital

II

ROME TO-DAY

The capital of United Italy, at first in Turin, where the first parliament met in 1861, was fixed at Florence in 1864, and in 1871 was transferred to Rome, which had fallen before the national army on the twentieth of September, 1870. It was one of the greatest testimonials to the power still exercised by the name of Rome that not only Italy but the sentiment of the world in general demanded the location of the modern capital in the seat of the ancient.

Rome to-day is approached by rail through Turin, Genoa, and Pisa from the northwest; through Como, Milan, and Florence from the north; through the mountains from Ancona and the east coast, and by two routes from Naples and the south, the older inland, and the newer the short line along the west coast. It lies on the Tiber seventeen miles from the sea, in the midst of a rolling plain called the Campagna, which includes in general the flat parts of ancient Latium. The Campagna is about forty miles wide from the sea to its north-and-east boundary, the Apennines, and is twice as long from northwest to southeast, with limits not so definite.

At twenty-five miles to the north of Rome the train from Florence passes Mount Soracte, made famous by Horace. The train from the Adriatic and the east, as it leaves the Apennines eighteen miles from Rome, passes through Tivoli, Horace's ancient Tibur, where the "headlong Anio," *praeceps Anio*, plunges its three hundred feet down from the

ROME TO-DAY

The view is toward the East, from the Dome of Saint Peter's. The Tiber and the round Mausoleum of Hadrian are in the background.

mountains into the plain.   The train from Naples, twenty miles before reaching Rome, skirts the Alban Mount, which rises out of the plain three thousand feet and forms the most striking feature in the Roman landscape.

The city of Rome to-day has a population of more than nine hundred thousand.   The Rome of ancient times may have contained above a million.   The area occupied by the modern city approximates a circle with a diameter of four miles.   The ancient city was somewhat less in extent, but more thickly populated.   The great wall of Aurelian, built by the Emperor Aurelian, who reigned A.D. 270–276, still stands, and is eleven miles in circumference, inclosing an area a little over three miles in diameter.   The city of to-day extends far beyond it in many directions, but only the northern half of the city inside the wall is densely populated ; the southern half is occupied by great areas containing only ruins and excavations, and by smaller areas containing modern houses.

We may think of the modern city as consisting of four parts.   First, there are the vast spaces of ruin and emptiness and partial occupation that compose the southern portion.   These include the Roman Forum and the Palatine Hill, maintained by the Government as national reserves, the Colosseum, and many other ancient monuments.   Second, there is the newer part within the walls, mostly in the north and northeast and belonging to the early decades of the past sixty years.   The railway terminus, dating from 1870, is in this part, on the broad plateau of the Quirinal and the Esquiline.   Third, there is the older part, from one to four centuries old, extending from the Capitoline Hill and the Tiber Island on the south to the Porta del Popolo on the north and including the entire Campus Martius, with Trastevere and the Borgo across the river.   Fourth, there

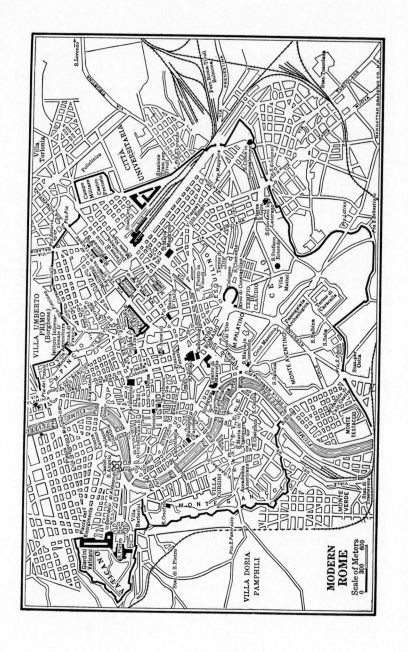

MODERN
ROME

Scale of Meters
0   300   600

are the newest quarters, mostly outside the wall of Aurelian, and all belonging to the past thirty years. These new portions include the Prati, near the Mausoleum of Hadrian to the north of Saint Peter's, the area outside the northeastern gates, and the district about the Porta San Paolo to the south. The population of the city has tripled in sixty years, and is constantly increasing.

Rome to-day is neither a great commercial city nor an industrial center nor a port, though it is a railway center. Its manufactures are few, and chiefly in the arts and crafts. Its trade is mainly of the slighter sort that ministers to the daily and occasional needs of a large permanent population increased by countless travelers. Rome is the national capital; it is the capital of the Roman Catholic Church; it contains the ruins of the capital of the ancient world; it is in Italy,

> "The garden of the world, the home
> Of all Art yields and Nature can decree."

Its greatest industry is the care of the stranger within the gates — of those who come from the ends of Italy to manage the multitudinous affairs of State and Church, and of those who come from the ends of the earth to see the world's most famous city.

III

THE RISE OF ANCIENT ROME

There was a time when Rome was not, and when the Seven Hills rose uninhabited out of a leafy and grassy wilderness. There was a time before that when there were no Seven Hills, but all the Campagna region was under the sea, and the mouths of the Tiber and the Anio were among the hills at the foot of the Apennines.

The Roman Campagna is a volcanic region. The living craters of Aetna and Vesuvius, and the dead craters of the Roman neighborhood, are the signs of a long line of weakness in the earth's crust. While a broad bay still rested over the future site of Rome, so geology tells us, upheavals and eruptions covered and elevated the bed of the sea until the land appeared above the waters. The surface thus formed was then furrowed by the abundantly flowing streams of geologic times and further modified by the volcanic rise of the Alban Mountains in its midst until the landscape was formed which we know to-day.

Into this rolling, hummocky plain of primitive times came the first dwellers in the Roman region. They were the wandering cave-men of the Old Stone Age, and they lived their scant and straggling life many thousands of years before Rome began. After them came the men of the Late Stone Age, a part of the wave that came over the Alps from France or up from Sicily and the south, and after these a wave from over the Alps, a part of the migrant movement that earlier peopled Greece with the Doric race.

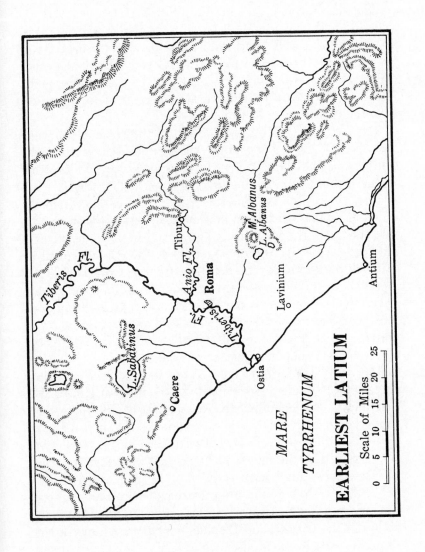

MARE

TYRRHENUM

EARLIEST LATIUM

Scale of Miles

0   5   10   15   20   25

This later wave was of Indo-European stock, and it blended with the Mediterranean race upon which it came as it spread throughout the Italian land. Its men were probably the first to settle on the Seven Hills beside the Tiber, a thousand years or more before the time of Livy and Virgil, who could only try, as we are trying, to see in imagination the earliest men of Rome.

The story of the rise and growth of the ancient city will best be told by setting down the various phases through which it passed. Seven may be mentioned here, in most of which Rome has a definite boundary marked by a wall.

First, there was the Palatine City. The earliest form of Rome came into existence when the strongest of the shepherd settlements which had already been made on the little heights along the Tiber by the race from over the Alps assumed a leadership, improved its defenses by building a wall of stone about its hill, and became known as Roma, the River City. This city was on the Palatine, the most inviting and most convenient of the hills. It was about one hundred and fifty feet above the Tiber level, had an area of forty acres, and was about a quarter of a mile square.

Second, the Septimontium. This form of the city included the Palatine and the skirts of the Caelian Hill to the east and of the Esquiline to the northeast. The five districts or precincts which now were added to the two precincts of the Palatine had probably hitherto been separate villages. It is likely that the added portions also were fortified, but with less substantial walls than those of the Palatine.

Third, the City of the Four Regions. The four regions, or wards, reached farther over the Caelian and the Esquiline, taking in the Oppian and Cispian, which were spurs of the Esquiline, and included also two new hills, the Quirinal and the Viminal. The names of the regions were Palatina,

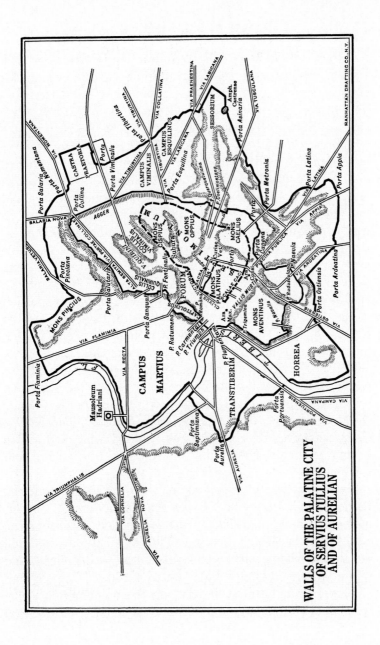

WALLS OF THE PALATINE CITY
OF SERVIUS TULLIUS
AND OF AURELIAN

Suburana, Esquilina, and Collina. The Collina, or Hill Region, consisted of the Quirinal and Viminal, which the Romans always called *colles*, hills, while they called the other hills *montes*. It is doubtful whether this form of the city was walled at every point.

Fourth, the City of Servius. The Servian City is named from Servius Tullius, the sixth king of Rome. It reached out to the south and took in the Aventine; to the north it included the remaining area of the Esquiline and Viminal and Quirinal; and to the west it added the Capitoline. The wall which inclosed it is still to be seen in about thirty fragments, some of them quite imposing. The most remarkable are near the railway station and at the south of the Aventine.

Fifth, the City of the Republic. By this is meant the city as it grew during the five centuries from the expulsion of the Tarquins in 509 B.C. to the time of Augustus and the Empire. There was no walling of Rome during this period, unless it is true, as has been suspected, that the defense called the Servian Wall belongs to the fourth century instead of the sixth when Servius reigned. The Roman State had by this time pushed its boundaries so widely into the outside world that the capital was far from danger. The city of Cato, who lived from 234 to 149 before Christ, had grown beyond its now useless walls, and numbered upward of half a million.

Sixth, the City of Augustus, or the City of the Fourteen Regions. This was the City of the Republic set in order, increased, and beautified. It was divided into fourteen wards, one of which was beyond the Tiber; it was well watered, perhaps fairly well lighted, and well policed, and was rapidly changing from brick to marble. The old wall of Servius was hard to find among the buildings of a city which had long since grown over and beyond it, and the legal city limit, extended more than once in the five hundred years of the Republic, was pierced at thirty-seven points by as many roads to Rome, and inclosed a city ten miles in circumference.

THE WALL OF AURELIAN

The greater part still exists. Here it borders the Protestant Cemetery, in which are the tombs of Keats and Shelley.

Seventh, the City of Aurelian. In alarm at the threats of invasion from beyond the Alps, Aurelian and Probus in A.D. 272–276 reared the mighty wall which bears the former's name and still exists. In brick and concrete twelve feet thick, rising sometimes to sixty feet, with loopholed galleries, and with parapet crowned in the course of its eleven miles by nearly four hundred towers, it was the last wall to girdle the city in ancient times.

It would be interesting to continue with other phases of the city — the sinking Pagan city that fell a prey to Alaric in A.D. 410; the Christian city rising in its midst; the ruined and empty Rome of the Middle Ages; the city of the Renaissance and Raphael, spreading from Saint Peter's into the Campus Martius at the bend of the Tiber, and surrounded by spacious fields made picturesque by ancient monuments; and the city of the pope-monarchs which had to yield when Italy knocked at the gates. Here, however, it is ancient Rome with which we are concerned.

In speaking of the city's earliest forms, the chronicler can use no dates at all, and very few names. There is little that is definite in the story of Rome before the Republic. That there were kings, and many of them, there is no doubt, and it is certain that the Etruscans at one time were its rulers for a hundred years or more. That the city began and grew in some such way as we have described, there is also no doubt. It has been agreed to speak of the founding of Rome as taking place on the twenty-first of April, 753 B.C., and the date is celebrated every year in Rome, and has been celebrated from time to time since ancient days. It has been agreed to speak of the last king's reign as ending in 509 B.C. These dates, and all the other dates and names and events of the Rome of the Kings, belong to legend rather than history; but there is no harm in supposing that legend here is a substantial indication of the truth. Of recent years, the tendency has been to see in the tales of Livy and Virgil something more than the story-telling of patriot and poet.

IV

THE RISE OF THE ROMAN STATE

It is our wont to speak of Rome as a conquering state, and to think of its expansion into the empire that ruled the ancient world as due to the calculating and selfish use of power. Conquest by force of arms, however, is only one of the many ways by which an empire comes to pass. There are also the interests of trade, the appeal of convenience or economy in administration, the feeling for language or religion, the desire for coöperation or the need of protection, or even mere sentiment begotten by some trifling incident that catches the fancy and stirs the hearts of men. All these, as well as the passion for power, may be the causes of a state's expansion.

Yet we may go even deeper, and think of the Roman State as a product of nature. In part, at least, it grew as any plant or other living organism grows, because of the irresistible urge of life whose law is growth.

The first expansions of Rome took place when the little communities on the neighboring hills were united with the Palatine City. We have seen the original city become the Septimontium, and the Septimontium expand into the City of Four Regions. It is likely that the annexations then involved were the peaceable arrangements of men who recognized the common interest.

This, however, is the expansion of the city, and it is the State which now concerns us. There was a period during which the territory covered by the city was identical with

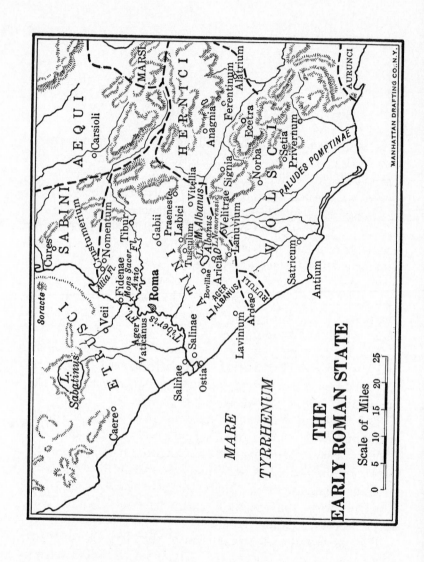

MARE
TYRRHENUM

**THE
EARLY ROMAN STATE**

Scale of Miles

0   5   10   15   20   25

the total area of the State; but this was very brief. The city soon established its formal rule over the neighboring pastures and tilth, and the real expansion of the Roman State had begun.

When Rome emerges from the legendary time of the kings in 509 B.C. as the Republic, its territory still is very small. The Etruscans across the Tiber hem it in from west and north, to north and east the still unfriendly Sabines and Aequians and Hernicans are only some twenty or thirty miles away, and to east and south the Latins are still masters of themselves. The Roman State consists of lands perhaps twenty-five miles by ten, bounded clearly by the Tiber and the sea, and less precisely by the mountain limits of the plain. In the Latin League of the year 500 B.C., the Latins, the nearest kin of Rome, have not yet admitted to their fellowship the city on the Tiber.

The expansion of Rome, however, is not long delayed, and, once begun, it has a sure and rapid progress. By 493 B.C., Rome is a member of the League. In 487 B.C. she breaks the Hernican power, and in 486 B.C. the Hernicans are with her against the Volscians and Aequians to their south and north. By 431 B.C. these two nations no longer oppose her, and she is the leader, if not the ruler, of all the peoples east of the Tiber to the Apennines and south of Mount Soracte to the sea. Her lands form a triangular territory some forty miles along the Tiber by seventy-five along the sea and about the same along the mountains. It is a territory whose bounds are set by nature and whose peoples have much in common.

The next expansion is into lands across the Tiber. The Etruscans who once controlled Rome are finally made less dangerous by the fall of Veii in the ten-year siege that ended in 396 B.C. The final and unsuccessful stand of Etruria in

ITALIA

Scale of Miles

0   50   100   150

Rhenus

Rhine

L. Venetus

Aenus

A L P E S

Mediolanum
(Milan)

Verona

Mantua
(Po)

VENETIA

ILLYRICUM

Aug. Taurinorum

Padus

G A L L I A

L I G U R I A

Genua

(Gulf of Genoa)

Luca

Arnus

Pisae

MARE HADRIATICUM

Rubico
Ariminum

Metaurus
Aesis

Florentia

Arretium

Sentinum

L. Trasumenus
Clusium

E T R U R I A

PICENUM

Asculum

Volsinii
Falerii

Narnia

FRENTANI

CORSICA

Tarquinii

Feronia

SABINI

Veii

MARSI

Caere

Luceria

SAMNIUM

A P U L I A

Roma

Ostia

Praeneste

Hernici

Sora

Aufidus

Tusc

Fregellae

LATIUM

Cannae

Anagnia

VOLSCI

Bovianum

Antium

Circei

Capua

Venusia

Caudium

Brundisium

Tarracina

Formiae

Tarentum

Misenum

CAMPANIA

CALABRIA

Cumae

Neapolis (Naples)

Pompeii

Paestum

LUCANIA

Heraclea
(Gulf of Tarentum)

MAGNA
GRAECIA

BRUTTIUM

Croton

SARDINIA

ERCTE M.

ERYX M.

Messana

AEGATES
INS.

Panormus

Mylae

Locri

Regium

CALATHA I.

Hippo Zarytus

Drepana

Lilybaeum

SICILIA

AETNA M.

Catania

Carthago

Utica

P. Mercurii

Agrigentum

Ecnomus

Gela

Syracusae

NUMIDIA

Bagrada

COSSYRA

Pachynum Pr.

A   F   R   I   C   A

295 B.C. leaves the river Arno at Pisa and Florence the northern boundary of Rome, and extends the eastward and westward limits until they include a hundred and fifty miles and reach almost from sea to sea. By the same date, the Samnites in Central Italy beyond the Apennines have made the last stand in their hundred years of rivalry with Rome, and the territory of Rome extends to the border of Magna Graecia at Venusia, later the native city of Horace. By 272 B.C., the fall of Tarentum delivers the south of Italy into the hands of the Romans, and Roman territory extends from the Arno to the Sicilian Straits and Brundisium and from the western to the eastern sea. This forms a state four hundred miles long by two hundred wide.

In 265 B.C., the crossing of the Strait of Messina by Romans in arms, to aid a band of their countrymen against the Carthaginians, began the career of Rome beyond the seas that ended in the control of the Mediterranean world. At the end of the First Punic War, in 241 B.C., she was mistress of Sicily. Sardinia and Corsica also soon were annexed. At the end of the struggle with Hannibal, the Second Punic War, 218–201 B.C., she found herself established in Spain, in the valley of the Rhone, and in northern Italy, and the sea was hers from Malta to the Pillars of Hercules, the ancient Gibraltar.

Next came the East. Conscious of her strength, even in the midst of the war with Hannibal Rome had answered an interference on the part of Macedonia by a declaration of war. With the battles of Cynoscephalae in 197 B.C. and Pydna in 168 B.C., the state that had risen under Alexander and the Philips crumbled before the assaults of the younger nation from the West. Greece was freed from the Macedonian, and after fifty years of troublesome protectorate became a Roman province with the taking of Corinth in 146 B.C., the year in which Carthage finally was destroyed and the north of Africa annexed. At this time the sway of Rome, though not in every part consolidated, extended from Spain to Syria and from the Rhone Valley to the coasts of Africa. The Mediterranean was a Roman sea, but not yet cleared of perils from pirates and the fleets of less irregular foes of Rome.

It was not until Augustus' time that this vast territory, with areas later added, was firmly knit together within the boundary which remained so long the definite limit of the civilized world. At the end of the Emperor's reign, in A.D. 14, the Empire's limit was marked on the north by the English Channel, the Rhine, the Danube, and the Black Sea, and was uncertain only as the eagles advanced beyond the Rhine. On the south, the Sahara was the bound, with the Nile Valley at its eastern end. On the west was the ocean, and on the east a line that never could quite be counted on, from the eastern end of the Black Sea to Syria on the south, and thus to Egypt, with allied states like Palmyra to mediate between Rome and the distant Armenians and Parthians in the north and the restless desert peoples in the south. The boundary of the Augustan Empire was practically the permanent limit of the Roman State for nearly five hundred years. It was altered once, when Claudius conquered Britain, for whose protection Hadrian and Antoninus built the walls on the Scottish border which are still to be seen; again, when Trajan in A.D. 106 annexed what is now Roumania, then called Dacia; and lastly, when the Euphrates was made more surely the eastern border. Aside from these changes, the line between Rome and barbarism was constant until the weakening of the fourth and fifth centuries resulted in its obliteration as the outside world came over the bounds to conquer and be blended with the older civilization.

The rise of the Roman State should not be thought of as merely the growth of a military power. During the thousand years or more of its experience as a rising and ruling state, its conflicts of arms with the enemy abroad were not its only or even its greatest struggles. While the struggle to advance the borders and to maintain the integrity of the State was going on along the far-flung battle lines of the Republic and Empire, another struggle was going on in the Roman Forum and in the Roman senate house. In this struggle it was not the right of the State to further territory that constituted the spoils of war, but the right of the citizen to further liberty.

The struggle was long and obstinate, and not without its victories. Here are some of the rights conceded only after long contention and frequent violence : the right of the people to be ruled by elected officeholders; the right to the control of the officeholders by means of tribunes with veto power; the right themselves to hold the various offices of quaestor, aedile, praetor, and consul; the right of the plebeian to marry into the patrician class; the right to limit the amount of land to be owned by the rich man; the right to share in the ownership of the land; the right to a reward from the conquered lands at the end of military service; the right to state support in the distribution of grain.

It took two hundred and fifty years for the common people of Rome to finish the series of struggles for the right of holding office by seating their first pontifex maximus. The question of land limitation against the rich and land privilege in favor of the poor runs through five hundred years of Roman history, and cost the lives of many noble men. The struggle between the orders was long and bitter, but from it the world came off with profit. The lessons of the Roman Republic were not forgotten in the Empire. They passed into the world's greatest code of law, and into the modern code of civic morality.

V

ANCIENT ROME AND MODERN TIMES

Now that we have become acquainted with Rome to-day as the capital of the United Kingdom of Italy and Sicily, and have seen the origin and growth of ancient Rome and the Roman State of which it was the center, and have thus constructed a setting for Eternal Rome, let us return to the statement with which we began, that Rome is different from other cities, and that we owe it to ourselves to understand what makes it so. Let us look more closely into the relation between ancient Rome and our own times.

To state at once and briefly this relation, the civilization in which we live is descended from that of ancient Rome. Our life to-day is a continuation of the life of the ancient Romans. The blood ancestry of America is to be found in various nations of Europe and other parts of the world, but our culture traces back to Rome. American civilization is essentially English. The present character of England's culture is due to the coming of the Normans in 1066, the date of the Battle of Hastings. The Norman culture grew out of the French, and the French resulted from Julius Caesar's conquest of Gaul in 58 B.C. to 49 B.C. The stream of history flows from Italy to France, from France to England, from England to America. It has flowed to us through other channels also—through France directly without passing to England, through Spain, through Holland, through Germany, and from Italy straight across the ocean; but

our language and our ways of thinking and acting have come
to us in largest part on the current that flowed from English
shores. We are Anglo-Romans, or Anglo-Latins. The
civilization of the United States and Canada is really Latin,
and only less unmixed than that of the Latin races.

But this claim will seem better founded if we look at our
modern culture in detail. What are some of the factors
that go to make up the cultural environment which makes
it possible for us to enjoy the life, liberty, and pursuit of
happiness which we call our inalienable rights, and what in
each case is our debt to ancient Rome?

First, there is language. About sixty per cent of the
words in the English tongue are descended, through Norman-
French, modern French, Italian, and Spanish, and directly,
from the Latin. You cannot read with the same precise
understanding, and you cannot speak or write with the same
intimate, accurate, refined, and rich command of English,
unless you know the language which lies at its foundation.
Nor is it true that the Latin part of English consists only
of long, stately, and unnecessary words, and that simple
Anglo-Saxon would and should suffice. Try sometime to
write or speak without using *pen* or *pin*, *date*, *fate*, *rate*, or
state, *class* or *glass*, *face*, *space*, *grace*, or *case*, *cause* or *clause*,
form or *grade* or *fact* or *grand*, or a hundred other words of
one syllable which are Latin; or try to get on without the
host of Latin words in two syllables, like *honor*, *glory*, *music*,
money, *language*. Try to write a paragraph or to talk a
quarter of an hour without using words of Latin origin at
all. English is the richest of the world's languages, and it
is the richest because it is a composite of many languages,
but chiefly of Latin and Anglo-Saxon, with all the resourcefulness in clarity, precision, rhythm, harmony, variety,
fitness, and freshness that belongs to a tongue abounding in

words and phrases of identical meaning but different in origin and character.

A PAGE FROM THE CODEX PALATINUS OF VIRGIL

Line 67 of Eclogue IX and lines 1–21 of Eclogue X. This manuscript, in the Vatican Library, is about 1500 years old.

Second, there is literature. We may dismiss this briefly by saying that English and American literature as a whole is very imperfectly read by those who are unacquainted with the Latin language and literature and with Roman history.   Milton, Spenser, Grey, Dryden, Byron, Thackeray, and Shakespeare himself, abound in contacts with Roman and Italian letters.   To remove from English literature all allusions, inspirations, and imitations due to ancient Rome would be to wreck it quite as badly as the language we speak would be wrecked if all its Latin words were canceled.

Third, there is the field of art.   Our sculpture shows at a glance its origin in Italy, Rome, and Greece.   The painting of the Italian Renaissance, from which all modern painting took its lessons, is rich with Roman subject matter and shows direct descent from the Roman Empire through the mosaics and manuscript illuminations of Byzantine and medieval times, and through the pictures on the walls of the catacombs and earliest churches.   Our architecture shows on every street how much we owe to ancient Rome. Our great capitol buildings, our banks and railroad stations, our university halls and our libraries, with their pillars and arcades and domes and vaults and coffered ceilings, all lead us back to Italy and Rome.   There is hardly a dome in America which is not to be traced either through the capitol at Washington and Saint Paul's in London to Saint Peter's in Rome and thus to ancient Rome, or to Saint Peter's directly and thus more quickly to ancient Rome.   If you live in a city of any size, you are never far from the visible influence of Rome.

Fourth, there is law.   The Roman State was the world's great laboratory of law.   The thousand years and more from the time the Romans emerge into history at the beginning of the Republic to the times of Justinian after the fall of the Western Empire represent the experience of a great race in the search for justice.   That experience, expressed in the great Code of Justinian, which was completed in A.D. 528–534, was Rome's greatest contribution to the world. Roman law is in operation still in Italy, in France, in Spain and Latin America, in Louisiana, Porto Rico, and the Philippines, and in the government of the Roman

THE GREAT HALL OF PENNSYLVANIA TERMINAL IN NEW YORK

The coffered vaulting, the great columns, the arches and mouldings, and the size make it similar to the Baths of Caracalla or the Basilica of Constantine, whose ruins in Rome have been the inspiration of many modern buildings.

Catholic Church. Even in the United States at large, in the British Empire, and in the Mohammedan countries, to which its descent was less direct, its influence is profound. With the migrations of the Latin and British peoples and with the spread of the Church, Roman law has touched every part of the world.

Fifth, there is religion. The Christian faith, spreading at first from Palestine to the cities of Asia Minor and Greece, emerges into the light at Rome in Nero's reign, and soon has

THE MISSISSIPPI STATE CAPITOL AT JACKSON

This and fifteen other State Capitol domes, with the National Capitol Dome, trace back through Saint Paul's in London to Saint Peter's in Renaissance Rome, and thus to ancient Rome.

its greatest center there. From Romans of every class, tired of the vanities and the selfishness and hardness of the old society, the new religion gathered its faithful; from the Roman house, basilica, and temple, it received the suggestions resulting in the architecture of its places of meeting; and into the vast framework of the Roman Empire the new life of Christian civilization gradually grew, to take the place of the old when Pagan civilization declined. "That the working of unspeakable grace might be spread throughout the whole world," wrote Leo the Great, Pope from A.D. 440 to A.D. 461, "Divine Providence prepared the Roman Empire."

Sixth, there is morality. The morals of our own day are the morals of ancient Rome. We owe their preservation and their currency to three things. First, the morality of pagan times passed into the Christian code of ethics. The enlightened ideas of Cicero in *De Officiis* were also the teaching of the Church. Second, Roman law itself was the embodiment of ancient ideas of right conduct, and brought them with it into modern law. Third, the Roman ideal of character has reached us in the history and literature that for countless generations have had a large place in the education of the ruling classes. Roman ideals of manhood and womanhood, of fatherhood and motherhood, of honor, faith, and patriotism, of loyalty and devotion, of personal bravery, of resoluteness and endurance, of purity and incorruptibility, have entered into the fiber of human character through the centuries.

The analysis of our modern civilization thus shows that we are still living in large part the life of ancient Rome. The civilization of to-day is not the work of to-day alone but an inheritance from the times when Rome was the Mother-city of the world. It is more than that; it is an inheritance from the total human past, for Rome herself transmitted to the nations of the modern world not only her own experience but that of the civilizations preceding her. Egypt, Chaldaea, Assyria, Greece, the nearer East, and Carthage, and ruder Germany, Gaul, and Spain, gave as well as received when they came under the sway of

Roman arms and institutions. Rome was the heir of the
ages. She became possessed of what the world had to give,
lived it into her experience, set her seal upon it, conserved
it, and bequeathed it to the medieval and modern world.
She is the connecting link between her forerunners, beginning with Egypt, "the eldest daughter of civilization,"
and her descendants, ending with the twentieth century in
the Americas.

"She gathered together the precious metal of ancient civilization,
fused and coined it anew, and put it once more into circulation.
She was the lens which received, condensed, and transmitted the
rays of human experience. She was the bridge to which all the
ways of the old pagan times converged, and from which diverged
all the ways of Christian times. She was the channel into which
the streams of ancient civilization flowed together to mingle their
waters before being swept on to divide and subdivide into the
currents of modern civilization. The legacy of preceding ages,
administered and increased by her, became the heritage of ages
succeeding. Whatever in the culture of our own day is held dear
— in art, literature, learning, in juristic or religious institutions —
is traceable first to Italy of the Renaissance, and then to ancient
Rome, where it either came into being or was adapted to the needs
of practical experience. The generations of to-day are still subjects of the empire of Rome. Her line is gone out through all the
earth and her words to the end of the world."

There is a building in modern Rome which stands as a
symbol of what we have said. It is the Church of Santa
Maria in Cosmedin, south of the Capitoline Hill and near the
Tiber. It is a church in use to-day like any other church,
and, by the uneducated or unobservant, might easily be
thought a building of to-day. If it is looked at carefully,
however, we soon become aware that its roof and stucco
veneer are all of the exterior that make it modern. Its
charming campanile belongs to the twelfth century; its

SANTA MARIA IN COSMEDIN

The campanile is of the twelfth century, and the church is built into and over an
ancient edifice, probably a temple of Ceres.

walls beneath the stucco are likewise medieval; the pillars of its portico and the lintels of its doors are ancient Roman. If we enter into the calm spaces of its interior, we soon see that the organ, the hangings at door and window, the chairs in use at the Mass being said in the chapel at one side, the finish of the walls, and the ceiling, are the only modern parts. The mosaic of variegated marbles on whose exquisite pattern we tread is of the twelfth century, and the marble which was cut to make it came from the ruins of ancient Roman buildings. The columns that make the aisles are pillars from ancient temples or porticoes. The walls whose finish gives them a modern look are really medieval, and imbedded in them at intervals are the ancient Roman columns that belonged to the building into and over which the church was reared. This is not all. Under the floor of the church are the rugged walls of some structure belonging to times before the temple or portico, just as the temple or portico belongs to times before the church. If we hearken to the Mass, we know indeed that its message is for the confirmation and the inspiration and the consolation of the people of to-day; but its language is the tongue of ancient Rome and its message unchanged by the passing of nearly twenty centuries.

The structure of modern culture is like the structure of Santa Maria in Cosmedin. The untaught and the un-reflecting accept it without thought as the creation of recent times, and even deny its dependence upon antiquity; and yet, were all that is ancient in its substance taken from it, the structure would collapse in terrible and hopeless ruin.

Such is the meaning of ancient Rome to modern times. Ancient Rome is not a remote and unrelated time and place. The ancient Romans are our ancestors in the direct line. To be acquainted with them is to know our family history and to receive its legacies and inspirations. To study the language, literature, and history of ancient Rome is to contribute not only to the formation of intellectual habit and to our understanding of the language we speak and write, but to our appreciation of the meaning of human life.

"Whatever men may babble about modern education," wrote the Dutch novelist, Maarten Maartens, "two influences, incomparable and consistent, confer on the human mind a free-masonry of refinement — the study of the classics, and the appreciation of Italy."

PART II

THE ROMAN

THE ROMAN

Thus far we have been occupied in contemplating the fact of Rome's existence, its long participation in the affairs of men, the nature of the land in which it stood and stands, the manner of its birth and rise to power, the growth of the State of which it was the capital, and the descent of its language, literature, art, law, religion, and morality through the ages and into the life of men to-day. We grouped these studies under the heading, Rome and Its Meaning.

The study of ancient Rome is at the same time an obligation and a pleasure. It is an obligation because we are more intelligent as men and citizens if we know what our forerunners have done and what their achievements have to do with life to-day. It is a pleasure because to meet our kinsmen in culture a long way off and in a distant time is an experience rich in human interest. Let us therefore enter actively upon a study of the ancient city and its life.

The best plan for our purpose will be to make acquaintance with the Roman. Let us first of all know him as a person. Against the background of the physical Rome in which he lived, let us try to see him as he looked on the street, let us become acquainted with the social structure in which he moved, let us enter his house and see how he lived, look on at his nurture and education, become acquainted with the woman who bore him and the woman he married, accept his invitation to dinner and share in what he ate and drank, and take some account of how he spent his time. All this will place distinctly before us the man and woman whose

43

lives went into the making of the culture to which our own is so much in debt.

When we have been thus introduced to the Roman, we shall be prepared to go with him into the scenes of business and pleasure which made up his life as a citizen of the Roman State and its capital city, and to become acquainted in detail with the life of the Roman people.

VI

THE CITY IN WHICH HE LIVED

Cicero lived from 106 to 43 B.C., Pompey from 106 to 48 B.C., Caesar from 100 or 102 to 44 B.C., Virgil from 70 to 19 B.C., Horace from 65 to 8 B.C., Livy from 59 B.C. to A.D. 17, and Augustus from 63 B.C. to A.D. 14. These are the great figures in whom our interest in ancient Rome will always center, and the city of their times, if we knew it well, would be the natural basis for our study of the ways of the ancient Roman and the life of his capital.

The city up to the end of the Republic, however, is less illuminated both by letters and by material evidence than the city of Augustus and the first emperors, and it will best serve our purpose to take as a basis not only the city of Cicero, Caesar, and the earlier years of Augustus, but the city of the whole first century after Christ ; keeping as near as possible, however, to the days of the Augustans and the great men of the Republic just preceding them.

The city of Rome in the time of Cato, who died in B.C. 149, contained about four hundred thousand persons. During the hundred years that led to Caesar's break with the Senate and to the dictatorship, in spite of wars abroad and at home, this number must have greatly increased. The three hundred and twenty thousand whom Caesar found enjoying free grain at the State's expense could easily represent a total of twice that population. It will not be far from right to think of Augustan Rome as containing more than five hundred thousand, and of the city at its greatest, in the

THE EAST END OF THE ROMAN FORUM RESTORED

From right to left: Basilica Julia, Temple of Castor and Pollux, Home of the Vestals, Temple of Vesta, Temple of Julius Caesar, Arch of Fabius, Temple of Venus and Rome. In the foreground, honorary monuments. The Imperial Palace on the Palatine appears above the Temple of Castor and Pollux.

latter part of the first century, as numbering at least a million.

There was no wall to inclose the city of Augustus. The wall called Servian had long since been obscured by the crowded buildings of an expanding capital, and was mostly inside the city limit. The limit or line that legally inclosed the Augustan city was nearly a circle about ten miles in circumference. At some forty points the line was broken by entrances at which the city tax on produce from without was levied — a manner of taxation employed by the cities of modern Italy up to its abolition in 1930. At points where the line was pierced by one of the great roads that came to the city from afar, doubtless the passage was marked by an archway or a gate. If it was a street or road of less importance, the barrier was perhaps less formal.

Yet the city straggled beyond even this ten-mile line. Julius Caesar's law providing that every owner for one mile beyond the gates should keep in repair the road that fronted his house was clearly evidence of much expansion in many directions, like that of Rome to-day.

All roads led to the gates of Rome, and through them to the Roman Forum or near it. Here was the heart of the city and the Empire, and here, to mark the fact, was the Milliarium Aureum, the Golden Milestone, erected by Augustus, a column sheathed in gilded bronze on which were engraved the names of the chief cities of the Roman world and their distances from the capital.

The streets that led away to become the great roads outside the city were like the spokes of a wheel. From the hill of the Capitol near the head of the Forum, there shot like an arrow to the north the Via Lata, which outside the city became the Via Flaminia and made for the Adriatic at Ariminum. Up the near-by depression between Quirinal and

Viminal ran the street called Vicus Longus, which emerged
from the old Colline Gate of the Servian Wall and as it left
the Augustan limit ran straight ahead toward Nomentum,
or turned to the left and made for the Via Salaria, the Tiber
Valley, and the upper Sabine country.   Leaving the Forum

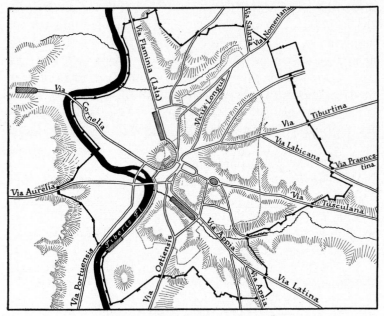

THE STREETS AND HIGHWAYS OF ROME

This map shows the Wall of Aurelian, A.D. 272–276, but the streets of the city were
more or less constant through the centuries.   The Circus Maximus is seen along the
Via Appia, the Circus of Caligula across the Tiber.   The Colosseum is also indicated,
and the polling-place on the Via Lata.

as the Argiletum, the Clivus Suburanus bent to the east and
went out at the Esquiline Gate as the Via Tiburtina, bound
for Tibur and the mountain country eighteen miles away.
Due east, the Via Praenestina, continuing the Via Labicana
inside the limits, made for Gabii and Praeneste, modern

Palestrina, on the mountain side, while the Labicana branched to the south in its own name. To the southeast, through the Servian Porta Capena and out along the level crest of a prehistoric lava stream, with sightly prospects, ran the most famous of Roman roads, the Appia, *Regina Viarum*, Queen of Ways, over the slopes of the Alban Mount and on to Tarracina, Capua, Beneventum, and Brundisium. The Via Latina, branching from it to the left, ran to the high divide in the Alban Hills past Tusculum, descending to the gap between Volscians and Apennines on the way to Campania. The Via Ostiensis on the left bank of the Tiber and the Via Portuensis on the right connected the city with the Tiber mouth. The Via Aurelia began at the Aemilian Bridge near the Forum Boarium, mounted the Janiculum, and led west and north into Etruria and on to Pisa and other coast cities. The Via Cornelia, farther north, ran west from the Tiber across the space later occupied by the piazza and church of Saint Peter.

Besides these longer streets that radiated from the city's center and were continued to form the network of highways that carried the goods and men of the Empire to distant parts of Italy and the world, there were the shorter streets that terminated at the city's bound; there were the streets that crossed from one thoroughfare to another or branched at lesser angles; there were the smaller streets that ran their narrow and irregular courses like canals through the masses of tall tenements in the denser parts of the city; and there were the alleys and little back streets belonging to every large town. There were broadenings of streets in places; there were the amplifications where porticoes bordered the way, with the shops that were sheltered by them; there were the market areas; there were the more splendid spaces for public business; and there were the gardens or parks.

It will be helpful here to set down the various names of the Roman thoroughfares and spaces. The *via* was usually the great road continued in the city; it may be called the avenue. The *vicus* was the ordinary street, large or small. The *clivus* was the *vicus* as it made one of the many ascents in the rolling city. *Plateia* was the borrowed Greek word denoting a broad passage or square — the later *piazza, plaza, place, Platz,* place. The *porticus* was the marble colonnade or arcade as it bordered an ample street and protected the walker from sun and rain, or it was the colonnade of four sides inclosing a market place, a theater and its space, or a temple and its area. The *forum* was a larger space devoted to trade or to the public business, and in the latter case contained or was bordered by state buildings and ornamental architecture. The main public square of any city in the West was likely to be called the forum, and the little towns that were nothing but markets were often called fora, as Forum Appi on the Appian Way.

The city, ten miles in circumference and three or more in diameter, that was crisscrossed and slashed and broken by these avenues and streets and alleys and porticoes and public squares was notable for variety.

It was varied, first, in density of population and buildings. The more thickly inhabited quarters were the Aventine and Caelian and southern Esquiline, with their slopes and intervening valleys, the district about the Capitoline reaching to the Tiber and south to the Aventine, and the depressions and slopes between the Quirinal and Viminal and Esquiline. The Palatine had always been a residence quarter, and with Augustus became the imperial quarter. The Capitoline was the seat of the two great temples of Juno and Jupiter, with a public square between them like the Piazza Campidoglio of to-day. The Forum was monumental and ornate

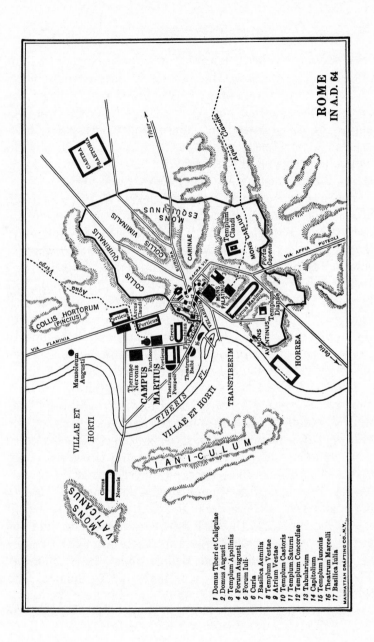

ROME
IN A.D. 64

1 Domus Tiberi et Caligulae
2 Domus Augusti
3 Templum Apollinis
4 Forum Augusti
5 Forum Iuli
6 Curia
7 Basilica Aemilia
8 Templum Vestae
9 Atrium Vestae
10 Templum Castoris
11 Templum Saturni
12 Templum Concordiae
13 Tabularium
14 Capitolium
15 Templum Iunonis
16 Theatrum Marcelli
17 Basilica Iulia

MANHATTAN DRAFTING CO., N.Y.

with senate, basilicas, temples, and honorary columns and statues. The Campus Martius was a place of magnificent distances and of buildings in the grand style. The high parts of the Quirinal and Viminal and Esquiline were occupied by the wealthy, and houses and palaces were interspersed with villas and gardens, public and private. The Janiculum towered above a popular but not yet crowded region called Transtiberim, the Trastevere of to-day.

The city was varied, next, in elevation. The spacious area of the Campus Martius, alluvial in origin, was as flat as a floor. The Forum, and the Velabrum leading south from it, lay at times deep in the shade of the buildings that towered above them on the steep and lofty Capitoline and Palatine. The central hills were 150 feet above the sea, the broader Caelian and Aventine about the same, and the long reaches of Esquiline and Viminal and Quirinal were about 200. The Janiculum, 292 feet, was the highest ground in Rome. The city rose and fell with a grand rolling of hill and valley that was only here and there abrupt.

That Rome was varied in its thoroughfares, we have already seen. It was varied also in its buildings. There were the temples of the Capitol rising against the sky, and two or three hundred others, large and small, scattered throughout the city, most of them in the Greek columnar style. There were the palaces of emperors and aristocrats on the Palatine, with unnumbered others on the hills to north and east. There were the Julian and Aemilian basilicas in the Forum, with the Rostra and the senate, and the arches of Augustus and Tiberius. There were the theaters of Pompey, Marcellus, and Balbus about the Capitoline. There was the Circus Maximus between the Palatine and the Aventine, and the Circus Flaminius near Pompey's Theater. There were the Forum of Julius Caesar and the

Forum of Augustus, with temples and colonnades, exuberant with the richest marbles. There were the shops for the wealthier trade in the city's heart, and there were the innumerable smaller shops all over the city for the use of the population at large — vegetable and fruit shops, clothing shops, shops for meats and cheese, restaurants and wine shops, barber shops, jewelry shops. There were jets and water-troughs here and there at the corners of the streets, fed by the seven aqueducts that brought cool waters from the mountain streams or the springs in the Campagna, many miles away. The chief of these were the Aqua Appia, built in 312 B.C., with its source ten miles east of Rome; the Anio Vetus, 272 B.C., coming from the Anio above Tivoli, forty miles long; and the Marcia, 144 B.C., from the Anio valley fifty-seven miles away. There were hundreds and perhaps thousands of wayside shrines of every size and character. There were the long lines of apartment houses and tenements that made up the solid mass of the ancient city, much as they do the modern, running at an even height of seventy feet, the Augustan building limit.

It was a city varied also in its population. Its old Roman stock touched elbows with Greek and Spaniard, with Gaul and Carthaginian, with German and Syrian. Its thoroughfares were thronged with plebeian and patrician, slave and free. Its business was as varied as its population.

But we shall in some future chapter see more intimately the business and the pleasures of the teeming, motley throng that filled the streets and houses of Rome. For the present, we are more concerned with the outward aspect of the capital city of the ancient world and the home of the Roman citizen. Let us conclude our attempt to bring it back to life by listening while the geographer Strabo, residing in Rome about 15 B.C., gives his impression of its grandeur.

A RESTORATION OF ROME AS SEEN FROM THE CAPITOLINE HILL

In the foreground are the Forum of Julius Caesar with the Temple of Venus Genetrix, and the Forum of Augustus with the Temple of Mars the Avenger. In the right background is the high ground of the Quirinal and Esquiline Hills.

"They have embellished the city with numerous and splendid objects. Pompey, Divus Caesar, and Augustus, with his children, friends, wife, and sister, have surpassed all others in their zeal and munificence in these decorations. The greater number of these may be seen in the Campus Martius, which to the beauties of nature adds those of art. The size of the plain is marvellous, permitting chariot races and other feats of horsemanship without impediment, and multitudes to exercise themselves at ball, in the circus, and the palaestra. The structures which surround it, the turf covered with herbage all the year round, the summits of the hills beyond the Tiber, extending from its banks with panoramic effect, present a spectacle which the eye abandons with regret. Near to this plain is another surrounded with columns, sacred groves, three theaters, an amphitheater, and superb temples in close contiguity to each other ; and so magnificent, that it would seem idle to describe the rest of the city after it. For this cause the Romans, esteeming it as the most sacred place, have there erected funeral monuments to the most illustrious persons of either sex. The most remarkable of these is that designated as the Mausoleum, which consists of a mound of earth raised upon a high foundation of white marble, situated near the river, and covered to the top with evergreen shrubs. Upon the summit is a bronze statue of Augustus Caesar, and beneath the mound are the ashes of himself, his relatives, and friends. Behind is a large grove containing charming promenades. In the center of the plain, is the spot where this prince was reduced to ashes ; it is surrounded with a double enclosure, one of marble, the other of iron, and planted within with poplars. If from hence you proceed to visit the ancient Forum, which is equally filled with basilicas, porticoes, and temples, you will there behold the Capitol, the Palatine, with the noble works which adorn them, and the piazza of Livia, each successive place causing you speedily to forget what you have before seen. Such is Rome."

VII

HOW HE LOOKED

Now that we have seen the city in which the Roman moved, it is time to look more attentively at the Roman himself. This will make necessary the study, first, of Roman dress.

The normal costume of the Romans consisted of toga, tunic, and shoes for men, and of stole, tunic, and shoes for women. Besides these, there were the occasional wraps or mantles for men called *lacerna*, *paenula*, and *synthesis*, and for women the *palla*. For the head there were various hoods and caps and hats and capes, but none of them in general use. Of course there was ornament, and there were styles of wearing hair and beard. It will be our business now to comment briefly first on these better-known features in the dress of men and women, and then on the variations due to material, station, calling, and place.

The tunic, *tunica*. This was worn by all classes and both sexes. It was the simplest of garments, having short sleeves and reaching to the knee or below. Sometimes it was worn with a girdle. The tunic of the women was very much like that of the men, but sometimes had longer sleeves. For both sexes it was the usual dress inside the house, and it was the usual dress of workers everywhere. Under it was worn a garment like short drawers or trunks, and women sometimes wore also a broad band of leather somewhat like the corset.

The *toga*. The toga was the characteristic garment of the Roman male citizen, and for a thousand years the sign

56

of his civic standing. It could not be worn by a foreigner.
It was the formal dress of the citizen on the street, at the
public function, and when he was borne to his last rest. It
was made of an elongated piece of goods, perhaps ten or
twelve by fifteen feet, normally
of wool in the natural white, and
of a cut and arrangement still
disputed in spite of the hundreds of examples on surviving
statues. The toga of consuls
and high magistrates in general
had a purple border. Citizens
running for office wore the plain
toga brilliantly whitened, *toga
candida*, and were called *candi-
dati*, candidates. Emperors,
and generals on the occasion of
their triumphs, wore the *toga
picta*, all purple and with gold
embroidery.

To put the toga on, the Roman draped it over the left
shoulder, allowing it to touch
the ground in front at his feet,
then drew its ample length
around his back and under the
right shoulder, and threw it
across the breast and over the

AN UNIDENTIFIED ROMAN
The toga is drawn up and hangs in a
short fold at the center.

left shoulder so that the end hung down his back. By
reaching under the fold across his breast, the wearer could
partially draw up the portion hanging in front and drape
it over the fold in such a way as to make it fairly secure.
In its simplest form and use, the toga was probably much

like a long, rectangular blanket. That it could have been very different in size and cut and manner of wearing, however, is indicated by the statues. Anything in dress so universal and so long in use was surely manageable, but in the extremes of fashion it must have been a difficult and expensive garment to wear and to keep in order.

A ROMAN LADY

She is draped in the stola, or tunica exterior, and palla, and seated in a cushioned chair.

The *stola*. This was the woman's formal garment corresponding to the toga. Another name, *tunica exterior*, suggests its nature. It was like the ordinary tunic, but ampler and more elaborate. From the girdle, or *zona*, at the waist to the top it was open at the sides, and the front and back pieces thus formed were fastened at the shoulders with buttons or clasps. When it was drawn up somewhat at the waist and overhung the zona in folds, its bottom just touched the ground. It had borders at bottom and top, and sleeves unless the ordinary tunic already had them.

The *palla*. The palla was the woman's mantle for out of doors, resembling in general the toga and worn in many different styles.

The *lacerna*. This was a short and light, sleeveless mantle or cape, sometimes with a hood, which was worn at first to protect the toga from rain or dust, and later sometimes took the place of the toga. It was open at the s and fastened at the shoulders. The *synthesis* was a fashionable dinner garment of fine material worn over the tunic, and was an indoor garment exclusively except on the Saturnalia holidays. The *laena* and *abolla* were cloaks of which little is known, and the *endormis* was a dressing gown used after gymnastics.

ROMAN SHOES

Found in the Roman border fort at Newstead, near the River Tweed not far from Melrose in Scotland. The two at right and bottom are of especially fine make.

On the streets of Rome on ordinary days, the uncovered head was the rule. In stormy weather, the outer wrap, or even the toga, could be drawn up for protection. There were head coverings of various sorts. The *pilleus*, a closely fitting, pointed felt cap for workers in the sun or rain, and the *petasus*, a Greek type of broad-trimmed hat for travelers, are the best known ; but the usual crowd in Rome and other cities of southern latitude would have been hatless.

For the feet, there were sandals and shoes. The sandal, *solea*, was much like the light leather footwear sometimes worn by children to-day, was varied in the manner of its fastenings, and usually worn only in the house. The shoe, *calceus*, was more substantial than the sandal, but was less convenient than the modern shoe. The tying of the senator's shoe was managed by means of broad pieces of leather attached to the soles and crossed and wound over the ankle and about the leg. For patricians there was a special shoe having a silver or ivory ornament called the crescent, *lunula*, on the outside of the ankle. The shoe of the ordinary man was more like modern footwear. There was rougher gear for laborers and soldiers, and there were wooden shoes. The soldier's boot was the *caliga;* the diminutive, *caligula*, was the nickname given to the prince, Little Boots, who became the Emperor Caligula. Women's sandals and shoes were different from men's only in their finer material and more frequent use of color.

For jewelry, the Roman man wore a ring which was usually of iron and bore a seal for use on letters and documents, and for the safeguarding of his cabinets or other places of keeping valuables. The gold ring was long the special mark of the equestrian class, but afterward became, like other rings, the sign merely of the free condition. Women used more jewelry than men. The museum cases display ornament in every material and form.

The dress of children, male and female, free and slave, rich and poor, was almost universally the tunic and short drawers and the simplest sandals and shoes. The boys and girls of the upper classes wore the *toga praetexta*, distinguished by the purple border—the boy until he reached manhood, the girl until her marriage.

Perhaps we should consider here as part of dress the care of beard and hair. Like dress, they had their variations in style. The shaggy hair and long beards of early times gave place to barbered heads and clean-shaven faces, but there were returns to the old manner. From the Scipio who destroyed Carthage in 146 B.C. to the Emperor Trajan, A.D. 98–117, the busts show beardless men with the hair well trimmed. Trajan and his circle wore their hair brought over the forehead. Marcus Aurelius and the Antonines enjoyed full beards and abundant hair. The Roman woman wore the long hair that the Apostle Paul declared was "a

Two Unidentified Romans and a Dacian
The bust at the left is sometimes called Sulla.

glory unto her," but in times of luxury she could dye and torture it or pile it high with the aid of artificial hair. Both little boys and little girls were lovely with hair that fell to their shoulders.

Such was Roman dress in its principal features. We should think of it further as having many variations.

There was the material, for example, varying with time and place and occupation and rank — silk, an article of great luxury from China; cotton, also from the East; linen, from Italy and Egypt; wool in great quantities from Italy and abroad; the skins of goats and sheep, worn by many in the country. There was the quality, coarse or fine according to the station of the wearer.

There was variation in color — the customary white, with the famous Tyrian purple as its most expensive and its most striking variation, and the crimson and violet produced in Italy from a certain shellfish. Purple, worn chiefly in the borders that distinguished the togas of magistrates and of boys not yet in the white toga of manhood, and in the broad and narrow stripes of the tunics of senators and knights, was the chief dye after Augustus, and almost the only artificial color before him. There was a great increase in variety and brightness of color, especially in women's wear.

Again, there were many variations depending upon position in the State employ. The wearing of the purple border and stripe, just mentioned, is an example. Purple was the distinctive color of the State, and became the imperial color.

There were the variations belonging to class and occupation — the populace in tunic and the ruling classes in toga; the slave in his cheap stuffs and coarse shoes; the patrician in his expensive and carefully kept toga and elegant footwear; the countryman in rough homespun; the soldier in military tunic and boots; the freedman and sailor in the conical cap; the respectable middle class in regulation tunic, toga, and sandals.

There were the variations due to race — the Northern captive in breeches; the African in his robe; the Egyptian, the Syrian, the Dacian, the Spaniard, each with something in garment, material, style, or color to betray his outland origin.

And finally, there were the accessories of costume, such as umbrellas and parasols, handkerchiefs, fans, purses, and gloves and mittens.

Before leaving the subject of costume, there are certain general characteristics that should be noted. First, the costumes of men and women were much more alike in Roman times than in our own. Secondly, the Roman costume went with the Roman eagles to the confines of civilization, and the toga was the symbol of the Roman spirit. Thirdly, the Roman costume, whatever it owed to Etruscan in early days and to Greek in the days when art and fashion seized upon it, appears with the earliest Roman, and endures unchanged through all the Roman centuries. Just as, amid all the variations of place and time, there remained a constant pattern of Roman character and conduct, so through all the diversities brought by rank and calling and race and time, there endured the Roma toga; and in the art and ritual of modern times its influence still persists. And, finally, the Roman costume as worn by the representative magistrate or citizen was one of pronounced distinction. The ample dimensions of the toga, its magnificent descending lines and sweeping curves, its variety, its massiveness and solidity, combined to make it a garment in the grand style, the fit cloaking of the lords and administrators of the World State and its capital city. Nothing more noble has descended in the portraiture of men than the dignified and stately processions of the Augustans on the Altar of Peace.

But dress is not the only factor in Roman personal appearance. We have not yet looked into the actual face of the Roman whose garments and carriage we have seen. If we do, we shall notice, first, that he may be of any shade of color from the ebony of the upper Nile to the rosy fairness of the Teuton. If we look only at the native of Italy and Rome, we shall note that his complexion is darker than the average of our American friends. It will vary from the weathered and swarthy bronze of the countryman and toiler in the sun to the soft and shadowed pallor of the worker within doors, but it will only by exception have the clear skin and blue eyes of the blond. In the second place, we shall notice that his features vary over the widest range. He may have the angular eagle-nose which the world calls Roman, but he is quite as likely to have some other, and we are compelled to abandon the conception of a typical Roman. The portrait busts that stand in scores against the museum walls are as remarkably individual as any portrait gallery of New England characters. In all but complexion, an assembly of elderly Roman faces in Cato's time would not have been greatly unlike the faces of our Puritan fathers.

On close acquaintance with the Roman authors, we realize that the personal resemblance noticed in statuary extends to character as well. The reader of our early American history will feel at home in the Roman stories of hardships willingly endured, of disaster bravely met, of devotion to ancestral faith, of temptation overcome and integrity preserved.

VIII

THE SOCIETY IN WHICH HE MOVED

The capital city of modern times is the convenient meeting place and seat of government, the creation and not the creator of the state, the servant and not the mistress of the state. The ancient state was a city-state, and the capital was identical with the state in a way not true of capitals to-day. All voters were enrolled in the voting groups at Rome, for example, and all who cast the vote were obliged to do so in the capital. In other words, representative government was not developed as in modern times.

Rome was not only the capital of the Roman State, but its beginnings were the beginnings of the State and the growth of the State was only the expansion of the city. However great the territory annexed, however great the increase in the number of citizens, the government continued to be the constitution of the city of Rome. The four voting tribes of the city of Servius had reached the maximum of thirty-five in 241 B.C., but all belonged to Rome and the immediate neighborhood. New voters thereafter were not made into new groups, but were distributed among the already existing tribes. Rome was an organic part of the Roman State as the heart is an organic part of the human body. The blood of the State was the blood of the city in circulation; the life of the State was the life of the city. The Rome of Augustus was to the Empire what the Emperor was to the citizenry. It was the Empire in action, as he was the Roman people in action.

Because Rome was the capital of the Mediterranean world, the society in which the Roman moved was varied far beyond the ordinary. Because she was also the heart that so long had given it life and determined its character,

THE PROCESSION ON THE ALTAR OF PEACE

The Ara Pacis Augustae was dedicated in 9 B.C. in honor of Augustus and Peace near the Mausoleum of the Emperor. Fragments of its sculpture are preserved in Rome, Florence, and Paris.

we must expect to find in Roman society a nucleus that was solid and constant. Let us consider what the social structure was into which Caesar, Cicero, and Virgil were born.

In the first place, as they were free men, each was born into one of the *curiae*, the thirty associations into which the free population of the State was divided. These associations, once of importance in religion, politics, and army affairs, were now only survivals, and need not be considered further.

In the next place, each was born into or assigned to one of the thirty-five tribes, *tribus*, of which four belonged to the

city and went back to earliest times, and the remainder
to the country. The importance of these also was soon to
be in the past, but their important function still was to meet
in their divisions, the *centuriae*, or centuries, for the election of magistrates and for other business involving the casting of votes.

In the third place, each of the three was born into a *gens*,
or family. The gens included all who bore a common family
name and traced their descent from a common ancestor.
There were different ranks of the gens, however. There
was the patrician gens, whose dignities and privileges, as
we shall see, set its members apart as the proudest of the
aristocracy; and there was the ordinary gens, which might
include the smallest and humblest groups of citizens. The
Virgilian gens and the Tullian gens, that is, the family groups
of Virgil and Cicero, were not of patrician rank; Caesar's
gens, the Julian, was patrician, and traced its origin back to
Iulus, or Ascanius, the son of Aeneas, the son of Anchises
and the goddess Venus.

Here should be mentioned the practice of adoption. The
head of a family who feared the dying out of his line, or who
for any other reason wished to include in his family the child
of another, could adopt by due process of law, giving the
adopted his own name, but adding to it in adjective form the
name of the family from which the adopted came. Publius
Cornelius Scipio Aemilianus, the younger Scipio who destroyed Carthage in 146 B.C., was by birth an Aemilius, the
son of Lucius Aemilius Paulus Macedonicus, victor over the
Macedonians at Pydna in 168 B.C., and was adopted by
Publius Cornelius Scipio, the son of the Scipio Africanus who
conquered Hannibal at Zama in 202 B.C. The importance
of adoption as a means of the preservation of old families
is easily seen. It might serve also as a means of giving home

and education to the son or daughter of a citizen in straitened circumstances.

But these groupings of curia, tribe, and gens have more to do with political classification than with the constitution of society, though membership in the gens might carry with  it social standing. It will be better to adopt some other plan of analysis.

There are certain classifications which occur at once. There was the free man and the non-free; it is a slave society with which we have to deal. There were the few extremely rich and the many extremely poor; Rome was a city in which one fourth the population received the dole while the wealthy engaged in the wildest extravagance. There were the aristocrats and the plebeians, with a middle class less numerous than is usual in modern times. There were the two political groups, the popular and the conservative, roughly identical with the plebeian poor and the aristocratic rich. There were the native Romans and Italians, and the foreign born. There were the citizens and the noncitizens. There were the constant and permanent parts of the population and the floating and transient.

AN UNIDENTIFIED ROMAN

Let us analyze, however, in the more thorough and usual fashion. According to this, we distinguish in Roman society the patricians, the knights or equestrians, the plebeians, the clients, the freedmen, the slaves, and the foreigners or strangers. A paragraph or two for each will serve to set them before us.

First, *patricii*, the patricians. The name was probably derived from the *patres*, fathers, who were the heads of the clans appointed by the king of the early State to form his body of counselors, the Senate. All who could prove descent from these "fathers" composed the patrician class, which was thus hereditary. At first in exclusive possession of all the offices in the State, they were in the course of time compelled to admit the plebeians to a sharing of them. For the most important period of the Republic, a comparatively small number of patrician families furnished the greater part of the consuls. By Caesar's time, however, patrician exclusiveness had arrived at the usual and natural result; the number of families had dwindled to about fifteen, and Caesar's policy of creating new ones by decree was adopted. Besides heredity, decree was the only means of entering the patrician class.

However, though the patricians were always the flower of aristocracy, their original importance as active heads of the State was early lost, and a wider aristocracy, called the *nobilitas*, succeeded them — one to which men of capacity, with less regard to birth, could aspire. From about 312 B.C., when the holding of any office in the State had at last become the right of all free men above the freedman class, entrance to the new aristocracy, or nobility, depended upon election to the curule aedileship. This brought with it the right to display in the state chamber of the house the wax masks of dead ancestors, the *ius imaginum*, a right practically necessary to success in standing for the higher offices of the praetorship, the consulship, and the censorship. Since election to one of the higher offices carried with it the right to a seat in the Senate, the possession of the "right of images" was really the sign of entrance into the nobilitas, the notables, the wider aristocracy above mentioned. It was composed almost exclusively of senators and was called the *ordo senatorius*, the senatorial order.

The senatorial order thus really took the place in political life which had been occupied by the patrician class. The patricians, fewer now and only a part of the Senate instead of the whole, retained their social distinction but not their exclusive power. The senatorial order, composed of the plebeian by birth as well as the patrician, had not the social quality of the earlier Senate, but for three centuries was all-powerful in the State. With the coming of Augustus and the reforms by which election to the senatorial office became dependent on the ruler's favor, the Roman Senate began its career as servant of the emperors.

Second, the *equites*, the equestrian class, or knights. The equites were in origin actual horsemen in the army. By the time of the Gracchi, 133–121 B.C., the equites had grown into a distinct class which was at the same time financial, political, and social. It was financial, because entrance into it depended on the possession of 400,000 sesterces, or about $20,000, and because its greatest activities were in financial enterprise. It was political, because it was an independent body of voters whose favor was much courted by politicians, and because it used its power to influence government in favor of moneyed interests. It was social, because its money raised it out of the plebeian class and made it the natural ally of the nobles, who usually with its aid controlled the Senate. The equites wore a gold ring and a tunic with narrow border, and at the shows had the right to seats in the fourteen rows next to the senatorial zone, which was nearest the arena or stage or race-course.

Third, the *plebs*, the plebeian class. This was composed

of all the free citizens who were not nobles and who did not possess the twenty thousand dollars conferring equestrian rank. Originally, the plebeians were the dependents of the patricians, and had no rights of their own. The process of their winning the various privileges of marriage, property, and office is a large part in Roman history.

Fourth, the *clientes*, clients or retainers. Clientes is a term of two meanings. For earliest Rome, it meant merely those who were free but not members of the patrician class and consequently not citizens. They were attached in a more or less formal and thoroughly honorable manner to the patricians, who were called their patrons, *patroni*, protectors; and received certain benefits for which they made a return by being in general at the service of their patrons. The clients of the time of Augustus and later were of a different kind. They are known to us from the Roman satirists as the crowds of mean-spirited men who every morning thronged about the doors of the arrogant and ambitious rich to receive the dole of food or money, in return for which they escorted and applauded and in other conspicuous or noisy ways supported their benefactors.

Fifth, the *liberti*, or freedmen. The liberti were those who had risen out of slavery. Many freedmen continued as clients their relations with former masters, and thus came gradually to perfect independence. A freedman became a citizen in the act of liberation from slavery, but did not at once acquire full rights. With his sons, he was barred from the equestrian order and from office, and was subject to discrimination in other respects.

Sixth, the *servi*, slaves. The slaves were a great mass at the lowest step of the social ascent. Besides the natural increase due to the union of slaves within their class or to irregular relations with the free, the chief sources of the slave

supply were the capture of tribes or towns in the great wars
of the Republic, or the insurrections and border troubles of
the Empire, and the traffic of the slave hunter. Pompey
and Caesar are said to have disposed of more than a million
slaves from Asia and Gaul. The slaves of early Rome were
captives from the Italian races, and principally employed
on the land. In Augustus' time the homes of the rich were
filled with slaves from many parts of the world, and all the
coarse work of the Roman world, together with much of the
professional and expert, was performed by them.

The slave could emerge from his condition by manumission due to a master's gratitude for special service, or to
purchase by the slave himself from his own savings. He
then became a *libertus*, and his master ceased to be *dominus*,
master, usually becoming *patronus* and remaining so until the
freedman had acquired fuller civic rights. Marcus Cicero's
private secretary, Tiro, whose system of shorthand was
called *Notae Tironianae*, the Tironian Notes, was a freedman,
and Quintus Cicero also liberated an especially capable slave
named Statius. Tiro was known after his liberation as
Marcus Tullius Tiro.

The keeping of slaves was not unattended by danger,
both to owners and to the State. Immorality, scheming,
thieving, running away, and murder of the master were
among the slave's offenses; hard labor at the mill or in the
mines, banishment to the lonely work of the farm, reduction
of rations, flogging, and death in cruel ways, were among his
punishments. There were sometimes slave revolts. In
the disorders from this cause in 134–132 B.C., and again in
104–101 B.C., there were hundreds and even thousands of
executions in Italy, and in Sicily it required whole armies to
quell the desperate uprisings against the lords of the plantations; cities were occupied and besieged, and great loss of

life occurred on both sides. The insurrection of the gladiators under Spartacus, in 73–71 B.C., involved upwards of forty thousand slaves in South Italy, and their defeat was followed by the crucifixion, at intervals along the road from Capua to Rome, of six thousand recaptured slaves.

If we mention, seventhly and finally, the *hospites*, the guests or strangers who might be present from outside the citizenship and bounds of the Roman State, and who in case

MARBLE STATUES IN THE NAPLES MUSEUM
At the left is Marcus Holconius Rufus, duumvir of Pompeii and rebuilder of the Great Theater.

of permanent or long-continued residence were likely to become clients of the more dignified sort, or even citizens, we shall have accounted for all parts composing the structure of the Roman population. About it as a whole it will not be unprofitable to make a few observations.

First, Roman society was composed of classes whose limits, compared with American society, were definite and fixed. It mattered a great deal whether one was on one side of the line or the other, both as to one's rights and as to the esteem in which one was held. For centuries before Julius Caesar, the patrician families formed a close corporation into which admission except by birth was impossible, and when Caesar created others, it was by a decree amounting to social revolution. Cicero by his election to the quaestorship acquired the right to sit in the Senate and thus passed from the equestrian to the senatorial order, and soon became consul; but the former consuls and the patrician senators did not welcome him to their society without reserve, and he was known as a *novus homo*, a new man. On the other hand, there were offices to which patricians could not be elevated. Before Clodius, the enemy of Cicero, could be tribune of the people and thus bring about the orator's banishment, he had to be formally transferred from the patrician to the plebeian status. The prosperous plebeian could become an *eques* only after his fortune reached the requisite four hundred thousand sesterces. The freedman at his manumission from slavery was not yet, either before the law or in the eyes of his neighbors, an equal of the freeborn. Horace makes a point of being an *ingenuus*, that is, of having been born after rather than before his father's manumission.

Yet it should be said that Roman society was after all not wholly inelastic. Men did frequently pass from class to class, and usually because of special capacities. Cicero himself is one of Rome's best examples of native ability winning recognition. Of equestrian and obscure provincial origin, he held every office in the round of the Roman public service. Horace was the son of a man who had come into the world a slave, and his recognition by the Augustan circle as poet and friend was a testimony to the possibilities of social elevation on the basis of talent and personal excellence. Even the slave, who, together with the work he performed, was held in contempt, could rise if possessed of talent or industry, as was proved by the numbers of freedmen who thronged the streets and business places of the city.

Again, Roman society was not stationary, but in continual process of change. The population of the city was increased by the coming of foreigners, slave and free, to fill the lower ranks. Foreigners of the best class were naturalized by action of the people in assembly; slaves became freedmen; freedmen became citizens of full rights; plebeians rose to the equestrian and senatorial orders; and the higher orders were depleted by failure, death, and the decay of families. The Romans by Augustan times had been modified in many respects, but chiefly in blood.

In spite of every change, however, the ancient ideals of blood and character persisted, and had their effect in notable men and times. Almost in the midst of revolution, Augustus took active measures to foster the old-style faith and morals. He had the women of his household spin the wool in the manner of the olden times. His diet was spare and simple, and he slept in the same room for forty years. Stern toward the members of his family, he was to some extent austere with himself. Antoninus Pius and Marcus Aurelius, a hundred and fifty years later, exemplified with greater success the Roman type. Maxentius, after another century and a half, names a son Romulus, erects a monument to the Founders of the City, and in his losing struggle with Constantine has his main support in the aristocratic or old Roman party. The last of all the emperors, Romulus Augustulus, bears a name that harks back to founders' days. The two most bitter of Roman prejudices, the feeling against the foreigner as represented by Juvenal, and against the Christians as manifested by the persecutions, were entertained most deeply by those who cherished most the ancient ideals of character and conduct.

IX

THE HOUSE IN WHICH HE LIVED

The ancient house, like the modern, varied according to country, climate, city, period, and the taste and condition of the individual. We shall concern ourselves with the house of the Roman in Italy in the first Christian century.

The house of this time with which we are most familiar is the Pompeian house. The ashes and light stones from Vesuvius which rained down upon the city in the famous eruption of A.D. 79 and buried it twenty feet deep have preserved for us the richest of all our sources of knowledge of the ancient house and its life. At Pompeii, then, we shall best begin a study of the house.

The houses of Pompeii were entered directly from the sidewalk. The door, *ostium*, in the case of the simplest houses, opened immediately into the main hall of the house, the *atrium*. In case the front of the house was occupied by shops, the door led to the atrium by means of a narrow entry passage, at one side of which there sometimes was a room occupied by the janitor.

The atrium was a large, square chamber in the middle of whose floor was a shallow square basin called the *impluvium*, into which, from an opening of like dimensions above it called the *compluvium*, the water from rains fell after running down the tile roofing that sloped inward on the four sides. The roof was supported at the lower corners of the compluvium either by four beams crossing one another, in which case it was called a Tuscan atrium, or by pillars rising from the corners of the impluvium, when it was called a tetrastyle atrium. The use of more than four columns made it a Corinthian atrium. When the roof sloped outward instead of inward, the atrium was called *displuviatum*. In rare cases the atrium was entirely covered.

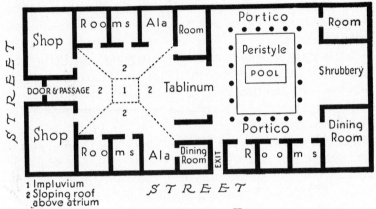

1 Impluvium
2 Sloping roof above atrium

STREET

PLAN OF A POMPEIAN HOUSE

This house has two dining rooms, and its peristyle is irregular in having rooms only on one side. The shops had windows and doors on the street which were closed at night by means of strong shutters.

The atrium was thus a spacious hall partly open to the sky, varied by sunshine and shadow in clear weather, and on wet days and nights by the patter of the rain in the impluvium as it fell straight through the open space or came streaming down the tile. About it were the various living and sleeping chambers, and facing one another across the end that was farther from the street were the *alae*, or wings, in one or both of which the man of family who possessed the "right of images" kept the waxen masks, the inscriptions, and the diagram of the family descent.

At the farther side of the atrium, between the alae and facing the ostium, was the *tablinum*, an ample room raised slightly above the floor of the atrium, from which it was only informally separated by a balustrade or hangings. Here the master of the house kept the strong box or *arca*, in which were his money and accounts of various sorts. Here he could receive his business associates, his clients, or his friends; or, by drawing the curtains, could shut out the world while he read and wrote, or passed the heated hours of the day.

Back of the tablinum, and separated from it again by hangings or by a wall with folding doors, was the peristyle, *peristylium*. At the simplest, this was a small space planted with flowers and shrubbery; at its richest, an elaborately landscape-gardened area fronted on all four sides by a colonnade supporting an inward-sloping roof of tile. From the colonnade, doors opened into the rooms of slaves or members of the family, and into the dining room and the kitchen. Above it were the rooms of the second story, occupied in a similar way.

The house thus described was the abode of a citizen of moderate means and good standing in Pompeian society. If we go in the direction of the poorer and less conspicuous, we shall find a one-story dwelling in the humbler quarters of the town consisting of the atrium, a sleeping room or two, and kitchen, with little else. If we go still farther, we shall find ourselves in the simple one-room house of the poorest. In the direction of greater wealth will be more pompous establishments in the style of Pansa's house, with shops fronting the street on three sides to insulate the life of the household from its noises, with many chambers about both atrium and peristyle for a household numerous in family and slaves, with a second story containing many chambers perhaps for rent, and with veranda and garden back of an elaborate peristyle. Such a house would be some 200 by 100 feet, with rich and colorful finishings and furniture.

To give reality to the house, we must think of the material that composed and made it habitable. Let us consider now the nature of its floors and walls, the furniture that garnished its rooms, the movable ornament that gave it variety, and the means by which it was lighted, heated, and supplied with water.

The walls of the house were usually of the mixture of mortar and broken stone or tile called concrete, surfaced with brick or a stone equivalent. Where they fronted the street or inclosed a room, they were finished with stucco and tinted. The tinting of the façade

A MOSAIC FROM POMPEII

The cat is killing a quail. Below are ducks, lotus buds, fishes, and shells.

was frequently made more brilliant by actual paintings, or on occasion was varied by the exhortations of the candidate for office; for example, *M. Marium aedilem facite, virum bonum, oro vos* — "Elect Marcus Marius aedile, he's a good man, I beg you." The façade might also be of plain gray stone without ornament.

The door, single or double, sometimes with a knocker, swung on a post or posts. The floors of entrance and atrium and various other rooms were of cement finished with mosaic. The mosaic varied from the mere relief of the cement pavement by the simplest and scantiest patterns in bits of enameled tile or cut stone to the brilliant pictures, elegantly bordered, which enriched the houses of the wealthy. The celebrated mosaic of Darius and Alexander in the Battle of Issus, found in the House of the Faun and now in the Museum at Naples, is 8 by 16 feet and contains some 17,000 pieces.

The walls inside the house were finished with the best quality of stucco and tinted in the deepest tones, the reds and yellows predominating. Pompeian red is a recognized color. Never without some manner of line or tracery to relieve it, the wall was frequently beautified by the use of bands or friezes, which might be enlivened with figures or scenes, like the famous Cupids at work and play in the House of the Vettii, or by the paintings, large and small, which are preserved in such numbers in the Naples museum or on the walls as they were found. The paintings of Pompeii now known are nearly four thousand. The use of delicate colored relief in stucco was also not infrequent.

The pillars of atrium and peristyle, their architraves, and the beams that crossed each other and formed the coffered or paneled ceilings and roofs of atrium, room, and peristyle, should be imagined in deepest colors and white and gold. Such splendor was found, of course, only in the houses of the wealthier.

It must not be forgotten that for its attractiveness the house depended much on movables. Among articles of furniture, there was the chair in many forms, of wood or marble or iron or bronze, with perhaps a deep-red cushion. There was the bench of metal or wood or marble against the wall of the atrium, or in the garden area. There was the table, varied in form and value, in atrium, tablinum, and

dining room and kitchen.   One famous table of citrus wood
in Cicero's house cost its owner the equivalent of twenty
thousand dollars, its material being the rare African citrus,
whose knots and roots were cut and fitted together with great
skill so as to display the wonderful markings for which the
wood was noted.   The cross section of a tree might also be
used.   There were the lounges, with arms and back and
pillows and cushions.   There were the beds, with mattresses
of straw or wool or feathers, supported by ornamental legs
and frames or resting on masonry, sometimes in small recesses, sometimes in the second story.   There was the
triclinium, the dining table of the rich, sometimes three
sloping banks of masonry on which the diners reclined while
being served from the central table inclosed by them, sometimes three movable couches of wood or fancy metal.   There
were cabinets for books, and wardrobes for the hanging of
clothes.

These articles, largely objects of daily use, varied in value
and beauty according to the taste and means of the master
and mistress of the house.   We may imagine other objects
less permanent and less utilitarian.   There were the hangings that no doubt graced the walls at times as well as the
openings of chamber and passageway.   There were the
vases of many shapes and sizes, of clay or bronze, that furnished pleasing relief to floor or wall.   There were the tall
candelabra of bronze or marble placed at convenient stations
throughout the main chambers.   There were the ornamental
lamps of bronze suspended from architrave or ceiling in
atrium and chamber.

The lighting of the ancient house was done by means of
lamps with one or more wicks, fed with the oil of the olive
or animal fat.   They were of iron, bronze, and terra cotta,
and of many beautiful and fantastic forms.   Their serene

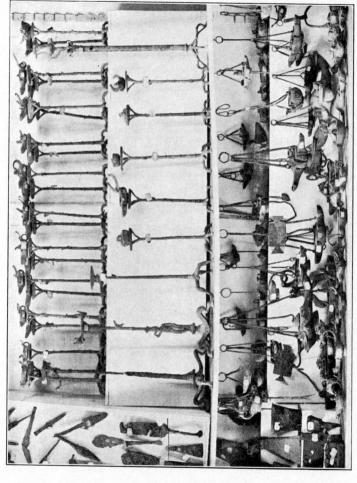

BRONZE LAMPS AND CANDELABRA FROM POMPEII

The lamps were set on the candelabra, or suspended from them by chains.

flames, singly and in clusters, were golden in the deep darkness of a house that had no windows in the lower rooms and
no communication with light except from the stars and
moon as they shone through the open roof. The slender
candelabra on which to set or hang the lamp one carried
were often of the rarest beauty.

THE PERISTYLE OF THE HOUSE OF THE VETTII IN POMPEII
The roof is restored, the ancient plants replaced, and the ornamental sculpture reërected.

The house as a rule was heated only by the rays of the sun.
The atrium in winter received the light when the sun was
high; the peristyle afforded in parts a sunny promenade;
there was in some houses a *solarium*, or sun room, and there
were houses with winter dining room to alternate with the
shaded one for summer use. Aside from the small pockets

of charcoal alight at mealtime in the kitchen, if any house was heated by artificial means it was by the brazier with its bed of glowing coals. In rare instances, the warmth came from a furnace whose heat circulated under a floor supported on little pillars of masonry, and through flat pipes that rose behind the plaster of the wall. At best, the house in the colder and sunless days of winter was not a comfortable place, and action in the out-of-doors must have been the citizen's escape from chill in the day, and early bed his escape at night. In the summer months, with awning above the impluvium, its twilight recesses were a charming refuge from the fervid sun of the South.

For water, the poorer houses depended on the woman with water pot on head who went to the nearest corner supplied with the always running jets belonging to the city system. In the richer houses, lead pipes in quite the modern fashion entered and supplied the kitchen, the bath, and the various fountains in peristyle or atrium.

To be complete, we should mention that the keeping of time was managed by the use of sundial and water clock. It is clear that the former would hardly serve on a sunless day; and neither indicated the time with the precision of the modern clock.

Such was the Pompeian type of house. It had many things in common with the modern house, but many things in great contrast.

The Pompeian house looked inward and not out upon the street. It had few windows, which were mostly in the upper story, but was more freely open to the air and made more use of the sun. It employed very little wood, whether in wall, roof, floor, or furnishings. Its wall paper was wall painting, its Persian rugs were mosaic pictures. It had no large mirrors on its walls, no ticking clocks, no gas or electric

POMPEIAN HOUSE INTERIOR RESTORED

Showing an atrium in the Tuscan style, with compluvium, impluvium, tablinum
and furniture, peristyle, and shrine.

light, no radiators or registers, no furnaces or kitchen ranges, no refrigerators, no rocking-chairs, no shelves of books in the modern fashion.

But the Pompeian house had its advantages. Secluded from the sight and sound of the busy street, spacious and airy, with vista including columns and light and shadow, varied with ornamental furnishings, warm with tinted walls and paintings and mosaic pavements, softened by the colored stuffs of cushions, rugs, and hangings, at its best it made a beautiful and stately home. In the better months of the year, its ample and varied spaces and airy freshness made it the ideal retreat, the dwelling in perfect harmony with climate. In the mild Italian winter, sheltered from the winds and inviting the sun into atrium and peristyle, it had a resourcefulness that went far toward tempering the cold and damp, which besides were felt less keenly by a people bearing them as a matter of course.

The Pompeian house, however, must not be taken to represent the houses of Rome. Pompeii was a southern Italian city sharing the culture of Magna Graecia, it was in even a milder clime than Rome, it was a provincial city, and it was a small city and uncrowded. Rome was a hundred and fifty miles farther north and fifteen miles farther inland; it was a city which in its early centuries of little contact with the world had grown into ways of its own, and it was a great capital in which building space was expensive.

No doubt there were in Rome some houses of the Pompeian sort. In a city which included and welcomed the ways of all the world, and in which so much was to be seen and heard that came from Greek lands, it would be strange if the Greek house also were not found. The one-story or two-story type of house, however, could hardly have existed in the heart of a city where space was in great demand, and where the Augustan limit of seventy feet proves that buildings approximated the height of the modern Roman apartment houses and palaces; and it probably did not exist in numbers, even in the less crowded parts of the city.

We shall be much nearer the truth if we think of the houses of ancient Rome as resembling the houses of modern Rome; that is, as buildings four or five stories high constructed about a court, with inside rooms looking on the court and outside rooms looking on the street, and with corridors running between the two the length of the wings. The excavations at Ostia are a proof that this is the reasonable view. In Ostia's more densely

THE STREET OF THE HOUSE OF DIANA IN OSTIA

The picture shows two stories and the character of brick construction. A small relief of Diana found in the house gave it the name.

built portions, the houses are several stories high and composed of apartments grouped about a court which is large enough to contain a fountain or well and to furnish light to the inner rooms. In some cases the court is more generous and becomes a garden. In the less crowded quarters of the town there are examples in the Pompeian style. Since Ostia was the port of Rome, a seaside resort of the Romans, and intimately connected with the capital, its building must have patterned after Roman building, and we are therefore justified in arguing from the surviving houses of Ostia as to the houses of Rome, with which we have little direct acquaintance.

So far we have been considering ordinary houses. A word may be said, in conclusion, of the extremes — the palace and the hovel — as they existed in Rome and its neighborhood. The hovel was a structure of cane, reeds, and straw, all one room and with only one entrance, the dirt floor occupied by table, bench, and bed, and other utensils of the simplest form, and by an open place for the fire, whose smoke escaped as best it might through a hole in the thatch or through the door. Meeting the bare needs of nature, it was occupied by the poorest and simplest people, and was the same rude shelter that had existed in the earliest times before Rome was founded. It is still to be seen occasionally in the lonely places of the Campagna or on the outskirts of cities, as rude as in the beginning. It was from this simple dwelling, the only type in primitive times, that the ordinary house and finally the palace developed, perhaps with some copying from the Greek house, which became known to the Romans from their campaigns and other movements in Magna Graecia and Greece itself. The Romans thought of Romulus and his men as living in such huts, and preserved on the Palatine a memorial called Casa Romuli, Hut of Romulus. The palaces in Rome were in part the houses of the Caesars on the Palatine, of which the Flavian is the only one well known, in part the residences of wealthy men among the tall apartment buildings along the crowded streets, and in part the luxurious homes in the more spacious garden quarters on the hills and on the rich country estates.

X

HIS CHILDHOOD AND EARLY TRAINING

We speak of education to-day as divided into primary, secondary, and higher, meaning commonly in America the eight years of the grade school, the four years of the high school or the private preparatory school, and the four years of college, often followed by three years of study for the higher degree or the diploma in medicine, law, or theology. The best way to understand Roman education will be to divide it as best we can in the same manner, and to see how it resembles, or differs from, our own.

We must treat the first or primary stage broadly by going back to the day of birth. Here we meet with something strange to us. At birth the Roman baby was laid at the father's feet for him to accept or to reject. The Roman *pater familias* possessed an authority over his children and the children of his sons which was practically absolute. Their lives and their earnings were legally his, and they were his property. He could make them slaves, for example, or punish them by death. This power was called *patria potestas*, and the Romans were proud of it as a chief cause of the solidarity of their society and State. It can hardly be supposed, however, that this authority was always put into practice. There were the natural feelings and public opinion to hold its exercise in check, and under the Empire it was even modified by law ; but its influence in the development of the loyalty, obedience, and discipline that lay at the foundation of Rome's greatness cannot be overestimated.

In case of rejection, the child was taken away and exposed. This points back to the primitive time when the infant might actually be left to die, after the manner of the Spartan State.   In the time which we are studying, it meant that the child was left where it would be found either by a chance comer or by some one who had a definite use for it, or even by some one known to have compassion. There were people who reared foundlings as slaves, and trained them in various occupations that gave them value in the market. Sometimes, in after life, the slave was recognized by a now repentant father or mother through possession of some ring or trinket left on the child at exposure. To-day, the foundling in Rome or elsewhere is likely to be cared for by some form of Christian charity.   It is not unlikely that there was something similar in ancient Rome, though on a lesser scale.

A Four-Year-Old Boy

Found in the Villa Livia at Prima Porta, seven miles north of Rome, where was found also the famous statue of Augustus in the Vatican.

If, as was usual, the child was taken up by the father and thus accepted, on the ninth day the family and friends met together in a happy gathering, a ceremony of purification and sacrifice took place, and little presents were given the child.   Among these was a string of playthings in various odd shapes, called *crepundia*, rattles, which were also to ward off the evil eye, known as *fascinatio*.   The father's gift was the *bulla*, a locket of gold suspended around the neck by a chain and containing some article or writing also directed against witchcraft or the evil eye. The bulla was worn until the boy became formally a citizen, and until the girl was married.

The ninth day was the *dies lustricus*, the day of purification, and was marked also by the giving of the name. The Roman name was composed of three parts, *praenomen*, *nomen*, *cognomen*, as in Marcus Tullius Cicero, Publius Cornelius Scipio. We have already seen how the addition of Aemilianus to the latter name signified adoption from the Aemilian gens.

The nomen was the name of the gens, the greater family including all who bore the name Cornelius, for example, and who traced their descent from a common ancestor Cornelius. The cognomen signified a branch of the family ; Publius Cornelius Scipio belonged to the Scipio branch of the Cornelian gens. The praenomen was the individual name given by the father on the dies lustricus. Cicero was thus a member of the Cicero branch of the Tullian gens who was given the name Marcus, as his brother received the name Quintus. It was usual for the eldest son to receive the father's praenomen. Among the best-known praenomina were Gaius, Lucius, Manius, Marcus, Publius, Sextus, Titus ; the total number was small, being in Cicero's time only eighteen. All were abbreviated by the use of the initial except Manius, which was written M'. Some of the most prominent nomina were Cornelius, Julius, Sempronius, Valerius, Claudius, Aemilius. The cognomina, as in Marcus Tullius Cicero, Gaius Julius Caesar, Publius Vergilius Maro, Tiberius Claudius Nero, appear in great variety, and sometimes suggest an origin in racial or personal peculiarity. The name Sabinus signified that the first of that line was a Sabine ; Benignus was good-tempered. The cognomen Cicero was thought to have been given first to some Tullius who either made a fortune from the *cicer*, a variety of pea, or bore a wart that resembled it.

An extended and official form of the Roman's name might include the name of his father, the tribe in which he was enrolled as a voter, and an adjective denoting that he had distinguished himself as governor or general in some province or in the taking of some city. Supposing Cicero to have had the name Marcus Tullius Marci Filius Palatina Tribu Cicero Asiaticus, we find in it that he was the son of Marcus, that he was enrolled in the Palatine tribe or division of citizens, and that he distinguished himself as a servant of the State in Asia. We have seen that the elder Scipio was called Africanus, and that Aemilius Paulus was known as Macedonicus; Scipio the Younger received the name Numantinus from his capture of Numantia, in Spain, in 133 B.C.

The first instruction of the child in the family of the old Roman type was given by the mother and father. The Romans were proud of their own instruction of sons and daughters in the ways of useful members of the family and the State. The mother was with her children constantly, and the son, as soon as years permitted, was much in his father's company. In the richer homes of the city, by Cicero's time, there were nurses and attendants, usually slaves of the household, and the bond uniting parents and children was relaxed; but on the whole we must think of the Romans as more than usually intimate with their children and more than usually wise in their use of this close relation in the forming of character as well as in practical instruction.

For the formal instruction not given by parents or relatives, there were the elementary teachers of reading, writing, and numbers. They might be slaves belonging to the house

and instructing within it the children of their master, sometimes with the children of other households included for the
sake of convenience and economy.   They might be teachers
conducting schools which were open to all children on payment of a monthly fee.   "Com-
ing on the Ides with the eight
coppers to settle their account,"
is Horace's reference to the
schoolboys of Venusia, whom he
describes also as "carrying tablet
and pencil cases on the left arm."

"With her small tablets in her
hand, and her satchel on her arm,"

is the picture of Virginia in
Macaulay's *Lays of Ancient Rome*
as she goes home from school
through the Roman Forum.

The apparatus of instruction
in the primary school consisted
of the wax tablet and the stylus, corresponding to the old slate
and pencil or the present paper
and pencil of America; papyrus
and pen for the more careful
work; the roll or book containing

A MOTHER AND SON
Perhaps Agrippina and Nero.

the poetry or prose in use; and the abacus, a counting
board of a sort still known and used in parts of the world,
by which reckonings in the higher numbers could be made.
The fingers also were used in counting, with other parts of
the body, but in a system too difficult to be recovered completely, though it was still in use in the Middle Ages.

The teachers in the primary work were the *litterator* and

the *calculator*, the "letter man" and the "pebble man";
the pebbles by this time meaning the calculi of the abacus
or the counters used without it. There was much memory
work, particularly the learning of the *Twelve Tables*, Rome's
earliest written laws, and of precepts of the sort given by
Benjamin Franklin in *Poor Richard's Almanac*, called *sen-
tentiae*. Sometimes, in the effort to make instruction pleasant, they used devices not unknown to-day — "as coaxing
teachers give pastries to children so that they will learn their
elements," writes Horace. Sometimes they were persua-
sive in other ways; Horace mentions also one *Orbilius
plagosus*, a teacher known for his whippings. Quintilian, a
famous educator of whom Pliny was a pupil about A.D. 75,
writes earnestly in disapproval of physical punishment, on
the ground that it destroys a boy's self-respect and is unworthy of a free man and a Roman.

It is likely that the Roman school was noisy. The children studied aloud, the schoolroom was frequently in open
air and in the din of the city, and the teacher consequently
raised his voice. In an epigram of Martial a schoolmaster
is addressed as "thundering with savage voice and beatings,"
making a noise worse than the metal worker forging a statue,
and shouting louder than the outcries in the amphitheater at
a gladiator fight. This is epigram and satire, however, and in
the ordinary school it was the studying aloud that was heard.

" What have you against us, you school-teaching villain,
   Detested by girls and by boys,
 That before crested cocks break the silence,
   Your blows raise that horrible noise?

" When a bronze-worker's putting a lawyer on horseback,
   The blow on the anvil's less loud;
 Milder yells in the great Colosseum
   The victor receives from his crowd.

" We next door wish to doze — during some of the night hours ;
  Entire lack of sleep makes us ill.
Let 'em out ; what they pay you for bawling
  We'll pay if you'll only keep still."

The schoolmaster in this epigram is spoken of as beginning his vociferous day "before crested cocks break the silence," and keeping the neighbors from their night's sleep. Juvenal, in the same generation, refers to boys sitting in school at an hour when no smith and no wool-carder would be at work, and to Horace and Virgil, that is, their school readers, begrimed and discolored by the sooty light of as many lamps as there were boys. No doubt the hours of school in the Roman cities were very early, but it should be remembered that in the rainy Italian winter months the darkness lasts far into the morning. In Rome to-day children are often taken to school when the streets are not yet in full day.

In an epigram to another harsh schoolmaster, Martial scolds about keeping the boys at work in the heat of summer. "The glaring days are hot with the flaming Lion, and glowing July is baking the parched harvest fields. Put away your whips of Scythian leather with their rough lashes, and your gloomy rods and your schoolmaster scepters, and let them sleep till the Ides of October ; if your boys keep well in the summer, they are learning enough." Here again are the words of the satirist, but it is likely that as little sentiment was wasted in the matter of summer heat as in that of early rising. There were no long summer vacations in Rome, but the frequency and length of holiday interruptions during the year made up for this. There were probably as many as a hundred holidays — Saturnalia, Lupercalia, Parilia, etc. — and it is likely that the Roman boy had as many free days as the modern boy, even counting the Saturdays and Sundays.

As we have been dealing with contrasts between ancient and modern, let us note here the greatest of all contrasts, namely, that the ancients had no school system supported like ours by the State and carefully organized to take the pupil from grade to grade and school to school from infancy to manhood, with the first years made compulsory. We need not suppose, however, that any father ambitious for his son was denied the privilege of securing practical instruction, for the earlier years of school were inexpensive, and setting up a school was the simplest matter. The great difference lay rather in the fact that education was neither compulsory nor urged upon all as it is in our own country to-day. Education was not the universal ideal, either in theory or in practice, that it is in most occidental countries in modern times. If anyone had proposed to Cato or Cicero or Augustus the compulsory education of every boy and girl in every station of life in all parts of the Roman realm for the primary years, not to say the years beyond, he might have been answered: "Why? It is not every man or woman that needs to be educated. Those in business and those in charge of public affairs should of course have command of the knowledge to make them competent and intelligent, and education for them may be left, as it always has been left, to the interest and ambition of individual, family, and class. The education of all would be a burden to the State, a hardship to the poor, an impossibility in the sparsely settled mountain districts, and a doubtful benefit either to the masses themselves, who would never exercise their knowledge, or to the Government. What the State wants on the part of the many is strength of arm, skill of hand, industry, and obedience, rather than a knowledge of which they make no practical use."

Because this ideal represents on the whole the thought

of the average Roman of either upper or lower class through the centuries that brought and continued the greatness of Rome, let us conclude this chapter here at the end of the primary and practical stage of education, which constituted the only education in anything like general use, and reserve the higher stages for separate treatment as belonging to the few.

CHILDHOOD SCENES ON A SARCOPHAGUS

The little boy is seen in several scenes, under the fig tree playing with a goose and a toy, and riding with his parents. The figure of the winged angel seems to prove this a Christian sarcophagus.

First, however, let us read two expressions of opinion which will help us appreciate the spirit of the Roman in the training of his children.

The one is from Tacitus, in whose *Dialogue on Orators* a speaker is recalling the virtues of earlier days.

"For in other days a man's son, born of a chaste mother, was brought up not in the chamber of a hired nurse but in the loving embrace of his mother, whose praise before all else was that she guarded the home and devoted herself to her children; or, some elderly woman relative would be chosen, to whose tried and approved character all the children of the same household could be entrusted, and in whose presence nothing was allowed that might seem unworthy in speech or improper in act. And not only their studies and school tasks, but their relaxations and their play, were watched over by their mother with a kind of holy reverence. In this way we are told that Cornelia, the mother of the Gracchi, and Aurelia, Caesar's mother, and Atia, the mother of Augustus, attended in person the bringing up of their sons and made noble men of them. This was a training whose strictness resulted in natures which were pure and without blemish and undistorted by any sort of defect, so that each one of them was ready straightway with all his powers to seize upon the honorable branches of study, and so that, whether he had inclined toward the army or to law or eloquence, he pursued that alone and mastered it completely. But in these days of ours the child is handed over at birth to some worthless Greek servant girl, to whom are added one or two slaves picked out of the lot, often the cheapest and those unfit for any serious service. With the stories and superstitions of such as these are the fresh and tender minds imbued, and nobody in the whole household has a thought for what he says or does in the presence of his child master."

It was about this same time that Juvenal wrote the famous line, *Maxima debetur pueris reverentia* — "the greatest respect is due to the child."

The other passage is Mommsen's résumé of Plutarch's characterization of Marcus Porcius Cato the Censor in the home.

"The old general was present in person, whenever it was possible, at the washing and swaddling of his children. He watched with reverential care over their childlike innocence, he assures us that he was as careful lest he should utter an unbecoming word in presence of his children as if he had been in presence of the Vestal Virgins, and that he never before the eyes of his daughters embraced their mother, except when she had become alarmed during a thunderstorm. The education of the son was perhaps the noblest portion of his varied and variously honorable activity. True to his maxim, that a ruddy-cheeked boy was worth more than a pale one, the old soldier in person initiated his son into all bodily exercises, and taught him to wrestle, to ride, to swim, to box, and to endure heat and cold.   But he felt very justly that the time had gone by when it sufficed for a Roman to be a good farmer and soldier; and he felt also that it could not but have an injurious influence on the mind of his boy, if he should subsequently learn that the teacher, who had rebuked and punished him and had won his reverence, was a mere slave.   Therefore he in person taught the boy what a Roman was wont to learn, to read and write and know the law of the land; and even in his later years he worked his way so far into the general culture of the Hellenes, that he was able to deliver to his son in his native tongue whatever in that culture he deemed to be of use to a Roman."

XI

HIS LATER TRAINING

Not even the first stage in Roman education, as we have seen, was the lot of every child. The part of it received in school instruction was far from being universal, and it is but natural to suppose that the part depending on the parents' interest was in many cases neglected.

We have seen also that, for the great majority of those who were provided for in school or at home, the training thus received was their only preparation for life except the living of life itself. The number of those whose elementary training was followed by formal instruction in higher branches was by comparison very scant. The falling off was much greater than that of to-day between the primary and the advanced.

The teacher of Roman youth in the second stage of Roman education was the *grammaticus*. As might be expected from the name, the training in this stage had largely to do with language. Its materials were the content of Greek and Roman books, and its exercises were concerned with the mastery of their content and with the use of the spoken and written word.

The school of the grammaticus was a natural step in the advance of enlightenment in a growing civilization which had begun with a little city-state of shepherds and farmers. When the Romans received in surrender the city of Tarentum in 272 B.C. and became the undisputed masters of Greek Italy, and when in 265 B.C. they crossed the Strait of

Messina into Sicily and incurred the enmity of Carthage, they entered upon a course which in less than a hundred years was to bring them into contact with the culture of all the Mediterranean world and to open their eyes to their own lack of the cultural graces. Many a Roman soldier during these years saw for the first time the cities of the older civilization, and many a Roman officer and envoy returned to the younger and ruggeder city on the Tiber with vivid recollections of an urban life brilliant with the architecture and sculpture and painting and drama of a long-established culture.

It was to this intercourse with Greek lands through the army, through commerce, through the Greek-speaking slaves who began to be common in Rome, through the Greek adventurers after fortune in the rising western city, that the amplification of the Roman ideal of education was due. The leading spirits in the movement were the elder Scipio who vanquished Hannibal, the younger Scipio who destroyed the city of Hannibal, and the friends who with them are remembered by history as the Scipionic Circle. The example they set was not without consequences. In time, Greek came to be in a limited way the fashion. The nursemaids of antiquity were likely to be Greek, as in certain modern countries they are likely to be French.

The first new schools were modeled in both language and content upon the schools of Greek lands. Their nucleus was Greek poetry, and especially Homer. The *Iliad* and the *Odyssey* were studied not only for their language and content, but were made the vehicle for instruction in geography, mythology, and morality, and for practice in composition and declamation. Like the humanities of to-day, this study of great literature in ancient times was either full of intellectual and spiritual richness or barren and unproductive, according as the teacher was well equipped and resourceful or unimaginative and arid.

The grammar schools in Greek were not alone. The grammar school in Latin also came into being. Having at first no Latin literature to form desirable subject matter, it

adapted the Greek. Livius Andronicus, a Greek boy who was brought to Rome a slave from Tarentum after its capture by the Romans in 272 B.C., and who became a teacher and literary craftsman, made a Latin translation of the *Odyssey* in the old Saturnian verse native to the Latins and often likened to the English nursery meter,

"The queen was in the parlor, eating bread and honey."

The first verse of the *Odyssey* came out something like,

BUST OF HOMER FROM
HERCULANEUM

This conception of the poet as bearded, old, and blind has prevailed since at least the fourth century before Christ.

"O Muse, sing me the hero, Ulysses wise and crafty."

By the time of Cicero, the plays of Terence, Plautus, and the tragic writers were added to the resources of the Latin grammaticus, and soon Virgil and Horace and Livy were to contribute still greater riches. With his country's heroic past now celebrated in epic, lyric, and history, the Roman boy of Augustan times in the grammar school had a wealth of inspiring matter in his own tongue as well as in Greek.

The variety of study possible in the use of literature alone is suggested by a sentence of Cicero in his work *On the Orator*, where he enumerates among the operations of the grammaticus in teaching, "the thorough treatment of the poets, the mastering of history, the interpretation of words, and a certain style in utterance." The possibilities of Roman history in the matter of character development are suggested by the work of Valerius Maximus, in which the lives of great Romans and stories from Roman history are made to illustrate the ideals of courage, endurance, abstinence, self-control, dutiful behavior toward parents, and friendship. The ministry of the poet to humanization in general is nowhere more richly expressed than by Horace in the first *Epistle* of the second book :

"The poet forms the tender and hesitating speech of the child ; even now he diverts his ear from impure talk, and presently also moulds his sentiments by means of friendly precept ; a corrector of harshness, envy, and anger. He tells of noble deeds, he edifies the oncoming years with well-known examples, he consoles the helpless and afflicted."

The end of the grammar period we have been considering must have coincided in many cases with the formal entrance of the Roman boy into citizenship. This important event took place at about the age of sixteen, though the age might vary, and it was usually the occasion for a celebration lasting the entire day. The day chosen was the 17th of March, called Liberalia, the feast of Liber, a deity of ancient Italian origin. Its events began early in the morning with a sacrifice to the household gods and the dedication to them of the now discarded bulla and purple-bordered toga of boyhood. The main feature of the day was the putting on of the plain white toga of manhood called *toga virilis* or *toga pura*. The family and friends then went in procession to the Forum and the appropriate office, presumably the Tabularium, or registry building, where the new citizen's name was added to the list of Romans with full rights. This formality accomplished, the procession continued up the Capitoline Hill to leave an offering at the shrine of Liber.

Marcus Tullius Cicero, the son of the orator, assumed the toga of manhood thus on the Liberalia in the year 49 B.C. at the age of sixteen, just as the struggle between Caesar and the Senate was beginning whose complications led to the tragic end of the father. The record of the event is preserved in two letters to Atticus. In the first, written at Formiae on March 11, while Caesar was blockading Pompey in Brundisium, Cicero says:

"I shall follow your advice and not retire to Arpinum at this time, although I wanted to give the toga pura to my Cicero there, and could have left this for Caesar as my excuse. But perhaps he will see offense in the very fact that I am not doing it rather at Rome."

The second is dated April 1, two weeks after Pompey had escaped from Caesar and crossed the Adriatic:

"Since Rome is no longer ours, I chose to give the toga pura to my Cicero at Arpinum, and our townsmen were much pleased by it. Yet all of them, and men wherever I go, I find gloomy and dejected."

The nephew of Cicero, Quintus Cicero Junior, also received the toga virilis at sixteen. He was at the time with his uncle Marcus Cicero, Governor of Cilicia, who wrote to Atticus about January 1, 51 B.C.: "I am asked to give the toga pura to your sister's son Quintus on my arrival at Laodicea." Virgil and the young Augustus were enrolled as Roman citizens at seventeen and fifteen, the former on October 15, the latter on October 18. The younger Antony was enrolled at fourteen. There were examples of the transition made as early as the twelfth year, and as late as the nineteenth.

The toga virilis and entrance into citizenship remind us of our modern "coming of age" at twenty-one. If we reflect that the event took place frequently on the 17th of March at the opening of spring, that it was under the patronage of Liber, an ancient god of growth, and that it symbolized the State's approval of the boy as a member of the civic communion, we may compare it also with modern Confirmation.

The next stage in Roman education is usually called the school of rhetoric. The students here were still fewer and more select. It was attended only by those whose ambition was to become orators, which meant those who aimed at the public career and its round of offices, ending in the consulship and the highest dignity in the State. It was of Greek origin; its teachers were the accomplished masters of composition and declamation who abounded in Athens and the cities of Asia Minor; its instruction was in both Greek and

BUST OF A GREEK PERSONAGE

Perhaps Sophocles.

Latin; and its whole concern was with the written and oral word, theoretical as well as practical, but mainly practical. Its two great devices were the writing of speeches put in the mouths of real or fancied persons, and the debate on some famous act or policy in history. It was not unusual for the ambitious young man to employ the rhetor in private, and the exceptionally talented were encouraged to finish their education in oratory by going to the best Greek teachers of eloquence on their own soil.

The importance of speech in the mind of the Roman can hardly be imagined in our day of careless enunciation and contempt for "rhetoric," a great art which we confuse with high-flown public speaking and "fine writing." We should remember that Rome to the time of Augustus was a State whose policy, and often fortunes, were determined by the able public speaker, that there were no printed newspapers, and that there was comparatively little publication; that the Senate, perhaps the world's most dignified assembly, was a body of several hundreds of men who were critical of speech as well as ideas; that the many-headed Populus Romanus in assembly was a hard body to dominate; and, not least, that much of the public speaking in Rome was in the open air or in large chambers, and required the expert management of voice.

The artificialities of training in rhetoric were of course pronounced, and did not escape the shafts of the satirist. Its themes especially were worn threadbare. "I too," writes Juvenal, "have urged upon Sulla to enjoy deep sleep as a private citizen." "Go your mad way and hurry over the terrible Alps," he says to Hannibal, "that you may please boys as a subject for declamation." Again, he represents the professor of rhetoric as complaining of the dull student whose miserable head is filled with the deliberations of Hannibal after the battle of Cannae, "whether he shall march on Rome, or, made cautious by the lightnings of a thunderstorm, he shall wheel his cohorts about all dripping from the tempest. Name any price you please and take it at once — what am I to give, for his father to hear the dunce as many times as I have heard him?"

On the other hand, the variety and richness of an orator's education when carried out in ideal fashion may be judged from the words of Tacitus as he writes of Cicero:

"Not content with the teachers that fell to his lot in abundance at Rome, he ranged over Greece also, and Asia, in order to make his own the entire variety of all branches of knowledge. For it is true that in the works of Cicero you may find proof that he did not lack in the knowledge of geometry, or of music, or of grammar, or, in a word, of any liberal branch of learning. He was a man who knew the subtleties of dialectic, the usefulness of ethics, the movements of nature and their causes. The truth of the matter, my dear friends, is this, that out of much learning in a great many subjects, and out of a universal knowledge, wells forth in its richness that wonderful eloquence of his."

The equipment of Cicero here described is really beyond the ordinary school of the rhetor, but no doubt represents the spirit of the best masters in the preparation of the orator for his work in life.

With our consideration of the training in rhetoric, we have really passed to the field of specialization, or professional preparation. There were no doubt some students in the schools of rhetoric whose purpose was only the general improvement of their faculties for whatever life they were to lead; but by far the greater number contemplated their studies as leading definitely toward the courts, or the schoolroom, or officeholding under the State.

In the matter of the professions in general, it is to be noted that in ancient Rome there were no colleges of law, medicine, engineering, and the like. The rhetorical schools were the nearest to the modern professional college, but even they were hardly the same. The Roman equivalent was the practical custom of *tirocinium*, apprenticeship. The young student of the law was loosely attached to some jurist of renown, went with him into court, sat with him as he gave advice, and perhaps was allowed to assist him in minor matters.

"After assuming the toga of manhood," says Cicero in the *Essay on Friendship*, "I was taken by my father to Quintus Scaevola, and, as long as I could and he allowed it, I never left the old man's side. Many wise discussions of his, and many brief and neatly turned utterances, I stored away in memory, and was eager through his wisdom to make myself more capable. After his death, I attached myself to Scaevola the Pontifex."

Caelius and Trebatius in later years were associated in the same manner with Cicero. In other professions, and in Roman occupations in general, especially in the arts and crafts, the same method of preparation was customary.

In conclusion, let us look briefly at a phase of education denied to all but the very few who gave quite special promise or who had more than average means. This was study abroad, the equivalent of study in European lands by young Americans.

The most renowned of cities in the ancient world was Athens — in Milton's phrase, "Athens the eye of Greece, mother of arts and eloquence." When Augustus ruled at Rome, its most glorious period was already four hundred years in the past, but it was still the intellectual capital of the far-flung Hellenic culture. Cicero, at the age of twenty-six, spent six months there, studying under its famous masters of eloquence. Horace was studying there in 44 B.C. when the news came that Caesar was assassinated. Marcus Cicero Junior was sent there at the age of twenty and cost his father no little money and anxiety. An account of this university student's career will be a fitting end to our study in higher education.

Young Marcus is already in the famous city in March, 45 B.C., when his father writes to Atticus, his banker and life-time friend, asking him to propose to the young man to keep within the thirty-five hundred dollars or so that came from certain rentals in Rome, and adding that he would wager other young men would not spend more. In August, Atticus reproached Cicero with having made his son's allow-

ance too generous for the boy's good, and the father replied
that, whatever young Marcus' record, it would be disgraceful to himself to have him hampered by lack of funds during
the first year. In the spring of the next year, one of the university officials wrote Cicero in a manner so little reassuring

GREEK AND ROMAN PORTRAIT BUSTS IN THE NAPLES MUSEUM
The third from the left in the upper row is Socrates; the fourth in the lower,
perhaps Hannibal.

that he thought of going to Athens to see for himself. In
May, 44 B.C., two months after Caesar's assassination, young
Marcus wants to go on a visit to Asia with Trebonius, one
of the conspirators, and to take with him Cratippus, his
professor of philosophy. Trebonius intercedes for him.
Requests for money continue, and finally Marcus is ordered
to get rid of Gorgias, a tutor distinguished quite as much
for immorality as for rhetoric. In August, he writes to his
father's private secretary, Tiro, a letter whose contents are

meant much more for Tiro's employer than for Tiro himself.

A glimpse into Marcus Junior's letter tells much about conditions in the University of Athens as well as about its writer. Among other things, we note the tutorial relationship between student and instructor. After telling in superlatives how very, very glad he was to get his dearest and kindest father's letter, and how his happiness was made complete by Tiro's own most delightful letter, he continues:

"I don't doubt that the reports you hear about me are pleasing and welcome, my dearest Tiro, and I promise you I'll do my best to have this good opinion which is being formed of me increased more and more as time goes on. So what you promise about your being the trumpeter of the esteem in which I am held, you can do with all assurance; for so much regret and torment have the mistakes of my youth brought me that not only does my soul shrink from the things I have done, but my ears also abhor their very mention. . . .

"Since therefore you were pained by me, now I assure you that your pleasure will be doubled by me. You will be glad to know that with Cratippus I am on very intimate terms — more a son than a pupil; for not only do I enjoy his lectures, but I am greatly attracted by his genial ways. I am with him whole days and often part of the night, for I am able to prevail on him often to have dinner with me. . . . What shall I say of Bruttius, whom I never allow to leave me — a man of simple and austere life with whom it is a great delight to associate, because we do not bar humor from our literary studies and daily philosophical discussions. I have engaged lodgings for him next door, and am supporting as well as I can from my scant means his needy condition. Besides, I have begun declamation in Greek with Cassius, but in Latin I want to have my exercises with Bruttius. I have as intimate friends and daily companions the fellows Cratippus brought with him from Mitylene, clever men whom he thinks very well of. I see a great deal also of Epicrates, the leader of the Athenians, and Leonides, and others like them.

"So much, then, for things about myself. Yes, and as to your writing about Gorgias — well, he was good in my daily declamation, but I have subordinated everything to being obedient to my father's directions; and he has written expressly for me to let him go immediately. I didn't want to argue the case for fear too much interest on my part would start some suspicion in him; and then this too occurred to me, that it was a serious thing for me to set up my own judgment against my father's. Nevertheless, your interest and good advice are very acceptable. . . ."

XII

THE WOMEN OF HIS FAMILY

To the average cultivated person, mention of the Roman woman calls up thoughts of dignity, nobility, common sense, and strength.   It calls up also the names of women remembered for these qualities, like Lucretia, Cornelia, Portia.

The women of Rome, like the men, were of many characters and conditions.   They were bond and free, native and of alien blood, rich and poor.   Like the men, too, they changed as the State grew older, larger, more powerful, and wealthier. The type we shall make the basis of our study will be the daughter, wife, sister, mother of the citizen in the times before the less worthy type began to be prominent.

The little Roman girl was given her name on the eighth day after birth, one day earlier than her brother.   The range of names available for her was even less than that in use for him, but probably more of hers are still employed to-day. The names of women do not yield so easily as men's names to classification or analysis, and were used with less formality and strictness.   We may distinguish various types, however. There were those like Cornelia, Caecilia, Valeria, Tullia, Julia, Terentia, Livia, Aurelia, Calpurnia, and Claudia, which were only the father's nomen, or gentile name, in feminine form.   There were those like Lucia, Publia, Gaia, Attica, and Paulla, which were the feminine form of the father's praenomen or cognomen.   There were some which indicated order in birth or importance, as Secunda, Maxima. There were diminutives, like Tulliola and Secundilla, formed

112

from Tullia and Secunda, and there were diminutives formed
from the father's name, as Agrippina, Messalina, Faustina.
The three-part name in use for men was not customary
with women.   One name usually sufficed, and when there
were two, the second was likely to be the possessive of the
father's cognomen, as Tullia Ciceronis.

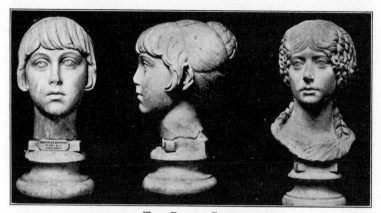

TWO ROMAN GIRLS

The one at the right may be Minatia Polla.   The other is seen in two views.

Up to about the age of six, the care and education and
dress of the girl were little different from the boy's.   During
the years that followed, the difference was greater.   As the
girl's destiny was marriage and the keeping of a home, her
attendance in the schools was shorter than her brother's, and
the portion of her education that consisted of training in the
duties of the home was greater.   Whether in city or country,
we must imagine her the companion and intimate of her
mother, learning to spin the wool into thread and to weave
the thread into the garments of the household, to sew, to
provide for the table, or, if the household was well-to-do, to
direct the work of the slaves.   In the more cultivated homes,

no doubt some of her time went into accomplishments, such as embroidery and other fancy work.

The time the Roman girl could spend in the studies of the school was further limited by the shortness of the time before she arrived at the age of marriage. This could be as early as twelve, but the usual age was probably later by several years. The women of Mediterranean lands are likely, other things equal, to marry at an earlier age than their northern sisters.

A ROMAN GIRL

It should be noted, first, that the Roman girl brought a dowry, the Latin word for which, *dos*, has passed into French as *dot*, and, humorously, into English as "dot." The dowry might be either money or belongings, and was furnished by the father or other head of the family; or, in case of independence, by the bride herself. The engagement was often made a solemn ceremony, with the formal dialogue which has been preserved:

"'Dost thou promise Gaia, thy daughter, to my son in marriage?'

"'The blessing of the gods rest upon it, I promise.'

"'The blessing of the gods rest upon it!'"

A ring was usual, worn on the third finger of the left hand, and the girl might also give some present in return.

For the marriage itself, only two acts were necessary : the formal consent of both parties, and the joining of hands in the presence of witnesses. No priest was necessary, and no official of the State. The wedding in a good family, however, was celebrated with many formal acts.

On the evening before her wedding, the bride had dedicated to the Lares her bulla and the bordered toga of her girlhood, and clothed herself, for the sake of good omen, in the tunic of one piece which was to be worn at the ceremony. In the morning her mother, no doubt attended by all the women of the household, arranged her hair in the traditional wedding fashion by dividing it with a spear point into six strands, a bit of symbolism with obscure meaning. She also fastened about the tunic a band in a manner called the knot of Hercules, this deity being a guardian of marriage and a patron of good fortune ; and draped her in the *flammeum*, the bridal veil, so called from its flame color. Its cloudlike nature was no doubt responsible for the verb *nubere*, related to *nubes*, a cloud, and meaning to take the veil, or to marry.

Thus costumed, and adorned with ribbons, jewelry, and a crown of flowers, the bride met the bridegroom, who had come to the house door in toga and chaplet, escorted by a wedding party of relatives and friends. After the omens of the sacrificial sheep had been reported favorable, she entered with him into the atrium, where the ceremonial clasping of right hands took place before ten witnesses and the wedding company. The matron who stood between them and somewhat behind to join their hands was the *pronuba*. The promise of the bride corresponding to our "in sickness and in health, etc., till death do us part," were, *Quando tu Gaius, ego Gaia* — "So long as thou Gaius, I Gaia." Our "Dost thou take this woman to be thy wedded wife?" etc., was represented in another form of marriage by the questions, "Dost thou will to be my *pater familias?*" "Dost thou will to be my *mater familias?*"

In the aristocratic wedding, the wedded pair next took seats at the left of the altar on the skin of the sacrificial sheep, while the Pontifex Maximus and the Priest of Jupiter, attended by an acolyte, made an offering to Jupiter and a

A WEDDING SCENE

The bride and groom clasp hands over the symbol of an altar, the pronuba, in this case Juno, standing behind them.   The remaining figures are probably deities, e.g. at the right are various gods of agriculture.

prayer to Juno, patroness of married life, and to the time-honored deities of the fields and their fruits whose blessing would bring a thriving family.   At this formal ending, the whole assembly crowded about the new man and wife with congratulations, or felicitations, expressed by *Feliciter!* — "with best wishes for happiness!"

There was of course the wedding feast; and, finally, after its termination at the end of the day, the procession escorting the bride to her new home.   This procession, called *deductio*, was an invariable feature of the wedding in high life, and served as well as the clasping of hands for the formal act required by the law.

The bridal progress was a spectacle of never failing interest to the neighbors and general public. The bride, separated by the groom from her mother with pretended force, found already marshaled in front of the house the various members of the procession, and heard the strains of the hymeneal song. Preceded by a boy with a whitethorn torch, she started on her way. At her side and holding her by the hand, were two other boys, all three no doubt in white, and behind her came first an attendant bearing the distaff and spindle that symbolized the character of the Roman matron ; then, carrying the holy emblems, the acolyte who had served at the altar ; and, finally, all the wedding party. The curious crowd, according to custom, cried out *Talassio!* though no one knew its meaning, shouted good-humored jests that sometimes reddened the bride's cheeks, and scrambled for the nuts, reminding us of rice, which the bridegroom scattered as he walked.

At the portal of her new home, the bride wound its posts with the symbolic wool, touched the door with oil and fat with a prayer for a life of plenty, as a precaution against the bad omen of a slip of the foot was lifted over the threshold, recited the formula, *Ubi tu Gaius, ego Gaia* — "wherever thou Gaius, I Gaia" — and was met in the atrium by the bridegroom, who presented her with the fire and water that symbolized the home and their life together. The bride lighted the waiting hearth with the whitethorn torch, and threw it, like the modern wedding bouquet, among the eager guests, to be carried off by the nimblest as a token of good luck. After a prayer by the bride, the pronuba conducted her to the *lectus genialis*, the couch which from that time on was to stand in the atrium as the symbol of union.

We have been witnessing what might be called the wedding in high life, like the modern aristocratic church wedding.

It was called *confarreatio*, from the sacrificial cake made of *far*, a certain kind of flour, and was the most formal, most aristocratic, and most ancient form of marriage. Its origin went back to times when the patricians constituted the State, were its only citizens, and married only within their own rank.

As the civic body grew larger and more complex, however, two other forms of marriage developed in answer to need. One was *coemptio*, or purchase, a ceremony distinguished by the pretended sale of the bride for a symbolic coin which was placed in actual scales. Another, called *usus*, use or practice, was based upon living together for one year. Both usus and coemptio were plebeian, and arose in times when the patrician marriage was the only form of citizen union. The details leading to the agreement of usus marriage, the terms of the period, and the formal acts at the end which gave the pact a final authority, all are lost to us; but, in the absence of complaint or comment, we may suppose that this most universal form of marriage was attended by obligations and safeguards which made it regular and of good repute, and that it was attended on occasion by ceremonies which made it as much an event in its own circles as the patrician marriage was in high society. Wedding celebrations of this kind may be compared with our home and civil weddings.

It has been noted that in early times only the patricians were citizens, and only the patrician marriage was recognized as legal by the State. When, toward the end of the Monarchy, the plebeians were made citizens, their marriages too were recognized as legal. It was not until 445 B.C., however, that marriage was legal between plebeian and patrician. By this time there were many plebeian families whose wealth and culture made them in everything but rank the equals or even superiors of the patricians, and the "mixed marriage" was not only legal but in many cases socially acceptable.

There were other mixed marriages. The union of a citizen with a noncitizen was legal, but the children were citizens only in case the father was a citizen. Again, in case of union between a citizen and a person from some race or community

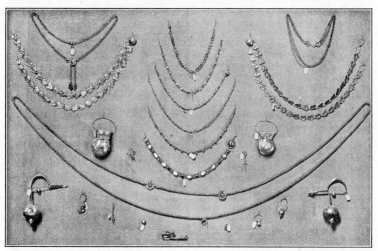

PERSONAL ADORNMENT IN GOLD
Chains, necklaces, ear-rings, brooches, and two bullas.

not having the right of marriage with Roman citizens, the act was legal, but the children were not citizens unless their father was.

A word should be said about property rights and about divorce. In the original confarreate marriage, the wife passed "into the hand" of the husband, and his rights over her and her property were the same as in the case of his sons and daughters, except the right over life. In the marriage called usus, the wife might pass into the hand in the same absolute manner, or she might marry, retaining membership and the usual property rights in her father's family. To do this, it was necessary for her each year to spend a period of three nights away from her husband. In the coemptio or purchase marriage, the other form of plebeian union, the passing into the hand was retained, an imitation of the confarreate union which may have been meant to carry social distinction. As time went on, however, marriage came to be more and more frequent without passing into the hand, and consequently without surrender of property rights to the husband.

This gradual but effective breaking of custom was both an accompaniment and a cause of the increase of freedom in Roman society. When the simple and strenuous period of early Rome had passed, and above all when the Punic Wars and the annexation of many provinces had brought the expansion of wealth and the increase of worldliness that went with racial and social experience, the absolute dependence of the wife on the old marital relation became distasteful first, and afterward unendurable. Economic and social freedom occupied more and more the minds of women, until by the time of Augustus divorces and illicit relations were so frequent as hardly to be scandalous. The Roman divorce was hindered legally only by the obligation on the part of the man to restore the dowry. The attitude of the family and the social circle no doubt served to restrain and to regulate, but at best the marriage relation, even in Cicero's time, was far from the dignity and constancy of the ideal union.

But it is not the purpose of this chapter to rehearse the scandals of the new-woman movement of ancient Rome. Let us not recount the usual stories of independence, arrogance, extravagance, ostentation, and abandonment, of mothers who refuse to rear their children, of women who

count the years by husbands instead of by consuls, of
noblewomen defiantly throwing away their names, of
princesses who disgrace their fathers, of empresses who
betray and poison their husbands; remembering in charity
that Slander, like Death, loves a shining mark, and may be
trusted to do injus-
tice even to the bad.
There is no doubt
as to a weakening
of character in both
the women and the
men of the late Re-
public and early
Empire. There is
no doubt also that
its causes had long
been coming with
the change of Rome
from the little rus-
tic State in Central
Italy to the State

TWO ROMAN LADIES

The lady on the right is Faustina, wife of Antoninus
Pius.

that included the Mediterranean world — with the increase in the number of woman slaves in the house and in
entertainment circles, and the increase in all the immorali-
ties that cluster about the institution of slavery; with the
increase in the foreign class and in all the fluidities and
irresponsibilities that belong to the alien and adventurous;
with the increase in wealth and its possibilities as the means
of defying opinion and authority; with the growth of a high
society that set aside the principles and laws that governed
the ordinary citizen. All this operated not only to encourage
relaxation of the moral bond in men, whose life by nature is
less restrained, but gradually to loosen the bonds of women,

who by reason of the limited field of woman's life are the more conservative sex.

Let us rather conclude by remembering that Roman womanhood included very many more than the few so fiercely assailed by the satirists, and that throughout the centuries of Rome's existence the ideal of the mother and wife and sister and daughter of the olden times was an ever present and living influence, constantly appearing in the flesh.

"Purity, loyalty, affection, the sense of duty, a yielding nature, and whatever qualities God has implanted in women" — is one of the many tributes to the Roman woman surviving in epitaphs.

"You were a faithful wife to me, and an obedient one," records another; "you were kind and gracious, sociable and friendly; you were ever busied with your spinning; you observed the religious rites of your household and your State, and allowed no foreign cults or degraded magic; you did not dress ostentatiously, nor seek to make a display in your household arrangements."

These are the sincere expressions that spring from the emotion of fresh bereavement, and their sincerity is confirmed by the less personal and more judicial record of the poet and historian. This is the manner in which the Roman Empire thought of the mothers of its early days, and this is the manner in which for fifteen centuries the later world has thought of the Roman woman.

But perhaps in our admiration for the loftier virtues of the Roman matron we have not realized as we should that the faithfulness and devotion which made her a blessing to her household were prompted by a heart that glowed with affection. Let the verses of two Romans far separated in time afford us a glimpse of the truth.

Statius, an admirer of Virgil who died at fifty-five in
A.D. 96, thus addressed his wife Claudia :

> "May that kind Power
> Who joined our hands when in thy beauty's flower
> Still, when the blooming years of life decline,
> Prolong the blessing, and preserve thee mine. . . .
> I saw thee, what thou art, when late I stood
> On the dark verge of the Lethaean flood.
> When, glazed in death, I closed my quivering eyes,
> Relenting fate restored me to thy sighs.
> Thou wert alone the cause ; the Power above
> Feared thy despair and melted to thy love."

Ausonius, born A.D. 310 in Bordeaux and reared there,
writes in a simpler strain to the wife whom he married at
twenty-four when she was eighteen, and who died at twenty-
seven. They have been married less than nine years when
he composes the touching lines :

> "Be life what it has been, and let us hold,
> Dear wife, the names we each gave each of old ;
> And let not time work change upon us two,
> I still your boy, and still my sweetheart you.
> What though I outlive Nestor ? and what though
> You in your turn a Sibyl's years should know ?
> Ne'er let us know old age or late or soon ;
> Count not the years, but take of each its boon."

At seventy, after nearly twoscore years, still lonely without her, he addresses her again, feeling the loss as if it were
fresh.

"Others in their sorrows are comforted by time ; these wounds
of mine are only deepened by the long years. . . . My hurt is
made the worse by the voiceless and silent house, in which there
is no one for me to tell of my griefs or pleasures."

XIII

WHAT HE ATE AND DRANK

The same soil was under and about the feet of the ancient Roman as lies about the modern Roman; the same blue sky in summer and shifting clouds in winter were over his head; the same waters washed his shores and carried his ships; he had the same physical needs and the same desires. To know for the most part what the common man ate and drank and how he lived, we have only to look upon modern Italy and the modern Roman. In reality there are many differences, but they depend less upon foods themselves than upon the manner of their use. Some of the differences most striking to us are due to the excesses of the rich which are made so prominent by the ancient writers of satire and epigram.

One of the two great feeders of the modern Roman is the land of Italy. It produces the wheat that makes his various forms of bread, his macaroni, and his pastries; there are other cereals, principally Indian corn and rice, but wheat is the chief, and in it the kingdom is nearly self-supporting. It produces the fruits that, each in its season, appear upon his table: the apples and oranges of winter, the strawberries and the cherries of late spring, the peaches and pears and apricots and melons and plums of summer, the figs and grapes of autumn. It sends him in autumn and winter the chestnut, to be roasted or boiled or made a dessert; and the hazelnut and almond, to be used alone or in confections. It yields the olive and its oil, one of the richest contributions to

THE GARDEN PLAIN OF ASSISI

From the Church of Saint Francis in Assisi, showing olives, elm-supported vines, orchards, gardens, and the Church of Saint Mary of the Angels, in which is preserved the earliest chapel of the Saint. The portico in the foreground is part of the Assisi church enclosure.

his diet and one of his country's greatest exports. It yields the varied and abundant vegetables natural to a mild and well-watered clime: the turnip, the squash, the beet, the bean, the pea, the cabbage and cauliflower, the artichoke, the cucumber, the onion, spinach, fennel, chard, garlic, the potato, the tomato. It gives subsistence to the herds and flocks and droves and swarms that furnish his beef, his mutton, his pork, his butter and milk, his endless varieties of cheese, his honey; it feeds his chickens and ducks and geese and turkeys; and shelters the hare, the thrush, the lark, the duck, and other wild things that constitute his game. The land of Italy nourishes the vine, which flows each year with nearly a billion gallons of wine in scores of kinds. From its mountains gush the springs that course to the city through the aqueducts, chief of which are the Acqua Marcia and the Acqua Vergine, bringing the same waters as in antiquity and over the same routes.

The other great feeder is the sea. From its nearer waters come the sole and the little mullet best known on the Italian table, with humbler and coarser kinds of fish, and from farther away the tunny, the herring, the anchovy, the sardine, and the cod. Over its paths come his imports in food and drink, which are not many, because his is a land of great variety as well as abundance, and because in the main he is content with what it offers.

The account of what the modern Roman eats and drinks, with a few corrections and comments, will serve for the ordinary Roman of ancient times. We note first that among his flour foods macaroni was not found, nor the bread and porridge made of Indian corn; and it is probable that his pastries were not the varied product of to-day, which is native to France and Switzerland rather than Italy. Among fruits, the orange was not the universal thing it is to-day;

the "golden apples of the Hesperides" of the ancient tales are a proof that the orange was not at home in Italy. Among vegetables, we must not think of potatoes and the tomato in ancient Rome. Among meats, beef should be mentioned as not so generally used as in modern times. Among dairy prod-

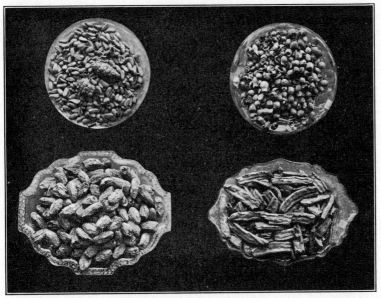

PRODUCTS FOUND IN POMPEII
Below, barley and St. John's bread or beans; above, perhaps rice and peas.

ucts, butter was little used and the oil of the olive was universal, as it is to-day. The place of sugar was taken by honey.

These are the chief differences as to the great body of the people. An enumeration of the luxuries brought in from other lands for the rich might add to the number of differences, but our impression would remain that ancient and modern food and drink, so far as the staples are concerned, are very much alike.

The meals of the Romans, like our own, varied with time, place, occupation, rank, and wealth. The ways of the Empire differed from those of the early Republic; the ways of the city were different from those of the country, the ways of the East from those of the West; those of the artisan and the laborer from those of banker and lawyer; those of the plebeian poor from those of the aristocrat and the rich.

AN ANCIENT MEAT MARKET

A customer or the proprietress with tablets, various cuts on the rack, cleaver, scales, butcher preparing a cut on the chopping block, receptacle for scraps.

There are four names for the Roman meals, and they correspond to our breakfast, lunch, dinner, and supper. *Ientaculum*, breakfast, is a word rarely met in Latin literature, and it disappeared with ancient Rome. *Prandium*, lunch, and *cena*, dinner, are very frequent, and survive in Italian *pranzo* and *cena* with the same meanings. *Vesperna*, supper, has also disappeared.

In the earliest times, when city and country were still a unit and classes were not pronounced, the universal custom was breakfast in early morning, light or substantial according to occupation, dinner at mid-day, and supper when the day was over. This was the natural sequence for a people leading an active life afield and in the open air of the city, and in the country it continued and still continues. In the city, the natural sequence soon came to be breakfast, the merest taste of something light; lunch, a fairly substantial meal; and dinner, the chief repast of the day.

These different sequences of Roman meals are exactly our own. Breakfast, dinner, and supper was the sequence for all in early American history, and remains so still for most of our country people. The order in the city, though by no means universal, is breakfast, lunch, and dinner.

With the average Roman of the city as the type, let us consider each meal of his day.

Breakfast for the ancient Roman in the city will consist of a roll or piece of bread, with a glass of water or wine. Of course he will have no coffee, tea, or cocoa. He will take his breakfast as soon as he rises, which will be at an earlier or later hour according to occupation. The bakers and the delivery boys and the laborers will be up at dawn, and will eat more substantially. The lawyers, senators, and the rich, with those in the professional and commercial callings in general, will rise later.

The Roman's lunch, in the middle of the day, consisted of bread, a substantial dish of eggs or meat, a vegetable or salad, a fruit, with perhaps cheese. He drank wine or milk.

The Roman dinner, at the end of the day's activities, was what might be expected after the light breakfast and simple luncheon above described. It was usually of three parts. First, there was the *gustus*, or *antecena*, which the French would call *hors-d'oeuvres*, the Italians *antipasti*, and Americans the appetizer. This might be set on in great variety, for the diner to choose from: eggs, salt fish, lettuce, radishes, etc., with a mild wine, sometimes sweetened with honey and called *mulsum*. Second, there was the main service, or cena, consisting of several successive plates or courses, including probably one of fish, one of meat, and one of vegetables. With the cena, ordinary wine was drunk, with water added, as is the universal custom also in modern Rome. Third and last, came the dessert, called *secunda mensa*. The possibilities for this were cakes of various kinds, pastries in general, apples and other fruits, and nuts, with wines appropriate to sweets. There were no cigars or cigarettes.

A LOAF OF BREAD FROM POMPEII
The baker's stamp is on it.

A simple dinner menu in Juvenal, about A.D. 100, is composed of : (1) asparagus and eggs; (2) kid and chicken ; (3) fruits. Martial, about the same time, has one made up of : (1) lettuce, onions, fish, and slices of egg ; (2) sausages, cereal, cauliflower, bacon and beans ; (3) pears, chestnuts, olives, toasted peas, green beans. It was so customary for eggs to appear in the gustus, and apples in the secunda mensa, that "from egg to apples" came to be the Roman way of saying "from start to finish."

The composition of Roman food and drink and the ways of Roman meals as given in this account will sound to most readers strangely sensible. We are so accustomed to being told of the scandalous luxuries and excesses of the Roman rich man — his nightingales' tongues, roast peacocks, and outlandish fish preparations — that we forget the sober and well-conducted people that lived about him and really were the people of Rome. The high life of the city belongs in a chapter to come, in which the life of Rome will be presented as seen by the satirist. In this chapter the object of our study is not the exceptional but the ordinary in the ancient Roman's life.

Where did the Roman eat his meals? In the earlier days, in the atrium, the large and only living room. In the country, and in every city house that had a garden in its rear, the table would have been set, for a large part of the year, in the open air, sometimes under the sky, sometimes under a leaning roof of wood or tile, sometimes under a trellis and vine. On the country estates and in the villages, many an evening would have found the family sitting in front of the house. It must not be forgotten that Italy is a Mediterranean country, that from May to October the warmth and sunshine prevail, and that through all these months there is almost never a drop of rain on Rome and the Campagna.

The fact of climate should be remembered also for the times when Rome had become the great capital and the Roman house had become an establishment with atrium and peristyle surrounded by many rooms, and with kitchen and dining room elaborately equipped and occupying space of their own. Many a restaurant in Rome to-day has its tables actually on the sidewalk for at least six months in the year. In the palace or on the street, the ancients no doubt made like use of the air and sun.

At least as early as the third century B.C., when Magna Graecia, or southern Italy, was annexed to the Roman State and brought its customs to the capital, the Roman dining room began to be called by the Greek name *triclinium*. The word, composed of "three" and "couch," describes the ancient equivalent of our dining table and chairs, and is applied also to the room containing them. It consisted of three broad, inclined couches about three feet high and ten

feet long, arranged about three sides of a table of rather small
dimensions in such a manner as to leave a fourth side entirely
free.   The entire room, in the house of Pansa in Pompeii, was
25 by 33 feet ; but this was very large.   The usual dining room
was little larger than the triclinium itself.   The couches were

A POMPEIAN TRICLINIUM

It is of masonry, with serving table and dinner ware.   The lectus summus and lectus imus, at right and left, are joined by the lectus medius.   On
either side of the angle made by the imus and the medius reclined the host
and the guest of honor, the latter on the medius.

of course comfortably mattressed, and draped according to
the standing of the family.   The triclinium might be movable, and in this case it consisted of three frames which, as
restored in the Naples Museum, make us think of bedsteads.
When permanent, it was composed of three solid and continuous banks of masonry, with round or square table built
in the same way, as seen among the ruins of Pompeii.   A rich

man's house might contain both a winter triclinium, built
where it could catch the sun, and a summer triclinium,
placed in a shady part of the house, or even on the second
floor.

The triclinium, as the name indicates, was a dining table
at which the diners reclined. The approved number of
diners was nine. More than this number was too many;
less than three, too few. "The number of guests," says
Cicero's friend Varro, "should begin with the number of the
Graces and go as far as the Muses; that is, it should begin
with three and end at nine."

The diners reclined upon the left elbow, three on a couch,
facing the table, which sometimes filled all the space between the couches and served the same purpose as the modern
table, and sometimes was only a serving table about which
the slave could move as he ministered to the diners' needs.
No cloth covered it, and it was often a beautiful and expensive piece of furniture.

Much of the food was served already prepared. The
diner used spoons of various kinds, but no forks, and the
knife but little. The fingers were much more freely used
than now, but it need not be supposed that table manners
were marked by less taste. Among the various features of
the table service, which had its delicate earthenware and its
richer and rarer bronze and silver and gold service, were
certain constant things, such as the goblets and pitchers and
mixing bowls for wine, the bread trays, and the *salinum*.
The salinum was an ornamental container for the mingled
meal and salt which was sprinkled on the family altar fire by
the master of the house at a certain stage of the dinner,
something after the manner of grace at table. In its most
pretentious form, it was of silver and an heirloom. This is
the kind which Horace has in mind when he describes the

happy man as one whose easy slumbers are not broken by
fear or sordid greed, and "on whose simple table gleams the
salinum." This seems to mean that even the poor possessed
the silver salinum as a matter of pride. The ordinary salt
container went by the same name.

The places at the Roman dinner were according to rank,
or to the preference of the host. The couches or wings of
the triclinium were known as the highest, middle, and lowest

CUPIDS IN A WINE CELLAR

The rustic dealer is handing the gentleman customer a sample; the careful and
anxious process of drawing it from the large amphora is seen at the right. From a
wall painting in the house of the Vettii, Pompeii.

— *lectus summus, lectus medius, lectus imus.* The imus was
occupied by the host and his family or by the humbler
guests; the medius and summus by the guests of greater
distinction. Each couch too had its summus, medius, and
imus, or first, second, and third places. The host reclined at
number one of the imus, and the guest of honor at his left on
number three of the medius, a place called *lectus consularis*
from its reservation for a consul whenever one was present.
One triclinium in Pompeii is provided with a children's seat
or bench, at the end of the imus.

Reclining at dinner, especially when the dinner was a social function, was probably universal in the city, and in the more pretentious houses in the country. It will be better to imagine the breakfast as an affair of little or no formality, and the lunch also as likely to be informal; and to think of the simpler households, and of the wealthier much of the time, as eating their meals in the sitting posture and in the free and easy manner that might be expected in the intimate life of the family.

An entertaining paragraph from Varro, the friend of Cicero just mentioned, will form a fit conclusion for our visit to the Roman dining room. The passage has been preserved for us by Aulus Gellius, the gentleman who lived in Athens and wrote for the benefit of his grandsons a miscellany called *Nights in Attica*.

"There is a most delightful book in Marcus Varro's *Menippean Satires* entitled 'You Don't Know What Late Evening May Bring.' In it he discourses on the proper number of dinner guests and on the service of the dinner itself. He further says that the number of diners should begin from the number of the Graces and go as far as the number of the Muses; that is, start from three and end at nine, so that when they are fewest they shall not be fewer than three, and when most, not more than nine. There should not be many, he says, because a crowded company in general makes confusion; at Rome standing, at Athens sitting, and nowhere reclining.

"The dinner itself, he says next, consists of four things, and can be regarded as fulfilling its purpose in every respect only if it gathers together a company of choice spirits, if the place is suitable, if the time is suitable, and if the service is not neglected. Further, he says, the guests chosen should neither be loquacious in their conversation nor dumb, because the place for eloquence is in the forum and before the jury seats, and silence belongs, not at a dinner party, but in a sleeping room. And so he recommends that the subjects of conversation should not be anxious and worrisome things, but pleasant and inviting matters, themes that improve and at the same time lead us delightfully on, so that our wit may gain in attractiveness and charm. This will of course be the result, he says, if we talk about the sort of things that have to do with our common experiences in living, matters that we have no time to discuss while occupied by public affairs and business.

"Further, as to the one who gives the dinner, he says, it is not so important that he be splendid as that he avoid anything mean; and not everything should be set before the guests, but rather such things as are wholesome and will be liked. He does not omit also to give us advice about the dessert and its nature."

XIV

HOW HE SPENT THE DAY

The world's greatest epigrammatist, Martial, a native of
Spain, who came to Rome in Nero's time at the age of twenty-
three and lived there for nearly forty years, describes in one
epigram the main features of the Roman day of his time.
The epigram was written sometime between A.D. 84 and 96,
the limits of Domitian's reign, and was addressed to Euphemus, the steward of the imperial palace, who was to present
a book of the poet's epigrams to the Emperor as he enjoyed
his wine at dessert. The day with which it deals is therefore
seventy years after the death of Augustus, and is concerned
with high life; but the day in general was much the same in
Rome throughout the first century of the Empire, and the
day in this short poem will therefore serve as background for
comments on the Roman's manner of spending his time. It
should be kept in mind, however, that with him the hour,
hora, meant one twelfth of the daylight or one twelfth of the
dark.

"The first hour and the second," writes Martial, "are given to
those who pay the morning call. The third hour exercises the
pleaders of cases until they are hoarse. To the fifth, Rome pro-
longs her various tasks. The sixth hour is rest for the tired; the
seventh will be its end. The eighth to the ninth suffices for the
sleek gymnasium. The ninth sends the diner to crush the high
mattresses. The tenth, Euphemus, is the right hour for my little
books, when your care watches over the ambrosial feast, and good
Caesar relaxes with heavenly nectar as he holds the sparing goblet
in his mighty hand. At that time admit my trifles; my Thalia
fears with bold step to approach Jove in the morning hours."

137

It is not easy to translate the hours of Martial precisely into modern equivalents, but he seems to divide the day in this manner: (1) During the hours ending at 7 and 8, the clients call to pay their respects and receive the dole, with orders for the day; (2) at 9, the business of the courts is under way; (3) the general business of the city goes on up to

REMAINS OF IMPERIAL PALACES ON THE PALATINE
The garden-like enclosure may go back to Domitian, the patron of Martial.

the 11 o'clock hour and through it; (4) at 12 comes the noon hour, with lunch and siesta, and the one o'clock hour ends it, or, perhaps, serves to wind up the day's business; (5) the two o'clock and three o'clock hours are for exercise and bath; (6) the three o'clock hour brings the time for dining out.

As Martial's purpose in this epigram is not the accurate analysis of a day but an exhortation to Euphemus to choose the most favorable hour at which to hand the poet's verses to the Emperor, it is not surprising that the divisions of the day are not distinct, and that its activities are not given in great detail. What he says in substance is: "The Emperor and the important people of the city are occupied until noon with the reception of clients, court duties, and other affairs. At the noon hour they are tired and want to rest. After that, they are finishing the day's business and doing their daily exercise and dressing for dinner. Nobody would be in the mood to hear verses at any of these hours. Wait until the Emperor and his friends are through with the day's affairs and sitting over their wine, and then present my book." The day here described is the day of the emperor, the high official, the aristocrat, the rich professional, and the commercial class.

The day of the middle-class man and of the lower classes exclusive of clients would have differed from that of the upper class in more than one respect. The early morning reception of clients played no part in it, and work took its place. Dining out was less frequent. With all the lower class, and with most of the middle class, the labors of the day did not cease with the seventh hour, but continued after the siesta until the setting of the sun.

The day of an average household of the middle class may be imagined somewhat as follows. It began at the rising of the sun, with slaves or servants already cleaning the floors. After a very light breakfast, which each took as was convenient, the children were accompanied to school, the master of the house went off to shop, office, or forum until noon, and the mistress directed or performed the tasks of the house, among them being a visit to the market for the day's provisions. At noon there was a light lunch at table in atrium, dining room, or peristyle, followed by quiet for an hour or two. The business or work of the afternoon was then resumed. At the proper hour the mistress or a servant went after the children and brought them home. A walk to the park, or a shopping expedition, or fancy work in the house occupied another hour, after which the remainder of the day was given to preparations in kitchen and dining

THE PERISTYLE OF THE HOUSE OF THE AMORINI DORATI, OR GILDED LOVES, IN POMPEII

The tiled roofing is a restoration, and the shrubbery is a reproduction of the ancient. Medallion-like ornaments are suspended in the porticoes. The house is named from little medallions of Cupids in gold foil found in the first room on the right.

room for dinner, private or with guests. The children were put to bed early, and the father perhaps went out for a social hour at a wineshop. At the end of the evening, the street door was locked and barred, the little lamps that rested on the candelabra were taken up to light the way to bed, and the atrium left in darkness.

This is the barest account of the Roman day, for our purpose up to this point is to realize only the general character of Roman daily life. In later chapters, we shall consider in greater detail the various occupations that made up the total of the city's work, and study also the diversions that were so large a part of its life. Let it be enough now to say that the work of the Roman citizenry was manifold, and that the round of the month and year was varied and lightened by many amusements — the play, the races, the swordsmen in the arena, the animal hunt, the juggler and mountebank in the street and parks, the Campus Martius and its games, the Tiber and its boating and swimming, the simple and natural amusements of the house, including the dinner itself, which occupied a larger place in ancient times than it does to-day.

It will bring the general character of the day into clearer relief if we employ again the method of contrast. There are several respects in which the Romans differed sharply from us.

First, their keeping of time was less precise than ours. So far as we can tell, there was no mechanical device for the keeping of time available to the public until 263 B.C., when a sundial was brought to Rome from Sicily, and with it the day of twelve equal parts as hours. There is mention of one thirty years before this, but it was at the Temple of Quirinus and probably not of general service. Up to the year 263 B.C., the measuring of time and the keeping of appointments must have depended upon the position of sun and moon, the casting of shadows, and perhaps other means unknown to us. Sunrise, sunset, and noon were the only certain points in the day. The amount of inconvenience and waste that had to be endured may easily be imagined. If the day was overcast, the meeting of obligations depending upon time must have been very uncertain.

The sundial itself is a very imperfect help. It is useless on cloudy days, it will not serve on any night, it is not portable, it will function only in the latitude for which it was designed, and even there it is but a clumsy and inaccurate means. The sundial brought from Catina, now Catania, in Sicily, though not correct for Rome, was used for ninety-nine years before a second dial was made, in 164 B.C., to suit the Roman latitude. Both were still in place on pillars behind the Rostra in the time of Cicero. Strange as it seems to us, the division of the day into twelve hours was not practiced at Rome before the sundial was introduced.

The sundial no doubt remained for some time comparatively rare, the few that were to be consulted being stationed near the administrative buildings, and corresponding to our clock on the city hall. Cicero in the defense of Quinctius pleads that his client "has always lived roughly and without regard for looks; has been of a gloomy and retiring disposition; has not spent his time at the Sundial nor in the Campus, nor in dining out."

A second step, and one of great importance, was the introduction to public use, in 159 B.C., of the water clock. This was a cylindrical container from which water was allowed to flow, and which was so graduated that the level of its contents, as they slowly fell, indicated the hour and even fractions of the hour. It might be of glass and transparent, or of metal, with the use of a cord and floating cork to regulate an indicator which moved up the graduated line. The "winding" of such a clock consisted in filling it with water at sunrise or sunset or noon, when the time was certain; and its repairing consisted in the accurate regulation of the flow that drained it. Its great advantage over the sundial was that it functioned day and night, and on cloudy days as well as clear.

Yet the water clock too was very imperfect compared with the clock of our times. Only on the March and September equinoxes are the days and nights of equal length, and the

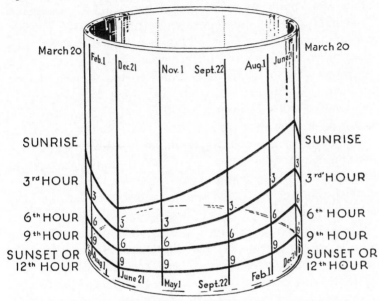

DIAGRAM OF WATER CLOCK

Filled at sunrise on the dates indicated to the points where horizontal and vertical lines intersect, as the water lowered by dropping away the clock showed the 3rd, 6th, 9th, and 12th hour of daylight, and by the use of additional horizontal lines could show other hours and fractions. By the addition of vertical lines it could be made to function on the other dates. By graduating the upper half it could be filled at sunset and become a 24-hour clock. Note that on March and September equinoxes the lines for day and night are of equal length, and that for every other day they are unequal. Their division into twelve parts consequently resulted in hours of equal length day and night only on the equinoxes. In summer months the twelve night hours were very short, and the twelve day hours very long.

twelve divisions or hours of equal length by day and by night. On all other days the light and the dark are of unequal length, and consequently their twelve equal parts are variations from the equinoctial hours. The earliest sunrise in Roman latitude is at 4.27 in summer and the latest at 7.33 in winter, and the length of daylight varies from 15 hours and 6 minutes on June 25 to 8 hours and 54 minutes on December 23; thus the hours vary from about 75 minutes in summer to 45 in winter. It is clear that if a water clock were made and operated for accuracy, it would have to be equipped with one graduated line for the two equinoxes, and with a separate line for every other day in the year, and that the amount of water supplied it would also vary. The water clock here described should not be confused with the water clock of the court and public assembly, which was a simple device like an hourglass used to limit the length of speeches and not to measure time as time.

With the introduction of sundial and water clock, and the more accurate calculation of time, it may be imagined that there was a great increase in public and private efficiency. This is proved by the very fact that sundials at length came into universal use. They have been discovered in every part of the Roman Empire, even to its very borders at the Sahara and at the limit of the northern wilderness. They were used in the more pretentious houses as well as in public. The distribution of the water clock, which was less durable and has left fewer remains, was no doubt even more general in the home if not in public life. The makers of water clocks were a regular artisan class, and their product continued in use far into the Middle Ages.

Universal as were the clock and dial, however, they were mostly stationary and always inconvenient. There were many who never troubled with them except as they were compelled by the law, which in some transactions involving time, as the use of water by the hour in irrigation, prescribed their use. Such persons went on in ordinary life regulating their movements by the use of sunrise; *mane*, or the first two hours; *ad meridiem*, or forenoon; noon; *de meridie*, or afternoon; *suprema*, or late afternoon up to sunset; and other more or less vague terms. In earlier times there were no doubt many who prided themselves on doing without the innovation, and others who half in earnest cursed the day it came to Rome with its bothersome precision.

Says a parasite in one of the comedy fragments of Cicero's time:

"May the gods destroy the man that first discovered hours, yes, and the man that first set up the sundial here, and took the day apart and smashed it for miserable me into little pieces. In the old days when I was a boy, a man's stomach was his sundial, and by a long way the best and truest of all your timepieces; at any time you felt that way, it told you to eat, except when there was nothing. Now, even when there is something, you don't eat unless the sun agrees to it. Yes, sir, the town these days is filled full of sundials, and most of the people in it are dragging around dried up with hunger."

The Roman day was thus very different from our own in the manner of its keeping time. It is hardly possible that this does not connote a great difference in the speed as well as the precision of doing business, and in the general tone of the city's life during the daylight hours. One would hardly have found the rapid nervous movement on the street or in the office that is the case to-day in America, or even in southern Europe. If besides we remember the Italian warmth of a great part of the year, we must imagine ancient Rome, even at its busiest, as leisurely and calm compared with the modern city. On summer noondays, indeed, the streets were almost silent and deserted.

A second difference between the Roman and the modern was the habit of early rising and early retiring. This was due entirely in the beginning, and indeed in great part in

later times, to nature. By nightfall the early Roman, both
in city and country, was tired out by the physical work of
long daylight hours. In addition, his house had the rudest
facilities for lighting, and there was little incentive for him
to make the evening long. The later Roman, in the more
purely urban life of Republic and Empire, was still without
the brilliant street illumination and the convenient house
lighting that have made the modern city more lively by
night than by day, and the modern home attractive for both
work and play far into the night. For those who have lived
a fireless winter season in modern Rome, it need not be
argued that the dampness and chill of the airy Roman house
on the evenings of the colder months encouraged an early
going to bed.

A third difference was due likewise to the lack of light.
The public amusements of the city — theater, amphitheater,
races — were all daytime shows. The Roman consequently
did not feel so strongly the urge to spend the evening out.
The most common of evening diversions, and about the only
one of which we are conscious in Roman literature, was the
dinner, and this was prolonged and frequent only in the life
of high society.

On the whole, the Roman day seems to have differed from
the day in our own large cities in six respects : (1) in its lack
of precision in the keeping of time ; (2) in the closer correspondence of its waking hours with the daylight and its
sleeping hours with the dark ; (3) in its longer midday
interval of rest ; (4) in its poorer lighting of street and house
at night ; (5) in the use of the daylight hours for amusements ; (6) in the prominence of dinner as the evening
diversion, and the lack of other night attractions.

It will be noticed that these differences depend chiefly
upon the presence of a warmer climate and the absence of gas

and electric illumination, and only in minor degree on differences in character and ideas.   The life of Rome was no doubt busy and crowded and noisy enough, and had its artificialities in plenty; but it was much more in harmony with nature than the life to which the increase of the world's population, with residence in colder climates and with modern inventions, has condemned the great capitals of to-day.

PART III

LIVING ROME

LIVING ROME

Our study of Rome and the Romans began with a visit to modern Italy and its capital. We found the Italian landscape unchanged and the city of Rome still sitting on the Seven Hills, with gigantic remnants of the ancient city rising in the midst of the modern. We went back to geological times, when vomiting volcano and surging sea and the mightily running river created the plain of Latium and fashioned it for habitation. We saw the first men settle by the Tiber, and traced the growth and changes of the city on its banks down through the ages and on to modern times. We saw how the Roman State grew strong and expanded from the Monarchy in Latium into the Republic that spread over Italy and about the Mediterranean, and into the Empire that made the Mediterranean a Roman lake and ruled the Western world. We saw how after the fall of the Roman Empire the sway of Rome continued — in language, in literature, in the arts, in law, in religion, in morality; so that the civilization of to-day is still the civilization of ancient Rome.

This was our setting for the Roman himself. Upon this stage and against this background of modern and ancient Italy and Rome and their importance in the affairs of the world to-day we placed the ancient Roman in person. We reconstructed the city of his time; saw how he was dressed and how he carried himself, and what the society was in which he moved; entered the house in which he lived; witnessed his rearing from babyhood, and his training up to the time of his entrance into manhood and the work of his world;

151

were introduced to his mother, sister, wife, and daughter, and were made to realize the splendid contributions of the Roman woman to her own and after times ; saw what he ate and drank, and took part with him in the life of his home ; and followed him in the round of the day from dawn to the setting of the sun. In all this, our purpose was to see the Roman as an individual figure.

We have thus completed the stage setting and introduced the principal one of the dramatis personae. In plainer words, we have made ourselves acquainted with the general appearance and general character of Rome and the Romans, and are now prepared for the special study of Roman life.

It will therefore be our purpose, in the chapters of the present section of our study, to follow the Roman of the upper classes in his career as the servant of the State or as the professional man, and to follow the common man to his daily work in the many skilled and unskilled occupations by which he gained his livelihood ; not forgetting the country and its life, so long at the base of the virtue and strength of earlier Rome. Having thus reviewed the careers of high and low, we shall try to give them color and vividness by telling the stories of representative Roman lives. In order the better to understand the meaning of life to the Roman, we shall make the much more difficult attempt to enter into his religious consciousness and to share his interpretations of the human lot. His diversions also will contribute to the appreciation of his inner being : the theater, the circus, the amphitheater, the baths, and the unorganized and simpler pastimes with which he garnished his existence. We shall find that he was a lively person and enjoyed the comic aspects of his environment. We shall note the follies and excesses that made him the target of bitterest satire on the part of his fellows. We shall not omit his excesses and crimes and the part they played.   We shall see him on his last bed of sickness, and follow in the train that conducts the mortal remnant to its last resting place.

The sum of these studies will be the collective life of the city.   Their result will be an appreciation of the human qualities of Living Rome.

XV

THE ROMAN CAREER

The great career in Rome was the career of the public man. It was the service of the State in the highest and most expert duties of the citizen. In its usual form it meant a period of some ten years in military service and lesser civil offices, and then the offices of quaestor, aedile, praetor, and consul. The consulship was the shining goal of Roman ambition. By the time the citizen reached it, he was forty-three at least, and a man much tested in the ways of the world.

The Roman career with its long, varied, and comprehensive experience was evolutionary, and thus the product of nature. The first form of the Roman State was tribal, and its chief was legislator, executive, judge, and priest all in one and might have said with greater right than the modern monarch, *L'état, c'est moi* — the State, it is I! With the growth of numbers, however, came the increase of duties and the sharing and delegation of their execution. The chief or king could not continue to be a specialist in every activity of the State. The council of fathers who advised him soon became the Senate that helped him make the laws. He had the prefect of the city to take his place during absences, the quaestors and duumvirs to arrest and try the criminal, and the tribune to command his cavalry. When the Republic took the place of the Monarchy, the powers originally in the king alone were still more widely distributed. There were the Senate and assemblies to create the laws, the con-

154

suls to act as judges and executives and to serve as leaders of the people and the army, the quaestors to attend to the city and State finances, and the dictator to give unity to effort in times of stress. Later, as the State's affairs became more complicated, the tribune was added to safeguard the common people's rights, the censor to act as corrector of public acts and morals, the praetor to conduct the courts, and the aedile to supervise the city's public functions and improvements.

The one-man State had thus evolved into the complex State with many offices. The Roman career, including as it did these offices, was the product of evolution quite as much as the Roman State.

The Roman who ran this career may himself be called a natural product. Each one of the offices of which the career consisted called for special abilities and was a special experience; the public man might, and frequently did, in his climb to the topmost round of the ladder, hold all of them; and it is easy to see that they conferred as well as required an unusual equipment of character and capacity.

But the Roman career was not created by nature alone. It was encouraged also by law. The succession of the offices which naturally led to the highest honor and usefulness in the State came in the course of time to be so customary that at last it was formalized. The Lex Villia Annalis of the year 180 B.C., named from its author Lucius Villius the tribune, provided that the offices usually held and the order in which they were usually held should thenceforth be the rule as well as the practice. From that date, chiefly as a result of the law but also in obedience to custom quite as strong as law, a definite order in the round of offices possible in the public career was established. By the end of the Republic, this round or succession of offices had so developed as to include the following possibilities: tribune of the soldiers, member of the board of twenty-six, quaestor, tribune of the people, curule or plebeian aedile, censor, master of the cavalry, praetor, interrex, consul, censor,

AN UNIDENTIFIED ROMAN ON A FOR-
MAL OCCASION

He has a roll or book in the left hand.

dictator; but it must not be supposed that any one man's career comprised them all, or that this order never varied.

As the dictator, the master of the cavalry, and the interrex were emergency offices, and the plebeian aedile and the tribune of the people were chosen exclusively from the plebs, and as the censorship was of little or no importance in the last century of the Republic, the round of offices, or legal *cursus honorum*, may be simplified to include the tribune of the soldiers, the board of twenty-six, the quaestor, the curule aedile, the praetor, and the consul. It is doubtful whether even the first two of these were obligatory before Augustus; at any rate Cicero, so far as we know, began the career with the quaestorship. In the year 81 B.C., additional legislation by Sulla had the effect of confirming an age limit, so that the quaestorship was not held before the age of thirty-one, the praetorship not before forty, and the consulship not before forty-three. Further, this legislation provided that between the successive offices two years should elapse, and that between two holdings of the same office ten years must intervene. The variations from this practice in the time of the Empire need not detain us at this point.

Let us now consider one by one the duties of the various offices in the cursus honorum. This will not only help us to appreciate the Roman career in its meaning to the Roman, but will indirectly describe the constitution of the Roman State.

First, the military tribunate. The requirement of service as officer in the army meant, of course, a period of at least several years in the military service, and was an expression of the Roman belief in soldierly capacity as a necessary qualification for the public man. At first appointed by the consuls, after 362 B.C. the *tribuni militum* were elected by the people, but their duties, which were purely military, remained the same. From 207 B.C., their number for some time was twenty-four, which provided six each for the four legions then constituting the levy. When more were needed, they were appointed by the consuls, who were the commanding officers and had the right. By the time of Cicero, the requirement of the military tribunate became simply ten years' service in the field or ten years' readiness to answer to the call, and it was possible to qualify with no actual service and with little training.

Second, the commission of twenty-six. The necessary qualification here was the holding for one year of one office from among a group of six. These six offices were places on six boards or commissions whose total membership amounted to twenty-six. They were: (1) the police commission of three for the arrest, trial, and punishment of criminals; (2) the commission of ten for the judgment of certain cases;

(3) the commission of four in charge of the courts in Capua, Cumae, and other towns; (4) the commission of three in charge of the mint; (5) the commission of four for the cleaning of the streets inside the city; (6) the commission of two for the cleaning of streets outside the city. These officers were all elected by the people. They might precede or follow the office of tribune in the cursus honorum. Augustus abolished the third and sixth groups, consolidated the others into a single body, and made the office the required first step in the cursus honorum.

Third, the quaestorship. The duties of this office were mainly the receipt and disbursement of the State's moneys, the care of the public records, and the oversight of details in the State's contracts. Besides the urban quaestors who had these duties, there were the military and provincial quaestors, who acted as quartermasters and paymasters, and the Italian quaestors, whose duties were performed at certain centers in Italy, one having charge of the grain supply at Ostia. The number of these officers increased from four in 421 B.C. to forty in 45 B.C. From the year 81 B.C., the date of Sulla's reform, they were entitled at the end of their tenure to a seat in the Senate. Cicero in 74 B.C. was therefore one of twenty new senators. As the number of additions each year was large enough to keep the Senate full, it was a body composed entirely of ex-magistrates.

Fourth, the curule aedileship. The curule or patrician aedileship was established in 366 B.C. to balance the plebeian aedileship which had existed from the early years of the Republic. Both were boards of two, and had similar duties — the superintendence of public places and buildings, such as the streets, baths, and temples; the care of the grain supply, with inspection of measures, weights, and foods, and fixing of prices; and the oversight of the games. The

aediles were thus the ancient equivalent of our street superintendents, building commissioners, and police boards. The
curule aediles were elected by the people, and the office
carried with it for the descendants of its holders the right
of keeping ancestral wax masks in the house. The plebeian
aediles were elected by the plebs alone and had no such
rights, but it was possible for plebeians in alternate years to
be elected curule aediles, and in time the plebeian aedile
won the right to a seat in the Senate.

Fifth, the praetorship. The office of praetor also began
in 366 B.C., its purpose being to relieve the consuls of judicial duties. Beginning with one urban praetor, who had
jurisdiction over suits involving citizens only, the praetorship was further represented in 242 B.C. by the praetor
peregrinus, who was concerned with cases in which one or
both parties were foreign, and later by four, six, and finally,
in Caesar's time, by ten, fourteen, and sixteen. In the later
years of the Republic, the praetors were occupied for their
year of office in judicial duties, and for a second year were
sent out as provincial governors. On entering office, the
praetor posted the principles of law and the forms of procedure by which he chose to be governed during his term.
As a usual thing, he continued his predecessor's policy, adding to it whatever he felt was called for by the circumstances
of the year. The sum of the urban praetor's edicts came in
the course of time to constitute a great body of civil and
criminal law. In the same way, the edicts of the praetor
peregrinus grew into a body of international law.

Sixth, the consulship. The duties of the consul at home
included presiding in the Senate and over assemblies of the
people, the introduction of bills before the people, the
nomination of a dictator when this was necessary, and
certain religious functions, such as the dedication of temples,

THE FORUM RESTORED AS SEEN FROM THE ROSTRA

At left and right: the Basilica Aemilia and the Basilica Julia. Facing us, the Temple of Julius Caesar and the Arch of Augustus. High on the right, the Palace of Tiberius; on the left, the Basilica of Constantine.

making sacrifices in the name of the State, and taking auspices. Away from Rome, the consuls were commanders-in-chief in case of war, and, unless employed in different fields, commanded each one day at a time. After 80 B.C., their commands were limited to Italy. They represented the State in treaties and other business, and received and presented foreign envoys to the Senate. They were sometimes given absolute power for the time being by decree of the Senate suspending the ordinary rights of the citizens. At the end of their tenure they became provincial governors.

Such was the round of public service through which the successful Roman usually went. Most of the offices in it were voted by the people in elections held by the *comitia centuriata*, the assembly by centuries; that is, the three hundred and seventy-three groups in which the voters were enrolled, each group casting one vote for its entire membership. Elections were held in an inclosure in the Campus Martius, and the voter wrote the name of his candidate and cast the ballot in secret.

As we have seen, there were other offices also open to the public man. In the first place, if he was of the plebeian class, he could be chosen one of the ten tribunes of the people. This office was created early in the Republic for the protection of the individual citizen, especially the plebeian, from the injustice of the patrician magistrate and the upper class in general. The tribune could block the action of any magistrate at any time by simply interposing his veto, could punish even with death a disobedient magistrate, and was free from arrest or punishment. This sacrosanctity of person and right of intercession gave him the most extraordinary power of obstructing Government measures, and made of the tribunate a storm center of Roman civic life.

Again, whether plebeian or patrician, the Roman in the

public career was eligible to the censorship, and so might be commissioned with the assessment of property, the supervision of the State's finances, and the revision of the Senate's membership. The censorship in its best days was a powerful restraint upon civic morals, but with the growth of the State in numbers and complexity was unable to maintain the control it exercised in earlier and simpler days.

Finally, in times of emergency the Roman career might include the offices of interrex, dictator, and master of the cavalry. The interrex was a senator appointed for five days when the State, on account of death or other cause, was left without consuls. His chief duty was to hold the elections for new consuls. In case no choice was made in the five days of his term, he appointed a second interrex. The dictator was appointed by the consuls, first authorized by popular vote, for a maximum of six months. The dictator's powers were absolute. The master of the cavalry was appointed by him as second in command. Both these essentially military offices had ceased to be customary after the Second Punic War, and were little employed until Caesar's time.

There were other offices to which the Roman might be called in his career — that of envoy, *legatus*, for example, or judge on some commission for drafting laws or trying cases. The mention of every possibility would involve us in too much detail. Let us rather try to appreciate the career in its total character.

The Roman career is paralleled in some respects by the national career in our American life. The American who aspires to the highest office in the land is usually a practitioner of law, and as a rule moves toward the goal of his ambition by a fairly definite path. He begins with training in the law school or law office, and looks for distinction first

in local affairs. He may be elected to municipal office as
attorney or judge or mayor, or to county office as district
attorney, or to a place in the State legislature as member of
the Assembly or senator. He develops a skill in public
address and in otherwise winning the good will of men.
After service in the legislature, he is elected member of
Congress; after that, perhaps governor. From the governorship, he is likely to be elevated to the national Senate;
and the natural ambition of the senator is the presidency of
the United States. This is one line of advancement. Another line, more purely legal, and with a different goal, is
from the lawyer's office to the place of municipal, county,
or State's attorney, from one of these to the bench as municipal or circuit judge, from this to the supreme court of
the State, and from the State to the national supreme court.

The American and the Roman careers, however, are far
from being identical. The Roman State was a city-state,
and the public men of the Roman Republic were the rulers
of a city which was the ruler of a world. They were not sent
from elsewhere to Rome as a convenient meeting place, as
our public men are sent to Washington, to remain there for
a period of two or six years in representing the voters who
elected them, and then to return to privacy or the conduct of
local affairs; but were born and bred in Rome or its neighborhood, were reared in the shadow of the Senate, were
educated with the State career never out of mind, and witnessed and felt the great moments of public excitement.
They advanced by difficult steps in the midst of passionate
competition, and were selected by blood and class and
fortune as well as by native ability and the art of handling
men. They received no salaries as such. When the highest
distinction had been reached in the consulship, they did
not retire, but went on to other service in the city or were

employed abroad in the governing of provinces, and in either case remained for life members of the Senate.

We must not think of the Roman career, however, as always exemplified by men of heroic figure. The Roman State was a democracy, the offices within its gift were nearly all elective, and the game of politics intruded then as now in the dignified affairs of statesmanship. There were the intrigues and the corruptions of the election campaign. There were enmities between classes as bitter as any between capital and labor to-day. There was incompetence raised to high places by blood or wealth. There was ignorance placed in power by the votes of the multitude. There were the rich rewards of provincial offices to tempt the greedy. There was the strain upon the State and upon the public man of meeting the new conditions of expanding empire. There was the unwieldiness of a Senate of three hundred, and there were the dangers of the divided rule of consuls and the abused power of the tribunate. There was the impotence of the censorship before the rising flood of immorality and extravagance that came with conquest, wealth, and immigration. There was the drain of war and luxury on the best blood of Italy. There was the weakening and the breaking of the Constitution, and its reconstruction in the Empire. There was the change from the responsible citizenship that made the Roman Republic great in character to the autocratic rule that made the Roman Empire efficient.

But we are concerned here with the Roman whose character and achievement lay at the base of Roman greatness in the day of Cato, in the stress of the Punic Wars, and in the earlier days of Rome's advance to the leadership of Italy — the Roman who rose above the faults of common humanity and the times, and ran with patience and success the race that was set before him from the toga of manhood to the consulship of middle age and the wise counseling of later life. The man thus born and bred and honored was a highly developed product. He was lawyer, soldier, orator, justice, legislator, administrator, and member for life of a body of three hundred men all of whom were ex-magistrates like himself, and most of whom were his equals in native capacity and knowledge of the world. In the breadth of his education and the breadth of his experience, he was one of civilization's best specimens of the man.

XVI

THE SENATOR

The Senate, according to Livy, was the creation of Romulus. After many men from the neighboring peoples had cast in their lot with the growing State by the Tiber and the king "began to be satisfied now so far as strength was concerned, he next provided for counsel to support that strength. He created a hundred senators, whether because that number was sufficient, or because there were only a hundred who could be created 'fathers.' At any rate they were called fathers from the distinction, and their descendants were called patricians."

The view of Livy that the Senate owed its institution and the senators their appointment to the king is not the only view. There are those who think that the Senate came into being naturally and without the intervention of authority through the counselings together of the men at the heads of the families or clans making up the community; and that it afterwards developed into the body called *senatus* whose membership consisted of one *senex*, or man of mature age and wisdom, representing each clan, chosen perhaps by the king, perhaps by the clan represented.

Whatever its origin, and whatever its earliest number, the Senate came eventually to have a normal membership of three hundred, to be composed of elderly men of proved capabilities, and to command in so high a degree the respect and obedience of the people and their elected officials as to be practically identical with the State. This is true in spite of the fact that the Senate, constitutionally, was never in its history other than an advisory council. Its decrees, *senatus consulta*, had the force of law only because the inherent authority of character had established an unbreakable tradition of obedience.

A GATHERING OF SENATORS
(From "Julius Caesar")

The Senate underwent many changes in the course of its long existence. At first composed of only one hundred, or at least some not very large number, the enrollment was soon extended, perhaps in the time of the kings. At first entirely patrician, early in the Republic it admitted plebeian members, and we are told by Cicero that the Ovinian Law, toward the end of the fourth century, made eligible *ex omni ordine optimum quemque*, the best men from every class. At first chosen for eminent qualities without formal regard to the holding of office, as their number increased they were appointed more and more because of conspicuous discharge of duty in a public capacity, until they became practically a body of higher ex-magistrates. By the time of Cicero's entrance into public life any citizen elected quaestor acquired by the act the right to a seat in the Senate at the end of his year of office, and held it for life unless disqualified at the revision of the roll called *census*.

Among the effects of these extensions of eligibility was naturally the increase of membership. In Cicero's youth the number increased under Sulla from three to about four hundred, and under Caesar it rose to nine hundred, to be reduced by Augustus to six hundred. Another effect was the lowering of the age limit, which was reduced to about thirty years because the quaestorship conferring the seat was reached at about that age. In Imperial times the limit became twenty-five. A third effect was that the patricians became fewer, both in reality and in proportion. Finally, the senatorial order arose, to form the wider aristocracy including not only patrician blood but plebeian blood that proved itself worthy by achievement in leadership.

There were two ways by which the membership of the Senate was lessened : by death and by action of the censors. There were three ways by which it was increased : by election of new magistrates, by regular action of the censors, and by special action of the dictator. The increases under Sulla and Caesar were dictatorial in character, and actuated by political interest. An addition to the roll by appointment was called *adlectio*.

From the institution of the censorship, about 443 B.C., the revision of the Senate roll occurred regularly once every lustrum, or five years. This was only one of the censorial

duties, but it was one of the most important. The procedure of the censors in making the revision was: (1) the
election of the *princeps senatus* for the next lustrum, up to
209 B.C. the oldest ex-censor, but later any ex-censor; (2) the
striking out of the names of the deceased, the disqualified,
and the unfit, including the
legally or morally delin-
quent; (3) the filling of the
vacancies, in earlier times
by selection from the lists
of former dictators, censors,
consuls, praetors, aediles,
and quaestors, in later times
by enrolling newly elected
quaestors; (4) the listing of
members in these categories,
from Sulla on, each according to official seniority, so
that for "asking opinions"
in Senate meetings there
was a definite roll and a
definite order of preced-
ence; (5) the reading of the
new list from the Rostra,
or, under the Empire, its
publication.

THE CURIA, OR SENATE HOUSE, TO-DAY

This is the Senate House built about A.D.
300, later converted into the Church of
Saint Hadrian. When the Forum level
had been raised by the débris of the ruined
city, the church floor was raised and a
new door built. The dark niches in the
lower part of the façade contained the
bones of monks interred in mediaeval
times.

As the offices through
which the senatorial seat at various periods was approached
were won by popular election, the Senate may be said to
have represented the choice of the people. The citizens
voting for Cicero as quaestor, for example, were conscious
that his election would carry with it after his year of service
a lifelong seat in the Senate.

When the senator came to take his seat, he had the right to the *latus clavus*, or broad purple stripe woven into the tunic from the neck downward to the bottom, to the red sandal with its peculiar buckle and straps, and to a reserved place at public entertainments. On the other hand, he was forbidden to engage in ordinary trade or to have Government contracts. His entrance into the ordo senatorius, unlike the rise to the equestrian rank, was not conditioned in the Republic upon financial standing; though Augustus inaugurated a senatorial property qualification of a million sesterces, about $50,000, contributing the sum in case the appointee did not possess it.

The meetings of the Senate, as befitted an advisory body, were at call, usually on the Calends or Ides unless the comitia were being held, and normally in the Curia Hostilia at the northwest corner of the Forum. The exception to this was in the month of February, when daily meetings were prescribed by law. The presiding officer and the issuer of the call in Ciceronian times was regularly one of the consuls. In a seat facing the door of entrance and also the assembly of senators, who seem not to have been assigned special places, after he had opened the session with sacrifice and inspection of the victim, the consul proceeded to the business for which the call had been issued, and which had been stated in the call; though he might previously make announcement of any appropriate news or communications received. The *relatio*, or presentation of the business, having been finished, he awaited the pleasure of the Senate.

In order to ascertain the Senate's wishes and bring them to the desired conclusion in a decree, the presiding officer began with the princeps senatus, at the head of the list, and addressed to him the formula, *"Dic, M. Tulli, quid censes —* Speak, Marcus Tullius, what is your opinion?" continuing

ROME FROM THE TEMPLE OF JUNO ON THE CAPITOL

At the left, fora of Caesar, Nerva, Vespasian; next, Curia, Basilica Aemilia, Colosseum; in center, Arch of Severus, Forum, Temple of Julius Caesar; at right, Tabularium, Basilica Julia, Temple of Castor, Palatine.

through the list in order of ex-censors, ex-consuls, etc. The senator addressed might either make a speech, as lengthy as he chose, or merely assent to whatever had been proposed, or in sign of assent pass to a seat beside the champion of the proposal. This process was called the *perrogatio*. On occasion there was debate, called *altercatio*. There seems usually to have been no formal counting of votes, but a declaration of result by the presiding officer. When the vote was close, there was a *discessio*, "a walking apart," or division. No quorum was required until Augustus' time, when it was necessary in case of a discessio, and absence was punishable by fine. There was no rule as to length of speeches, or relevance. In Cicero's *Seventh Philippic*, the first three lines and the last seven words are on the business of the day, and the remainder is devoted to Antony, the enemy of the State. After the vote had been taken, the Senate was dismissed and the president with the framer of the decree and the one or two most interested in it remained to write the formal draft, which was deposited in the treasury.

Among the matters which came before the Senate were the fixing of taxation amounts and contracts for their collection, the verification of accounts, the discussion of bills and lists of candidates before their submission to the people, the control of provincial administration, the sending and the hearing of envoys, the ratification of wars or treaties voted by the people's assembly, and the suspension of the law in moments of crisis such as that when Cicero and his colleague were commissioned to see to it "that the Republic took no harm — *ne quid res publica detrimenti caperet.*"

The Roman Senate was the most distinguished of the world's deliberative assemblies. Sprung from a conservative and deeply religious society; composed of members from prominent and long-standing families, members of seasoned age, of capacity tried and proved by experience, and with lifelong tenure; called upon to meet the emergencies of a constantly expanding State and a constantly changing society — in its best days the great council was rich in the wisdom which was the product of earnest and capable living, made cumulative by the consistency and continuity and permanence of its character. When Livy declares of it that "he who said it was composed of kings had the true impression of its appearance," he describes the dignified and grave exterior which was the fit expression of that character. Nor need we think that the ideal thus described has nothing to do with the times of Cicero. Whatever the failings of the Senate in its later day, its greatest orator himself and many of the senatorial friends who stood with him were the worthy successors, whether in capacity or in character, of the Catos and the Curii and the Decii by whom they never ceased to be inspired.

XVII

THE VOTER

Cicero was a member of the Senate from 74 B.C., the year after his quaestorship in Sicily, to his death in 43 B.C., a period of thirty-one years beginning with the end of his thirty-second, when the conclusion of his quaestorial duties entitled him to a seat in the great deliberative council. Though the senatorship was not directly an elective office, it was due to the votes of the people who had made him quaestor. It will therefore be of interest to study the election methods of ancient Rome.

The voters' assembly at which Cicero's election to the quaestorship took place was the *comitia tributa*, the assembly of the 35 tribes. There were two other popular assemblies, the *comitia curiata*, the assembly of the original 30 *curiae* or divisions of the patricians, which had ceased to have any great importance, and the *comitia centuriata*, the assembly of 373 *centuriae*, divisions originally meaning a hundred men but later merely the number made convenient by the total roll of citizens entitled to vote. Both the comitia tributa and the comitia centuriata had certain law-making and court powers as well as the electoral function. Their difference in electoral jurisdiction lay in the fact that the centuriate assembly elected the consuls, praetors, and other major magistrates, and the tribal assembly the plebeian aediles, the quaestors, the commissioners of the mint, the street superintendents, and the many other minor office-holders.

174

The election procedure at both assemblies was much the same. First, the consuls and Senate determined beforehand the date on one of the hundred and ninety days not forbidden by religious provision, and within a fixed period in the summer. Next, at least seventeen days before the election, a herald proclaimed the coming event, which was to take

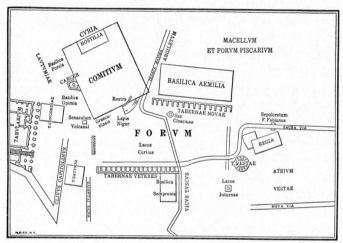

THE FORUM OF THE REPUBLIC

The time is before 46 B.C., in which year Julius Caesar's basilica replaced the Tabernae Veteres and the Basilica Sempronia. The shops, tabernae, on both sides show how ordinary trade filled the Forum in earlier times.

place early in the morning, usually in the Campus Martius. Thirdly, if the auspices taken before dawn on the day appointed were favorable, criers and trumpeters gave the final call to assemble, and the voters came together and grouped themselves by tribes or centuries as the case required, each body taking its position in the proper section of the voting inclosures called the *Saepta*. The Saepta Julia, planned by Julius Caesar for the centuriate assembly and erected by Augustus, was meant by the Dictator to be a marble inclosure surrounded by a mile of portico, and was probably so constructed. A voting precinct called the *Ovile*, or sheep-pen, preceded it. The comitia tributa met in the Forum. Fourthly, after the religious preliminary consisting of a sacrifice, the presiding officer, normally the consul or other magistrate who had issued the election call, read to the voters the list of candidates. In Cicero's time, the number of quaestors to be elected was twenty, which Caesar was to increase to forty.

The next step in the process was the casting of the vote. This was done in the tribal assembly by each of the thirty-five tribes as a unit, and in the centuriate assembly by each century as a unit. In either case the division determined its vote by ballot in the section assigned it in the Saepta, each voter writing or pricking on a blank tablet the name of his choice and depositing it in the *cista*, or urn, under the eye of the election official. When the vote of one tribe, chosen by lot to be the first, had thus been determined and had been declared, the remaining tribes went through the same process all at the same time, and the results were announced in an order determined by lot. The number of voters present in each tribe depended upon the interest of the individual and, in the case of the citizen living in a distant part of Italy, upon his willingness to sacrifice time and money in a journey to the capital.

The election of Cicero to the consulship, which occurred in July twelve years after his elevation to the quaestorship, took place at the comitia centuriata in the Campus Martius. At this election the voters were grouped by centuries in the smallest inclosures of the Ovile or Saepta, one century was chosen by lot to cast as a unit the first vote, and the remaining centuries followed. As in the tribal assembly, the voters filed through a narrow passage, each leaving in the urn a tablet on which he had written or pricked his choice, to be taken out and counted by *diribitores*, the enumerators, who handed the result to the magistrate presiding.

Cicero's campaign for the consulship began at least a year in advance. In July, 65 B.C., he is already writing Atticus concerning the prospects of his candidature. He names a half dozen possible competitors, one of whom is Catiline, and declares his intention of beginning to "lay hold of," *prensare*, or canvass, on July 17, the date for the elections of that year. Catiline will be in the race, he says humorously, if the sun does not give light at noonday, referring to the fact that Catiline was facing trial for extortion and was sure to be convicted and therefore disqualified from running.

The game of politics in the days of Cicero was much the same as it is in our own. The words *prensatio*, laying hold of or soliciting, and *ambitio*, going about, are themselves indicative of the manner of running for office, but a much more eloquent testimony as to the art of getting votes is preserved for us in the *Commentary on Running for Office*, thought to have been addressed by Quintus Cicero to his brother Marcus early in the year 64 B.C. A few extracts from it will suffice to show how little the methods of the office-seeker change as the centuries pass.

"Think what State you belong to, what office it is you are running for, who you are. Let hardly a day pass without rehearsing to yourself as you go down to the Forum: 'I am a New Man; it is the consulship I am aiming at; this is Rome.' The newness of your name [a *novus homo* was a man not of patrician birth who had risen at least to the aedileship] you will counterbalance in largest part by your fame as an orator. That gift has always brought with it great consideration. A man considered fit to be the patron of ex-consuls cannot be regarded as unfit for the consulship. Since therefore you will have this reputation to begin with, and since

whatever you are you owe to this, see that when you speak you
come prepared for it as if in every case the matter at issue were
your own ability. . . .

"And so see to it that you make yourself solid with all the centuries by many various friendly connections.   In the first place,
what anyone can see, win over the senators and the equites and the
active and influential men of all the other classes.   There are a
great many enterprising men in the city, and many freedmen of
influence and energy in public life whom as far as possible through
your own efforts and those of your mutual friends you must make
your backers.   Do your best; seek them out, win them over,
show that you are appreciative of their great favor to you.   In the
next place, have regard to the city as a whole, to all the guilds, the
precincts, the neighborhoods.   If you can win over to your friendship the leaders of these groups, you will easily get the support of
all the rest through them.   After this, see that you have all Italy
in mind and memory, laid out and listed so that there will be no
city or colony or prefecture or place in the whole country left by
you without its assurance of the necessary support.   Go through
them thoroughly and search out the men in every locality; get
acquainted with them, solicit them, make them solid for you, see
that in their own neighborhoods they canvass for you and become,
so to speak, candidates in your behalf.   They will want you as
their friend if they see that their friendship is sought after by
you. . . .

"These remarks occurred to my mind concerning those two
morning reflections which I spoke of when I said you must go down
to the Forum every day rehearsing to yourself: 'I am a New Man;
it is the consulship I am aiming at.'   The third remains: 'this is
Rome,' a city made up of the coming together of nations, a city of
many traps, much trickery, and many vices of all kinds.   You
will have to put up with arrogance, with insult, with ill will, with
haughtiness, with hatred and attack, on the part of many, many
persons.   I can see that it will require great good judgment and
skill for one meeting with so much that is greatly offensive on the
part of men of all sorts to avoid collision, to avoid scandal, to
avoid secret attack, to be the one man accommodating himself to
so great a variety of character, expression, and feeling.

"Keep on therefore, I say it again and again, in the course you

THE ROMAN FORUM TO-DAY

The open court of the Vestals is in the left foreground; the Basilica Julia is beyond the three columns of the Temple of Castor and Pollux. At the farther end are the Temples of Saturn and Vespasian and the Arch of Severus; beyond them, the Tabularium, the Capitoline Tower, and the Dome of Saint Peter's.

have begun. Excel in eloquence; by this men at Rome are both held and won, and kept from attempts to hinder and to harm. And since our commonwealth is most especially vicious in this respect, namely that it is wont to allow bribery to make it forget worth and standing, see to it that in this you take good account of yourself; that is, that you realize that you are one able to strike into your competitors the greatest fear of the risk of a prosecution. Let them understand that they are being observed and watched by you; they will have a great fear not only of your diligence, and the authority and power of your eloquence, but surely also of the devotion of the equestrian order to you."

Trials for *ambitus*, bribery, were frequent in Cicero's time; his own defense of Murena was in such a case. A law against public solicitation of votes was passed as early as 432 B.C. In 181 B.C., a law provided that those convicted of ambitus should be barred for ten years from running for office. Within Cicero's lifetime at least four laws against the offense were enacted. The parties to bribery, besides the candidate and the voter, were the *interpres*, who made the bargain, the *sequestris*, who held the money, and the *divisor*, who delivered it. Other technical names in political matters are *nomenclator*, one who hired himself to the candidate to prompt him as to the names of the persons he canvassed or met; *candidatus*, so called from the white toga which signified to the public the candidate's ambition; *petitor* and *competitor*, also meaning candidates; *optimates* and *nobiles*, the conservative or senatorial party, and *populares*, the popular or democratic party.

XVIII

THE LAWYER

The great Roman profession, as we have seen, was the career of public service. We have seen, too, that it embraced a wide range of qualifications and called for the discharge of duties in many different fields. The Roman whose career culminated in the consulship and perhaps continued in the censorship was lawyer, soldier, parliamentarian, justice, legislator, administrator, and probably had also a special knowledge of religion as connected with affairs of the State.

It is apparent that in antiquity as well as to-day the lawyer's calling was closely identified with the public career. The duties of the praetor in Rome could hardly be administered by one not bred in the law, though the office was less technical and more like that of a presiding officer than is the judge's office to-day. The duties of consul and of governor in the province were likewise best administered by those familiar with the law.

The law in antiquity, however, was much more exclusively in the hands of public men than is the case to-day. The technical lawyer of the modern kind, or the specialist in a single field, could hardly be said to exist in Cicero's time. Of what we call the practice of law, outside the circle of public men who already held or were running for the offices of the Roman career, there is little evidence. The great scholars in the law up to Cicero's time, as well as the greatest figures in the Roman courts, were also men who actively conducted the State's affairs. Quintus Mucius Scaevola, author of special treatises on wills, contracts, etc., and one of the founders of legal science as it exists to-day, held all the offices in the cursus honorum, was praetorian governor of a province in 98 B.C., consul in 95 B.C., and an orator of repute. The Scaevolas were the leading family of their time in knowledge of the law, and most of their members were prominent in the public service. Servius Sulpicius, the friend of Cicero who wrote the beautiful letter of consolation after the death of Cicero's daughter Tullia, was the author of a special work on dowries and of two books on the praetorian edicts, and one of the deepest scholars of law, and yet had held all the offices in the cursus honorum, had been governor of Achaea, or Greece, and contracted his last illness while on an embassy from the State to Antony.

Like the public career itself, the prominence of the Roman public man in the courts of law was the product of evolution. When the Roman State was in its early days, the patricians were the governing class. They were the source of the law, its interpreters, and, through the king and his officials, its executors. The rights they exercised as the only citizens were accompanied by responsibilities to the *gentes* and noncitizen dependents who looked to them for protection. The powerful who made and knew the law were in humanity and honor bound to help the ignorant and weak. Even into historical times and down to the days of Cicero, when the exclusive rights of the patricians had long since been shared by the general body of citizens, the ideal responsibilities of the governing class to the commoner survived. The law of Cincius, passed in 204 B.C., forbade the lawyer to accept a fee for his services. Nothing of course could prevent grateful clients rewarding their lawyers by political support, and there were no doubt many evasions of

THE SOUTH SIDE OF THE FORUM RESTORED

From left to right: front of the Temple of Julius Caesar, Temple of Castor and Pollux, Julian Basilica, Temple of Jupiter on the Capitoline Hill.   The Arch of Janus is in the right foreground.

the Cincian Law ; but its passage was evidence that in theory the possessor of legal experience was bound to place his knowledge at the service of the people, and its renewal as late as Augustus, with an amendment by Claudius allowing limited fees, proved that the ideal was being held to, despite the decline of public spirit. The interest aroused by a decree of the Senate in Pliny's time forbidding fees but allowing a money present at the end of the case, is further evidence, though the present may amount to five hundred dollars. The reason for this leniency may be seen in the fact that the political support customary under the Republic could not serve as reward under the Empire, when office was gained rather through approval by the emperor and his powerful friends than through the votes of the people.

Having seen who were the practitioners and students of the law, we must next try to understand the workings of the law in court. The year 366 B.C., marked by the creation of the praetorship, was one of the most important dates in the history of law. From now on, the trials which had hitherto been conducted by the overburdened consuls and their advisers, the pontifices, could receive more expert attention. Another important change took place in 149 B.C., when the first permanent special court was established, for the trial of magistrates charged with misappropriation of funds and financial abuses in general. The most frequent charge was extortion in the provinces. The first known trial for this offense took place in 171 B.C., when the people of the two Spanish provinces complained of their governors. The case was brought before a praetor. The growing number of similar cases soon called for a court of its own. A second standing court was formed not long afterward, this time with jurisdiction over cases of attempt to murder. This was called the Court on Stabbers and Poisoners. Still

later, Sulla established special courts on acts partaking of
the nature of treason, on forgery, on corrupt election practices, and on the embezzlement of public moneys. Such
courts, and the location of branch courts in Italy with representatives of the praetors at Rome to sit in judgment, made
necessary the increase of the number of praetors, who in
Sulla's time were eight, and in Augustus' reign were sixteen.

Besides the praetors, or judges, there were the *iudices*,
the juries. The iudices were from the first a feature of the
praetor's trials, and had originated long before the creation
of the praetor's office. The establishment of the special
courts naturally carried with it the providing of juries for
them. In the case of the court on extortion, from the time
of Gaius Gracchus the equites were privileged to form the
jury. Sulla, recognizing the tendency of the equites to be
severe with senatorial offenders and lenient with their own
class, gave the seats on these juries to members of the Senate,
who in their turn were lenient or severe according to sympathy. The law of Aurelius Cotta, in 70 B.C., attempted
a juster arrangement by giving the jury rights to senators,
equites, and tribunes of the treasury. Thereafter, the juries
were drawn from a list made up by the urban praetor, which
Cicero tells us consisted of nine hundred citizens. The
number is thought to be too low; the court on extortion
alone had had a list of four hundred and fifty. The names
were kept by the praetor in a book called the *album*.

In the number of jurors chosen to act in various trials,
there was great variation. Cicero's mention of the number
ranges from 50 to 75. The method of empaneling or select-
ing a jury also varied, but its general outlines may be seen
in the provision of the Acilian law on extortion, 122 B.C.,
which specified that the prosecutor should choose from the
album of 450 jurors 100 names, and that the defendant

should then strike out 50, leaving the remaining 50 to sit on the case. This is essentially the method of the modern jury court.

A strikingly different method was employed by Pompey when he was sole consul and in charge of the political trials. In the trial of Milo, he summoned the entire 360 who were on the list of the court on assaults. The 360 heard the trial up to the last day, when 81 were chosen to hear the pleas of the opposing lawyers, and the remaining 279 discharged. Each side then challenged or struck off 15, leaving 51 to render the verdict. This was Pompey's way of preventing bribery; the uncertainty as to the final composition of the jury would baffle the attempt to buy them up.

The prosecuting lawyer was regularly the person who brought the charge. In some cases the magistrate himself had brought the charge and was both judge and prosecutor. Any citizen could bring suit, and many a citizen, like Cato, brought suits as a means of becoming prominent, as well as from civic motives. The accused could conduct his own case or have a patronus act for him, and there might be friends called in as advisers, the *advocati*, or advocates.

The conduct of the Roman trial, like that of the modern trial, included the testimony of witnesses, the speeches of lawyers, and the cross-examination of witnesses, with great liberty permitted the lawyer in his questioning. The rules of evidence in general, in comparison with American and English procedure, were exceedingly lax. The familiar modern objection to an attorney's questions as "incompetent, irrelevant, and immaterial," was wholly lacking. The modern rules excluding "facts irrelevant to the fact in issue, as being connected with it only by resemblance," "hearsay," "opinion," and "character," had no parallel in the Roman court. The issue of a trial in Cicero's day seems to have depended almost as much upon the reputations of the parties as upon the facts deduced from testimony. All sorts of sensational appeals were allowed, including the going about of the accused in the toga of mourning and the presence of imploring relatives and friends at the trial. The evidence of slaves was taken under torture.

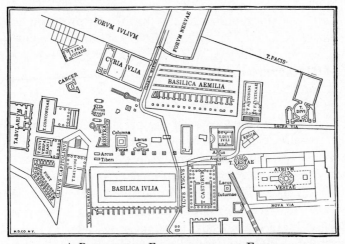

A PLAN OF THE FORUM UNDER THE EMPIRE
The two great basilicas show how the law business centered in the Forum.

At the end of the testimony of witnesses and the speeches of the lawyers, the jurors were asked individually whether or not they were ready to vote. Those who thought the court should adjourn and the case be further argued were then dismissed, providing they were not more than one third of the total, and the remaining two thirds, without a judge's charge and, so far as we can tell, without discussion or consultation, delivered the verdict by secret ballot. Each had received a two-sided wax tablet four inches square, on which was traced an A, for *absolvo*, "I acquit," and a C, for *condemno*, "I convict." This tablet, with one or the other letter erased, he dropped into an urn in full sight of the court, and in such manner that all might see the erasure but not the unerased letter, and thus know that he really voted. Finally, a juror chosen by lot extracted the tablets and read the letter on each one. A majority determined the verdict.

This was the manner of the verdict as provided in the Acilian Law of 122 B.C., which governed the court on extortion, whose jurisdiction was over criminal cases. The manner of procedure in civil cases or in later times may have been modified, but it was in substance as above described when Cicero frequented the courts.

Elsewhere we shall treat of the various kinds of offenders who appeared before the Roman courts, and of the penalties they had to suffer. It should be mentioned here, however, that a great difference between ancient Roman and modern American courts is to be seen in the matter of appeal. When the ancient party to a suit was convicted or otherwise lost his case, there was no such thing as another trial in a higher court; when the case was adjudged, that was the end so far as the courts were concerned.

This does not mean, however, that the losing party was always punished. There were methods of interference which were often effective in rescuing the accused from trial, or, if not from trial, from the execution of sentence after trial. In the first place, a higher magistrate could prohibit a magistrate of lower rank from proceeding with a trial. The dictator, consul, or tribune of the people could forbid the jurisdiction of the praetor. In the second place, there was the veto power belonging to higher and to equal magistrates against the execution of sentence. This right of *intercessio*, intercession, might be exercised personally by the magistrate after the accused had made an appeal in person. The officer most frequently exercising such power was the tribune of the people. It could be employed at any point in a trial or when the trial was over and the accused was facing the actual imposition of the penalty.

The jury trials in the regular praetors' courts and in the permanent special courts were not the only trials in which the decision depended upon the votes of a body of citizens. The tribunes could and frequently did impeach generals and other public servants and call them to trial before the people met in the centuriate assembly. It was this kind of trial which resulted in Cicero's banishment in 58 B.C.

We need next to imagine the place where the courts were held. The Roman climate was mild, and the Roman practice allowed the spectator free access to trials. The business of the courts was for long in the open air in the Comitium, an area in front of the senate house, and in the Forum, on which the Comitium fronted. Here, sometimes large and permanent, sometimes smaller and temporary, and even portable, was the tribunal, a platform on which the praetor or other magistrate presiding took his seat in the curule chair denoting authority, while beside him and in front on seats or benches were his assistants and the jurors. The Tribunal Aurelium in the Forum is mentioned several times by Cicero. It was a permanent structure, and was approached by steps. In front of the tribunal, standing or sitting, were the parties to the suit and their witnesses and friends, with patrons and advocates if they did not conduct their own case. Standing about in a semicircle were the spectators attracted by the case, who were called the *corona*, the crown, or garland.

As time went on, great halls called *basilicae* occupied the

borders of the Forum — the Basilica Porcia, erected by
Marcus Porcius Cato in 184 B.C., the Aemilia in 179 B.C.,
the Sempronia in 170 B.C., the Opimia about 121 B.C., the
Julia in 46 B.C. These buildings usually consisted of a
great central hall or auditorium, which could be divided
into separate areas for use by several courts sitting at one
time, surrounded by arcaded porticoes opening on to the
Forum or street, so that entrance and egress were easy, and
seeing and hearing from outside not impossible.

SCENE ON ONE OF TWO MARBLE BALUSTRADES IN THE FORUM

At the left, the emperor addresses the citizens from the Rostra ; at the right, from
a tribunal he extends an act of benevolence to some class represented by a mother
and child. A fig tree and a statue of Marsyas which stood in the Forum are seen at
the right, and the background shows the Aemilian Basilica, one of the great law
buildings, on the north side of the Forum.

Besides the open-air tribunals and the basilica, there
were other places used on occasion for legal business. The
fate of the accused in the conspiracy of Catiline was decided
by the Senate at a meeting that chanced to be held in the
Temple of Concord at the west end of the Forum. On the
day of Caesar's death, he was listening to petitions in a part
of the buildings connected with Pompey's Theater in the
Campus Martius. Neither of these events, however, was a
trial. The emperors had their private court rooms, usually
in the palace.

Some glimpses of actual court scenes are afforded by Pliny
the Younger, a great admirer of Cicero who practiced law

about A.D. 100, in the reign of Trajan. The court before which he appears is the centumviral court, normally consisting of one hundred and five jurors, sitting in the Julian Basilica on civil cases involving property rights.

" I had gone down to the Basilica Julia," Pliny writes, "to hear those to whom on the next sitting three days afterward I should have to answer. The jurors were in their seats, the decemvirs had come, the advocates were ranged face to face. A long silence, and finally a messenger from the praetor. The centumvirs are dismissed, the day is left free; to my joy, for I am never so well prepared that I am not glad of a postponement. The cause of the delay was the praetor Nepos. He had posted a short edict, giving notice to prosecutors and defendants that he was going to enforce the contents of the Senate's resolution. The resolution was attached to his edict: all persons having business with the court must take oath before beginning action that they had not given, promised, or provided for any fee to any person on account of services as advocate. In these words and a thousand others, it was forbidden to buy or to sell such services. After cases were concluded, however, a money gift of ten thousand sesterces was to be allowed."

Pliny calls the centumviral court his arena — " especially in my arena, that is, before the centumviri."

"Recently when I was to speak before the centumviri," he writes in another letter, "there was no way for me to get to my place except through the tribunal and the jury itself; so great a crowd occupied every other space. More than this, a certain distinguished young man who had got his tunics torn, as sometimes happens in a crowd, stood there covered by his toga only, and seven hours at that; for I talked that long, with great effort and greater advantage."

The centumviral court did not always consist of the original one hundred and five members; and it sat in some cases as a whole, and at other times was divided into four panels. "There were a hundred and eighty jurors sitting,"

writes Pliny of the case of Attia Viriola, a lady unjustly
disinherited by an eighty-year-old father who had married
a second time; "for the four panels combined amounted
to that.   There was a huge array of advocates on both sides,
the public benches were crowded, and in addition to this a
dense corona of bystanders extending around the vast court
room in a circle which was many deep.   More than this,
the platform of the tribunal was packed, and even from the
galleries of the basilica women as well as men were leaning
over with a great anxiety to hear, which was difficult, and
to see, which was easy."

A court room scene not quite so suggestive of respectability is presented by Cicero in the letter to Atticus which
describes the trial of Clodius on the charge of having attended
in disguise a religious meeting, exclusively for women, in
61 B.C.

" But if you want to know what the trial was like," he writes,
"it had an outcome which is incredible.   For, after the challenging
was finished in the midst of the loudest clamoring — because the
prosecutor like an upright censor rejected all the worst characters
and the defendant like a kindly trainer of gladiators removed all
the reputable people — as soon as the jurors were in their seats
decent people began to have decided misgivings.   There never was
a more disgraceful lot sitting in a gambling resort — senators with
befouled names, knights without a cent, and tribunes of the doubtful sort.   Yet there were a few honest people among them, those
that he was unable to get rid of by his challenge; and they sat
there sad and sorrowful in company not of their own sort, feeling
painfully their contact with baseness. . . .   There wasn't a man
who didn't think of Clodius as convicted a thousand times rather
than merely accused.   And when I was brought on as a witness
and his supporters began to hoot, I think you have heard how the
jury all rose together, how they gathered around me to offer their
throats to him in defense of my life. . . .   Nobody thought that
Clodius would appear and answer.   'Tell me now, O Muses, how

then first fell the fire.' You know Calvus. . . . In two days
with one slave, and an ex-gladiator at that, he fixed the whole
business. He called them to him, he promised, he gave security,
he paid cash down. . . . Well, even with honest men all with-
drawing and with the Forum full of slaves, there were still twenty-
five jurymen brave enough in the face of the greatest risk to prefer
death to letting everything go wrong; and there were thirty-one
who were moved more by hunger than by honor. Catulus saw
one of them and asked him: 'Why did you ask us to give you a
guard? Was it because you were afraid the money would be
taken away from you?' There you have, as briefly as I can tell
it, the kind of trial it was and the reason for the acquittal."

XIX

THE TEACHER

When we speak of the learned professions to-day, it is usually with the lawyer, the teacher, the doctor, and the clergyman in mind. The same four existed in ancient Rome, and the differences between ancient and modern are of much the same character in all four.

We have seen that the Roman lawyer up to the time of Cicero was not a highly specialized product, but a man of experience and skill in practical public affairs, and that even those who went deeply into law and wrote scientific treatises on it were consuls and governors as well as praetors. Of the three other professions, it may be said that at least those of education and the priesthood were like the practice of law under the Republic in being closely connected with the duties of citizenship and in not being developed into specialized and separate callings. The pontifex, the flamen, and the augur were officers of the State like consuls and praetors, and in most cases had won their places in the religious service because of distinction in political or military life. The education of the Roman boy and girl through all the early period was of the scantiest and most practical kind and given by father or mother or some one in the house; and in later times, when the teacher was so common that education, at least in the first stages, was within the reach of practically all citizens, a great part of it still was dependent upon the contact of the young with the practical affairs of their fathers and mothers and with public affairs observed in company with them. The doctor's calling was more distinct.

The teacher in the lower schools of ancient Rome can hardly be called a person of standing. He was frequently a slave or the son of a slave, and at best an ill-paid citizen. We have pictures of him on the walls of Pompeii as he plies the switch in his open-air school under a public portico. Horace, as we have noticed, saw the little boys of Venusia on the way to their lessons with the teacher's pittance of eight coppers for the Ides in their book-bags, and made the name of one teacher, Orbilius, memorable by attaching to it the adjective *plagosus*, the wielder of the whip. He tells us also of the *doctores blandi*, the teachers who use cookies to make the children willing to learn their A-B-C's. Juvenal, a century later, speaks of "drawing back the hand under the ferule." No doubt there were many faithful and inspiring teachers, and many people who appreciated the potential and the actual nobility of the calling, but on the whole the teacher in the primary schools was a humble if not a servile member of the community. When Horace eloquently describes the effect of poetry on the young, there is no suggestion of the teacher as the medium of that effect.

The teacher in the grammar school was a person of greater consequence. His pupils were select and farther advanced, and he was no doubt frequently the master of a private school enjoying a reputation for character and effectiveness. It was to secure instruction of this type that Horace and Cicero were at an early age taken by their fathers to Rome; "that I might be taught the same things as any knight's or senator's son," Horace says.

More fortunate still were the teachers of the select few who studied philosophy and rhetoric in preparation for the career of the public man. These were Greeks and Romans

of reputation, who were much sought out and well rewarded.
At their best, they enjoyed a fame that extended throughout
the Roman State. In Greek cities, above all in Athens,
there were many of them, and Cicero in his sojourn in the
East in 80–79 B.C. sought out the principal ones and studied

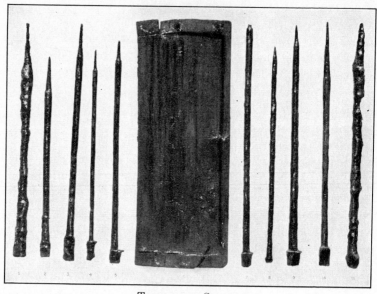

TABLET AND STYLUSES

Found in the Roman border fort at Newstead, near the River Tweed not far from
Melrose in Scotland. The tablet, about 5½ × 2½ inches, is one of two wings which
folded together and enclosed the writing on the wax.

under them. With some of them he had already studied
in Rome. Three of them mentioned by him as being in
Rome were Diodotus the Stoic, who lived many years in
Cicero's own home and died there in 59 B.C.; Philo the Aca-
demic, who was a refugee from the Mithridatic War; and
Molo of Rhodes, an envoy to the capital. Philo and Molo
both were teachers of Cicero at Rome in 88 B.C., when he

was eighteen years old, and Molo again nine years later in Rhodes. Molo was also Caesar's teacher soon afterward. The well-known Archias was not so great a man, but from Cicero's words in his praise it is easily seen that Archias was a type of the capable educator in liberal arts.

In spite of their ability and fame, however, the Greek teachers in higher education were more or less the humble objects of patronage on the part of wealthy and influential Romans. Not everyone believed in the training they represented, and the great mass of the Roman people distrusted Greek culture and despised the Greek character. Few Roman teachers were able or cared to vie with them in their field. The persons from whom Cicero acquires his special knowledge and inspiration in Roman subjects are not professional Roman educators, but public orators and officials to whom he is attached in a sort of apprenticeship or whom he follows about and observes in their daily public achievement : the two wise and learned Scaevolas, the finished and elegant Crassus, the unpolished but forceful Antonius. The only professional educator of note furnished by Rome was Quintilian.

Marcus Fabius Quintilianus was a Spaniard from the banks of the river Ebro in Spain, born A.D. 35. He was sent to Rome for his education, returned at the age of twenty to practice law and teach rhetoric in his native town of Calagurris, and went back at thirty-three to Rome, where, after about twenty years as teacher and lawyer, he wrote *The Training of the Orator*, a very sensible, solid, and high-minded work in twelve books, published about A.D. 95, when its author was sixty. Quintilian was the first appointee to the professorship in Latin rhetoric established by Vespasian when the already famous teacher and orator was about thirty-five. He was a great admirer of Cicero, and it is to be noted also that he was teacher and lawyer in one, and was thus another illustration of the union of public and professional life in Rome.

PAQUIUS PROCULUS OF POMPEII AND WIFE
The lady has folding tablets and a stylus; Paquius, a roll-book or volumen. This is a wall-painting.

Quintilian's ideal of education for the orator is a process beginning in the home, continuing in school and beyond school in life, and based on the broadest general culture. A few short quotations will contribute to an understanding of both Quintilian himself and the thoughts of his time on education. We are told that at this time a good teacher of oratory received about $100 per year from each pupil. A primary teacher had something like $3 from each pupil, and a grammaticus about $20. That there were wide differences in masters and schools and methods, is easily seen from Quintilian's work.

THE LANGUAGES

"I prefer that a boy should begin with Greek, because Latin, being in general use, will be picked up by him whether we will or no; while the fact that Latin learning is derived from Greek is a further reason for his being first instructed in the latter. . . . The study of Latin ought therefore to follow at no great distance and in a short time proceed side by side with Greek.   The result will be that, as soon as we begin to give equal attention to both languages, neither will prove a hindrance to the other."

The Age of Beginning

"Some hold that boys should not be taught to read till they are seven years old, that being the earliest age at which they can derive profit from instruction and endure the strain of learning. . . . Those, however, who hold that a child's mind should not be allowed to lie fallow for a moment are wiser. . . .   Why should we despise the profit to be derived before the age of seven, small though it be? For though the knowledge absorbed in the previous years may be but little, yet the boy will be learning something more advanced during that year, in which he would otherwise have been occupied with something more elementary."

The Very Young

" I am not, however, so blind to differences of age as to think that the very young should be forced on prematurely or given real work to do.   Above all things we must take care that the child, who is not yet old enough to love his studies, does not come to hate them and dread the bitterness which he has once tasted, even when the years of infancy are left behind.   His studies must be made an amusement: he must be questioned and praised and taught to rejoice when he has done well; sometimes too, when he refuses instruction, it should be given to some other to excite his envy; at times also he must be engaged in competition and should be allowed to believe himself successful more often than not, while he should be encouraged to do his best by such rewards as may appeal to his tender years."

Education and Morals

"I would urge that the lines which he is set to copy should not express thoughts of no significance, but convey some sound moral lesson.   He will remember such aphorisms even when he is an old man, and the impression made upon his unformed mind will contribute to the formation of his character. He may also be entertained by learning the sayings of famous men and above all selections from the poets, poetry being more attractive to children."

A ROMAN BOY BEING TAKEN TO SCHOOL

He wears the toga praetexta. The slave paedagogus, in tunic and sandals, carries his tablets.

PRIVATE OR PUBLIC SCHOOL

"But the time has come for the boy to grow up little by little, to leave the nursery and tackle his studies in good earnest. This therefore is the place to discuss the question as to whether it is better to have him educated privately at home or hand him over to some large school and those whom I may call public instructors. The latter course has, I know, won the approval of most eminent authorities and of those who have formed the national character of the most famous states. It would, however, be folly to shut our eyes to the fact that there are some who disagree with this preference for public education owing to a certain prejudice in favor of private tuition. These persons seem to be guided in the main by two principles. In the interests of morality they would avoid the society of a number of human beings at an age that is specially liable to acquire serious faults : I only wish I could deny the truth of the view that such education has often been the cause of the most discreditable actions. Secondly, they hold that whoever is to be the boy's teacher, he will devote his time more generously to one pupil than if he has to divide it among several. . . . But morals may be corrupted at home as well. There are numerous instances of both, as there are also of the preservation of a good reputation under either circumstance. . . . There is nothing to prevent the principle of 'one teacher, one boy' being combined with school education. And even if such a combination should prove impossible, I should still prefer the broad daylight of a respectable school to the solitude and obscurity of a private education."

Strain and Relaxation

"All our pupils will require some relaxation, not merely because there is nothing in this world that can stand continued strain and even unthinking and inanimate objects are unable to maintain their strength, unless given intervals of rest, but because study depends on the good will of the student, a quality that cannot be secured by compulsion. . . . I approve of play in the young ; it is a sign of a lively disposition ; nor will you ever lead me to believe that a boy who is gloomy and in a continual state of depression is ever likely to show alertness of mind in his work."

Flogging

"I disapprove of flogging, although it is the regular custom and meets with the acquiescence of Chrysippus, because in the first place it is a disgraceful form of punishment and fit only for slaves, and is in any case an insult, as you will realize if you imagine its infliction at a later age. Secondly, if a boy is so insensible to instruction that reproof is useless, he will, like the worst type of slave, merely become hardened to blows. Finally, there will be absolutely no need of such punishment if the master is a thorough disciplinarian."

Reading

"In this connection there is much that can only be taught in actual practice, as for instance when the boy should take breath, at what point he should introduce a pause into a line, where the sense ends or begins, when the voice should be raised or lowered, what modulation should be given to each phrase, and when he should increase or slacken speed, or speak with greater or less energy. In this portion of my work I will give but one golden rule: to do all these things, he must understand what he reads. But above all his reading must be manly, combining dignity and charm; it must be different from the reading of prose, for poetry is song and poets claim to be singers. But this fact does not justify degeneration into sing-song or the effeminate modulations now in vogue: there is an excellent saying on this point attributed to Gaius Caesar while he was still a boy: 'If you are singing, you sing badly; if you are reading, you sing.'"

Applause in School

"I strongly disapprove of the prevailing practice of allowing boys to stand up or leap from the seats in the expression of their applause. Young men, even when they are listening to others, should be temperate in manifesting their approval. If this be insisted upon, the pupil will depend on his instructor's verdict and will take his approval as a guarantee that he has spoken well. The audience no less than the speaker should therefore keep their eyes fixed on their teacher's face, since thus they will learn to distinguish between what is praiseworthy and what is not: for just as writing gives facility, so listening begets the critical faculty. But in the schools of to-day we see boys stooping forward ready to spring to their feet: at the close of each period they not merely rise, but rush forward with shouts of unseemly enthusiasm. Such compliments are mutual and the success of a declamation consists in this kind of applause."

LETTERS AND THE ARTS

We have just taken account of the profession of teaching, and in former chapters we described the education of children and the advanced training of older boys and of young men destined for public life. This gave us some insight into the mental habit of the Romans, but only as it was connected with formal instruction in the schools and under tutors. If we are to make a truthful estimate of their intellectual life, we must know more concerning the occupation of their minds in the leisure hours of adult life. What did the Romans read, and what place in their lives did the fine arts occupy?

Compared with most modern nations of Europe and America, the masses of ancient Rome read little. Education was not universal, there was no printing press, publication was greatly limited, and the condensed, periodic, artificial language of literary and professional Latin was even farther removed from common speech and understanding than the serious literature of to-day is from the matter of cheap journalism. Horace, Lucretius, and Livy, and even Virgil and Cicero, for the ordinary man, were hard reading. On the other hand, the Romans who did use books were of the serious sort who read with conscious appreciation.

Let us look for a moment at what they read. Up to 240 B.C., when Livius Andronicus, a former slave brought captive to Rome from Magna Graecia after the fall of Tarentum in 272 B.C., translated the *Odyssey* into the Latin language for purposes of school instruction, there was practically no Latin literature. The *Twelve Tables*, dating from about 450 B.C., and some of the speeches of Appius Claudius the Blind, consul in 307 B.C., are all that the historian of literature takes account of, and they were hardly deserving of the name of art.

THALIA, MUSE OF COMEDY

The tympanum, pipe, and vine leaves in the hair, are symbolic of Dionysus, or Bacchus, in whose honor drama was produced.

When Cicero and Caesar were young men, Latin literature was therefore less than two hundred years old. What there was for them to read for purposes of study or diversion consisted of something like this : in epic, the *Odyssey* in the rugged Latin of Livius Andronicus, the *Second Punic War* of Naevius, and the *Annals of Rome* of Ennius; in drama, the adaptations and imitations of Greek tragedy by Livius, Ennius, Naevius, Pacuvius, and Accius, and of Greek comedy by Caecilius Statius, Plautus, and Terence; in satire, the miscellanies of Ennius and the social and political attacks of Lucilius; in oratory, the speeches of Appius Claudius, Cato the Censor, and others; in history, the poetic exploitations of Ennius and Naevius, the *Origins* of Cato, and the works of several writers on the Punic Wars; in the didactic, Cato's *On Agriculture;* in jurisprudence, a number of commentaries marking the beginnings of scientific study of the law. It will be seen by this, first, that Roman literature was greatly indebted to Greece, a fact which would be more noticeable if form as well as subject were considered; second, that aside from the drama, which was a public spectacle supplied by the State in the grand style, this literature, whatever its form, sprang from the life of the Roman people; and, third, that it was a practical literature, lacking almost entirely the lighter contribution of the lyric, and concerning itself largely with the interests of the State.

To supplement this not very abundant national literature, there was available, for those who were fired by intellectual or professional ambition, the rich legacy of Greek literature. From the time of the Scipios, about the middle of the second century B.C., the ideal education included instruction in both tongues and a finishing in Athens. There was a Greek library in Rome under Augustus, and another under Trajan.

By the time of Cicero's death, Roman literature had been enriched by the lyrics of Catullus, the great poem of Lucretius *On Nature,* the *Commentaries* of Caesar, the encyclopaedic learning of Varro, the legal treatises of Mucius Scaevola and Servius Sulpicius, and the wide variety of Cicero's own magnificent contribution. In a few years the *Eclogues* or *Pastorals* of Virgil were added, bringing to his practical countrymen the fresh and delightful experience of the poetry of Theocritus, the Greek whose *Idylls,* published two hundred years before Virgil's time, are the world's most famous short poems on the life of the country. By the time the menace of Antony and the East was removed at the battle of Actium in 31 B.C., Virgil's *Georgics* were near completion, and Horace was known for satire and somewhat for lyric. In five years Livy at the age of thirty-three was to begin the great *History of Rome*, the appearance of whose parts from time to time brought fame to him and crystallized the ideal of Roman character in the minds of his own and future generations. The *Aeneid* was given to the world soon after its author's death in 19 B.C.

The deaths of Virgil and Horace in 19 B.C. and 8 B.C., of Maecenas and Augustus in 8 B.C. and A.D. 14, and of Livy in A.D. 17, close the account of the great Augustan writers and the chief patrons of Augustan letters. Ovid's versatility and ease in the *Metamorphoses*, the *Amores*, and the *Heroides*, the exquisite love poetry in elegiacs by Tibullus and Propertius, and even the less fortunate product of others in a court circle where it was the fashion to write, deserved the fame they won, but these authors are not to be ranked with the great names of Cicero, Caesar, Virgil, Horace, and Livy, at whose mention the world is reminded, not of the anxieties and conceits and graces of the young poet about town, but of the Roman State and of the Roman character that lay at its foundations.

The century after Augustus' death added much to literature. There were the two Senecas, the elder who wrote on rhetoric, the younger who contributed philosophical essays, the *Moral Epistles*, and a number of tragedies which in the Renaissance served as the link between ancient and modern serious drama. There were the historian Tacitus, and Quintilian the professor of rhetoric, and the satirist Juvenal, and the epigrammatist Martial, and the encyclopaedist Pliny the Elder, whose *Natural History* is a mine of information of all sorts, and the letter-writing Pliny the Younger, who emulated Cicero, and the picaresque novelist or satirist Petronius, and Lucan the poet of Pharsalia, and

Silius Italicus and Statius, the ambitious authors of tedious epic.

No doubt there were works of less permanent nature in circulation, but there was nothing remotely resembling the flood of books and magazines and journals that inundates the reader of the twentieth century. There were libraries from Augustus on, and twenty-nine are known in the period from his time to Hadrian. The library at Timgad in Roman Africa is estimated at twenty thousand books. This is little, however, compared with modern times. What survives of Roman literature corresponds to the serious and solid literature of modern times which we call standard or classic, and was read, as the classics to-day are read, only by the fit and few whose intellectual and moral equipment enabled them to read and enjoy. The striking differences between the two reading publics are, first, that the few who composed the ancient public suffered less from the distractions of too many books, and, second, that the great mass of the lower reading public was lacking altogether. As regards publication, it may be added that public readings by authors, so frequent as to invite the

A LADY WITH STYLUS AND TABLETS
Painted on a wall in Herculaneum. She has gold ear-rings.

satirist's attack, were in part a substitute for the issuing of
books.

Regarded as material for liberal training in the school
and for liberal culture on the part of the adult serious reader,
the literary product of Rome during the two centuries from
Cicero's youth to the deaths of Pliny, Tacitus, and Juvenal
in the reigns of Trajan and Hadrian compares on the whole
not unfavorably with that of similar periods in the histories

A TRAGIC MASK

Found in the Villa of Hadrian, fifteen miles
from Rome.

of other peoples. It rivaled
Greek oratory in Cicero,
and Greek history in Livy
and Tacitus. It surpassed
Greek satire in Horace and
Juvenal, and furnished the
world's greatest epigram-
matist in Martial and
greatest letter-writer in
Cicero. It did as well in
the lyric and epic as Greece
of the fifth and fourth centuries. If we miss the sup-
pleness and ease of the
Greek tongue, there is compensation in the precision,
dignity, vigor, and sonorousness of a language that was
the fit instrument for the lords of a world. If the philosophy of Plato, the criticism and science of Aristotle, the
epic of Homer, and the Athenian drama found nothing Roman to rival them, it was because their richness was too
great for rivalry and could inspire only its transfer from
tongue to tongue.

Much has been said of Roman lack of originality in letters
and the arts. The drama indeed was especially indebted

to the Greek stage. Greek plays were imitated, adapted, and even translated, as French or Italian plays have been for the English and American stages. They were great plays, they were of the great past of a great race, they lent themselves to the purposes of the Roman aedile to produce on state occasions an impressive piece of tragic pageantry or a polished comedy of intrigue. The timely, the local, the realistic, belonged no more to State theater representations in the grand style than the jazz piece to a symphony concert. At the most, the slighter forms of drama, if used at all out of their proper place in unofficial shows, were curtain raisers to the higher forms of art. Yet no one thought of the Greek play in Latin as plagiarism, or blamed it as unoriginal. Quite the contrary, the use of Greek literature for Roman purpose conferred distinction on the user. To know both tongues and use them, to be versed in Greek literature, had long been the ideal before the times from Augustus to Marcus Aurelius made it the fashion. The men who could make Greek letters accessible to their fellow countrymen were benefactors to be thanked for their cleverness. The first men to do it claimed the credit of pioneers. Cicero, Virgil, Horace, and Ovid write with the assurance, and sometimes the assertion, that their use of the form and substance of Greek literature will bring them everlasting fame.

In other fields than the drama, the debt of Roman literature is not so direct and so overwhelming, though to deny it in general would be like denying the general dependence of American letters upon European. But the declaration that Roman letters are indebted to the Greek must not mislead us into the too common view that Roman literature is not an expression of Roman life and Roman character. Those who argue best that the *Georgics* and *Eclogues* and

Aeneid of Virgil and the *Odes* of Horace are only "pale reflections" of Hesiod, Theocritus, and Homer, and of the Greek lyric poets, are the mechanical scholars who are patient in the finding of sources and parallels, have had no experience of Italy, and are unaccustomed to read an author as a whole. With such critics it is hard to argue. To the reader who has carried his authors in Italy or read them after his return, it never occurs to think of Latin literature as anything but the expression of Roman and Italian experience. Whatever the borrowings of Cicero in *De Amicitia* and *De Senectute*, in both of them the reader feels that the friendship and the old age are Cicero's own and are charged with the authority of his sixty-two years of living. Whatever the form of Horace's *Odes*, they are warm with Italy and Roman life.

But let us pass to the arts. The art most constantly present to the Roman eye was architecture. Here again, reminders of the Greek were everywhere. The temple, the basilica, the baths, the portico or colonnade, the theater, the amphitheater, the circus, the inclosure or group called forum, the triumphal arch, the honorary column, the palace, the administrative building, all displayed in varying degree the column and architrave and the moldings and other ornaments belonging to the Doric, Ionic, and Corinthian styles of building.

Of the various buildings in Graeco-Roman architecture, the temple was least removed in character from the Greek. The other buildings were likely to be Greek only in their decorative aspects, and even there made abundant use of the semicircular arch. The great façade of the Colosseum is an example ; the three Greek orders are used on it purely as ornament — a modified Doric on the first zone or story, the Ionic on the second, the Corinthian on the third, and a

The Temple of Juno Moneta on the Capitoline Hill in an Artist's Restoration

modified Corinthian on the fourth, all employed in conjunc-
tion with the arcade. The reality of the Colosseum and most
of the great Roman buildings was the vault, practically
unused in Greece. This was the living principle that made
the Roman structures stand; the Greek columns and architraves and moldings were only beautification, applied
ornament not needed for stability. Without the vault,
the towering masses of brick and concrete made necessary
by the bigness of Roman civilization would not have been
possible. In the temple and elsewhere, the Corinthian
was the favorite style; with moldings enriched and multiplied, from Augustus on it satisfied, better than austere Doric
and restrained Ionic, the Roman love of the exuberant and
splendid.

Some Roman buildings, like the aqueduct and the bridge
and the fortification wall, had nothing to do with Greece
either in reality or appearance. The triumphal arch and
column seem to have been Roman inventions, though employing Greek detail. The earlier centuries, without marble
and of simple needs, showed little that suggested Greece.
All in all, Roman building is in essence like Roman literature. It is an art at its greatest in examples inspired by
the State, with one form, the temple, like the drama, more
closely imitative than others; with many borrowed details
for beautification, but with substance and structure in
general solidly its own.

The painter's art of Roman times as it has been preserved
consists almost entirely of wall decoration in the houses of
Pompeii. The contributions of Herculaneum, Ostia, and
Rome are slight in comparison. From this decoration and
from the writings of Pliny the Elder it is evident that there
was also an independent art of painting and that easel pictures were produced; but painting was never so great an

art in Ancient Rome as it became in the Renaissance. Its subjects ranged from street scenes and ordinary life to tales from Homer and Greek tragedy. Mosaic, usually for floor decoration, with its birds and beasts and fruits and flowers, sometimes rose to great excellence, as in the battle scene of

ALTAR FRAGMENT FOUND IN ROME

The branches of the plane, or sycamore, are a marvel of realistic beauty.

Alexander and Darius. The elder Pliny's mention of doves reproduced so faithfully as to show their reflection in the water is verified in Pompeian mosaic.

Sculpture was of greater importance. Two kinds of demand called forth its production. The rich and ambitious capital had either seized or acquired by purchase much of the art of Greece, and its presence inspired the order of many copies, adaptations, and imitations of famous Greek works for the adornment of gentlemen's villas and houses, and for the public buildings and gardens. Much of this product was poor, and little of it was original; yet, though it does not flatter the artist's invention or skill, it is an evidence that the Romans appreciated the value of art. In the second place, there was the demand of consuls and emperors and others among the great or the pretentious for portrait busts and statues, and for pictorial sculpture in relief to commemorate their exploits in war and peace. The reliefs on the arches of Titus and Constantine, the columns of Trajan and Marcus Aurelius, the balustrades in the Forum, and the museums filled with portrait sculptures, many of them belonging to the world's best art, are examples of this. The excellence of Roman art in the historical relief and in portraiture can hardly be overstated. Sculpture again is a demonstration of the close connection of Roman art with life, and especially the public life.

Such in the main were the arts and the literature which graced the strenuous living of the Roman people. Perhaps the art of the garden, public and private, now called landscape architecture, should be included. It was no doubt as important in ancient as in Renaissance Italy. Music seems hardly to have existed as an independent art. Most references to music in ancient times relate it to the flute or pipes in religious ceremonial or to accompaniment in dramatic representation, or to the shell or lyre in connection with lyric poetry, or to the horn and trumpet in war. The great singing and instrumental music of Italy were still many centuries away.

The Romans are often called a matter-of-fact and inartistic people, with the implication that they were also without taste. This is not quite just. Rome from Augustus on was a monumental and magnificent city with a wealth of statuary brought from the East or executed in the capital.

For two centuries at least it had had its coteries of Hellenists, and for two centuries more the Greek tongue was the mark of intellectual distinction. No doubt there were great numbers of Romans who did not give a thought to art, and much or most of the art in the city was the work of Greek minds and hands; but this does not prove a national want of appreciation. The society that made its capital a city of architectural splendors and a vast museum of the arts, that produced the faultless urbanity of the Augustan literary and intellectual circles, that recorded in Livy its appreciation of the noble traits of men, and that evolved the Ciceronian prose and the Virgilian verse, is not lightly to be charged with want of culture.

XXI

THE DOCTOR

The Roman physician, like the Roman teacher, was likely to be a Greek or of Greek descent, and was frequently a freedman or even a slave. When Cicero says, as he writes of the various callings, "Those fields of knowledge in which either there is a greater intelligence or from which the benefit sought is out of the ordinary, as medicine and architecture, are honorable for those to whose rank they belong," he is probably not thinking of patricians or equestrians, or even of plebeians of Roman blood, but of a profession largely filled by foreigners of the freedman class.

The elder Pliny, quoting an earlier writer, states that the first physician to come to Rome was Archagathus, an emigrant from the Peloponnesus in 219 B.C. who was given Roman citizenship and an office purchased at the State's expense. This was seventy-two years after the religion of Aesculapius, the god of healing and the patron of physicians, was brought to Rome and located on the Tiber Island, an event which no doubt marked an active beginning of interest in Greek medical skill. The office of Archagathus seems to have been a surgeon's clinic: "They say he was a surgeon and that his coming was at first much liked, but that soon his cruelty with the knife and cautery gave him the name of butcher, and brought the art and all doctors into bad repute."

The Greeks were never popular in Rome, and Archagathus probably suffered for his nationality as well as for the indifference to other people's pain with which he was charged. Old Cato liked the doctors no better than the rest of the Greeks, and is said to have declared that they had conspired to kill the Romans off. There were those, however, who won the confidence of the Romans and rose to greatness. Asclepiades from Prusa, a friend of Cicero who had a pleasing address and some skill in oratory, was highly esteemed, made a fortune, and founded a school. Antonius Musa, the favorite physician of Augustus, was of Greek blood and a freedman.

The prejudice against the Greek practitioner was not so keen as time went on. Julius Caesar, we are told by Suetonius, "presented with citizenship all who professed medicine at Rome, and all teachers of the liberal arts, in order to make those already there more willing residents of the city, and to attract others to come." Yet Pliny can say of medicine a hundred years later: "This is the only one of the Greek professions which Roman dignity has not yet taken up; very few indeed of the Romans have shared in its great advantages, and they have straightway gone over to the Greeks. Yes, and to tell the truth, the untaught also and those who know nothing of the Greek tongue have no faith in any doctor unless he practices his calling in Greek, and they have the less faith in what is done for their health if they understand."

There were nevertheless many Roman physicians, and some of considerable fame. Marcus Artorius rose to be physician to Augustus, and Cornelius Celsus, under Tiberius, wrote a manual of eight books on medicine which is Rome's authoritative contribution to medical literature.

As might be expected, the practice of the healer's art in Rome was both general and special. There were oculists, aurists, dentists, and surgeons; there were specialists in ulcers and ruptures; there were specialists in women's diseases; there were the water-cure doctors, of whom Antonius

ÆNEAS WOUNDED

A wall painting from Pompeii, showing Aeneas wounded in the thigh, the surgeon
dressing the wound, Ascanius weeping, and Venus appearing with the magic herb.
The scene is from *Aeneid* XII 383–424.

Musa was one, and the wine-cure doctors. There were male doctors and female doctors; there were doctors maintained in the larger houses, there were court doctors. There were doctors for slaves, for gladiators in training, and for soldiers' barracks and the army. There were doctors who received the enormous salary of $30,000 a year; there were communal doctors in the smaller towns who received very little; and there were quack doctors.

The practice of medicine in Rome by the ignorant and unskilled was an easy matter. There were no medical colleges giving diplomas, no examining boards, no licenses. "There is no penalty for their ignorance," says Pliny. "They learn at our risk and get their experience by the death of their patients, and a doctor can kill a man with entire freedom from punishment." Medical education was by apprenticeship; the learner helped the doctor in his office or clinic and accompanied him on his rounds, and in due time was either taken into partnership or given permission to practice independently. "I was feeling low," writes Martial in an epigram addressed to Doctor Symmachus, "but you came straightway to me with a hundred of your students. A hundred hands chill with the North wind felt my pulse. I didn't have the fever before, Symmachus, but I have it now." The drug business also was more or less unregulated; there were sellers of medicine, but no scientific pharmacies, and the doctor kept his own stock of drugs. If there are abuses in our day of careful regulation, it is hardly to be supposed that there were not greater abuses in Rome, with the profession largely made up of the servile and the foreign, who had less to lose and more to gain than the reputable Roman.

We should not be too hasty, however, in concluding that medicine was in irresponsible and incompetent hands. The

Greeks had a long experience in medicine and surgery behind them.   There were probably in Alexandria and other enterprising cities superior facilities for a really scientific preparation ; there were medical treatises for the basis of study — and apprenticeship is after all a very practical and very effective

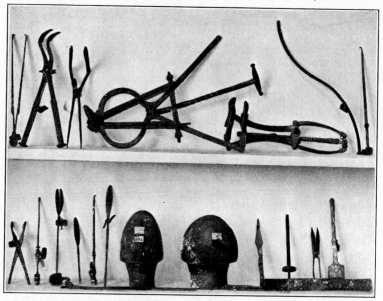

SURGICAL INSTRUMENTS FROM POMPEII

Nippers, forceps, dilators, catheter, tenaculum.   Below, from the right : clyster pipe, for injections ; scissors ; cannula, or drain ; bleeding-cups ; spathomele, for preparing applications.

method which still exists in the use of clinic and interneship for the training of the young physician.   It should not be forgotten, too, that what may be called the standard diseases and the standard remedies were known and treated in simple and practical fashion from the earliest times, and have always remained substantially the same.   Most of all, we should not forget the wonderfully complete equipments of ancient surgical instruments — forceps, needles, scalpels, knives, lancets, catheters, sounds — which have been found, and which have astonished modern surgeons by their identity with those in use to-day. Among these collections, one is of Pompeian origin and preserved in the museum at Naples, and another was found near ancient Vindonissa, a Roman legionary post of the second century after Christ in Switzerland, in the remains of a permanent military hospital belonging to the post. Besides the ruins, the instruments, and various little boxes containing drugs, an inscription was found, "To Tiberius Claudius Hymnus, physician of the Twenty-first Legion, and to Claudia Quieta (his wife)," placed by his patron, Atticus.

HIPPOCRATES, THE FIRST GREAT
GREEK PHYSICIAN

The Oath of Hippocrates is still taken
by graduating medical students.

Dentistry was not the universal thing it is to-day in America, nor even the less universal thing it is in Europe, but gold work of some sort was known in Rome at a very early date. This is indicated by a fragment of the tenth of the Twelve Tables, dating about 449 B.C., mentioning "teeth joined to or with gold."

Considering the prominence of the Greeks in medicine and surgery in Rome, it is not going too far to assume that Hippocrates of the island of Cos, about 460–360 B.C., called the father of Greek medicine and esteemed by Plato and Aristotle in Athens, was a great influence in Roman medicine. The physician's oath as preserved in Hippocrates' work on medicine is still administered in our own time to the graduating classes of colleges of medicine, and was no doubt a part of the formality of admitting the apprentice student to practice in Rome. An attentive reading of it will suggest much as to the practice as well as the ethics of the Roman physician.

The Oath

"I swear by Apollo Physician, by Asclepius, by Health, by Panacea and by all the gods and goddesses, making them my witnesses, that I will carry out, according to my ability and judgment, this oath and this indenture. To hold my teacher in this art equal to my own parents; to make him partner in my livelihood; when he is in need of money to share mine with him; to consider his family as my own brothers, and to teach them this art, if they want to learn it, without fee or indenture; to impart precept, oral instruction, and all other instruction to my own sons, the sons of my teacher, and to indentured pupils who have taken the physician's oath, but to nobody else. I will use treatment to help the sick according to my ability and judgment, but never with a view to injury and wrong-doing. Neither will I administer a poison to anybody when asked to do so, nor will I suggest such a course. Similarly I will not give to a woman a pessary to cause abortion.

"But I will keep pure and holy both my life and my art. I will not use the knife, not even, verily, on sufferers from stone, but I will give place to such as are craftsmen therein. Into whatsoever houses I enter, I will enter to help the sick, and I will abstain from all intentional wrong-doing and harm, especially from abusing the bodies of man or woman, bond or free. And whatsoever I shall see or hear in the course of my profession as well as outside my profession in my intercourse with men, if it be what should not be published abroad, I will never divulge, holding such things to be holy secrets.

"Now if I carry out this oath, and break it not, may I gain forever reputation among all men for my life and for my art; but if I transgress it and forswear myself, may the opposite befall me."

One or two extracts from the same work will show us tne physician actually at work.

"I urge you not to be too unkind, but to consider carefully your patient's superabundance or means. Sometimes give your services for nothing, calling to mind a previous benefaction or present satisfaction. And if there be an opportunity of serving one who is a stranger in financial straits, give full assistance to all such. For where there is love of man, there is also love of the art. For some patients, though conscious that their condition is perilous, recover their health simply through their contentment with the goodness of the physician."

"The dignity of a physician requires that he should look healthy, and as plump as nature intended him to be; for the common crowd consider those who are not of this excellent bodily condition to be unable to take care of others. . . . The prudent man must also be careful of certain moral considerations — not only to be silent, but also of a great regularity of life, since thereby his reputation will be greatly enhanced; he must be a gentleman in character, and being this he must be grave and kind to all. For an overforward obtrusiveness is despised, even though it may be very useful. . . . In appearance, let him be of a serious but not harsh countenance; for harshness is taken to mean arrogance and unkindness, while a man of uncontrolled laughter and excessive gaiety is considered vulgar, and vulgarity especially must be avoided."

"Such, then, should the physician be, both in body and in soul."

Finally, the ancients were already using the jokes about the doctor which are so familiar to-day. Here is one of ours: "What profession do you follow?" "The medical; I'm an undertaker." This is not so very different from one of Martial's epigrams:

> "An undertaker now is Brown,
> Doctor no more;
> His work is really still
> What 'twas before."

And here is another from Martial:

"Though he bathed with us yesterday, dined with us, too,
  And was quite in the pink of condition,
Ancus died this A.M., — of a dream that he'd asked
  Hermocrates to be his physician."

XXII

THE MONEY–MAKER

The money of the ancient Roman was a coin system whose unit was the *as*, a copper piece worth about two cents. The next larger coin was the silver *sestertius*, between four and five cents; the next, the silver *quinarius*, between eight and ten cents; the next, the *denarius*, also silver, between sixteen and twenty cents. The *aureus*, of gold, had a value of between four and five dollars. Roughly speaking, the coins of Rome corresponded to our nickel, ten-cent piece, quarter, and five-dollar gold piece. The sestertius was the unit in ordinary calculations; in large transactions the reckoning was by thousands of sesterces. By Cicero's time the *as* was little used, but fractions of it were coined.

The original money of the Romans was their cattle, as the word *pecunia*, from *pecus*, testifies. Their original coin, at first mere crude metal and then stamped, was the unwieldy copper as weighing a pound, whose bulk was gradually reduced until at the end of the Second Punic War in 203 B.C. it weighed an ounce, and finally half an ounce. The coinage of silver in Rome began in 269 B.C., the mint being located in the temple of Juno Moneta on the Capitoline Hill. The word "Moneta," used as an epithet of Juno and perhaps referring to some fancied warning or admonishment from the goddess, soon began to mean the mint, and then the coin or money which was the product of the mint. The word has descended to our times as Italian *moneta*, French *monnaie*, and English *money*. The coinage of gold,

COINS OF THE LATE REPUBLIC AND EARLY EMPIRE

Coin *e* was struck by Mark Antony about 37 B.C.; coin *f* by Augustus about A.D. 6. Both are *aurei*, gold; the latter is inscribed, Caesar Augustus, Divi F[ilius] Pater Patriae. Coin *g* is a *denarius* of Trajan, about A.D. 107, with the River Danube on the reverse. Coins *i, j, k* are of Tiberius and Nero.

first occurring in the war with Hannibal, and introduced as a war measure, was discontinued soon after, but resumed by the time of Augustus. The Roman supply of silver was principally from the Spanish mines near Nova Carthago, now Cartagena, where forty thousand miners were employed as early as Polybius, the Greek historian of Rome, 210–128 B.C. Gold came from the Tagus in Spain and the Pactolus in Asia Minor; copper from Etruria and various more distant sources.

The word "moneta" also meant sometimes the stamp or die which was used in the process of coinage. The Roman coins of all metals and all periods which fill the museum cases of every land are stamped with the figures of gods and goddesses, the features of consuls, generals, and emperors, and with the monuments they erected, and are a wonderful means for the study of the Roman past. The issuing of money until 15 B.C. was controlled by the Senate. At that date the emperor assumed charge of the mintage in silver and gold and relieved the Senate of all but the coinage in copper. The duties of actual minting were at first in charge of special boards and later of the *tres viri monetales*, the commission of three on the mint.

The dealings of Roman business in the last centuries of the Republic brought contacts with the money systems of many different states. Conquest, the movement of troops, provincial administration, the interchanges of trade, the importation of the grain supply, the slave traffic, and the increase of travel set money into circulation and frequently took it far from home. No port or other city of size was without its thriving money-changers to convert the stranger's or the returning citizen's foreign coin into the local currency. No city of importance was without its money-lenders and bankers to accommodate the borrower and to issue bills of exchange or letters of credit to those with business abroad. Deposits bearing interest were received and funds were subject to check. By the time of the Empire, the financial life of Rome was on a scale and of a character

surprisingly like that of modern times. There was even a panic in A.D. 33, which the Emperor Tiberius allayed by the distribution of four million dollars of State funds among the banks.

The man who was ready to be changer, lender, buyer and seller on commission, and in general to play the part of the modern banker, was the *argentarius*, the money-man, from *argentum*, silver. Another name for the money-broker, which was applied also to the tester of metal before it went into coinage, was the *nummularius*, from *num-*

LUCIUS CAECILIUS JUCUNDUS

Jucundus was an auctioneer. This bronze portrait was found in his house in Pompeii, where was found also a box which contained 127 tablets recording accounts of his sales.

mus, a coin. The name for one who was more exclusively a lender was *foenerator*, from *foenus*, interest. When Cicero borrowed to buy his mansion on the Palatine, he found it easy to get money at six per cent, and said he was regarded as good security because of his successful consulship of the year before. This was probably less than the usual rate. Much higher rates of interest are heard of, but under unusual conditions.

If we inquire into the active financial life of Rome, we find that, aside from the ordinary mercantile operations natural to the business of a city, the money transactions were largely in the hands of the equestrian order; that is, those citizens not of senatorial rank who possessed four hundred thousand sesterces, about $20,000. These men were the active money-making class from the time when their order was formed by Gaius Gracchus in 123 B.C. Besides banking and commercial business, they undertook State contracts, such as the importation of grain for the city, the provisioning of the army, the construction of public buildings and aqueducts, and the raising of the taxes.

It is in connection with the taxes that we hear most frequently of the financial career of the equestrian order. The Roman State did not collect its taxes through the office of a State treasury department, but sold to the highest bidder the contract for collecting the amounts due in the provinces or territories assessed. If the successful bidder did not, in the fear of not getting the contract, bid too high, he was able to collect from the people a sum large enough to satisfy the government claim and to give him a large profit. The persons who served as actual tax-collectors, the *publicani*, were much disliked; those who would reproach Jesus called him "a gluttonous man, and a winebibber, a friend of publicans and sinners." Sometimes the bidder or bidders — for the agent was frequently a business firm or a stock company — overreached themselves by contracting at too large a sum, and on realizing their mistake applied to the Senate for a cancellation of the contract.

Since the support of the equites as a class was much valued by the senatorial or conservative party, requests like these for special favors might be embarrassing. Cicero writes to Atticus in December, 61 B.C.:

"Yes, another fine proposal from the equites that is just about the limit — and I not only tolerated but even actively stood for it! Those who had the contract for Asia from the censors complained in the Senate that in their eagerness they had gone too far and agreed to impossible terms, and asked for a cancellation. I was the foremost among their champions, or rather the second; for Crassus was the one who put them up to be bold enough to make the demand. An unpleasant business — a shameless proposal, and a confession of lack of judgment. There was the greatest danger of their being wholly alienated from the Senate if they did not get what they wanted."

Crassus, who stood behind the equites on this occasion, belonged to their order and was one of the wealthiest men of the time, and it is not unlikely that he was financially interested in the company or companies appearing before the Senate as above described. The city was probably full of investors on a smaller scale.

The importation of grain for Rome and other cities was another constant opportunity. The days when the peninsula sufficed for itself were past, even in Cicero's time; in 75 B.C. his duties as quaestor in Sicily included the sending of wheat cargoes to Rome. Over a century later, Tacitus writes: "Once Italy exported supplies to the legions in distant provinces, and it does not suffer now from unproductiveness. But we draw rather on Africa and Egypt, and the life of the Roman people is allowed to depend on ships and chances at sea."

Other opportunities for investment are illustrated by the career of Atticus, the friend of Cicero. Besides extensive lending to Cicero and his friends and to various Greek cities, he engaged in publishing and in the training of gladiators.

So far in our account there is nothing in the business life of Rome that is unfamiliar to modern times in America, unless it is the restriction of financial operations so largely to one order in society. The money connections of the patricians and the senatorial class who were not patrician were of a different sort. The theory of Roman society was that men of good family and senators were not engaged in money-making but in the service of the State. We have seen that the offices in the public career carried with them no salaries, and that services to the citizenry in general were gratuitous. This was a matter of tradition from the earlier times when the chief men of the gentes found all their occupation in the management of public affairs and of their own estates. Tradition was strengthened by law. Livy, for example, tells of the unpopularity of the consul Flaminius "because of a new law [about 220 B.C.] which Quintus Claudius, tribune of the people, had carried in opposition to the Senate, with Flaminius as the one senator supporting him; a law forbidding the possession by any senator or any senator's son of a sea-going ship of more than three hundred amphorae capacity [about seven and a half tons]. This was regarded as enough for the carrying of produce from the land; all money-making was looked upon as unbecoming to senators." We have already noted the Lex Cincia de Muneribus of 204 B.C. prohibiting the acceptance of payment or gifts for service in the courts.

It must not be supposed, however, that either tradition or the law kept senators and patricians from financial contagion. In the first place, it is hardly possible that the Cincian Law was not in numerous instances evaded. There were various ways in which the genuinely grateful citizen who had means could discharge the obligation he felt toward the man of rank or family who had helped him through a difficult business in the courts. There was legacy; there was the throwing of business opportunity in his protector's way; there was support in the next elections; and there might be an actual payment kept secret. In all but the last mentioned, it could be claimed that the letter of the law was not violated; and as time went on and the city became crowded, and the great families found their fortunes

FORUM AND CAPITOL RESTORED

At the left: Temple of Vesta, Temple of Castor and Pollux, Imperial Palace (in background); center: Temple of Julius Caesar, Arch of Augustus, Basilica Julia; right: Arch of Tiberius, Temple of Vespasian, Temple of Saturn, Temple of Jupiter (on hill). Back of the Temple of Vespasian is the Tabularium.

on the decline, and more and more of the governing class were men of scant means, it could be claimed that to observe scrupulously the spirit of the law as well as the letter was to attempt the impossible and to be unjust.

Cicero affords an example. From all we can know, on his entrance upon the public career the orator was a man of moderate fortune. He was always in debt, yet apparently always able to indulge the most expensive tastes. To explain how he could buy a house for one hundred and seventy-five thousand dollars, support a son in Athens at three thousand dollars a year, own half a dozen country places, and lead a life to correspond, is difficult unless it is assumed that his constant activities in public life met with some reward. In England, a modern aristocratic country, the fiction of no charge by the barrister is maintained, while every client expects to pay a fee and is not left uncertain as to its amount.

In the second place, the owning of landed property was neither forbidden nor of ill repute. This also was a tradition from the earlier and simpler day. The estates outside the city grew larger and came into fewer hands after the importation of grain reduced the profit of ordinary farming. Cattle, wine, oil, and fruits took the place of grain, and an equipment of slave labor the place of the numerous small farmers.

In the third place, the public career led in the majority of cases to the provinces, where by fair means or otherwise the fortunes of the propraetor or proconsul and the numerous friends or relatives under his patronage found ample means for increase. We hear much about extortion and other abuses, but it need not be supposed that there were not also honorable means of profiting by the governorship. Every successive increase of Roman dominion opened up new fields for investment, and the governor and his administrative train were first on the ground. Even at home in the capital, there was the opportunity to participate in provincial enterprises by investment.

We may conclude therefore that, directly and indirectly, the nonsalaried and noncommercial nobility as well as the equestrian financiers were able to share in the worldly advantages of the constantly expanding State.

XXIII

THE COMMON MAN

We have followed the public man in the career of service
to the State as civilian and soldier, and have followed him
also in his service to the individual citizen in the capacity of
lawyer or advocate. We have seen the activities of somewhat humbler men in teaching and medicine, the activities
of the equestrian class in commerce, contracts, and financial
adventure in general, and the participation of the aristocratic class in money-making by way of investment, speculation, and exploitation of the provinces.

These careers, political, legal, financial, pedagogical, and
medical, correspond in general to the professions of to-day,
though we have seen that the callings of teacher and doctor
were of less distinction than they are in modern times. Let
us now pass to the other occupations that went to make up
the life of the ancient city, mentioning first those which we
usually associate with the intellectual or professional callings, and afterward the more common sort which depend
upon skill of hand or upon mere labor.

The employees in and about the government offices will
make a good beginning. There were, first of all, the *scribae*,
the scribes. This class included the secretaries of individuals, commissions, the courts, and the Senate, the numerous ordinary and expert accountants, and in general all
those usually meant by the term "clerk." Horace was for
a time clerk in the State treasury. Cicero had a private
secretary named Tiro, an expert in shorthand, as has been

noted.   Besides the army of clerks, as great in ancient times as now, there might have been found every morning in ante-chambers and offices of the Government a great number of attendants : the janitors and ushers, who let the visitors in and out, ran errands, and facilitated in general the busi-

ANCIENT WRITING MATERIALS

Wax tablets, styluses, ink-well, and fragment of pottery with Greek spelling exercise.

ness of their superiors; the lictors, who accompanied the magistrates, carrying the fasces symbolic of authority; and the various messengers.   A collective name for this little world of clerks and attendants was *apparitores*.

As having business with this class, the stationers and booksellers may be noticed here.   The material for sale by the stationer was the paper made from the papyrus plant and called *charta*, manufactured in large quantities by cutting the stalk into strips, moistening, pressing, and finishing; pens made of reeds and split at the point like the old-fashioned quill pen; wax tablets consisting of wooden frames with coating of wax; styluses with point for writing in the wax and blunt end for smoothing out or erasing; black ink for ordinary use and red for headings and ornamental features; ink-wells; and pen or stylus cases. In the bookseller's shop were the rolls of papyrus which constituted the volumes, *volumina*, or books. The Sosii Brothers, in the Argiletum, a street leading from the north side of the Forum near the Senate, were the sellers of Horace's works.

There were also the publishers of books. Atticus, the friend of Cicero, included among his many activities the publishing business. The place of printing press was taken by the copyist, perhaps a trained slave, who repeated the author's work in as many copies as were desired. In the case of a firm publishing many books, there would be a large force of these copyists. The use of a number of dictators, each in a room with a hundred copyists, could bring out a large edition with little delay; or the transcription could be done individually. Cicero writes Atticus in June, 60 B.C., about the work he had written in Greek on his own consulship, "If you like the book, see that it is to be had at Athens and the other cities of Greece." In 45 B.C., after changing the *Academica* from two books to four and making other changes, he writes Atticus, who had already had the work copied in part: "You will not let yourself be disturbed by the loss from having had copied the parts of the *Academica* in your hands. In the new form the work will be more distinguished, briefer, and better."

In the field which we should call the fine arts, that is, painting, sculpture, architecture, and the finer handicrafts, there were of course many at work. They were in most part of Greek origin, were artisans rather than artists, and left no names of the first class. Architecture was the greatest of the arts employed by Rome. The public and private building of Augustan times, when Rome was changing from brick to marble, brought commissions to many experts and work to many artisans. The number of men employed in building, painting, molding and chiseling, pottery, and in the general beautification of the city during its prosperous and growing days, must have been very great.

Even in music, an art of less prominence in antiquity than it now enjoys, there were many

THE TOMB RELIEF OF THE HATERII

The sculpture shows a crane, whose ropes and pulleys were operated by the large tread-wheel. The building is a tomb in two stories, the lower for burial and the upper for use as a chapel. On a couch above reclines perhaps a lady of the Haterian gens who is interred in the tomb. The crane may be the sign that the Haterii were contractors.

teachers and performers. There were the flute-players attached to the theaters, where the plays had parts which were accompanied, and to religion, at whose sacrifices they contributed to the ritual, and in whose processions they formed a part. There were the players of stringed instruments, such as the lyre and the harp, who accompanied the recitation of the ode or the choral parts of the tragic drama. There were the trumpeters and cornetists of the army and of public functions. There were teachers not only for the training of these musicians but for such young people as included music in their education, whether instrumental or vocal.

Again, the business of amusement furnished occupation to many. There were the actors and attendants at the theater; the gladiators and trainers and keepers of the beasts in connection with the amphitheater; the grooms and jockeys and attendants at the races in the circus; and the employees at the baths, which were already an institution in Augustus' time.

There were the occupations connected with the eating and drinking of a million people. There were the carters who brought the produce from country or warehouse to the vegetable market, the cattle market, the fish market, and other centers of sale. There were the dealers in the markets, and the shopkeepers. There were the drinking places and the restaurants. There was the baker, who was usually his own miller, and bought the wheat, ground it in the stone mill turned by donkey or slave, made the flour into dough, and baked it in the big oven resembling our Dutch oven, all in his one place of business. The tomb of the baker Marcus Vergilius Eurysaces, at the Porta Maggiore, is built of kneading jars and decorated with a frieze displaying all the operations of his business: the purchase of the grain, the grinding of the flour, the mixing of the dough, its preparation for the oven, the baking of it, the sale of the bread.

There were the occupations that furnished and cared for

the dress and ornament of the citizenry. There were the
spinners, with distaff and spindle, such as may be seen in
the humbler homes of Italy to-day, and there were the
weavers, with loom and warp and web and shuttle, equipment likewise still employed. Both were to be found in

OVEN AND MILLS

A miller and baker's establishment in Pompeii. The mills of lava rock, turned by
slave or donkey power, flank the brick and concrete oven, in which fuel was burned
until the heat was sufficient, when the fire was raked out and the loaves put in.

the household, and worked also in factories or shops. There
were the dyers, the fullers or laundrymen, the tailors, the
hatters, the shoemakers. "Let the shoemaker stick to his
last," was a Roman saying — *ne sutor supra crepidam.*
There were the barbers, and the makers and sellers of razors,
brushes, and combs. There were the jewelers who made

and sold the rings, brooches, necklaces, bracelets, and diadems that beautified the rich, and the cheap and flashy ornament worn by the poorer. The little stores and shops of the ancient city were multitudinous. When the wooden and iron shutters were put up or drawn at close of day, and

A Cloth Sale

Two salesmen are displaying a piece of goods in a portico on the market place, before two gentlemen with slaves.

when they were taken down in the morning, it was a noisy process, and the street underwent a great change in appearance.

There were the handicrafts. There were the carpenter and the mason and the decorator and mosaicist, to execute the plans of the architect. There were the cabinetmaker and the lampmaker and the potter and the worker in bronze to furnish and light the house.

There were the marble workers, who sawed and cut the beautiful material of which public buildings and many private houses were made or with which they were veneered. There were many kinds of marble, from distant quarries, some of them in beautiful tints — the ruddy, deep-toned, mottled *africano*, and the gold-and-purple *giallo antico*, or Numidian antique yellow, both from Africa; the peacock marble from Phrygia; the black from Euboea, the island north of Athens; the pure white Pentelic from the famous mountain near Athens, and the sparkling white from the island of Paros; the marble of Luna from near Pisa, where there are still great quarries that ship to far parts of the world; the granites and porphyries of Egypt. A treatise on Roman marbles records more than two hundred varieties. Marble working is a craft much practiced in Italy to-day. The marble of Luna is now called Carrara.

There were the clay workers, who made the brick and tile that went into the vast bulk of Roman building. The largest clay pits were across the Tiber beyond where Saint Peter's now stands, and are still in use on the same extensive scale. In earlier times bricks were dried in the sun; by the time of Augustus they were dried in kilns. Many were stamped with the name of the owner, the maker, or the reigning emperor, and thus give much evidence to the archaeologist and historian. The ordinary brick wall was composed of only a surface of bricks, usually three-cornered, the interior of the wall being concrete, a mixture of broken stone and old tile with mortar made from lime and a crumbly material brought from pits in the Campagna.

There were the workers, slave or free, employed by the great contractors in the erection of buildings — the carriers and tenders, the operators of the great derricks and rope-

and-pulley devices pictured on the tomb of the Haterii
Brothers in the Lateran Museum. The simpler tools have
changed little, but machinery has developed enormously.
One great difference between ancient and modern building
employment is in the greater number of hand laborers in
antiquity and in the use of slaves.

LOADING A GRAIN SHIP

From a painting in Ostia. The ship is named Isis Geminiana, and has
on board the captain, Farnaces Magister, Abascantus the owner, a stevedore emptying a sack, another stevedore with hand upraised, and a fifth
person. It has two steering oars.

There were the people who carried the wares of the great
city; the boatmen who came from Ostia up the Tiber,
the loaders and unloaders at the wharves and warehouses
by the Aventine, the draymen and pushcarters who distributed to the retail trade the cargoes from across the seas
and the produce from Italian farm and garden. There
were the cabmen and the chairmen and the muleteers and
donkey drivers.

Nor should the men be forgotten who kept the streets
in condition and safe. There were the pavers and the
cleaners, and there were the police, called *vigiles*, who included also the firemen. In the time of Augustus there

were some seven thousand five hundred police, a number comparable to the nine thousand of London.

Finally, there was the household service: the janitor, the hall porter, the chambermaid, the lady's maid, the children's attendant or *paedagogus,* the steward, the cook, the gardener.

If to the aristocratic and other distinguished callings described in earlier chapters we add the more ordinary callings just considered, we are able to realize the variety of occupations and men that went to make up Living Rome. It remains to compare once more the ancient with the modern.

In the first place, a great share of the city's business was done by slaves and freedmen. From the common drudgery of the streets to the care of a consul's or an emperor's household, there were few occupations in which the slave and the recently emancipated were not found. The professions of medicine and teaching and the fine arts were largely in the hands of men who had been slaves and who were still in the semi-independent position of the freedman who looked to his former master for protection and patronage. It was only the governing class that was wholly composed of the freeborn and citizens, and in many instances the freedman or the slave was so influential with master or patron as to be substantially in control. The result of such surrender of the professions and arts to men of servile origin was a lack of respect for the professional callings themselves which must have impaired their effect and retarded their progress.

In the second place, it is to be noted that the work of ancient Rome was done, not by machines, but by pairs of hands. The tasks that were done and the goods that were supplied were performed and supplied by the individual.

This had two effects. One was that the number of contacts and the intimacy of man with man were greater. The city was full of small tradesmen and small artisans and special workers. From the shoemaker to the surgeon, learning was by apprenticeship, and even in preparation for law and public life there was something very like apprenticeship. The other effect was that the pace of life, however quick and nervous it seemed to a Juvenal, a Martial, or a Horace, was far more leisurely than is the case in our age of mass manufacturing, mass training, rapid transit, and instantaneous communication. Yet neither slowness nor the human contact was peculiar to Rome or to Roman times. It is not more than a hundred years since the day of the apprentice was ended by the advent of the industrial machine, and there are still nooks where the chain store and the factory and the professional and technical college do not function.

A MERCHANT'S TOMBSTONE

The inscription reads : Marcus Antonius Trophimus, of the Augustal priesthood, dealer in mantles at Puteoli and Naples, erected this monument to himself and to Julia Irene, his wife of rarest character, and to Antonia Jucundina, their daughter, and to their freedmen and freedwomen and their descendants, and to Julia Euphemia and her descendants.

In the third place, the work of the ancient world was not only minute, but the workers were minutely organized. For every occupation, from the unskilled to the highly skilled and intellectual, the *collegium*, or guild, was the usual thing.

There is nothing more interesting in the life of Rome than the guilds, the *collegia*. When history begins, there are already eight of them in existence : the fullers, the cobblers, the carpenters, the goldsmiths, the coppersmiths, the dyers, the potters, and the flute-blowers. The number multiplied until in the Empire it probably would have been difficult to find a worker unattached to one of them. There were the porters, the masons, the castanet-players, the pastille-makers, the ragmen, the flask-makers, the bridle-makers, the cab drivers, the coopers, the stonecutters, the purple-dealers, the woolcombers, the plumbers, the perfume-sellers, the fruiterers, the pearl-dealers, the auctioneers, the leather-dealers, the bakers, the clothmakers, the wood-makers, the armorers, the artillerymen, the boatmen, the sailors, the ass drivers, the muleteers, the hornblowers, the porters, the pavers, the saltfish-dealers, the gladiators, the household slaves, the grocers, the tanners, the inn-keepers, the pallbearers, the hunters. Even the professions, such as medicine and the stage, had their guilds. There were the physicians, the actors, the oculists. There were guilds of various nationalities, of soldiers. For Rome alone, there are twenty-five hundred inscriptions known which indicate more than a hundred guilds, and there are inscriptions showing guilds in four hundred and seventy-five towns elsewhere. The bulk of this evidence belongs to times later than Caesar, Cicero, and Virgil, but conditions were different only in degree, and not greatly different even in that.

The mention of these numerous guilds in the field of labor, variously referred to as colleges, clubs, associations, corporations, or unions, naturally suggests the methods and purposes of organized labor in modern times. We should be wrong, however, if we concluded that the ancient guilds existed for the sake of a "labor" party or for the spreading

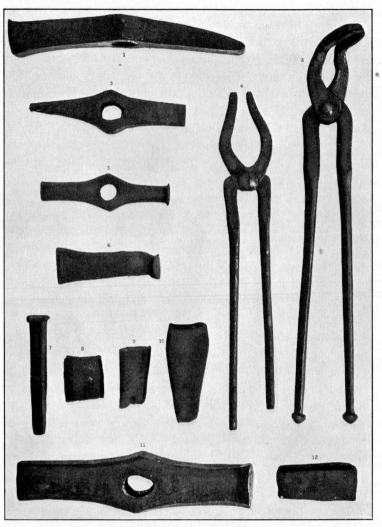

BLACKSMITH'S TOOLS

Found in the Roman border fort at Newstead, near the River Tweed not far from Melrose in Scotland. The tongs are 16 and 18 inches long; the hammers, 11 inches. No. 10 is an anvil, no. 7 a punch for making holes in hot metal.

of a "labor" gospel. There was a quarrel in 43 B.C. between the union and nonunion pallbearers, but beyond this the question of the open shop in ancient Rome does not appear. The withdrawals of the plebeians to the Sacred Mount outside the city and to the Aventine in the early Republic were in the nature of general strikes, but their purpose was the winning of civic rights rather than the improvement of labor conditions. There is evidence of an outbreak of the workers in the mint and the death of seven thousand people in the disorder, but this is an isolated occurrence dating from the time of Aurelian, A.D. 270–276, and could hardly have been a strike in the usual sense.

CUPIDS AS FULLERS

From left to right: treading the new-made cloth in water, to remove oil and cleanser; carding or combing to bring out the nap, which was sheared down; inspection; folding. From a wall painting in the house of the Vettii, Pompeii.

It is possible that in the earlier times of the Republic the guilds were an attempt at exclusiveness and trade protection, but their great purpose at all times, so far as may be judged, was the very natural one of human solidarity. The members of the guild met and ate and drank together, exchanged ideas, perhaps on occasion did something to improve the conditions of their calling, agreed on mutual support in certain matters, and in general felt the glow of sympathetic fellowship. There were officers elected; we hear of *patres, tribuni, fratres, sorores, magistri, curatores, praefecti*, titles which suggest imitation of a city government. No doubt the flatteries of self that were felt by those accepted in membership, to say nothing of election to office, were a potent cause of the favor in which the associations were held. Sometimes the guild calls itself sonorously a "most honorable and distinguished order" — *ordo amplissimus et splendidissimus*. It has an initiation fee, in one case $5.00 and a flagon of wine; dues, in the same case, ten cents a month; and fines — for example: "if anyone shall have spoken disrespectfully to a flamen, or laid hands upon him, he shall pay two denarii. . . . If anyone shall have gone to fetch wine, and shall have made away with it, he shall give double the amount." The chief purpose of the fund is the insurance of decent burial and respect after death. By the middle of the second Christian century the guilds are quite generally known as funeral guilds, that is, associations for mutual burial insurance.

A guild at Lanuvium, twenty miles south of Rome, had among its regulations regarding burials the following:

"It has pleased the members, that whoever shall wish to join this guild shall pay an initiation fee of one hundred sesterces, and an amphora of good wine, as well as five *asses* a month. Voted likewise, that if any man shall not have paid his dues for six consecutive months, and if the lot common to all men has befallen him, his claim to a burial shall not be considered, even if he shall have so stipulated in his will. Voted likewise, that if any man from this body of ours, having paid his dues, shall depart, there shall come to him from the treasury three hundred sesterces, from which sum fifty sesterces, which shall be divided at the funeral pyre, shall go for the funeral rites. Furthermore, the obsequies shall be performed on foot."

Various bits of legislation still surviving indicate that the guilds were sometimes suspected. They were left unmolested under the Republic except when nocturnal and secret, until in 64 B.C. a decree of the Senate was passed which aimed to suppress them. From then to the end of the Empire, the rights of association were jealously guarded by the Government, and it is suspected that the prevalence of burial guilds was due to evasion of restrictions of the law on the regular industrial guild. In the end, we are told that in the general decay of the Empire the member-

CUPIDS AS GOLDSMITHS

From left to right: anvil work, weighing for a customer, counter with three drawers and scales, a goldsmith at work, a furnace adorned with the head of Hephaestus, and two workers, one with pincers and blowpipe, the other engraving a piece of goldware. From the same source as the preceding picture.

ship of the guilds fell off, and that the Government made enrollment in them compulsory, thus converting their members and members' descendants into serfs bound to the occupation into which they were born.

Finally, it should be remembered that, besides the infinite variety of workers in Rome, there were the unemployed. The list of those receiving the dole of grain or its equivalent in Caesar's time is said to have been three hundred thousand, and this does not include the clients of the rich and aristocratic patrons. The number of the idle in the city was always notorious.

We may conclude by relating the amusing story of the guild of Roman flute-players told by Livy.

"I would pass over as not worth mention an incident of this same year [311 B.C.], did it not seem of consequence as regards religion. The flute-players, not liking it because they had been prohibited by the last censors to dine in the Temple of Jupiter, long a traditional privilege of theirs, went off in a body to Tibur, so that there was no one in the city to furnish music at the sacrifices. The Senate, constrained by respect for religion, despatched envoys to Tibur to arrange for the men's being returned to the Romans. The citizens of Tibur, having good-naturedly promised the favor, summoned the players to their council chamber and urged them to return to Rome; but, finding that they could not be prevailed upon, adopted a plan of dealing with them which was quite consistent with human nature. Choosing a holiday, they invited them variously to various houses on the pretext of wanting music for the banquets of the day, filled them with wine, of which their class is very fond, threw them in their drunken sleep into wagons, and carried them off to Rome. They did not come to their senses until the wagons had been left in the Forum and the dawn overtook them still in their drunken state."

XXIV

THE FARMER

In our account of the many occupations having to do with the life and living of Rome, no mention has been made of the country Roman; and yet the farmer, the gardener, the fruit grower, and the shepherd of Latium were for the early centuries at the very base of the city's sustenance and comfort.

It is true, of course, that the farmer does not live in the city; and it is true also that Rome by the time of Cicero was a city of over half a million surrounded by acres whose produce was but a trifle in the feeding and clothing of its citizens. The acres which supported it had for a long time been far away — at first in Italian fields beyond the mountains that circled the Latin plain; then, in Sardinia and Sicily; still later, in Africa and Spain and Gaul and Egypt. But there had been a time when the lands that lay about the capital were intimately connected with the city and shared its life, and when to think of the State was to think of the landed properties and their owners outside the gates as well as of the teeming streets of the city.

The Roman State in origin was a commonwealth of shepherds and farmers, and it was not until it was well on in the conquest of the outside world that it ceased to retain a rustic character, and ceased to have what might be called a peasant aristocracy. Nor would it be right to suppose that even in the days of the emperors, when the active cultivation of the Campagna was long in the past and its acres given up to the large estate and the rich man's villas, there was no connection between the city and the country. The landed estate never ceased to be held in esteem as the least sordid and the most dignified of the forms of holding property. Whatever the fate of the Campagna as an agricultural area,

THE CHURCH OF SAINT FRANCIS AND THE PLAIN OF ASSISI
The precise nature of planting garden, vineyard, and orchard is to be noted.

Italy herself was as much the garden of the world in the time of Virgil and Horace as it was in the time of Byron and is to-day.

Partly, then, because the bond between Rome and the soil has always been close, but especially because of their intimate union in the earlier times of the Roman Republic, to include the farmer among the men of Living Rome is not only appropriate but necessary.

The memory of those earlier times was vivid still in Cicero's day. "The senators in those days lived in the fields," he has old Cato say, in *De Senectute;* "because Lucius Quinctius Cincinnatus was at the plow when the message came that he had been elected dictator. . . . Curius and the other elders used to be summoned to meetings of the Senate from their villas, and that is why those who served the summons were called *viatores.* . . . It was when Curius was sitting at his fireside that the Samnites offering him a great sum of gold were repulsed."

The words in which Cato is made to express in the same essay his love of life on the soil will make a fitting introduction to the ancient farmer's life:

"Could old age be called pitiable in these men, who found joy in the cultivation of their acres? Really, to my thinking, one could hardly conceive of an old age happier than this, not only in the service it renders, because the tillage of the soil is beneficial to all mankind, but also in the delight of which I have spoken, and in the fulness and abundance of everything necessary to the life of men and the worship of the gods. . . . For the capable and careful owner always has his wine cellar and oil cellar and granary as full as can be; the whole farmhouse is richly supplied, and abounds in pork, kid, lamb, fowl, milk, cheese, and honey. And then there is the garden, which the farmer calls his second meat supply; and all these things I mention are made more savory still by bird snaring and hunting in unoccupied hours. Why should I go on to speak of the green meadows or the rows of trees or the beauty of the vineyard and the olive grove?"

To these words could be added the praise of Virgil for the fruitfulness of his native land:

"There is no cessation. The year is always rich either in the fruits of the orchard, or in the increase of the flocks, or in sheaves of corn, the gift of Ceres; it burdens the plowed fields with increase and exceeds the bounds of the granary. . . . The Sicyonian olive is bruised in the mill, the swine come home glad from their acorns, the wood yields its fruitage of arbute berries; and autumn lays her varied fruitage at his feet, and aloft on the sunny rocks the gentle grape is ripening for the vintage."

> "But fruitful vines, and the fat olive's freight,
> And harvests heavy with their fruitful weight,
> Adorn our fields; and on the cheerful green
> The grazing flocks and lowing herds are seen. . . .
> Perpetual spring our happy climate sees,
> Twice breed the cattle, and twice bear the trees,
> And summer suns recede by slow degrees."

Horace and Tibullus are as much in love with Italy as Virgil. " Golden Plenty from a full horn is pouring forth her fruits upon Italy," is Horace's description of the year as he writes to Iccius. What more charming picture of the countryside is there than his second *Epode?*

"And so he either weds the tall poplars with the fullgrown trailers of the vine, or in the secluded vale looks forth upon his wandering flocks, or prunes away with his hook the useless branches and grafts more fruitful ones in their places, or stores away in the fresh jars the honey pressed from the comb, or shears his helpless sheep. Or, when Autumn rears from the fields her head decorous with mellow fruits, how happy he is as he takes from the tree the grafted pear, and from the vine the grape cluster vying with the purple!"

But the beauty and fruitfulness of Italy require no proof. Let us pass from poetry to the practical, and attempt to look upon the land as it produces, and upon the farmer at his work.

In modern Italy there are three methods of managing the land. In North Italy, in the great plain of the Po, the farms approximate in size the American farms of a hundred acres to a quarter section, and are either rented or owned by the farmer living on the estate. In South Italy and Sicily, the land is in large holdings owned by absentee landlords and much neglected. In Central Italy the average holding is about forty acres, and is rented for so long a time as practically to amount to ownership, in the system called *mezzadria*, or halving; the tenant receiving half of everything

CAMPANILE AND LANDSCAPE AT SAN SEVERINO
This picturesque village is on the east side of the Apennines near Ancona.

produced. The farm of Central Italy is not so large but that its work will all be done by the tenant and his wife and children, with occasional exchange of work with neighbors. In France the system is called *métayer*.

The ancient farmer as he appears in the pleasant pictures of the poets, and also as he is seen in the more sober pages of Cato's *On Agriculture*, or of Varro's *On Farming*, or of

Columella's twelve books, the tenth of which is in verse, has much to remind us of modern Italy, and, above all, of Central Italy. Let us look at him and his affairs in Cato's page. It will tell us indirectly as well as directly much about the Roman husbandman.

The farm of a hundred *iugera*, or about sixty-six acres, says Cato, should consist of a good vineyard, a garden that can be irrigated, an osier bed, an olive orchard, a meadow, a grain field, a bit of woodland, an orchard, and an acorn grove. It should have buildings well constructed, large oil cellars and wine vats, and plenty of casks to provide storage in case of the need to wait for better prices. There should be elms along the road and by the hedges. The wood will come handy, and the leaves may be stripped for the oxen and sheep. The vines must be wedded to the trees.

The size of this estate and its variety of products are strongly suggestive of the Tuscan farm of to-day. The wedding of the vine to the elm which Cato recommends is a charming figure, just as appropriate now as two hundred years before Christ. Who ever forgets his journeyings in Italy through fields in which rectangles of garden and golden grain stretch endlessly between rows of fronded elms festooned from tree to tree with swinging green vines already heavy with promise?

And here is the olive farm of a hundred and sixty acres, which is fitted out with overseer, housekeeper, five field hands, three ox drivers, one ass driver, and one shepherd; and with three yoke of oxen, three asses with paniers for carrying manure, an ass for the mill, and a hundred sheep. The overseer must be the first up and the last to bed, and the housekeeper must be no gossip or gadabout, but keep the house and hearth well swept, and have plenty of chickens and eggs and preserves. The slaves are to have meal,

bread, figs, olives, wine, pickles and vinegar, salt, and clothing in specified quantities. A peck of salt is enough for
the year.

"If an ox begins to ail, give him right away one hen's egg raw ;
make him swallow it whole. The day after, pound up the head of
a leek with a half pint of wine and make him drink it. Pound up
standing on your feet and give from a wooden container, and have
the ox himself and the one who gives the dose be on their feet.
You must be fasting when you give it, and the ox when he takes
it. . . .
"Make your threshing-floor this way. Dig out the place where
you are going to make it. Afterward, sprinkle it with olive
dregs and let the ground soak well. Afterward, pulverize well
the lumps. Then level off and tamp down with beaters. Afterward, sprinkle again and let dry. If you do it this fashion, ants will
not damage it nor grass grow up in it. . . .
"If you have a dislocation, you can cure it with this charm.
Take a green reed four or five feet long, cut it in two and have two
persons hold the parts to your hip bones. Begin to chant, *daries-
dardaries-astataries-dissunapiter* [a nonsense rhythm], and at the
same time try until they come together. . . . Wave a knife above
them. When they have come together and the one touches the
other, take the knife in your hand and cut the pieces to right and
left, bind them on the dislocation or fracture, and it will be cured.
But repeat every day this incantation, or the following in place of
it, *huat-hauat-huat, ista-pista-sista, dannabo-dannaustra.* . . ."

Here is Cato's recipe for cheese cake. Mash up two
pounds of cheese, pour in a pound of corn meal, or a half
pound of flour, and mix well with the cheese. Add an egg,
and beat it well. Pat into a cake, place on leaves under a
dish on a hot hearthstone, and bake slowly.

The care of oxen and wagons, the harvest of the olive and
the making of the oil, the vintage, and the treatment of
slaves, are other themes in the simply and roughly written

treatise of Cato. Its homely wisdom, its intensely practical
spirit, its mixture of common sense and superstition, represent well the character of the small farmer in Italy, ancient
and modern. His knowledge and practice do not depend on
books or institutions of learning, but on the experience
handed down from generation to generation on the same
acres.

The basis of Cato's experience was his own estate on the
slopes of the Alban Hills near Tusculum. The town of
Monte Porzio Catone, where

> "Up rose the golden morning
> Over the Porcian height,"

in Macaulay's *Lay*, whether the name means anything or not
as to place, is not distant from his holding. Olive, vine, and
garden are rich on the rounded hillsides, and the more level
fields of the Campagna floor are near. The farming of Cato
was that of Central Italy.

The manner of such farming changed little during the
centuries. Two farmers' calendars of the later Empire
giving the data for each month would have served as well
in the time of Cato, except for the different number of days
they give certain months. If the truth were known, they
would probably be found the direct descendants of almanacs
in the Censor's day. They are bronze cubes, containing
three months in three columns on each vertical side, with the
signs of the zodiac heading the columns. Below the sign for
each month are the numerical data regarding days and hours,
the names of the sign and the patron deity, the special farm
activities of the season, and the appropriate religious observance. The month of January in the *Menologium Rusticum
Colotianum*, for example, reads:

MONTH
JANUARY
DAYS XXXI
NONES ON THE FIFTH
THE DAY, HOURS NINE AND ONE HALF
THE NIGHT, HOURS FOURTEEN
THE SUN
IN CAPRICORN
TUTELAGE
OF JUNO
STAKES
ARE SHARPENED
WILLOWS
REEDS
ARE CUT
SACRIFICE
TO THE GODS
OF THE HEARTH

But the modest estate of the rigid old patriot was not the only sort. There were also the great plantations and ranches in other parts of Italy and in the provinces where lands were ampler. Flavius Vopiscus, a writer of much later times, tells of an estate with 500 slaves, 2,000 cattle, 1,000 horses, 10,000 sheep, and 15,000 goats. Pliny, in the first century, mentions one with 4,117 slaves, 3,600 yoke of oxen, and 257,000 other beasts. These were great contrasts with the farms of Cato's neighborhood, or the Sabine Farm of Horace, which the poet says " sent its five good fathers to Varia," meaning the five overseers or tenants in charge; or the home of Martial's country friend so appreciatively described a hundred years after Horace:

"In every corner grain is stacked,
    Old wines in fragrant jars are packed:
    About the farmyard gabbling gander
    And spangled peacock freely wander:
    With pheasant and flamingo prowl
    Partridge and speckled guinea-fowl:
    Pigeon and waxen turtle-dove
    Rustle their wings in cotes above.

> The farm-wife's apron draws a rout
> Of greedy porkers round about;
> And eagerly the tender lamb
> Waits the filled udder of its dam.
> With plenteous logs the hearth is bright,
> The household Gods glow in the light,
> And baby slaves are sprawling round.
> No town-bred idlers here are found."

It would be interesting to follow up in Marcus Terentius Varro's *On Farming* the various activities already described by Cato but not at length. Varro makes us better acquainted with the details of equipment and operation; with the seasons, and the work best adapted to each; with planting, cultivating, harvest, and garnering; with the technique of livestock breeding, and of bees, and of domestic and wild fowl. Much might be said also of the vicissitudes of the soil and its tillers from the days of the peasant aristocrat, whose last example of note was Cato, through the times of large estates which Pliny the Elder called the ruin of Italy, to the later centuries when the tillage of the soil was a serfdom, large parts of the country were malarial, and the miseries and unsafety of the Dark Ages were approaching.

But Italy and agriculture are everlasting, and through all the centuries and in all the authors we should find the eternal verities of life in the unchanging country. Let us rather be content with a few paragraphs on the most characteristic products of the ancient Italian farm.

First, there was the grain, principally wheat. In spite of what is usually said of the importation of grain and the cheapening of Italian wheat, it is unlikely that the Italian farmer did not grow wheat for his own need and for the neighboring market. In its production, we must imagine the same processes which are to be seen to-day in the little villages and plains of Italy. The plowing was done with the ox, and the plow made of a beam from the woodlands. The reaping was done with the sickle, and all the household went to the field, with perhaps the neighbors. The threshing was done with the flail, or with horses or oxen trampling the grain on the circular threshing floor. " Thou shalt not muzzle the mouth of the ox that treadeth out the corn." The trampling or flailing done, the mingled straw and chaff and wheat were tossed in the wind with the winnowing fan until the grain was ready for the sack and the granary. "Whose fan is in his hand, and he will throughly purge his floor, and will gather the wheat into his garner; but the chaff he will burn with fire unquenchable."

In the second place, there were the fruits and the vegetables, always easy to grow in Italy, and with no foreign market to fear. In Roman times there were no express trains and refrigerator cars for the transportation of perishables to another country.

But the richest resources of the peninsula were the olive, the grape, and the products of meadow and pasture. The change from small to large estates had no effect on these, unless it was to encourage them.

The olive, not native to Italy, was introduced from Greece. It was prepared in brine or vinegar in various ways, but its great use was for oil — oil as food, oil as fuel in lamps, oil as the basis of unguent and perfume. Gathered by picking late in autumn, the berries were allowed to mellow for a few days in heaps, and then crushed in the olive mill of hard, rough stones revolved by donkey power. The pulp thus formed was then pressed, the oil allowed to settle in the jars that caught it, and ladled off into other jars for sale or storage. The modern yield of oil in Italy is upward of fifty million gallons a year, from over five million acres, or about one fifteenth the peninsula, and is one of the chief exports. The groves are found on many a mountain side which would hardly serve another purpose. In ancient times, the invader in time of war was always a threat to the olive orchard because its laying waste meant the loss of income for many years.

AN OLIVE CRUSHER AND A HAND-MILL FOR GRAIN
The crusher was revolved by hand, and separated the pulp from the stones.

The grape, like the olive, was introduced from Greece at an early time. It was eaten as fresh fruit and dried as the raisin, but chiefly used in the form of wine. In the early Republic, when Italy was producing a full grain supply, the demand for wine had to be met in part by importation from southern Italy and Greece, but by A.D. 81 there were so many vineyards that a limit to their planting was set because of agricultural needs. The varieties most mentioned in Latin authors are the Formian, the Falernian, the Massic, and the Caecuban, all produced on the west coast about a hundred miles south of Rome. A century after Horace's birth, there were eighty-five wines, and the Italian product was sent to distant countries. To-day the annual yield of wine is about three quarters of a billion gallons, and wine is an export of great consequence. About one seventh of Italy is planted with the vine.

The vineyard could be either on the southward-facing hillside or in the plain. For support, there were the elms, kept fairly small by trimming back, and prevented, by the same means and by stripping of the leaves, from intercepting too much sunshine; and there was the trellis made of cane. Both methods are still in use. The vineyards that cover the slopes of the Alban Hills like a great green garment consist of endless rows of vines rearing themselves to catch the sun on cane arrangements that look like stacked muskets. The branches clamber from stack to stack on other cane laid horizontally. With either method, the ground must be frequently worked.

The vintage, in late September or October, was a busy and a genial season. The grapes were gathered, in the case of the elms by the aid of ladders, and carried in baskets and carts to the treading vat, where bare feet crushed them to a juicy mass. The press received them next, operated either with windlass turned by levers or with the use of wedges driven by mallets. The juice, drained into great terra cotta jars that held a hundred gallons and were half embedded in the floor of the storeroom, was left uncovered for several days until fermentation was complete, and then, after final expert treatment, sealed in the proper amphorae and stored for the trade.

One more permanent feature in the life of Italy must be mentioned — its animals: the sheep, the cattle, and the goats, that furnished the wool, the leather, the mutton and beef and kid, the milk, and the cheeses that no doubt existed in as many varieties then as they do now. Nothing in Italy to-day is more striking than the beautiful cattle with immensely spreading horns, black muzzle, great liquid eyes.

PLOWING IN MODERN ITALY

and silvery-gray or white flanks. They were there at least in the time of Trajan, who is said to have brought them from Pannonia, and perhaps they were the *albi greges* of Virgil, the white herds of the Clitumnus. If the gods must have their sacrifice, no nobler victim can be imagined. The poet Carducci found in the ox the inspiration for a magnificent sonnet:

> "I love thee, pious ox; a gentle feeling
> Of vigor and of peace thou giv'st my heart.
> How solemn, like a monument, thou art!
> Over wide fertile fields thy calm gaze stealing,

Unto the yoke with grave contentment kneeling,
To man's quick work thou dost thy strength impart.
He shouts and goads, and answering thy smart,
Thou turn'st on him thy patient eyes appealing.

"From thy broad nostrils, black and wet, arise
Thy breath's soft fumes, and on the still air swells,
Like happy hymn, thy lowing's mellow strain.
In the grave sweetness of thy tranquil eyes
Of emerald, broad and still, reflected dwells
All the divine green silence of the plain."

Nowhere better than in the unchanging country can one
feel the permanence of human affairs and the nearness of
ancient Roman days. The Tuscany of to-day is the Etruria
of yesterday. The life of Virgil's *Georgics* is the life of the
Italian countryside to-day. Let us listen to an Italian-
born essayist, Charles W. Lemmi.

"To me the *Georgics* are not ancient literature; they are the
record of my boyhood and youth. . . . Turn, now, and look.
Two huge, snow-white oxen, their spreading horns garlanded with
red tassels, are bending to the creaking plow, breathing mightily.
Stooping over the plow-handle, a brown-clad figure struggles after,
with uneven steps, in the lengthening furrow. Behind him, an old
man, white of hair and beard, with sweeping gesture and steady
stride, scatters the grain from the basket on his arm. Oh, do you
not know, as you look, that you are in Virgil's country? Do you
not remember?

'In the birth-tide of spring, when melt from the mountains the ice and the snow,
And the crumbling clods are breaking down as the west
winds blow,
Then let the bull begin to groan at the plow deep thrust
as he strains.'

Do you not remember? Come and see; nothing has changed.
"The old man smiles gravely as we approach; the young plowman straightens up, and with a rough grace pulls off his battered

hat. Look, it is the same wooden plow as of old. . . . '*Questo è l'aratro,*' says the old man, smiling. '*Questo è il timone. Questa, la stiva. Quelli? I bovi, sono.*' To be sure. *Hoc est aratrum. Hic est temo. Haec stiva. Illi boves sunt.* We know them all, I warrant you. Plow and pole and handle and oxen; we know them all. When was it — yesterday, that Virgil described them to us? . . .

A MODERN PLOW NEAR ROME

The simple plow sometimes found where little ground is cultivated. It is practically the same as that described in Virgil's *Georgics*.

"Still as of old, a red moon is of evil omen; still the new moon betokens rainy weather when it clasps the old moon in its arms; the countryman still rejoices when the stars shine clear and sharp. Unquestioning faith in what tradition teaches — that is the plowman's credo; that, the reaper's. Science may smile, but when the moon is waning, the sower sows no grain. . . . They have no doubts; their philosophy is immemorial tradition. As Cato and Virgil cultivated their fields, so do they cultivate theirs."

XXV

ROMAN PORTRAITS

We have surveyed the chief occupations that went to make up the total of Living Rome. By way of summary, and for the purpose of lending reality to our survey, it will be of advantage now to contemplate the lives and characters of a number of actual Romans. Let us look briefly at Cicero, the public man and orator ; at Caesar, the soldier and statesman ; at Horace and Virgil, poets from the South and North ; and at Marcus Aurelius, the philosopher at the head of the State.

Marcus Tullius Cicero was born on January 3, 106 B.C., in a charming valley of the Apennines about seventy-five miles to the southeast of Rome. The Cicero home was at the point where the little Fibrenus flowed into the Liris, a swift stream that to-day turns many mills. Three miles away, and high on the rocks, was Arpinum, then as to-day the chief city of the neighborhood. Much running water, frequent rains, a mild climate, and the sheltered location, make the valley a paradise of foliage and flowers.

Marcus Tullius Cicero the father and Marcus Tullius Cicero the grandfather complete the Cicero ancestry so far as known, and Marcus Tullius Cicero the orator's son will bring the line to an end. The name Tullius suggests a jet of water ; the name of Cicero, as we have seen, a chickpea, or a facial blemish resembling one. The family belongs to the equestrian order, the modest home is an older house improved, the father is not robust and is devoted to letters. Helvia, the mother, is of respected family and a thrifty house-

267

hold mistress. The people of Arpinum have been Roman citizens since 188 B.C. The near-by town of Sora is the birthplace of heroes: of Regulus, who kept his word and returned to Carthage to die; of Decius, who rode into the battle and voluntarily sacrificed his life to bring victory to the

MARCUS TULLIUS CICERO

Roman army; of Marius, a distant connection of the Ciceros, who drove back the Teutons and Cimbri when Cicero was five years old.

Of the little boy Cicero nothing is known. He may be imagined about the house with his father and mother or at a neighboring school, learning the usual things. At ten or twelve, he may be imagined in Rome, perhaps at the house of an uncle, Aculeo. He has been brought to the capital to receive in more stimulating surroundings the best education possible. It includes Greek as well as his native tongue, and its aim is cultural as well as practical, but in the background of it all is the practical ambition of turning it to account in the career that leads to the consulship. About him in the streets and in the Forum, in the courts and on the Capitol, in the houses of his uncle and his father's friends, the eager young student sees the prominent men of Rome — foremost among them the urbane Crassus and the direct and vigorous Antonius, both about forty-five and at the height of their fame as pleaders.

After taking the toga of manhood, the sixteen-year-old

Cicero was introduced by his father to Quintus Mucius Scaevola, the most learned lawyer of the time, at whose consultations, decisions, and discussions he never missed an opportunity to be present. This Scaevola was an augur, and on his death in about 88 B.C. Cicero began to follow Scaevola the Pontifex Maximus in the same manner. In this year he also studied under Molo of Rhodes, a famous teacher of oratory who was visiting Rome. Philo of Athens and Diodotus the Stoic were other teachers of his youth.

In the midst of these studies, the war between Rome and the Italian subjects demanding citizenship broke out, and Cicero spent the year 89 B.C. in the field. It may be supposed that this experience broadened and deepened his character and by the quickening of the manly faculties more than compensated for loss of time from study.

The civil war between Marius and Sulla from 88–83 B.C., and the dictatorship of Sulla from 83–78 B.C., kept Rome in a state of uncertainty, but Cicero's preparation did not halt. In 81 B.C., at the age of twenty-five, he delivered in a civil case the first of his orations which has been preserved. In 80 B.C., he won the case for Roscius, falsely charged by a protégé of Sulla with murder. This won him a reputation for courage, besides recognition as an orator, but also alarmed his friends, who warned him of Sulla's displeasure. Partly as a measure of caution, partly because of physical weakness, but mostly for the sake of further study and training, Cicero left Rome for the East. First spending six months at Athens in study with Antiochus the philosopher, he visited and received instruction from all the teachers of repute in the province of Asia, and concluded the tour by studying again with Molo of Rhodes, who had instructed him in Rome.

After his return to Rome in 77 B.C. at the age of twenty-nine, with his formal education completed, Cicero married Terentia. Sulla was dead, and the State, for the time at least, at peace. The young orator began actively to realize his ambitions. He was quaestor in 75 B.C. in the western half of Sicily, was prompt in his handling of the grain supply to Rome, and won the confidence of the Sicilians. Returning to Rome in 74 B.C., he took the seat in the Senate to which the year of the quaestorship entitled him, and went on with his career in the courts, winning among others the case for the Sicilians against Verres, the unscrupulous praetor of Syracuse from 73–70 B.C. In 69 B.C. he held the aedileship. In 66 B.C. he held the praetorship, and in 65 B.C. might have been, had he not preferred his life and calling in Rome, the governor of a province and a rich man. In 63 B.C. he attained to the consulship, the highest office in the cursus honorum.

Natural talent and character, aided somewhat by the need of the senatorial party for a safe and able candidate, had brought Cicero to the peak of his ambition. The triumph was the greater because he was the second *novus homo* in the consulship for three generations; that is, he was the second man not of patrician blood in three generations to hold the consulship. Marius was the first, winning by reason of military genius what Cicero won through genius as an orator and through personal quality.

The remaining twenty years of Cicero's life were uncertain, varied, and trying. The execution of the conspirators in 63 B.C. resulted in his exile in 58 B.C., a blow that caused him the intensest suffering. He was elected augur in 52 B.C., was governor of Cilicia in 51 B.C. with a record for just and capable administration, was placed in charge of Campania by Pompey in 49 B.C. when Caesar marched on Rome, and for the last year of his life was the leader of the Senate and the defenders of the old régime. His great ambition to keep the senatorial and equestrian orders united as the ideal party, his ability as lawyer and orator, and his sense of justice, made him throughout an influential factor in every effort to preserve the Republic.

A strenuous political life, however, did not claim all of Cicero's time and interest. He continued his active life as advocate. Above all, he continued the intellectual and literary life. His letters fill two large and closely printed volumes, a golden treasury of information and of the sentiment of the times. He transmitted in his essays the philosophy of the Greeks whom he admired. He wrote four books on ethics, which are among the world's most enlightened utterances on conduct. He wrote the immortal essays *On Old Age* and *On Friendship*. He left several works on rhetoric and the orators, and the treatises *On the Republic* and *On the Laws*. All these, with the *Orations*, form a body not only of eloquence but of information which would be difficult to match in the life of any man in history. In the end, on December 7 of the year 43 B.C., at the age of sixty-three, he was deprived of life by the agents of Mark Antony, the man against whom he had stood as the leader of the Government in its last days.

The life of Cicero is exceptional in many respects : in his rise from the position of an ordinary provincial to the consulship and augurship ; in the ideal nature of the preparation for his life work ; in his comparative independence of military connections ; in the disinterested character of his provincial administration ; in the general purity of his life and motives ; in his vivid and lifelong intellectual curiosity ; in his genius as master of the spoken and written word. Yet all this is a matter of degree, and does not prevent our seeing in him an illustration of the general content of the Roman

public career: in education, in the holding of the offices of
the cursus, in the connection with law and the courts, in
oratory, in provincial service, in the soldier's experience, in
devotion to the life of the State.

With Cicero's life as background, the career of Caesar may
be surveyed in fewer words.   Born in Rome, of patrician

blood and of prominent family, he is without the handi-
caps of Cicero.   If we accept
with Mommsen the date of his
birth as 102 B.C., he assumed
the manly toga at fifteen and
was married at sixteen to
Cornelia, daughter of Sulla's
enemy, Cinna.   At twenty,
ordered to divorce her, in defiance he flees into Samnium,
but is later allowed to come
back.   At   twenty-one,   he
joins the army in the East,
and at twenty-two is decorated with the civic crown
for saving a citizen's life.

GAIUS JULIUS CAESAR

At twenty-four, he is with Servilius Isauricus against the
Mediterranean pirates.   On the news of Sulla's death in 78
B.C., he returns to Rome.   He loses his first cases at law,
goes to Rhodes for training by Molo, on the way has an adventure with the pirates, who first capture him and then are
captured by him, and is back in Rome in 74 B.C., at the age
of twenty-eight.   In 70 B.C. he probably is concerned with
the political defeat of the senatorial party which was formed
by Sulla.   In 69 B.C. he is elected quaestor, and in 68 B.C.,
at thirty-four, discharges the duties of that office in Spain.

In 65 B.C. he is aedile and spends upwards of $800,000, on one occasion providing 320 pairs of gladiators for a people's entertainment. In 63 B.C. he is made pontifex maximus and takes part in the deliberations on the case of the conspirators; in 62 B.C. he is praetor, and in 61 B.C. governor of Spain; and in 60 B.C. is elected consul, giving up a triumph in order to run for the office, which he holds in 59 B.C. For the next ten years he is in Gaul. In 49 B.C. he begins the civil war which results in the death of Pompey, the defeat of the senatorial armies in the East, in Africa, and in Spain, and on March 15 of the year 44 B.C., in the midst of reforms and plans for further conquest, is slain at a meeting of the Senate.

This is the career in which the military element predominates. Let us now survey two lives of the quieter type.

Quintus Horatius Flaccus was born in Venusia, in the southeastern part of Italy, on December 8, 65 B.C. His father, once a slave, had been freed before Horace's birth, and was engaged in a humble calling. From Venusia, where there was only the little school attended by the sons of the centurions in the garrison, and their like, he took his son to Rome for an education that should be the equal of that enjoyed by sons of the equites and senators. He went farther, and sent Horace at the age of twenty to Athens, where he began his studies in the usual courses of philosophy, mathematics, etc. In the midst of these studies, however, came the news of Caesar's assassination, and, not long after, Brutus himself arrived and began to interest young Romans in the cause of the liberators.

Horace joined the patriot army, was made tribune, fought in the defeat at Philippi in 42 B.C., and in the course of time found himself in Rome with property confiscated and no prospect in the world. He was given a place as clerk in the treasury, attracted attention by his talent for writing, got acquainted with Virgil and Varius, and was introduced by them to Augustus' friend and counselor, Maecenas, who gave him at the age of thirty-two the Sabine Farm, thirty miles from Rome in the high and secluded valley of the Digentia. He began to write poems at about twenty-four, and his first volume of *Satires*, published at thirty, was soon

AN UNIDENTIFIED ROMAN

This bust is labelled Pompeius Magnus, but August Mau thought it represented Quintus Horatius Flaccus.

followed by a second book of *Satires* and the *Epodes*. At forty-two he published three books of *Odes*, at forty-five a book of *Epistles*, at fifty-two a fourth book of *Odes*, and at fifty-five a second book of *Epistles*. On November 27th of the year 8 B.C. he died, and was buried on the Esquiline Hill.

Horace was not patrician, and belonged neither to senatorial nor to equestrian order. His was a life with no ambition for oratory, no running for office, no soldiering except by accident, no straining after fortune in the usual sense.

Yet it was a life of much experience and many contacts — of country village beginnings, of excellent education, of study abroad, of army experience in a lost cause, of bureaucratic occupation, of acquaintance with the best men of the Augustan State.

Virgil, too, was of plebeian rank, and born far away from Rome, at Andes, probably near modern Pietole, three miles from Mantua, on October 15, 70 B.C.; but his father, a common laborer or a potter who married his employer's daughter and made his home in the country, sent his son to school in Cremona at the age of twelve, to Milan at the age of sixteen, and finally to Rome. Virgil was thus later than Horace in his arrival at the capital, and richer in provincial and country experience. His studies in Rome were chiefly rhetorical, the usual preparation for the civic career, at which he aimed. A dubious account names his teacher as Epidius, and calls Epidius also the teacher of Octavius, the future emperor. In his twenty-first year, it is possible that the poet was enrolled in Caesar's army, whose strength was drawn largely from Cisalpine Gaul, where Virgil had lived.

When Virgil came to enter on his chosen profession as advocate, he appeared in court once, lost his case, and gave up the ambition for public life. Leaving Rome at about the age of twenty-two, he went to study with Siro, an Epicurean philosopher of repute, at Naples, where he had as friends three distinguished young men, Plotius Tucca, Varius, and Quintilius Varus. He spent little time after this in the capital, preferring the region about Naples, where most of his writing was done. When the confiscations of land took place after the battle of Philippi, his property in the Mantuan region was taken to be given the veterans of Antony. An appeal to Caesar not only brought a restoration of his land, but led to intimacies with the young Augustus and his friends. Maecenas became his patron, and in 38 B.C. on Virgil's introduction became the patron of Horace also.

Relieved, like Horace, of the cares of earning a livelihood, Virgil devoted himself to the poetry which had already been his passion for ten years or more, and which Augustus and Maecenas were shrewd enough to see would be an asset in their work of reconstructing the Roman State. He had written from early youth, but his genius did not mature early.

By the time he published the *Eclogues*, or *Bucolics*, which established his reputation, he was thirty-three. These ten pastorals were imitations of Theocritus, who lived three centuries before, but full of the charm of Italy. At the age of forty, he had completed the *Georgics*, four books filled with praise of Italy and the love of nature. For the next

THE YOUTHFUL MARCUS AURELIUS

eleven years he was occupied with the *Aeneid*, which was still unfinished when he became ill on a visit to Greece and died in Brundisium on the way home.

Virgil was buried at Naples, in or near which he had lived for more than twenty years. He was tall and dark, of a rustic look, delicate in health, diffident and retiring, and slow of speech. The *Aeneid*, with which he was not satisfied and which he wished destroyed, was placed by the Emperor in the hands of Varius and Tucca, and published in 17 B.C., two years after his death, substantially as he left it.

The last portrait will afford a contrast. Marcus Aurelius Antoninus, born in Rome on April 26, A.D. 121, was the son of the praetor Annius Verus, and the nephew and adopted son of the Emperor Antoninus Pius. Surrounded by relatives and teachers of excellent character, he had an ideal rearing and education. Herodes Atticus and Cornelius Fronto taught him rhetoric, a distinguished jurist taught him law, and among his teachers of philosophy were Sextus of Chaeroneia, grandson of Plutarch, and Junius Rusticus, his adviser when he came to the throne. For these and for others, the Emperor in his *Meditations* thanks the gods. He was an earnest student and a hard worker, abstemious and self-denying, even to the damage of his health. He was at home with arms and in the law. At twenty-five he married Faustina, the daughter of Antoninus Pius, and at forty, in A.D. 161, he became emperor.

The reign of Marcus Aurelius was marked by the Parthian War in A.D. 165; by a great pestilence which spread over the west of Europe; by Teutonic attempts to break into the Empire in A.D. 174; by the revolt of a general, Avidius Cassius, in A.D. 175; by persecution of the Christians at Lyons in France in A.D. 176, and by the war with the Northerners which ended in their defeat in A.D. 179 and in the Emperor's death at fifty-nine years in A.D. 180 from an illness contracted the year before. The wars at the northern frontier he led in person, and he died in camp. He was a faithful son and husband, and a loyal pupil. Many of the letters between him and his favorite teacher survive. One of them will be of interest.

"Hail, my sweetest of masters," he writes Fronto. "We are well. I slept somewhat late owing to my slight cold, which seems now to have subsided. So from five A.M. till nine I spent the time partly in reading some of Cato's *Agriculture* and partly in writing not quite such wretched stuff, by heavens, as yesterday. Then, after paying my respects to my father, I relieved my throat, I will not say by gargling — though the word 'gargarisso' is, I believe, found in Novius and elsewhere — but by swallowing honey water as far as the gullet and ejecting it again. After easing my throat I went off to my father and attended him at a sacrifice. Then we went to luncheon. What do you think I ate? A wee bit of bread, though I saw others devouring beans, onions, and herrings full of roe. We then worked hard at grape-gathering, and had a good sweat, and were merry and, as the poet says, 'still left some clusters hanging high as gleanings of the vintage.' After six o'clock we came home. I did but little work and that to no purpose. Then I had a long chat with my little mother as she sat on the bed."

Marcus Aurelius adopted the Stoic philosophy, and put it into practice in the spirit of a religion.

"Of human life the time is a point, and the substance is in a flux, and the perception dull, and the composition of the whole body subject to putrefaction, and the soul a whirl, and fortune hard to divine, and fame a thing devoid of judgment. And, to say all in a word, everything which belongs to the body is a stream, and what belongs to the soul is a dream and vapor, and life is a warfare and a stranger's sojourn, and after-fame is oblivion. What then is that which is able to conduct a man? One thing and only one, philosophy."

MARCUS AURELIUS IN TRIUMPHAL PROCESSION
A Victory hovers above him, and a trumpeter goes before.

The dead Emperor was honored by deification, and in a way became a saint. Many kept by them his statue or bust, and in the time of Capitolinus, his biographer of long afterward, it stood among their household deities.

The many surviving portraits of the philosopher statesman, in statue, bust, and relief, of which the most famous is the equestrian statue on the Piazza Campidoglio in Rome, present the Emperor with full beard and plentiful hair, and with grave, dignified, and serene countenance in keeping with the character of the *Meditations*.

XXVI

THE WORSHIPER

It is time something was said about the religion of the Roman. To know of his environment, person, and occupations is not enough; we need to know of his thoughts and behavior before the mystery of life. This is a difficult matter; the inner life of men is always the last thing in their composition to be appreciated.

The religion of the Roman when it first comes into sight has already been greatly influenced by contact with other religions. Before that time, he was like other men of imperfect culture; he saw and felt spirits everywhere: in the beasts of the field, in the trees and stones, in the wind and thunder, in all the objects, animate and inanimate, with which he was surrounded. To keep his relations with them right, to turn aside their wrath or to win their favor, he devised special words or acts. This is the stage of belief called animism.

As his experience grew, however, his vision also grew. He became familiar with what was nearer at hand; only that which was more remote from contact retained its mystery. The number of spirits which especially concerned him became smaller. From animism he passed to polytheism, the faith in a number of distinct gods. He worshiped Faunus and Fauna, the protectors of his animals in field and wood. Janus was the god of all beginnings and of the turn of the yearly season. Jovis was in the sunshine, the rain, the lightning, the thunder. Vesta was in his hearth and home.

Consus protected his horses, and Saturn the seeding and the harvest.

But some of these are deities little heard of in historic times. Before the Romans prayed to Jupiter and Juno and other gods familiar to Virgil and Cicero, further development was necessary.

A VESTAL VIRGIN

As the Roman absorbed the races near him and came into close relations with Volscian, Etruscan, and Samnite, and finally brought both them and the Greek of southern Italy and Sicily under his sway, contact with other men and other religions broadened his outlook, and modified his acts of worship. From the simple polytheism of the fields and the open air of Latium, he passed to the polytheism of the older and more thoughtful Greeks. From deities without form or shape and altars in grove and pasture, he passed to the temples and images of Etruscan and Hellenic gods. The image of Diana in the temple on the Aventine in King Servius' time was the first statue of deity worshiped by the Romans. With the reign of the Etruscan kings, the gods of Etruria also entered Latium. By 217 B.C., all the Greek gods and goddesses had been brought to Rome and had blended with the native deities. The Greek gods received the Roman names, and Greek ideas and ceremonial were modified by Roman thought and practice. Zeus and Hera became Jupiter and Juno; Poseidon and Athena became

Neptune and Minerva; Ares and Aphrodite, Mars and Venus; Apollo and Artemis, Apollo and Diana; Hephaestus and Hestia, Vulcan and Vesta; Hermes and Demeter, Mercury and Ceres.

These are the gods who appear in the pages of Cicero and Virgil and Horace and in the statuary descended to us from Greek and Roman times. It must not be thought, however, that they were the only gods of the Roman people. They were indeed the representative deities of the State, the most frequently heard of, the most impressive to look on, and the most cosmopolitan; they were the world deities of Roman civilization. But in thinking of religion as a force in the life of Rome, we must remember the faith of the individual at the hearth and as he went about his ordinary living. In the homes on the farm and in the villages of Latium and Central Italy, in the old-fashioned homes of the capital itself, there were still in Augustan times the gods of early Rome: Vesta and the Penates, protectors of the family; Faunus, protector of the flocks; Saturn, god of the planted crops; and many another of the kindly guardians from times when the gods of Olympus were yet unknown.

Nor were the Graeco-Roman and the old-fashioned Italian faiths the only ones. There were also the gods, not yet regarded quite with favor, of the many foreign groups that had come to be a part of the great city. There was the Great Mother, for the Orientals; there was Isis, for the Egyptians; there was Mithras, for the Persians. There were philosophers who interpreted the gods in new ways to suit themselves. There were astrologers and fortune-tellers for the superstitious.

It will not be possible to follow out in detail either the beliefs or practices of Roman religion. Let us attempt only to understand its general character.

First of all, the religion of the Roman world was not the same in all places and in all times. It varied according to city and country and race, and it changed from century to

THE TEMPLE OF THE GREAT MOTHER OF THE GODS ON THE PALATINE HILL

Its high foundations are covered by a grove of ilex trees. Augustus restored the temple, which was about 100 × 50 feet. The fragments are of volcanic rock called peperino, and were coated with stucco to make them appear marble.

century. The Latin tribes, the Etruscans, the Umbrians and Samnites, and the Greeks had modified it, the Egyptians and Orientals were a growing influence in the city of

Augustus' time, and the Christians were soon to come with the greatest leaven of all.

In the next place, it was a religion which was formally a

part of the State. It would be wrong to speak of religion and the Roman State as an alliance between two separate things, for religion was a function or department of the State. The temples and priests, the sacrifices and expiations, the various processions, and the celebrations of holidays were under the control and at the expense of Government. This is not said of personal and private worship, of course, which might be carried on at any time or place. The temples were open to everyone, and every-one was free to erect

MARCUS AURELIUS WORSHIPS BEFORE THE TEM-
PLE OF JUPITER ON THE CAPITOL

An acolyte holds the incense casket, the Emperor sprinkles from it on to the altar fire supported by the tripod, an attendant plays the pipe, and the sacrificial animal and the *popa* (the priest with the axe) wait.

his own altar or shrine and to sacrifice in the manner he chose.

Third, it was a religion represented by many places of

worship, and by many reminders to the eye. In Rome there were some three hundred temples, nearly the number of churches there to-day, and Augustus was the restorer of eighty of them. They were stately edifices with colonnades, vivid with tinting and flashing with metal ornament. The priests at their altars were robed in gorgeous vestments, and the solemn processions moving through the street and forum were among the great spectacles of the city. There were also the smaller places of worship. There were thousands of little shrines and separate altars in the city, by the side of the country road, and on the farms. The flowers and candles and kneeling devotees so frequent in Italy to-day all had their equivalent in ancient times, and the priest at the altar in the open air was a much more frequent sight.

Fourthly, it was a religion highly organized and with a multitude of functionaries. At its head was the college of pontifices, an ancient body self-elected and holding office for life, headed by the pontifex maximus. It exercised authority over sacred observances in general, such as interpretation of portents and decisions regarding festivals of prayer or sacrifices in expiation. There were the flamens, or priests officiating at sacrifices, of whom the flamen of Jupiter was the most prominent. There were the Vestal Virgins, a sisterhood of six chosen in girlhood by the pontifex maximus, in charge of the worship of Vesta, deity of the hearth and symbol of the inner life of the State. There were the Fratres Arvales, a brotherhood of priests who prayed for the fruitfulness of the fields; the Luperci, protectors of the flocks and herds; and the Salii, custodians of the sacred shield, who appeared in procession every March, leaping and clashing their armor. There was the college of augurs, experts in the lore of signs from Jupiter. There were the quindecimvirs, the board of fifteen in charge of cults introduced from abroad, with special oversight of the Sibylline Books and the worship of Apollo. There were the septemvirs, the seven in charge of feasts in honor of the gods.

As might be expected from the number of its temples and priests and from the number of its gods, it was a religion of many festivals. To mention only a few, there were the Ludi Romani, a season of two weeks in September, sacred to Jupiter; the Saturnalia, in December, in honor of Saturn; the Lupercalia, February 15, to prosper the flocks; the Cerealia, April 19, for the grain and wine spirits.

In the fifth place, the religion of the Romans was one of numerous formal details and of great strictness in their observation. Every movement at the altar, every phrase, and every syllable must be preserved in all exactness; an omission robbed the ceremony of all effect, and might bring down upon the priest or the State the wrath of the offended god. The Salic priests in Cicero's time repeated at the altar formulae which they scarcely understood themselves, so ancient was the wording of the rite. The flamen of Jupiter was not allowed to mount a horse, to have a knot in any part of his dress, to wear a ring unless it was broken, or to take an oath.

Sixthly, it was a religion of signs and portents and omens and auguries and visions and dreams. Its theory was that deity had its way of manifesting itself to mortals, if mortals could only understand. In public and private, no citizen entered upon an undertaking with confidence unless he had taken the auspices, that is, performed a sacrifice and noted the signs in the victim, or otherwise made formal observations, and found that the gods were not against him. The Roman priesthood had treasured up from earliest times the lore of the flight and the notes of birds, the eating and drinking of the sacred chickens, the markings and movements of the sacrificial victim's entrails, the behavior of the lightning, the interpretation of dreams, the signification of the unusual in nature. Cicero's treatise *On Divination* is a discussion of methods in learning the will of the gods. Especially in times of trouble, such as war or the plague, some strange dream

A ROMAN SACRIFICE

The priest pours incense on the altar flame, the priestess assists with a bowl of incense, and the *popa*, or holy executioner, with sacrificial axe, brings up the victim. The Roman priest kept the head covered during sacrifice.

or freak of nature or fancied vision in the sky might call for consultation of the Sibylline Books, or a season of prayer and purification, or the introduction of a new cult. Such things as these were of less authority in the days of Cicero and Caesar than in earlier times, and were kept up rather because of long custom and popular belief than because intelligent men believed in them; yet Caesar's colleague in the consulship, Bibulus, could still keep measures from coming to the vote by resorting to the ancient procedure of " watching the sky." Caesar himself at last put Bibulus and the obstructionists aside, but with people less enlightened and resolute, and in the backward places of the Roman realms, the lore of superstition and the blind observance of tradition never ceased.

Seventhly, it was a religion of material sacrifice. It has even been said, though not with entire truth, that it was a religion of bargaining and devoid of spiritual value. The worshiper prayed for a material benefit, and promised a material payment. The flowers and fruits were laid on the altar, the libation of wine was poured, the lamb or kid or ox was slaughtered, and the gods received a share of the feast. The general departing for the wars, the trader setting sail with laden argosy, the pontifex in behalf of the State, promised the gods a gift of gold, a lordly victim, or a definite per cent of the spoil or gain. If the person promising fulfilled his part of the contract, the deity was bound to grant him his desire. There was no demand for belief or faith, no subscription to creed; the scrupulously correct performance of ritual was all that was required. It may be objected also that the slaughter of helpless victims at the altar, the sight of blood, and the reek of burning flesh must have been revolting to the senses of many Romans, as their mere mention is to us. It was a religion of uncleanly practices.

That the Roman's faith was entirely without spiritual aspiration or spiritual communion is in the nature of things hardly possible. The spiritual experiences of the ancients may not have been so common as those of modern times, and they surely were not so frequently set forth in literature, but they existed, even as without being spoken of and unsuspected they exist in many a modern life. If this is not true, how could such a passage be written as that in Minucius

Felix? " In communion with and filled with the divine, our priests foresee that which is to come, give warnings against danger, healing to the sick, hope to those who are cast down, help to the unfortunate, solace to those in calamity, relief in time of trouble."

A BOY SOCIETY HONORS DIANA

Four boys burn candles before the goddess, who stands with quiver in hand on a pillar between two torches. Four others, who carry baskets of fruit and standards tipped with busts and supporting grape clusters, are being marshalled for a procession. The painting was found in Ostia.

Yet the charge of formalism is doubtless in a measure justified. All religions, when reduced to system and established, soon suffer from it. The official religion of the Roman State remained for centuries unchanged in much of what appeared to the eye, and its forms were stereotyped and mechanical. It owed its security in part to the very fact that it was old and fixed by the practice of generation after generation, that its temples had a venerable past, that its priests in their ministry were impressive with the sanction of time, that its colorful and stately processions were rich with mystic symbols of other ages and another world.

Eighthly, it was a conservative religion. Here again, it was like religion in general, which is always slow to change, and, like religions employing many forms and much ceremony, it was especially slow to change. It had not only the conservatism of inertness, but was conservative consciously and with a purpose. Its priests, its patrons, the magistrates, the elder citizens, the aristocratic families of the old Roman blood, the stolid folk of the unchanging country, with the many whose temperament unaided by reason set them against all change, formed a great body whose argument for a thousand years was always the same. The State was founded and has risen to greatness under the protection of the gods, they insisted. Its fortunes have been due to obedience, its misfortunes to disobedience or mistake. Our temples, our priests, our ancient ceremonies, represent the long experience of our sires and grandsires in the search after knowledge of the relations between the human and the divine. To cast all this aside, or to relax in the strictness of our observances, would be to bring ruin upon the State and all its members. For the sake of respect for tradition, for the sake of patriotism, and for the sake of safety, let us follow in the steps of our ancestors.

" Thou shalt continue to atone for the sins of thy fathers, O Roman," says Horace, as he surveys the ruins of the Roman State which Augustus is trying to rebuild, " until thou shalt have reërected the falling shrines of the gods and replaced the images foul with blackening smoke. It is because thou art obedient to the gods that thou art set over men. To this refer every beginning; to this, every end. It is neglect of

the gods that has brought many woes on mournful Hesperia."
Four hundred years later, the same sentiment is on the lips
of Symmachus, the gentleman and patriot of the city soon to
be entered by Alaric : " If long existence confers authority
upon religions, the faith of so many generations is worthy of
preservation, and we ought to follow our fathers as they with
such good results followed theirs."

Ninthly, the Roman religion was one which included many
varieties and degrees of faith. We have seen that with the
growth of the Roman State the religion of the Greeks was
blended with the native faith, and that the religions of Egypt
and Asia followed. Not only were various religions brought
together to form one body under the State, but the individual
citizens might vary in their interpretations and beliefs. This
is a condition which must exist when religion has grown into
a system with much conservatism and formalism. There
were the extreme conservatives who took religion literally
and frowned on every departure from the rule. There were
the timid who were cowed by tales of priests about the after
life in the lower world. There were those who saw in the
old tales a deeper and spiritual meaning ; Jupiter was the
sky, Juno the earth, the fruits of the earth their children, etc.
There were the Stoics, who found the old religion insufficient
but would not abandon it, and based upon it an enlightened
system of belief and conduct. There were those who found
in Isis and Mithras the satisfaction they did not feel in Apollo
and Minerva. There were those who were faithful to forms
but felt no moral restraint, and behaved as they pleased.
There were those who did not believe, but looked upon religion as a necessary instrument in the affairs of men ; like the
modern political philosophers who say that if the people had
no religion we should have to invent one. There were the
skeptics who denied all reality in religion. There were the

superstitious who regulated themselves by inessentials, and whose lives were full of little suspicions and dreads. Religion was not the same thing to all people in ancient Rome, as it is not in any country or church to-day.

It will make clearer the place of religion in the Roman consciousness if we consider the attitude of various individuals toward the divine.

Caesar, as we have seen, in his consulship broke away from the long-standing regard of the public man for augury. His whole career was in the same spirit. " No regard for religion of any sort ever frightened him out of an undertaking or even made him hesitate," Suetonius says. He had held the office of pontifex maximus three years before the consulship, but the fact had nothing to do with religion as we conceive it. Caesar was a free liver and spendthrift, and stood for the office because it would help him into favor and out of debt. His regard for religion was the regard of the practical man for an instrument to use in his own advantage or that of the State.

In Cicero may be seen better the attitude of the average public man toward religion. The names of the gods are often on his tongue, and he never speaks or acts with disrespect of them; but he also gives no evidence of the prayerful spirit or of participation in the acts of worship, though this is not necessarily proof of the lack of loyalty to religion. His belief in the immortality of a better world is grounded, not in faith, but in reason; if indeed it does not depend entirely upon Plato's doctrines always fascinating to him. His inspiration is philosophy rather than religion. The Stoic teaching has the greater attraction for him, and he never misses the opportunity of disapproving the Epicurean, but he does not subscribe without reserve to any system. Had you asked him his thoughts upon religion, he would very probably have said that it was a proper and necessary thing in the life of the State, that it would be a waste of time to debate its usefulness either there or in the life of the individual citizen, and that the individual citizen's duty was to continue in the ways of his ancestors. If he had gone on to discuss, it would have been as a philosopher and spectator rather than as a worshiper.

AN EARLY ROUND TEMPLE IN ROME

This is one of four temples excavated since 1924 in the south portion of the Campus Martius. They were worshiped in by the Romans of Hannibal's time and earlier.

If we look into the religious beliefs of Horace and Virgil and Lucretius, we shall find three types. Horace is the spectator, Lucretius the aggressive and passionate skeptic, and Virgil the religious by temperament.

Horace calls himself an Epicurean, but in a humorous manner which indicates no very deep conviction. The morality which he preaches, and for the most part lives, is

Stoic. His poems addressed to Apollo, Minerva, Venus, and Diana, and his references to deity in general, are those of a man who acquiesces in religion, does not debate it, has no passion for it, but admires the virtues of devotion and uprightness, and enters into sympathy with the worshiper. His ode to Faunus is an exquisitely clear portrayal of the simple and familiar faith of the country:

> "Oh, wont the flying nymphs to woo,
>   Good Faunus, through my sunny farm
> Pass gently, gently pass, nor do
>   My younglings harm.

> "Each year, thou know'st, a kid must die
>   For thee; nor lacks the wine's full stream
> To Venus' mate, the bowl; and high
>   The altars steam.

> "Sure as December's nones appear,
>   All o'er the grass the cattle play;
> The village, with the lazy steer,
>   Keeps holiday.

> "Wolves rove among the fearless sheep;
>   The woods for thee their foliage strow;
> The delver loves on earth to leap,
>   His ancient foe."

The ode to Phidyle, another picture of the country, suggests the moral and spiritual elevation of which the Roman religion was capable. Were not our communication with the mind and heart of the common people of Roman times so badly broken, we might be told of unsuspected riches.

> "But raise thy hands, O rustic Phidyle,
>   Under the new-born moon outstretched to heaven;
> Only do thou thy household gods appease
> With greedy pig or fruit of this year's trees
>   Or incense given:

"Then shall the wind that bringeth pestilence
　　Blast not the fertile vine, thy tender crops
No blighting rust, thy gentle nurslings fear
No sickly season when the Autumn sere
　　Its apple drops.

ON THE ALBAN MOUNT

Monte Cavo, 3,200 feet, is here seen from Tusculum.　The scenes in Horace's
poem to Rustic Phidyle were probably in the Alban Hills.

"The victim grazing on the snowy height
　　Of Algidus, in oak and ilex glade,
Or fattening on grassy Alban plain,
Marked for the altar, with his blood shall stain
　　The pontiff's blade.

"Thee it availeth naught with sacrifice
　　Of many a yearling lamb to make thy plea
Unto thy gods, thy little gods, if thou
But crownest them with fragile myrtle bough
　　And rosemary.

> "Lay but a spotless hand upon the altar,
> No costly gift enhancing its appeal,
> And it shall calm thy little hearth-gods' ire
> With simple salt that crackles in the fire,
> And holy meal."

Lucretius also is the declared Epicurean, but one who is filled with the passion of the reformer. The gods have no concern for men, is his vehement message; they are created beings like men, in nothing different save their deathlessness and unconcern. With man, and all other existing things, they are the blind creations of a primeval, whirling, colliding chaos of atoms. There is no immortality; the soul is made of atoms and mortal like all else, and the everlasting sleep of death is the end of soul as well as body. There is no after life of either misery or blessedness. Temples and priests, altars and offerings and prayers, the tales of another life— all are false and unreal; and the chief cause of the miseries of man is the belief in them that brings fear into his heart. Death is not an evil; it is only the beginning of never ending repose. Epicurus is the savior of mankind from the enslaving fears of the religious life and the dread of death.

Virgil represents the religious temperament, and Roman religion at its best. Taught by Epicurean masters, an admirer of Lucretius' *On Nature*, he knows the physical doctrines of Epicurus, but in mind and soul he is too generous to be confined by any sect. He feels the tragedy of death, whether in Dido and Euryalus, or in the cattle of the field or the birds of the air. He feels the mystery of life, and the presence of the infinite unknown in all the spaces of heaven and earth and sea and in all their creatures. He admires devotion to friends, to family, and to State, and reveres the old and the established practices of the Roman worshiper. Religion with him is not a mere convention; he associates morality with it. He feels that the good man will be rewarded and the bad punished, on earth and in another world. He feels that Rome and the Roman citizen have a destiny, and that this world and its affairs were ordered by a divine plan.

A NOVEL VIEW OF SAINT PETER'S
This is taken from the rear, looking toward the city.

He feels the solemnity of the human being consciously an instrument in the divine hand.

Rome is called the Holy City, and rightly so. It did not first become the Holy City, however, with the advent of Christianity; it was the holy city of paganism before it was the holy city of Christianity. Camillus is made by Livy to say in 390 B.C., when it has been proposed to move the capital

to Veii: " We have a city founded and established by the
will of the gods through signs.   There is no spot in it not full
of religious associations and the presence of gods.   The
places, no less than the days, for sacrificial observances are
fixed.   All these gods, public and private, are you going to
desert, my fellow citizens? "   Sallust calls the Romans
religiosissimi mortales.   Cicero writes that in religious
matters his countrymen are superior to other peoples, and
that they have overcome all the nations of the world because
they have realized that the world is directed and governed
by the will of the gods.

XXVII

ROMAN HOLIDAYS

There are two reasons why the subject of religion should be followed by the subject of holidays. In the first place, the public holidays of Rome were almost all associated with religion. A holiday was a holy day. In the second place, the manner in which men and nations employ their free time is, next to religion itself, the best indication of their character. Further, the subject of amusements is soon to claim our attention, and amusements depend largely upon holidays. It was on the days or series of days in honor of the gods called *ludi*, — plays, sports, or games — that the drama, the races, and the gladiatorial exhibitions took place which are the best-known entertainment of the Roman populace.

A TRAGIC MASK FROM THE VILLA OF HADRIAN

Such masks are the common ornament of theaters to-day.

The association of religion and amusement came about in a natural way. When the Romans in the primitive little city on the Palatine and in the rustic communities under its sway met together around their common altars to honor and propitiate the deity for whom the day was set aside, no legal business could be transacted, and work of every kind was suspended. The prayer and sacrifice concluded, the remainder of the day was given up to rest and merry-making. In the country, there were the dance and the simple trials of strength and skill that always belong to rustic gatherings and always remain the same. In the city, these simple beginnings soon developed into formal entertainment. As the city grew to be a great capital, the entertainment came to be an end in itself, and assumed enormous dimensions.

The chief public holidays during the middle years of Cicero's life were the Ludi Megalenses, April 4–10, in honor of the Great Mother of the Gods, seven days; the Ludi Cereales, April 12–19, in honor of Ceres, the grain goddess, eight days; the Floralia, April 28–May 3, in honor of Flora and the flowers and fertility, five days; the Ludi Apollinares, July 6–13, in honor of Apollo, eight days; the Romani or Magni, September 5–19, in honor of Jupiter, fifteen days; the Sullani, or Ludi Victoriae, October 26–November 1, instituted by Sulla to celebrate his victory, seven days; the Plebeii, November 4–17, founded to conciliate the common people, fourteen days.

These holidays, all classified as ludi, or festivals of which public entertainment was the great feature, amounted to 64 days. The functions were in charge of aediles, who sometimes made them the means of their ambition by contributing heavily from their own money. The number of days devoted to ludi had increased from 64 to 87 by the reign of Tiberius, the successor of Augustus; was 135 in the time of Marcus Aurelius; and is said to have been 175 in the middle of the fourth century. Sometimes there were special ludi; as after the taking of Jerusalem by Titus in A.D. 70, when they lasted 100 days, or in A.D. 106, after Trajan's conquest of Dacia, when they continued 123 days. These larger numbers included gladiatorial combats, which were at first called *munera gladiatoria* and were not officially ludi.

The ludi, or games, were not the only holidays in the Roman year. There were other festivals which swelled the number in Cicero's and Virgil's time to over one hundred. The name for all holidays was *feriae*, or *dies festi*; feriae being the origin of our word "fair," and dies festa the origin of Italian *festa* and French *fête*. The ludi are thus to be

CUPIDS IN A CHARIOT RACE

Six trees serve as *metae*, goal posts. Three scenes are portrayed: the start, an accident, the victor with palm branch. From a wall painting in the house of the Vettii, Pompeii.

defined as feriae on which plays and circus races were featured by the State.

Of the feriae which were not ludi, the one which appeals most to the modern is the Saturnalia, many of whose usages found their way into the Christmas of the Church. Originally one day only, December 17, but grown by Cicero's time to seven, the Saturnalia was celebrated by calls on friends, the giving of presents, including wax candles and pastry images, and the treatment of slaves as equals. The Saturnalia was at first a festival of the farm, but in the city lost its rustic character except that it preserved a public sacrifice at the Temple of Saturn at the head of the Forum, which was followed by a banquet ending with cries of *Io Saturnalia!* by the banqueters. It was a season of unrestrained merrymaking, during which a great deal of license was allowed and the slaves especially enjoyed taking liberties with their masters. The seventh of Horace's second book of *Satires* is a scolding given the poet by his slave Davus, who has followed his master to the country on the Saturnalia.

There were many other holidays marked by religious observances and general amusements. There was the Paganalia, January 24–26, in honor of Ceres and Tellus [Earth], the patrons of the seed sown in autumn and to be sown in spring. There was the Lupercalia, February 15, with a sacrifice of goats and a dog at the Lupercal cave beside the Palatine, where Romulus and Remus had been found by the she-wolf. Its main feature was the sacred race about the hill by two noble youths who as they ran struck all women standing near with strips of hide taken from the victim. The scene in Shakespeare's *Julius Caesar* is historical as to substance:

Caesar.	Calpurnia!
Calpurnia.	Here, my lord.
Caesar.	Stand you directly in Antonius' way,
	When he doth run his course. Antonius!
Antonius.	Caesar, my lord?
Caesar.	Forget not, in your speed, Antonius,
	To touch Calpurnia; for our elders say,
	The barren, touched in this holy chase,
	Shake off their sterile curse.

On the Parentalia, February 13–21, all Rome visited its dead with flowers and offerings of wine and honey and milk, in a sort of family communion. On the first of March, the day of Mars, once the Roman New Year, the twenty-four priests called Salii went leaping and dancing in procession through the streets. On the Liberalia, March 17, the Roman boy put on the toga of manhood.

The Parilia, April 21, in honor of Pales, the goddess of pastures and flocks, was celebrated in the city also as the birthday of Rome. On the 29th of May was the Ambarvalia, with its procession of all the people around the fields, and the sacrifice of a pig, a sheep, and an ox for the purification of the crops and animals — a celebration still surviving in another form in the Christian Church. The Vestalia, June 9, was in honor of the goddess of the hearth, whose worship originated in the time when the primitive village maintained a common fire from which at need the hearths could be renewed, and when the daughters of the chieftain were in charge of it.

The feriae in July were old-fashioned, and their origin obscure even to the ancients. On August 19 was the Vinalia Rustica, when perhaps the Flamen of Jupiter plucked the first fruits of the vineyard and offered prayer and sacrifice for the coming vintage. In September the fifteen days of the Ludi Romani were almost the only feriae. On the Fontinalia, October 13, the wells and springs were decorated with garlands of flowers.

November was another month with few feriae besides the ludi. The Ides of every month were sacred to Jupiter, the Calends to Juno; the Ides being the 13th except in March, May, July, and October, when the date was the 15th, and the Calends being the first. Every ninth day, the *nundinae*, was market day, and the farmers came to town, but it is uncertain whether these days were feriae.

Not even these are all the festival days without ludi which are known; but if they are added to the sixty-four days of the ludi, the impression is quite strong that the Roman year had a great number of holidays. This is the fact, but not to the degree that might be thought. In the first place, many of the festivals of which we have evidence in the surviving calendars were either little noticed or practically obsolete. In the second place, it should be remembered

that there was no Sunday in pagan Rome. If we add to our
fifty-two Sundays the various national and State holidays,
we shall have about sixty days on which business is not transacted, as against the more
than a hundred in the Rome
of Cicero. If we count the
Saturday afternoons taken
by the banks and profes-
sional classes, it will increase
the free days by twenty-six.
In Europe the total is even
greater. In the third place,
the Roman feriae were not
always observed by absten-
tion from labor and business.
Writers on farm affairs, including Virgil and Cato, tell
us that to work at certain
tasks on festival days is not
an offense against either
human or divine law — "to
lead the water into the fields,
to fence the grainfield about,
to lay snares for the birds, to
burn the brambles, to bathe
the flock in the health-giving
stream." If this was true
of the country, in the city

An Aedile Giving the Signal at
the Games

He has a scepter as a symbol of authority in the left hand, and a handker-
chief or cloth in the right.

many a festival went by with little effect on the day's
business.

We may conclude this account of the holidays by saying
something about the Roman calendar. The Roman year
for a long time began with March, the month of Mars, pro-

tecting deity of a race of warriors, whose birthday was on
the first of the month.   This is why the months which for us
are ninth, tenth, eleventh, and twelfth — September, October, November, December — bear the Roman names of
"seventh month," "eighth month," "ninth month," and
"tenth month"; and why July and August, before Julius
Caesar and Augustus, were Quinctilis and Sextilis, "fifth
month" and "sixth month."   It is supposed that the change
to January 1 as the official first day of the year took place
in 153 B.C.   It was on this date that the consuls began to
enter upon their duties on the first of January instead of on
the first of March.

In the year 46 B.C., another and a more important change
took place.   Up to this time, there had always been in the
calendar the difficulty caused by the difference between the
sun's year, which is 365 days, 5 hours, 48 minutes, and 48
seconds, and the year of twelve moons, which is 354 days,
8 hours, 48 minutes, and 35 seconds.   If, for example, the
Vinalia Rustica is celebrated on August 19 by the lunar
calendar, it will occur eleven days earlier each time in the
solar year, and there will be no grapes for the flamen to offer.
The arrangement by which this disagreement was corrected
for several centuries before Caesar's dictatorship consisted
of a four-year cycle, in which a year of 355 days was followed by a second of 355 plus 22, a third of 355, and a
fourth of 355 plus 23, the extra periods being inserted after
February 23.   This reminds us of our extra day every four
years in February.

Even this device, however, was not perfect, and by
Caesar's time the calendar was badly out of harmony with
the sun and moon.   The Dictator's remedy was first to bring
the calendar dates into correct relation with the sun and
moon by prolonging the year 46 to 445 days, and then to

begin the year 45 with the new system called after its founder
the Julian Calendar, according to which the year consisted
of 365 days, with one day added after the 23d of February
every fourth year. This system, with a correction by Pope
Gregory XIII in A.D. 1582, is in use to-day in America,
Europe, and most of the rest of the world, though the
Gregorian feature is not quite universal.

According to Livy, the Roman calendar was first published in 304 B.C., in the Forum, "in order that it might be
known when business according to law was possible." Its
publication after Caesar's time, with dates, indications of
festivals, and annotations, was common in Rome and elsewhere. There are in existence parts of thirty calendars or
more, fourteen of which were found in or near Rome, and
one of which is practically complete. Most of them are
incised in stone.

Besides their indications of the various holidays of the
Roman year, the calendars also set down against each day a
certain mark. There are eight of these marks, of which
three should be mentioned here. These are the letters F, N,
and C, meaning Fastus, Nefastus, and Comitialis. The
Dies Fastus was a day on which business with the civil
authorities, and especially matters in the courts, could be
transacted without offense to the gods. The *Dies Nefastus*
was the opposite; on a day marked N no business was legal,
whether because the day was consecrated to the gods or
because by reason of defeat, disaster, or other sinister event
in time past the date was ill-omened. The *Dies Comitialis*
was one on which it was legal for elections to be held as well
as for business to be transacted.

The number of days in the Julian Calendar marked F
and C, and thus under divine approval for business purposes,
was 239. The remaining 126 were nearly all marked N, and

in most cases coincided with religious festivals. It should be added that in some cases the annotations F and C are found with festival days; not every religious holiday was denied to business. The Italian elections to-day are held on Sunday.

XXVIII

THE THEATER

In Rome as well as in Athens, the giving of plays was a function of the State, was under the sanction of religion, and occurred on religious holidays. In Athens the patron deity was Dionysus, the great spectacles in tragedy and comedy took place at the main festival of the god on the opening of spring, and three plays at least were presented on a single day. In Rome under the Republic there were four State festivals at which literary drama was produced: the Ludi Megalenses, April 4–10; the Ludi Apollinares, July 6–13; the Ludi Romani, September 5–19; the Ludi Plebeii, November 4–17. Plays were given on occasion also at triumphs and at funeral games. The number of holidays in which the theater had a part increased until in the late Empire there were about a hundred. One drama each day was the practice, beginning in the middle of the day and lasting about three hours. Before the times of separate theater buildings, it took place in the Circus or near the temple of its patron deity, just as the medieval Christian play took place at the church door. The aediles contracted for the play with a *dominus gregis*, master of a troupe, who acquired the right of the play from its author. Wigs, masks, and the properties in general were in use. Female parts were usually done by men, many actors and managers were slaves or freedmen, and the social standing of the profession was low, though the best talent commanded the respect of all.

There were in Rome by the last five years of Horace's life

three theaters of the first class. The Theater of Pompey, erected by the great general in 55 B.C. and restored by Augustus in 32 B.C., perhaps after damage by fire, was the first permanent theater in Rome. It was of stone, marble, and stucco, at the south end of the Campus Martius, and seated some ten thousand persons. It was part of a building group including also temples, a portico, and the hall in which the Senate met on the day of Caesar's assassination —

> "And in his mantle muffling up his face,
>   Even at the base of Pompey's statua,
>   Which all the while ran blood, great Caesar fell."

The next theater was dedicated in 13 B.C. by Lucius Cornelius Balbus, its builder, a friend of the Emperor, and had seats for about eight thousand. It stood farther south and nearer the Tiber, and its ruins are under the present Piazza dei Cenci and surrounding buildings. The third was also dedicated in 13 B.C. and named after Marcellus, nephew and adopted son of Augustus, who died at the age of twenty in 23 B.C. It also was near the Tiber, not far south of the Theater of Balbus. After a medieval and modern existence as fortress and palace of the Pierleoni, Savelli, and Orsini, and after recent service in one of its parts as residence of the American Ambassador to Italy, the Theater of Marcellus is now an impressive national monument. It had some fourteen thousand seats.

The erection of these playhouses all within the last fifty-five years of the pagan era does not mean that the drama had not hitherto existed in Rome. Quite the contrary, its active history began nearly two hundred years before the building of Pompey's theater. In the year 240 B.C., in order to celebrate in unusual fashion the close of the twenty-four years of the first war with Carthage, the aediles commissioned Livius Andronicus, a teacher and writer who had been brought to Rome as a slave boy in 272 B.C. from Tarentum in Magna Graecia, to put on as features of the Ludi Romani a tragedy and a comedy adapted from the Greek.

THE THEATER OF MARCELLUS IN ROME

For centuries it served as fortress and palace and for many shops. It has recently been disengaged and made a public monument.

The history of the Roman stage before Livius, who represents the literary drama, is obscure. According to Livy, stage representation began in 364 B.C. with the introduction of actors from Etruria, and Varro sees the remotest origins in such community gatherings as the Lupercalia, after the manner of the rise of Greek drama from the festivals of Dionysus.

Livius was among the captives from Tarentum, whose fall meant the passing of Greek Italy under Roman control and a great impulse to Greek culture in the capital. Livius and his successors, Ennius, Naevius, Pacuvius, and Accius, the last of whom died in 86 B.C. and was acquainted with Cicero, produced a great body of Roman tragedy based on the Greek plays of Sophocles and Euripides. A similar body of Roman comedy based on Menander, Apollodorus, Diphilus, Posidippus, and other writers of the New Comedy in Athens, was produced by Plautus, 254–184 B.C., Caecilius Statius, 219–166 B.C., and Terence, 195–159 B.C. America using the plays of England or France, and England using the dramatic material of France or Italy, are partial parallels.

The tragedy of the Roman authors of the Republic is preserved only in fragments, though we have nine tragedies by Seneca written in Nero's time. The comedy is preserved in six plays of Terence and twenty-one of Plautus. Both tragedy and comedy in Rome are of great importance in the history of drama, because on the one hand the Greek New Comedy without Plautus and Terence would not be represented by a single complete play, and on the other hand without Seneca modern tragedy would have missed its chief inspiration. The history and production of drama has been a continuous tradition from Athens through Rome to Renaissance Italy and the capitals of modern literary culture.

It is difficult to explain how Rome could have been interested enough in drama for two hundred years to produce the numerous plays just referred to and still not have provided at least one permanent theater. During all this time we are to imagine a temporary stage erected, when the date of the ludi approached, at the foot of the Palatine or other slope, and the audience standing or sitting in curved rows on the rising ground. The usual explanation is that the theater with seats was regarded as a luxury which would lead the Roman people in the path of decadence trodden by the Greeks, who were held in contempt as unmanly and unreliable by their Roman patrons and conquerors. A permanent theater of stone begun in 154 B.C. was torn down by order of the Senate, and for a few years at least the people were forbidden to be seated at the shows. If the reason advanced is true, we must imagine the austere ideas of Cato the Censor, who died in 149 B.C. at the age of eighty-five after lifelong hatred of Greek fashions, as held by a very considerable part of Roman society. Yet it is hardly possible that the scores and hundreds of Roman plays had nothing back of them but the patronage of a governing few who were specially interested in Greek drama; the plays of Plautus and Terence were read and are referred to as if enjoyed by the Roman public, and all evidence goes to show that the drama in general was in high esteem. We must conclude that the prejudice against the theater with permanent seats did not extend to the plays themselves.

The era of the great writers of Roman drama was thus past before the city's first playhouse was built. Plays were still being written in the times of Cicero and Augustus, but none of them has survived, and they seem to have been written more as a literary fashion than for actual use on the stage. Cicero's brother Quintus, for example, wrote tragedies while serving with Caesar in Gaul, and many of the Augustan courtiers tried their hands at it. The record of Quintus Cicero was four plays in sixteen days. That plays were produced in abundance in the latter part of the first century before Christ is indicated by the erection of the three theaters. In by far the larger part, they were the tragedies and comedies of a century and a half before — the Sophoclean and Euripidean adaptations made by Ennius and Pacuvius, above mentioned,

> "Presenting Thebes or Pelops' line
> Or the tale of Troy divine,"

and the comedies of Plautus and Terence adapted from Athenian plays by Menander and others of the fourth century B.C.

The productions were not entirely of the old, standard sort, however. There were some plays containing Roman subject matter and played in Roman costume and with Roman scenery. A serious play of this kind was called *praetexta*, from the purple-bordered toga of its costume.

A Comic Actor and His Masks
This is sometimes called Menander and his favorite, Glycera.

Romulus, Aeneas, Decius, are some of the titles. *Octavia*, with scene in Nero's time, is the only complete praetexta surviving. The chief character, Octavia, is the daughter of the Emperor Claudius, and the bride of Nero, in whose affection she is supplanted by Poppaea, with the tragic result of exile. There were also comedies with Roman content called *fabulae togatae* because of the toga, the native costume, just as the Greek adaptations were called *fabulae palliatae* from the *pallium* of the Greek costume. Some of the titles of the togata were *The Lady Lawyer, The Defeated Candidate, The Divorce*. Afranius, the chief writer of the togata, wrote forty plays. There were mimes, short and scandalous plays in which the stock characters were the unfaithful wife, the deluded husband, and the gay coquette. *The Twins, The Wedding, Lake Avernus*, are titles of mimes by Decimus Laberius, of Caesar's time. Another mime writer of the time was Publius Syrus. Sometimes there was the Atellan Farce, with its broad comic characters, Pappus, Maccus, Dossennus, and Bucco, like the Punch and Judy characters who are suspected of descent from them. Pomponius and Novius are the only authors who raised the Atellana to the literary level, and some of their titles are *The Farmer, The Village Barber, The Campanians*. The Atellana was displaced by the mime, and the mime specialized in gesticulation so successfully that it developed into pantomime.

The stage in the times of Cicero and Horace no doubt offered a variety of entertainment. We may be sure that comedy was more welcome to the people than tragedy, and that the grossness of the mime was attractive to many who found too quiet the polished urbanity of Terence. We may be sure, too, that there was much entertainment of a dramatic nature which never reached the stages of the great theaters or the public programs of the ludi. There were jugglers and acrobats, and the ancient equivalents of the vaudeville acts.

Even in the presentation of the standard plays there were often liberties taken for the sake of pleasing the multitude. Cicero attends the opening plays in Pompey's theater, and writes a friend: "The sight of so much apparatus on the stage took away all pleasure, and I have no doubt you were quite content to miss it. For what delight can one take in six hundred mules in *Clytemnestra*, or in three thousand mixing bowls in *The Trojan Horse*, or in the various arms and trappings of infantry and cavalry in some fight? These things drew the admiration of the people, but would have given you no pleasure." The *Clytemnestra* here referred to is that of Accius, at that time dead thirty years, and *The Trojan Horse* is probably a play by Livius Andronicus written nearly two centuries before.

The liking of the people for dumb shows and noise at these plays attended by Cicero is to be seen in a passage of Horace also. He satirizes in his smiling way the untaught and stolid plebeians in the audience clamoring in the midst of a play for "a bear, or the boxers, and ready to fight it out if the equites don't agree; for the bear and the boxers are what the dear common folks like."

"But all taste of the equites, too, has left the ear, and is now in the empty pleasure of the roving eye. For four hours or more the curtain is kept lowered [the modern 'raised'] while squadrons of cavalry and companies of infantry fly across the stage. Presently unhappy kings are dragged past, their hands bound behind them, chariots career along, and carriages, and wagons, and ships, and loot of ivory and Corinthian bronze. If Democritus [the laughing philosopher] were on earth, he would laugh to see a cross between a camel and a leopard, or a white elephant, capture the eyes of the crowd. He would find himself giving more attention to the audience than to the play itself, as affording more of a spectacle by far. He might think the author was staging the play for a deaf ass. For what words can rise above the din of our theaters? You would think the forests of Garganus roaring in the storm, or the Tuscan sea, with such noisiness are plays witnessed, with their display of rich and outlandish costumes. The actor comes on to the stage loaded down with them, and the clapping of hands begins. 'Is he saying anything yet?' 'Not a thing!' 'Then what is it they are applauding?' 'The gown he has on, done in Tarentine violet!'"

There were other features of ancient dramatics resembling the modern. There were favorite actors, of course — the stars.

There was Aesopus in tragedy and Roscius in comedy, both among Cicero's acquaintances, and both said to have been his models in gesticulation, and observers in their turn of the lawyer Hortensius in court. Roscius, who died when Cicero was forty-four, was defended by the orator in the speech *Pro Roscio Comoedo*, and was said by Cicero to be so perfect in his art that a person excelling in anything was called a Roscius.

Aesopus had retired before 55 B.C. and was honored by a recall to the stage on the dedication of Pompey's theater, but with unfortunate results. "There had returned to the stage, for the sake of distinction, those who I supposed had left it as a mark of distinction," Cicero writes his friend Marius. "Your favorite Aesop was in such a state that nobody would have objected to his retiring. When he had begun to take an oath — you know the passage, 'if wittingly I prove false' — his voice failed him."

The century before, there had been Ambivius Turpio, the star of Terence's comedies, of whom Cicero in *On Old Age* has Cato make a simile: "As the spectator in the first row enjoys Ambivius Turpio more, though those in the last row also enjoy him, so perhaps youth because nearer to pleasures takes keener delight in them, but old age too, though at a distance, delights as much as need be wished." Later, in the time of Domitian, there were Demetrius and Stratocles, famous in comedy, "the former very fine in the parts of gods, young men, good fathers and slaves, matrons, and serious old women, and the latter better in the parts of cross old men, tricky slaves, parasites, panders, and livelier characters in general. The voice of Demetrius was pleasanter, the other's carried better."

There were sometimes jests from the audience at the expense of the actor. An undersized Hector came on, and some one called out: "That is Astyanax! Where is Hector?" A tall actor was greeted with: "Step over! You

A ROMAN THEATER AT MERIDA IN SPAIN

The architecture and sculpture indicate a fine building of the times of Marcus Aurelius.

don't need a ladder!" A heavy one was advised, "Be careful of the stage!"

Sometimes the position is reversed, and there are personalities from the stage. "What! Are you beginning to scowl because I said this was going to be a tragedy?" cries Mercury in the prologue of Plautus' *Amphitruo*. "I'm a

god; I'll see to having it changed." The prologue to the
Captives is quite as familiar. "Do you get this? Very
well, then. Yes, but the fellow away off yonder in the back
says he doesn't. Come along up! If there isn't a place for
you to sit, there's room outside. Because you're making the
actor go begging. I'm not going to burst myself on your
account, don't think it!"

The Mediterranean basin is dotted with the ruins of
ancient theaters. In or near almost every city of size in
Italy and Sicily, and in the principal ancient Roman centers
of Africa, Spain, and France, the theater is one of the objects
to be visited. Some of the examples even in lands more
Greek than Roman show the construction of Roman times.

The Roman theater differed from the Greek in having
the orchestra semicircular instead of circular. In other
respects the differences were of little consequence. The
parts of the theater were the *scaena*, scene, or stage; the
orchestra, in earliest Greek times the circle in which the
chorus chanted and danced; and the *cavea*, or auditorium.
The larger of the two theaters at Pompeii, which may serve
as an example, had two *tribunalia*, equivalents of the modern
box, above the entrances at right and left of the cavea rows.
Here sat the magistrates, Vestals, or other dignitaries. The
seats in and next to the orchestra, and consequently nearest
the stage, were reserved for the senators in Rome and for
the town councilors in provincial cities. Fourteen rows
were reserved behind these for the equites, according to the
Roscian Law of 67 B.C. The more distant sections were
occupied by the common crowd of soldiers, women, minors,
and plebeians in general. The stage at Pompeii was 120
feet long, 24 feet wide, and 5 feet high. The curtain rolled
downward into a deep groove at the beginning of the play,
and upward at its close. For the background, there were

normally two permanent houses with alley between and exits to right and left. The exit at the right of them was understood to lead into the city; the one at the left, to the harbor and foreign countries. There were painted scenes in use, some like the modern sliding scenes, and some at the sides on large three-faced prisms which were revolved when a shift was desired. A ticket or check seems to have been used for seating. On hot days awnings might be stretched over all and the air cooled by sprinkling, sometimes even with perfume.

There was little writing of drama after Augustan times, and none after Hadrian's. Acting also came to an end, so far as high-class entertainment was concerned, and the last centuries of the Roman Empire saw nothing on the stage but mimes and pantomimes, rope dancers, sleight-of-hand artists, and the like. The clergy of the Christian Church were forbidden the theater altogether, and no Christian could be an actor or marry one of the acting class. The disapproval of pagan Rome, expressed up to Nero's time in a law excluding the actor from civil rights, was continued in Christian Rome.

Beyond A.D. 533, nothing by way of the stage is traceable in the West. When the drama appeared again, it was at the altar of the Church, in the liturgical play which developed into the mystery play and the Morality. When the interest in this had opened the way, the old classical drama of Greece and Rome came back again in the languages of Italy, Spain, France, England, and Germany, and the modern stage resulted. The study of the drama leads inevitably to Rome, and from Rome to Greece.

XXIX

THE RACES

The most ancient, the longest continued, and the most popular of the public amusements of ancient Rome was the chariot race, which took place in the elongated space curved at one end and straight at the other called the circus. Livy assumes that its first occurrence was in the time of Romulus, who, in order to get wives for his womanless State, "got up games in honor of Equestrian Neptune, named them Consualia," and invited all the neighboring communities, with secret instructions to his men to seize their unmarried young women.

The actual laying out of a circus ground and the organization of the races into a yearly festival, the *Ludi Circenses*, Livy attributes to Ancus Martius, the fourth king. "The sports," he says, "were horses and boxers brought from Etruria. They became the custom, and then kept their place as a yearly festival, called variously 'Romani' and 'Magni.'" We may suppose either that the races began with the holiday gatherings of drovers and farmers at which they tried the speed of their animals, or that their origin was in military exercises and displays, or that they were introduced already developed from Etruria, which was advanced in its contacts with the East and with Greece.

Up to 364 B.C., when players from Etruria are said to have given the first dramatic entertainment, the races were the only amusement provided by the State. The Circus Maximus, on the long, low, level space between the Palatine and the Aventine, from the beginning and throughout was the largest assembly place in Rome, and with the beginning of the Christian centuries had a seating capacity of at least 150,000. It was not the only circus. There were also the Circus Flaminius, erected in 221 B.C. at the south end of the Campus Martius near the Capitoline, and visible in large part up to the sixteenth century, since when it has disappeared in the buildings of modern Rome; the Circus Vaticanus, built by Caligula in A.D. 37–41, used by Nero for his notorious torment of the Christians, and disappearing at the erection of Saint Peter's; and the Circus of Maxentius, A.D. 309, a distance outside the gates on the Appian Way, near the tomb of Caecilia Metella.

The craze for the races which existed in Nero's time was still notorious when Ammianus wrote of it in A.D. 359. The ears of Rutilius Namatianus, as he sails down the Tiber and away from Rome in A.D. 417, are filled with the echoing cheers of the multitude for the winning charioteer; and it is not until A.D. 549, with the Gothic chieftain Totila's celebration in the Circus Maximus, that we cease to hear of the races. Even the Christians yielded at times to the popular enthusiasm, and justified themselves by referring to Elijah's going up by a whirlwind into heaven with a chariot of fire and horses of fire.

The Circus Maximus was about two thousand feet long and five hundred feet wide, and its exterior rose in three stories of marble-veneered arcades. It extended on both sides to where the slopes of Palatine and Aventine began. Within the lowest arcade were a long promenade and the entrance doors and stairways. The east end was somewhat curved, and its walls impressive with high towers. The vast interior consisted of three parts: the *spina*, the track, and the *cavea*, or seats.

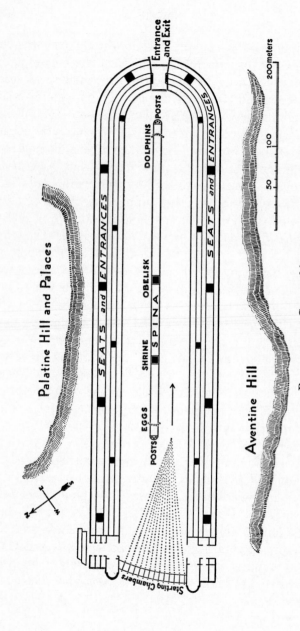

Palatine Hill and Palaces

Aventine Hill

SEATS and ENTRANCES

SEATS and ENTRANCES

Entrance and Exit

POSTS

DOLPHINS

OBELISK

SHRINE

SPINA

EGGS

POSTS

Starting Chambers

200 meters

100

50

PLAN OF THE CIRCUS MAXIMUS

Entrance was by means of stairways in the body of the building reached from the vaultings which supported it.

The spina was a slender but massive barrier of ornamental masonry about one thousand feet long with three cones of gilded bronze, the *metae*, or goal posts, at either end, and with seven marble eggs at one end and seven dolphins at the other for keeping tally on the laps of the race. A famous fountain near the Colosseum was called Meta Sudans, the sweating goal post, from its shape and the manner in which the water behaved. On the spina were several shrines and statues, and an obelisk seventy-eight feet high brought by Augustus from Heliopolis near Cairo in Egypt, and now standing in Piazza del Popolo at the north gate of Rome. The obelisk now at the Lateran Church, one hundred and five feet high, was placed on the spina of the Circus Maximus by the Emperor Constantius, A.D. 337–361.

The arena, between the spina and the seats, was bounded at the end where the start was made by the slightly curving row of *carceres*, barriers or cells for the chariots as they stood waiting for the signal to go. At the other end the boundary was the curved line of the seats, pierced by the Triumphal Gate, through which at the end of the race the victor splendidly passed. The arena here, as well as in the amphitheater, got its name from the *arena*, sand, with which the ground was strewn.

The immense banks of seats, divided into zones and sections by means of passageways and stairways, were approached through numerous *vomitoria*, discharges connected with flights of stairs leading from the ground under the lowest arcade. The space next the track was occupied on both sides and at the curved end by a massive bank of masonry supporting a platform divided into sections which were splendidly fitted up as boxes for the spectators of highest rank. On the side of the Palatine, where the imperial palace rose high above the Circus, was the loggia or balcony of the emperor and retinue, so constructed as to be entered directly from the palace. The seats were marble, at least in greatest part, and at their top it is likely that a gallery ran. The end occupied by the starting chambers contained, above them and the main entrance, a balcony and seats for

THE HEAD OF A CIRCUS DRIVER

the president or giver of the races, *dator ludorum*, and his retinue and friends.

The chariot races were the great feature of all the principal festivals, though they are most associated with the Ludi Romani or Magni in September. On the morning of the races, the eager and excited crowd streams from every direction toward the monster building. The neighborhood is noisy with vendors of all sorts, and bookmakers crying their bets. There is no admission price, for the games are at the State's expense, and many are in their seats long before the time set.

When the endless expanse of white seats is alive with colorful humanity and the scattered crowd of gesticulating enthusiasts that dotted the arena has also disappeared into the great assemblage, all eyes begin to watch the monumental entrance way at the east end, and all ears are attentive. Presently, from the direction of Forum and Sacred Way, the sound of trumpets is heard. The roar of the talking multitude decreases, the sound grows louder and nearer, and every eye is focused on the entrance, through which in a moment march with jaunty step the brightly costumed players of

the horn and the pipes. Following them on to the yellow
sand and along before the brilliant boxes filled with color
and life at the foot of the never ending ranks of spectators,
preceded by his twelve lictors, rides in his chariot the consul
who is to preside for the day, a lordly figure in white and
purple and gold with ivory scepter in hand and with golden
garland held above his head by an attendant. Behind the
consul and his retinue come the many four-horse chariots
entered for the races of the day, which sometimes amount to
twenty. The drivers are bright, each in the color of the
faction for which he is driving — red, white, blue, green,
purple, or gold — and the chariots and horses also display
the colors. The factions are the rival companies that furnish the races from great horse-breeding and horse-trading
establishments, and the partisans of the various colors
representing them are frenzied in their applause as the
brilliant parade passes, including images of various deities
on platforms carried by men, with the priests and attendants
belonging to their service.

The procession completes the course amid the yells and
screams and clapping of hands and waving of handkerchiefs
and scarfs, and at its end quickly disbands. In a few moments the consul is at his post in the balcony above, the
chariots are in the starting stalls below, with attendants at
the barriers that separate the horses from the arena. The
multitude is silent and strained; the consul rises and displays at arm's length the white signal cloth. In another
second, with all eyes on him, he lets it fall, the barriers drop
or are moved aside, and the chariots plunge forward toward
the track to the right of the spina. The stalls are so situated
that each is equidistant from the point toward which they
plunge, so that the "start" is made from the stalls, is fair,
and is not repeated.

The Roman circus race had nothing to do with breaking records of time. As in the pony races of the Palio at Siena to-day, which are started in the same way by the dropping of the cable barrier, the sole ambition of the driver was to be first at the finish. As is the case at Siena, too, everything on the course was fair. As the chariots career down the track, each driver as he exhorts and lashes his horses keeps his eye on the coming turn about the three gilded goal posts at the end of the spina. If he can come sharply around, all but touching them, he will have a great advantage, but he will do it at the risk of collision, whether he cuts in ahead of his rivals or they cut in ahead of him. If he fails, his careering and excited horses, the outermost one of which on either side is only loosely attached, may pile up with the rival teams in a mass of poles and wheels and men, and plunging, snorting animals, and crush him to death; or his chariot may strike another and be overturned and the horses gallop on, dragging chariot and driver in horrible disaster; for in order to drive well he must wear the reins tied fast round his body, and he may not be quick enough to sever them with the knife he carries for the purpose.

The fate described is what happened to Orestes in the tragic race at Delphi, in the *Electra* of Sophocles.

"Orestes had passed safely through every round, steadfast in his steadfast car. At last, slackening his left rein while the horse was turning, unawares he struck the edge of the pillar; he broke the axle-box in twain; he was thrown over the chariot-rail; he was caught in the shapely reins; and, as he fell on the ground, his colts were scattered into the middle of the course. But when the people saw him fallen from the car, a cry of pity went up for the youth — now dashed to earth, now tossed feet uppermost to the sky — till the charioteers, with difficulty checking the career of his horses, loosed him, so covered with blood that no friend who saw it would have known the hapless corpse."

At the passing of the goal posts — "the goal post shunned by the glowing wheel," of Horace's first *Ode* — one of the marble eggs behind the posts is taken down. At the other end, where the first of the seven laps is completed, one of the dolphins is taken down. Without this tally, and with all the rapidity and excitement, there would be no end of misunderstandings. When the seventh egg is down and one dolphin still in air, the chariots do not turn as they pass the dolphin, but make for the chalk line straight ahead near the starting chambers, and complete the race. The distance run in the seven laps is less than three miles. The decision is proclaimed, the devotees of the

A CHARIOTEER AND HIS HORSE
He is tightly strapped, and has tattooing on his arms. A mosaic.

winning driver and color bellow and scream their satisfaction as he rides before them with the palm of victory in his hand and disappears through the Gate of Triumph. The horses are taken away to their stables, the course is cleared, and the next race called.

The successful driver is the darling of his faction and the populace. His races and in some cases his victories reach into the thousands, and his winnings into the millions. Diocles the Spaniard in twenty-four years ran 4,257 races, won 1,462 victories, and received for them $1,800,000. Marcus Aurelius Liber won 3,000 times. Horses as well as drivers were favorites. Crescens, a Mauretanian driving for the Blues, won his first victory in the twenty-fourth race on a birthday of Nerva with the horses Circius, Acceptor, Delicatus, and Cotynus, and so recorded the facts in an inscription found at Rome in 1878.

The subject of the races may be concluded with a few references from the authors. The rivalry between the factions had not reached its height in Augustan times, when there were still only three colors, the Reds, the Whites, and the Blues. In Cicero's time only the Reds and Whites contended. When Horace makes beautiful use of the chariot race as a simile of life's race for wealth, the circus is still primarily a sport and a spectacle: "The avaricious man strains to pass this rival and that (for he finds ever a richer rival as he hastes), like the charioteer, who, when the hoof whirls along the chariots just released from the starting chambers, presses upon the horses that have passed his own, and pays no heed to him he has left behind among the last in the race."

It is not long after this that speculation, the craze for the colors, and the passion for betting convert the sport of the circus into the frenzied institution it remained throughout the Empire.

"All my time these days," writes Pliny the Younger, "I have been spending in the most delightful quiet with my tablets and books. But you say, 'How could you manage it, in the city?' Why, the circus games were on, a kind of show that does not attract me in the least. There is nothing new in them, nothing different, nothing that does not suffice forever if you have seen it once. That is the reason why I wonder the more that so many thousands of grown up men can have so childish an eagerness again and again to look on at horses running and men standing in chariots. If they were only attracted by speed on the part of the horses or by skill on the part of the drivers, there would be some excuse for it; but the fact is, it is a color they applaud, and a color they are in love with, and if in the middle of a race the one color should suddenly be exchanged with the other, the support and applause would also be transferred, and straightway people would abandon the horses and drivers whom they were following from far away and whose names they were shouting. So much influence, so much authority is there in a worthless tunic, I will not say in the eyes of the common crowd, which is cheaper still than the tunic, but in the eyes of even some persons of character. And when I think of their sitting there so insatiable in their enthusiasm for so empty and frigid and hackneyed an entertainment, I take a certain pleasure because a pleasure like this does not take me."

When Ammianus Marcellinus, a veteran soldier and a visitor to Rome, writes of the races and the people in A.D. 359, almost three centuries later, neither has changed.

"These men," writes Ammianus of the common people, "spend their whole lives in drinking, and gambling, and brothels, and pleasures, and the public spectacles; and the Circus Maximus is their temple, their home, their public assembly; in fact, their whole hope and desire. And you may see in the Forum, and roads, and streets, and places of meeting, knots of people collected, quarreling violently with one another, and objecting to one another, and splitting themselves into violent parties. Among whom those who have lived long, having influence by reason of their age, their gray hairs and wrinkles, are constantly crying out that the State cannot stand if in the contest which is about to take place the skillful charioteer whom some individual backs is not foremost in the race, and does not dexterously shave the turning post with the trace-horses. . . . And when the wished-for day of the equestrian games dawns, before the sun has risen, they all rush out with headlong haste, as if with their speed they would outstrip the very chariots which are going to race; while, as to the event of the contest, they are all torn asunder by opposite wishes, and the greater part of them, through their anxiety, pass sleepless nights."

Three centuries and a half before this, Ovid, in Augustan times, was attending the races. In one of the short poems called *Amores*, we find him in the Circus Maximus waiting for the day's events to begin. Chance has given the flirta-

RESTORATION OF A SCENE AT THE RACES

The race is in full career, before the Emperor's box. Three of the seven dolphins are to be seen on the spina. The porta triumphalis is at the farther end, with the Alban Mount fifteen miles beyond.

tious poet a seat beside a nice-looking young lady whom he immediately begins to cultivate.

"I'm not sitting here because I'm interested in famous horses," Ovid says to her, "though I hope the one you bet on will win. I came to talk with you, and to sit by you. You can look at the races, and I'll look at you. Why do you edge away from me? It will do you no good. The line compels us to sit close together. That's the advantage of the circus, with its rules as to space.

"But now the procession is coming. Keep silence all, and attend! Now is the time for applause — the golden procession is coming. First is Victory, coming along with wings outspread. Come here, goddess, and help my love to win! Cheer for Neptune, you who put all your trust in the waves! I want nothing with the sea; my native land for me! Cheer for your Mars, soldier! I detest arms. Peace is what I like, and love that is found in the midst of peace. And Phoebus — let him be for the augurs, and Phoebe for the huntsmen! Minerva — let the craftsmen clap their hands for you! You that live in the country, rise to Ceres and tender Bacchus! Pollux — for the boxers! and Castor — for the rider! But we — we are for you, lovely Venus, for you and your Cupids mighty with the bows! Smile on my undertakings, O goddess, and change my beloved's mind. Make her accept my love!

A CHARIOTEER WITH THE PALM OF VICTORY

His body is protected by a casing of leather.

"But your feet are dangling. If you like, you can stick your toes in the grating. The circus is clear now for the greatest part of the show, and the praetor has started the four-horse cars from the even barrier. I see the one you are eager for. He will win if he has your applause, whoever he is. The very horses seem to know what you want. O dear me, he has circled the post in a wide curve! What are you doing? The next is hugging close with his axle and is gaining on you. What are you doing, you wretch! You will lose my girl the prayer of her heart! Pull, pull, the left rein — with all your might! We are standing for a good-for-nothing! — but call them back, citizens! Toss your togas in signal from every side! Look, they are calling them back.

"The starting chambers are unbarred again and the gates are open wide; the many-colored troop is flying out with reins let loose. This time, at least, get by them, and get down to work on the open space!

"The charioteer has got his palm; my palm is yet to be won."

In the scandalous *Art of Love* also, Ovid includes the races, and in terms much like those we have just read.

> "Thus love in theaters did first improve;
> And theaters are still the scene of love.
> Nor shun the chariots, and the courser's race;
> The Circus is no inconvenient place. . . .
> But boldly next the fair your seat provide;
> Close as you can to hers, and side by side. . . .
> Then find occasion to begin discourse;
> Enquire whose chariot this, and whose that horse.
> To whatsoever side she is inclined,
> Suit all your inclinations to her mind.
> But when the statues of the deities,
> In chariots rolled, appear before the prize,
> When Venus comes, with deep devotion rise.
> If dust be on her lap, or grains of sand,
> Brush both away with your officious hand.
> If none there be, yet brush that nothing thence,
> And still to touch her lap make some pretense. . . .
> Light service takes light minds, for some can tell
> Of favors won by laying cushions well."

XXX

THE GLADIATORS

At mention of the gladiator, no reader or hearer fails to associate with the word the massive building known since the Middle Ages as the Colosseum, and called in Roman times the Amphitheatrum Flavium because it was erected by Vespasian and his son Titus, the first two emperors of the Flavian dynasty, whose third and last reigning member was Domitian.

The Colosseum was opened by Titus in A.D. 80. It was located in the depression between the Palatine, the Esquiline, and the Caelian Hills, and occupied part of the vast area, a mile square, in which Nero had built the combination of palaces, porticoes, gardens, baths, and ponds called *Domus Aurea*, the Golden House. It was elliptical, about 600 feet by 500 in diameter, and 160 feet high, and its arena measured 280 by 175 feet. Its capacity was about 50,000.

The first gladiatorial combats in Rome are said by Livy to have taken place in 264 B.C. They had existed before this in Etruria and Campania, and their origin is to be sought in the funeral customs of the early Mediterranean peoples. Achilles putting Trojan captives to death at the burning of Patroclus' body as a sacrifice to the soul of his friend, suggests the manner of their beginning. If on such an occasion the captives, instead of being slain by their captor, were paired off and permitted to fight for their lives, a triple purpose might be served: the sacrifice to the dead, the addition of an event to the entertainment of the funeral games, and the stimulation of the martial spirit on the part of the spectators, who were almost wholly members, present, past, and future, of the army, the most important part of the State.

The gladiatorial exhibitions at Rome ceased after the first hundred years to have a strict association with funeral games,

THE COLOSSEUM

Mighty as it is, about two-thirds of its bulk has disappeared, much of it in the building of Saint Peter's.

and became the people's most exciting entertainment — "that kind of spectacle," says Cicero, "to which every sort of people crowds in the greatest numbers, and in which the masses find the greatest delight." During the last hundred and fifty years of the Republic, they were given and paid for by men who for the sake of office or other reason were seeking the popular favor. Under the Empire they were one of the emperor's great resources in the conciliation of the people, whether at Rome or in the provinces. They were consequently due throughout to private initiative rather than to the State as such, were given at irregular intervals rather than on fixed dates, and varied greatly in the number of days.

At the first exhibition of gladiators, for the funeral games of Brutus Pera in 264 B.C., there were three pairs, but under the emperors the number might be hundreds or even thousands, in shows lasting for weeks or months. Up to the time of the Colosseum, the permanent amphitheater of Statilius Taurus, erected in 30 B.C., was the usual scene of the shows. Before that, temporary seating in the Forum or elsewhere was provided in case of need.

The best way to appreciate the character and significance of the most notorious of ancient Roman sports is to imagine ourselves attending an afternoon's exhibition. The time may be supposed to be toward the close of the first century after Christ, when the gladiatorial combat was at its highest in skill and popularity.

We have learned of the date of the exhibition and other details through a general announcement, perhaps painted in red letters, like the following from a wall in Pompeii: "Thirty pairs of gladiators furnished by Gnaeus Alleius Nigidius Maius, Quinquennial Duumvir, together with their substitutes, will fight at Pompeii November 24, 25, 26. There will be a hunt. Hurrah for Maius the Quinquennial! Bravo, Paris!" Maius was a rich man of about A.D. 50, and Paris perhaps a gladiator. On another wall appears: "Twenty pairs of gladiators furnished by Decimus Lucretius Satrius Valens, permanent Priest of Nero, son of the Emperor, and ten pairs of gladiators furnished by Decimus

Lucretius Valens his son, will fight at Pompeii April 8–12. There will be a regular hunt, and the awnings. Aemilius Celer wrote this, alone and by the light of the moon." In the first, the substitutes insuring the show, and the wild-beast hunt, *venatio*, are to be noted. In the second, there is a promise of the great canvas awnings to protect the spectators from the sun. Sometimes there are promised also *sparsiones*, sprinklings of saffron water, to modify the heat. Celer is a professional billposter.

The better to follow the events of the day, we have bought and are bringing with us a program containing the names of the swordsmen, their mode of fighting, the number of times they have already fought and won, the name of their patron or owner, and the name of the personage who gives the exhibition. From this program we know whether or not to expect good quality in the fighting, and on it we shall record the score of the day.

Early in the afternoon we find ourselves in one of the eager and talkative human currents flowing from every direction through the various streets that lead to the great building. As we approach the façade, we cast a glance of appreciation on its three stories of travertine arcades, framed in the Doric, Ionic, and Corinthian styles, and the fourth story, still of wood and supporting the sockets for the masts to which the canvas is attached. One of the numerals on our ticket indicates the numbered arch through which we must pass into the two corridors running about the interior in order to reach most conveniently the right one of the many stairways whose zigzagging flights conduct the crowd to the vomitoria, the openings through which the interior of the building is reached. As we suddenly emerge among the countless lines of seats encircling the arena and reaching far above us as well as below, we feel very small. An usher helps us find our section and place, and rents us a cushion to temper the hardness of the marble seat.

After getting settled, we begin to take account of what is before and about us. First, so far below us that we feel dizzy, is the freshly sanded arena. Back of the strong fence separating it from the spectators and protecting them against any possible violence from man or animal in it, is a platform of masonry twelve feet high supporting many splendid seats, all of them like thrones and some of them really thrones. A bronze balustrade borders the side of the arena. Here we shall presently see the emperor and his suite, the chief officials of city and State, including senators, and the many other important personages to be found in a great capital. These are the "boxes" of ancient times.

Separated from these places by balustrade and aisle rises a girdle of thirty-six rows of seats, the first fourteen of which are for the equestrian order and the rest for others distinguished by wealth or station. These thirty-six rows are inclosed by a high wall with doors and windows, back of which is one of the entrance passages encircling the cavea, and above which begins the widest girdle of seats, those for the ordinary crowd. The girdle, including a narrower girdle at its outer edge for women, whose attendance is not encouraged, reaches to the inclosing outer wall of the building at its summit.

Every part of the vast area of seats is rapidly filling. Vociferous conversation, the shouting of vendors, and the flapping of the great stretches of canvas fill the place with a mighty din. The bright light and heat of the day are tempered by the shade of the canvas.

A blare of trumpets and a cheering announce the arrival of the imperial party. The emperor, or other person who gives the entertainment, called the *editor*, is in his place at the most prominent point on the band of seats nearest the arena. He gives the signal, there is the sound of music in marching time, and from one of the four gates leading into the arena comes the procession of those who are to face death for our pleasure, and who quite possibly will be

"Butchered to make a Roman holiday."

As they pass before the emperor, they halt for a moment to address him with the dramatic *morituri te salutant* — "the doomed to die salute thee!" and pass on and out to the chambers in which they are to await the summons to their places on the program.

After a short preliminary with blunt weapons to prepare the performer and the audience for the serious business of the spectacle, the first pair is announced. Perhaps its two fighters are Samnites, the original heavy-armed type in crested helmet and greave for one leg, with oblong shield and short sword. Perhaps they are the light-armed Thracians, with helmet and small round shield, dagger or very short curved sword, and greaves for both legs to make up for the smallness of the shield. Perhaps they are the type called Gauls or *murmillones*, also heavy-armed, or the type in British costume fighting from chariots. Perhaps two different types are matched, as the Samnite and the Thracian; or the fight is by several on a side; or there are the novelties, themselves by this time grown familiar: the *retiarius*, with trident, net, and dagger, against the *secutor*, with shield and sword, whom he tries to envelop and render helpless in the net, and whom in case of failure he has to run from until he is able to recover the net and cast again; or the blindfold with two swords; or the fighters with the lasso; or the dwarf; or even a woman.

The excitement of the crowd rises to wonderful heights,

and sweeps us away with it again and again.   There are some
pairs evenly matched and of extraordinary skill whose dexterity and form arouse frenzied cheering.   They fight to
the draw, and the crowd rewards them at last by approving
their discharge.   A loser suddenly turns what is almost defeat into victory, and the applause is deafening.   Another,

GLADIATORIAL ARMOR
Helmet, shoulder-pieces, leg-protectors.

for some real or fancied fault in form or spirit, is disapproved,
and there is a storm of hostile yells that goes far toward
bringing his defeat.   When at last he is disabled and face
to face with death, his appeal to the giver of the games or
the emperor for mercy is answered by a wave of the hand,
giving over the right of deciding to the populace, who with
shouts of abuse turn their thumbs down.   He stands to the
stroke, collapses on the sand, soaking it with his blood, and

is dragged away through the death-gate. The red spot and red trail are sanded over afresh, and the next pair called.

The vanquished who has been true to form and fought a good fight is recommended to mercy by applause and the waving of handkerchiefs. The spiritless, the unwilling, and the rebellious have sometimes actually to be driven into combat. We hear our neighbors behind talking of one who, while being brought to the amphitheater this very day, feigned drowsiness, and thus let his head be caught in the wheel of the cart and his neck be broken. The crowd at the moment cheers itself hoarse for a favorite; at another, it rages with revilement of a craven or some fighter of no appeal; and at another sinks back in the silence of fatigue or indifference. At the end of each combat we mark the names on our program with a V for "Victor," a P for *Periit*, "Perished," or an M for *Missus*, "Let go." Some spectacles are *sine missione*, and then the fight is always to the death.

When the last match between the swordsmen is finished, there is an interval during which we discuss the events just witnessed, and relax, while the attendants of the amphitheater hurriedly make ready for the *venatio*, the hunt. In this, beasts taken captive in distant parts of the Empire are hoisted in elevators from their dens under the arena, and suddenly released on its sands to face a human enemy who is expert with arrow, spear, or sword, or to fight one another. It may even be that men and women guilty of some crime, or known to be of the Christian faith, will be made to meet unarmed the fiercest animals.

By the time the program is over, the sun is low and the lessened light under the great canvas shows it. The crowd as it slowly disperses through the many exits is much less lively than when it came. Soon the streets of the city are filled by the streams of those returning home, discussing as they go the merits and demerits of the dead and the living who furnished their afternoon's amusement.

The amphitheater was sometimes also the scene of naval combats, though these fights belonged properly to an arti-

A REPRESENTATION OF THE VENATIO

The scene is in the circus, whose parts the sculptor merely indicates: the emperor and empress, or sponsors of the games, in their box; the seven eggs; a column and statue on the spina. A swordsman and a spearman are fighting a tiger and a lion. A man has been killed.

ficial lake, called *naumachia* after the name of the battle itself. Such an exhibition could hardly have taken place in the Colosseum except before the many rooms, dens, and passages were constructed under the arena.

Such were the sports of the arena in the capital and in almost every city of size in the central and western Medi-

terranean basin.   There are notable specimens of the amphitheater still to be seen in Verona, Capua, Pompeii, and
Pozzuoli; in Arles, Nîmes, and Bordeaux, in France; at
Cagliari in Sardinia, at Pola and Spalato on the east side of
the Adriatic, at Italica near Seville, in Spain, and at El
Djem in Africa, where the fifth in size of these buildings
overshadows a whole Tunisian village; to say nothing of
many smaller ruins.   The amphitheater in Verona is still
used for concert and drama, and those at Arles and Nîmes
for the bullfight.

When we contemplate the number of the amphitheaters
in the Roman world, and remember the ten thousand gladiators who fought in the exhibitions of Augustus alone, the ten
thousand who fought in four months at Trajan's celebrations
of the conquest of Dacia, and the numerous hardly less extensive shows that took place in the capital under every
reign until the sport declined and died in the fifth century,
we are compelled to charge ancient Roman society with a
monstrous aggregate of heartless cruelty.   However, before
concluding that the amphitheater and its sports were due
simply and only to the lust for bloodshed, we should consider
the gladiatorial combat in all its aspects.   Let us summarize.

First, let us recall its origin in the natural hardness of
primitive Mediterranean peoples whose normal condition
was warfare, and who believed in the propitiation of the dead
by the sacrifice of their enemies at the tomb.

Let us recall in the next place that in warring civilizations
hardness as well as courage and skill in the practice of arms
is a virtue, and that gentleness and compassion are qualities
dangerous to the State.   When the gladiatorial combat was
introduced at Rome, the Romans had been a warring race
for five hundred years, and were to continue a warring race
until the times of the Empire and the Pax Romana, two

hundred and fifty years afterward. The spectacle of men
expert in the use of arms, self-possessed in the moment of
mortal danger, and unflinching before the final stroke, could
easily be regarded as a contribution to the soldierly expert-

THE INTERIOR OF THE COLOSSEUM TO-DAY

Only a small part of the arena has been left by the excavators, who have exposed
the corridors, chambers, cages, and elevator arrangements below it. The bases of
the imperial and senatorial boxes are seen bordering the arena. They are encircled
by the substructures that supported the other banks of seats.

ness and soldierly spirit of every man of military age and
every youthful legionary-to-be who witnessed it.

In the third place, it is to be remembered that the amphitheater served the State at least in part as a means of
criminal discipline. Many of the fighters were noncitizen
malefactors condemned for the more outrageous crimes, and

given this chance of redeeming their lives by prowess in arms or by the appeal of personal quality to the emperor and the multitude. "Sentenced to the arena" was no doubt a familiar phrase in the courts of the Roman Empire; the more desperate and the more unfit being sent to the lions, and those of better physical quality to the training schools to be made ready for combat with their kind.

In the fourth place, there was the element of sportsmanship. The captive in war might easily prefer the chance of victory and freedom to the certainty of sale into lifelong slavery in the mines or galleys or on the distant plantations. The man who had won safety and freedom might easily be attracted by the glamour of applause and by genuine love for the excitement of the life to continue as fighter or trainer. The enthusiastic populace admired the good sportsman and the good fellow, and many a man who was intimate with sporting circles was drawn by sheer coveting of notoriety into the gladiatorial career. To be the victor in a hundred combats, the champion confident against all comers, to feel the admiration of fifty thousand glowing pairs of eyes, to hear the applause of fifty thousand straining throats and fifty thousand pairs of clapping hands, to look up and around at the waving of fifty thousand fluttering handkerchiefs and scarfs and togas, to be aware, and perhaps even to be careless, of the eager good will of senator and magnate and emperor, could carry the gladiator as well as the charioteer, in Horace's phrase, "as lord of the earth to the gods above." And there were also the humbler but not unappreciated favors. Celadus, in Pompeii, is the "glory" and the "sigh" of the girls, *puellarum decus, suspirium puellarum;* and Crescens is their adored, *puparum dominus.* That there were rewards in money as well as in fame, it is hardly necessary to remark.

But these considerations, while they may explain how the gladiatorial combat originated, how its introduction among the Romans could be tolerated, and how it might justify itself to a degree in the minds of its defenders, do not wholly account for its lodgment in Roman society as an institution, and its becoming one of the two greatest holiday amusements of a world at peace and a State no longer in fear of enemies or depending upon the skill and valor of the citizen-soldier. There are two reasons for its growth and permanence which have nothing to do with religious belief, the military spirit, or sportsmanship, but which are grounded in its use as an instrument for other ends.

The first of these reasons was the usefulness of the gladiatorial combat as a political and personal instrument. By the time of Cicero and Caesar, it was frequent for men who stood for office to outbid one another in courting the people by means of gladiatorial shows. Not only did the gladiators exhibit themselves in the service of their candidate patron, but accompanied him as a bodyguard, and did not hesitate to commit disorderly and violent acts in the streets at his command. The letters of Cicero contain many references to the high-handed behavior of the bands of gladiators and other roughs employed by Clodius and Milo during the quarrels that resulted in the death of Clodius in 52 B.C. The Senate was so uneasy because of Caesar's plans for exhibitions in the campaign for the aedileship in 65 B.C. that it limited him to three hundred and twenty pairs. One of Cicero's vexations during his governorship in Cilicia was the insistence of his young friend Caelius Rufus, curule aedile, on Cicero's shipping him panthers. Patiscus has sent Curio ten, and Cicero should send Caelius ten times as many. As for the emperors, good and bad, there was no limit to their giving of gladiatorial shows, whether for the sake of personal glory or for the sake of keeping their subjects contented. At the dedication of the Colosseum in A.D. 80, Titus provided gladiators and five thousand beasts. In A.D. 249, Philip celebrated the thousandth anniversary of Rome by providing a thousand pairs of gladiators, thirty-two elephants, ten tigers, sixty lions, thirty leopards, ten hyenas, ten giraffes, twenty wild asses, forty wild horses; ten zebras, six hippopotami, and one rhinoceros. Probus in A.D. 281 provided one hundred each of lions and leopards from Libya and Syria, three hundred bears, and one hundred African lionesses.

The second cause for the tenacious hold of the amphitheatrical sports was their utilization for commercial purposes. Like many abuses, ancient and modern, they paid. The day that politicians began to see in him an advantage, the training and furnishing of the gladiator was already on the way to becoming an industry. The industry soon had its contractors, barracks, trainers, agents, and recruiters. The erection of the first amphitheater, the kindred sports of the naval battle and the animal hunt, the arrival of the imperial régime with its increase in the demand for men and beasts, the building of the Colosseum, the solicitude of the ruler for the popular good will, all went toward the firmer lodgment of the deadly sport in the life of the Empire and its capital. Its abuses were terrible. They included the slaughter of the captive and the criminal for the entertainment of an idle multitude already surfeited with blood; the wrongful condemnation of the unfortunate and friendless who were guilty at most of only minor crimes, the impressment of the innocent but helpless, the compulsion of the slave, all in the desperate search for human material to supply the demand of the shows and keep them interesting; the breeding of cruel indifference to suffering; the encouragement of gambling and of all the triviality and waste and degradation that associate themselves with a brutal sport; the corruption of politics; the arming of a dangerous and unscrupulous class of men; and, not least, the glorification of wrong ideals and the obscuration of the right in the minds of the rising generation.

THE AMPHITHEATER AT VERONA
Concerts and opera in the grand style are given here every summer.

Of course there were persons not attracted by the amphitheater, and there were those who rose above it. There was Cicero, who wrote to his friend Marius in Pompeii concerning the sports he missed by being away from Rome: "Why should I think you regretted missing the athletes, you who despised the gladiators? . . . And I must tell you, lastly, about the beast-hunts — two a day for five days;

magnificent, no one denies. But what pleasure can it be to
a man of cultivation when either a poor, weak human being
is torn by a most powerful beast, or a splendid beast is run
through with a hunting spear? If these things are to be
seen, after all you have seen them many a time ; and I, who
was there to see, saw nothing new. Last came the day of the
elephants, by which the ordinary crowd was greatly im-
pressed, but without showing any pleasure. Quite the contrary, a certain pity was aroused, a kind of feeling that the
big beast was kin in some way to the human race." Not
only does Cicero here speak of Marius as despising the
gladiators, but shows repeatedly in the *Orations* by contemp-
tuous allusions to the gladiator that he assumes on the part
of Senate and jury and people the same feeling he entertains
himself.

Yet the fairly human Younger Pliny can praise his friend
Maximus for promising the people of Verona a gladiatorial
exhibition, and can commend the act as a suitable honor to
the memory of his dead wife. The literature of pagan Rome
is practically without protest against the amphitheater.
The average Roman took it for granted, and the remon-
strances of those who did not were ridiculed, or drowned in
counter protest, or went unnoticed. The numbers and the
argument of those who admired the fight as a science and the
spectacle as an art, who wanted excitement as an escape
from the monotony of life, who saw no use in opposing what
seemed the natural and inevitable thing, who profited
directly by contract or indirectly by the trade of the crowd,
who argued that the shows increased the business of the city
and the unity of the Empire, were overwhelming.

It took three centuries and a half of the growth of the
Christian spirit, and almost as long a period of general worldly
decay, to accomplish the extinction of the bloodiest of

sports. The last gladiatorial fight in the Flavian Amphitheater in Rome took place in A.D. 404, the last known wildbeast hunt in A.D. 523. The great building began at that time the career of ruin by earthquake, natural decay, and the hand of man which converted it into a quarry for the building of medieval and Renaissance Rome and left it only a third of its former self before the sentiment of modern times was aroused to protect it.

The Colosseum is the ruined and empty monument to an unlovely phase of the life of ancient Rome. The deadly swordsmanship that soaked and stained its yellow sands with crimson no longer ministers to the curiosity, the love of excitement, and the greed of men. Yet let those who gaze upon it as belonging wholly to the past reflect upon the many features the life it represents has in common with the life of modern times, and upon the mingling of the good and the evil, the beautiful and the ugly, the logical and the illogical, that is always present in human behavior. Let them think of the American national game, its excitements, its accidents, its scandals, its raging crowds, its heroes and their salaries, its vested interests. Let them think of the Spanish national sport, with its golden sands and bright-hued crowd, its brilliant processions, its dexterity and its art, its perils and its gallantries, its idolized and princely *matadores*, its amphitheater in every town, its scientific breeding and training farms, its frenzied applause and its heartless derision, its cruelty to horses, its Sunday and saint's-day performances, its heedlessness of protest, its permeation of every mind. Let them think of the chase and the coursing of hare and hounds. Let them think of the glittering and flattering splendors of the cinema palace, its cheap and coarse crowds, its capable and unscrupulous managers, its boastfully expensive and coarsening pictures, its pretentions to virtue as educator and moralist, its undisguisable commercialism, its enthusiastic defenders and its bitter enemies, and the thousand economic ramifications that invest it with permanence. Let them think of student athletics, the million-dollar stadium, the dependence of the college upon the winning team, the corruptions and hypocrisies of recruiting and retaining the champion, the interest of the college in the gate receipts, the interest of the community in the money-spending crowd, the tyrannies of training, the farce of the study requirement for men whose time and strength and attention are demanded first of all by the game, the general debauchery of mind and tongue as the time for the contest approaches, the mob of the old grads returning to see the team cover itself and Alma Mater with glory, the betting and the extortion, the frenzied silliness of cheer-leader and rooter "helping to win the game," the mingling of brawn and brains in the bruising, crushing, desperate effort to get through, the jeers and insults and threats and abuse for referee or player or rooter, the pandemonium of exit, the "good time" of the evening and night, the apathy and languor of the days that follow, the assumption that without it all the college would go to ruin. Let them think, finally, of pugilism: of the genius employed in its management and advertising, of racial and class feeling sweeping over the country and over other countries, of its gigantic crowds and its admission charges in the grand style, of its betting, of the mingled curses and prayers and exhortations yelled at the ringside, of the delirium of applause at the sight of the successful blow and at the sight of blood, of the willingness for death itself rather than the defeat of the favorite and the loss of stakes, of the prizes in money and fame that come to the winner, of the thousands of smaller champions and the cliques that center about them, of the promoters who ex-

ploit them, of the wholesale conversion of society to toleration by the astute advertising of the scientific side of the
"art of self-defense" and the ignoring of its brutal side.

Reflections like these, with the comparisons they suggest,
may quite properly leave us unshaken in the conviction
of the gains humanity has made since the amphitheater
saw its cruel killings, but they will not leave us quite so sure
that the dead and empty ruins are all that survive in modern
society of the ancient life they represent.

XXXI

THE BATHS

There exists to-day no exact equivalent of either the ancient Roman baths or the ancient Roman custom of the bath. The word to-day denotes, in the singular, merely an act of cleanliness; in the plural, a health resort with springs having curative properties, or a thermal establishment for the treatment of the ailing. There are hot baths, sulphur baths, mud baths, Turkish baths. To think of the Roman baths, *balnea, thermae,* in any such way would be to see only part of the truth.

The description of an ancient example of the baths will make clear both the building and its uses. Let us take for the purpose the baths of the Emperor Diocletian, the huge remnants of which are still to be seen as one comes from the railway station in the northeast part of Rome. These baths, opened in A.D. 306 after the abdication of the Emperor, were the largest in the Roman Empire and the last but one to be erected in Rome. They differed from the baths in Rome and Pompeii of three hundred years before in size and appointments, but not in essential characteristics.

The Baths of Diocletian measured about four hundred and fifty yards, or a quarter of a mile, on a side. The establishment consisted of an inclosing wall of concrete faced with brick and probably covered with stucco. At two corners of this girdle were two large circular chambers with solid brick walls, flanked each by a rectangular room, and between them the girdle wall projected in a semicircle. One of the dome-

352

like chambers is now the round church of San Bernardo, and
the other also has a modern use. The limit of the semicircle of wall is preserved in the curved façades of the build-

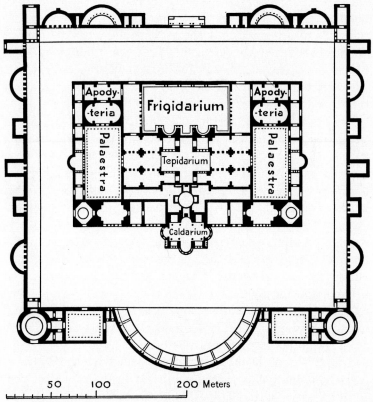

PLAN OF THE BATHS OF DIOCLETIAN

ings fronting the Piazza dell' Esedra. On the remaining
three sides the wall accommodated smaller semicircular and
rectangular rooms.

Inside the inclosure, the bather found himself facing the
building proper, which was surrounded by a spacious

promenade, and arcaded in two stories in the Ionic and
Corinthian styles. It measured about 300 yards by 175, and
contained the three essential parts of the Roman baths.
These were the *frigidarium*, or cold bath; the *caldarium*, or
hot bath; and the *tepidarium*, or tepid bath. The caldarium has disappeared, but the tepidarium, over 200 feet by
80, has been since Michelangelo's time the transept of Santa
Maria degli Angeli, one of the largest churches of Rome.
The vestibule of the church is an ancient circular chamber
that stood between the caldarium and the tepidarium.

Besides these three regular chambers, the largest of which
was three hundred feet long, there were the usual dressing
rooms, *apodyteria*, the open-air porticoes for games and other
physical exercise, *palaestrae*, and many smaller chambers for
a variety of uses — libraries of Greek and Latin once housed
in the Forum of Trajan; lecture halls and lounges; additional baths and gymnasiums and dressing rooms; store-
rooms for the usual bath supplies of towels, perfumes,
unguents, and strigils for the removal of oil and sand;
offices for the stewards; rooms for the attendants and
helpers, waiting rooms for the slaves and sedan-chair men;
refreshment rooms, and perhaps quarters for masseurs and
medical advisers. The large semicircular space now forming
the Piazza dell' Esedra was used as a theater.

The Baths of Diocletian were supplied by the Marcian
Aqueduct, built 400 years before and bringing water from
57 miles away in the Sabine Mountains. Accumulated outside the establishment in a capacious reservoir 300 feet long
and 50 wide, the water was distributed through larger and
smaller pipes to all the tanks and pools and tubs and jets
with which the chambers were supplied. The cold, hot,
and tepid rooms had tanks at ends and sides and probably
pools in immense round basins of marble and granite sup-

ported on bases at convenient places on the pavement. There were large tanks for plunging, smaller ones for quieter bathing, many individual baths in the smaller rooms, and many portable tubs for use on the larger floors. The main pool in the frigidarium of Caracalla's baths, built ninety years earlier, was about 80 by 170 feet. The exercise porticoes were also supplied with convenient plunges.

The air and water varied in temperature in the three main parts of the building. The caldarium walls were lined with hot-air ducts of tile behind the stucco and near the surface, the tepidarium walls were constructed in the same way but with the ducts set deeper so that the heat was slower, and the frigidarium was left unheated. The caldarium was further heated by hot air circulating under the floor, which was supported by many slender brick pillars.

This slow but even and sensible method of heating is employed in the American Episcopal Church in Rome and in one of the churches in Liverpool. Instead of streaming through registers or rising from radiators to the ceiling, the heat begins in the pavement and permeates directly the total volume of air.

The graded heating of the water for the caldarium and the tepidarium was provided by placing the furnace nearer the former. In earlier and smaller establishments, the air was sometimes tempered by a large brazier, such as survives in Pompeii, though the hanging floor was invented a hundred years before Christ, and the heating of the walls soon followed.

The opening of the baths in Rome was fixed in Hadrian's time at two o'clock, but varied according to period, place, and circumstance. The manner of their use varied also. Earlier or later in the day, according to the hour at which his business left him free, the bather appeared, alone or attended by a slave with the necessary towels and other articles. If he was vigorous and had the serious purpose of keeping fit, he began in the palaestra with bowling or ball, or other more or less strenuous exercise; then stripped in the dressing room and was given a rub with perfumed oil, or, if he had

THE CALDARIUM OF THE STABIAN BATHS IN POMPEII

The little brick pillars by which the floor was supported are seen partly restored in the foreground. Some of the floor with the pillars entire occupies the background. Hot air circulated under the floor thus suspended.

stripped for the exercise, was relieved of the dirt and oil by the use of the strigil; went into the tepid room for a first bath; took a sweat and a second bath in the hot room; finished with a cold plunge and a rub, dressed, and was ready for other recreation or for dinner. If he had no settled program, he might make the operation short by exercising, using the strigil, rubbing, taking a cold plunge, and dressing; or might prolong it in any way his fancy prompted.

Not every patron of the baths came to them for the same purpose. There were those who came for mere cleanliness, and there were those who came for the recreation of a tired body. There were those who came for the relief of ailments, and those who came as a preparation for dinner. Some came to enjoy the luxury of being worked over and to see who else was there. There were some who had appointments, social or business or literary. Sometimes, according to the satirists, the poet was there, reciting his verses in the midst of the defenseless bathers. "How pleasantly the vaulted space echoes the voice!" he says to himself in Horace.

Such was the building that housed the ancient Roman baths, and such was the institution of the baths. Like other institutions, it was a growth. It began in rustic Latium with the ordinary custom of country people, a daily washing of the dirt from hands and face and feet, and at intervals a wash all over. With the growth of the city and development of urban tastes, the richer, the cultivated, and the traveled not only bathed every day, but made the daily bath the correct thing socially. The homes of the wealthier included ever more elaborate baths, and the growth of demand among the less wealthy of the middle class soon brought into being the public bath. Its attractions were increased first by the addition of conveniences to the bath itself, and then by the addition of hygienic, medical, and athletic features. The bath became not only a social requisite, but a cure and a recreation. With the addition of other facilities, such as lounges, lecture rooms, reading rooms, and porticoes for games and promenades, it became an amusement and a luxury. For the classes of highest rank and greatest wealth, it became the usual preliminary to dining. With the expansion of the Empire, the general increase of prosperity, and the rise of standards of living, the numbers of the common people who used the baths increased throughout the Roman world, but especially in the capital. Not only did contractors build them as an investment, but the ambitious, the patriotic, the philanthropic, the public-spirited citizen, and, above all, the benevolent or anxious emperors, provided the means for their erection; and many were built at the public expense. They were rarely free of charge, but prices were scaled in such a way that none but the absolutely penniless were denied the pleasure; and there were times when some one's generosity removed the fee entirely.

The number, size, and splendor of the great bathing

A RESTORATION OF THE INTERIOR OF CARACALLA'S BATHS

This may represent the tepidarium. Fountains, plunges, pools, and basins were conveniently distributed.

resorts in the city of Rome is an impressive testimonial to the prominence of the bath in ancient life. The list of the major establishments includes the baths of Agrippa, opened in 19 B.C. near the Pantheon; of Nero, A.D. 64, in the same neighborhood; of Titus, A.D. 80, near the Colosseum; of Trajan, some time in A.D. 98–117, also near the Colosseum; of Sura, a friend of Trajan, on the Aventine; of Commodus,

who reigned A.D. 180–193, on the Caelian; of Septimius
Severus, A.D. 193–211, on the Caelian; of Caracalla, in
A.D. 216, south of the Palatine; of Alexander Severus, who
in A.D. 228 rebuilt the baths of Nero; of Decius, in A.D 250,
on the Aventine; of Diocletian, in A.D. 306, on the farther

A FRAGMENT OF THE BATHS OF DIOCLETIAN

This is the first prominent fragment of ancient Rome to be seen by the visitor
emerging from the railway station.

Quirinal and Viminal; of Helena, mother of Constantine,
on the farther Esquiline near the present Church of Santa
Croce; of Constantine, A.D. 312–337, on the sloping end of
the Quirinal.

Most of these establishments were still in existence, and
many of them in use, when the last was built. The Baths
of Diocletian had a capacity of three thousand; the Baths

of Caracalla, sixteen hundred. They were solidly built in concrete faced with brick, and splendid with stucco and marble veneering and decoration, with paneled vaultings and ceilings in gilt and color, polished walls, and brilliant floors in mosaic. Many were rich in sculptural pieces. The Farnese Bull and the Farnese Hercules were among the finds in the ruins of Caracalla's baths; the Laocoön was discovered in the Baths of Trajan. Both these establishments are still represented by monster ruins, and many of the others exist in considerable fragments. Nothing is more familiar on the many sites of ancient Roman towns in remotest parts of Europe and Africa than the great heaps of ruined concrete walls and vaults, long ago collapsed, that bring us witness of the most universal and the least vicious luxury of Roman civilization.

And yet these ruins of major establishments do not represent the whole truth. We are told that the generosity of Agrippa in 33 B.C. provided for free bathing in a hundred and seventy establishments in Rome. These places have left no name, and there were others like them in every city, large and small. A nameless village near Pliny's Laurentine estate had three public baths.

There were also, in places widely scattered over the Roman world, the curative baths that were visited principally by those in search of health — the sulphur baths still used at Bagni, near Tivoli; the baths at Aquisgranum, now Aix; at Aquae Aureliae, now Baden-Baden; at Bath in England. These do not properly concern us here.

The ancient baths were thus far more than the means of cleanliness. They were that, but they were also hygienic, pathological, recreational, athletic, social, intellectual, cultural. They were the ancient city club, Y. M. C. A., golf, community center, gymnasium, playground, amusement

park, beauty parlor, business men's rendezvous, country
sojourn, and bathing beach.   They were warm and comfort-
ing in winter; in summer they were thronged with seekers
for relief from heat and fatigue.   The modern Roman in the
dog days goes in thirty minutes by huge electric trainloads to
the beach at Ostia, twenty miles away, cools himself in the
sea and toasts himself on the sands, meets friends, indulges

BATH RUINS AT CARTHAGE
One of the many giant remnants of the baths found everywhere in Roman territory.

mildly in the less wholesome diversions of the beach resort,
and returns to his home refreshed if not unfatigued in the
incomparable cool of the Roman summer evening.   The
tired business man of ancient Rome was at least two hours
from the sea, but he had the baths at his door.

It remains to enliven our imagination of the Roman bath
by letting a Roman himself discuss the subject.   Let us look

over the philosopher Seneca's shoulder as he writes, not many years before his death in A.D. 65, to his friend Lucilius. Directly and indirectly, he will tell us interesting things.

"Hang me if silence is as necessary as people believe to a man who has shut himself away to study. Here I am, with all kinds of noises sounding from every side. I am in lodgings right over a bath. Imagine for yourself now every manner of noise that can be hateful to the ear. When the more strenuous are going through their exercises, swinging their hands heavy with weights of lead and either putting lots of muscle into it or making believe they do, I can hear their gruntings as they hold in and then let out their breath, and then their wheezy and labored blowing. And when it is my luck for the fellow to be one of the lazy sort who is satisfied with just a nobody's rubbing down, I hear the smack of the hand as it crashes on to his shoulders, varying in sound according as it comes down flat or hollowed. But if one of your ball-scorers happens along and begins to keep count of the balls, it's the finishing touch. Then add the tough, and the thief caught in the act, and the fellow who enjoys the sound of his own voice in the bath; and then add to them the fellows who jump into the tank and hit the water with a mighty splash. Besides these, whose voices, if nothing else, you can't object to, think of the hair-plucker continually squeezing out his thin, scratchy voice in order to get himself noticed, and never stopping his noise except when he is jerking the hairs from someone's armpits and making him yell instead. And then there is the cake-seller and his various cries, and the sausage man, and the pastryman, and the whole tribe of vendors from the cookshops, everyone hawking his wares in his own particular tune. . . . Yet I swear to you that this racket bothers me no more than the waves of the sea or a waterfall."

Again, Seneca writes of a visit to the country estate of Scipio Africanus at Liternum in Campania, north of Naples. The name Villa Literno has been given to a station in the neighborhood on the new line from Rome to Naples via Formia.

"I am resting at the country house which once belonged to Scipio Africanus himself. . . . I have inspected the house, which is constructed of hewn stone; the wall, which encloses a grove; the towers also, buttressed out on both sides for the purpose of defending the house; the well, concealed among buildings and shrubbery, large enough to keep a whole army supplied; and the little bath, buried in darkness according to the old style, for our ancestors did not think that one could have a hot bath except in the dark. It was therefore a great pleasure to me to contrast Scipio's ways with our own. Think, in this tiny recess the 'terror of Carthage,' to whom Rome owes thanks that she has been captured but once, used to bathe a body wearied with work in the fields! For he was accustomed to keep himself busy and to cultivate the soil with his own hands, as the good old Romans were wont to do. Beneath this dingy roof he stood; and this floor, mean as it is, bore his weight.

"But who in these days could bear to bathe in such a fashion? We think ourselves poor and mean if our walls are not resplendent with large and costly mirrors; if our marbles from Alexandria are not set off by mosaics of Numidian stone, if their borders are not faced over on all sides with difficult patterns, arranged in many colors like paintings; if our vaulted ceilings are not buried in glass; if our swimming pools are not lined with Thasian marble, once a rare and wonderful sight in any temple — pools into which we let down our bodies after they have been drained weak by abundant perspiration; and finally, if the water has not poured from silver spigots.

"I have so far been speaking of the ordinary bathing establishments. What shall I say when I come to those of the freedmen? What a vast number of statues, of columns that support nothing, but are built for decoration, merely in order to spend money! And what masses of water that fall crashing from level to level! We have become so luxurious that we will have nothing but precious stones to walk upon.

"In this bath of Scipio's there are tiny chinks — you cannot call them windows — cut out of the stone wall in such a way as to admit light without weakening the building; nowadays, however, people regard baths as fit only for moths if they have not been so arranged that they receive the sun all day long through the widest of windows, if men cannot bathe and get a coat of tan at the same time, and if they cannot look out from their bath tubs over stretches of land and sea. So it goes; the establishments which had drawn crowds and had won admiration when they were first opened are avoided and put back in the category of venerable antiques as soon as luxury has worked out some new device, to her own ultimate undoing.

"In the early days, however, there were few baths, and they were not fitted out with any display. For why should men elaborately fit out that which costs a penny only, and was invented for use, not merely for delight? The bathers of those days did not have water poured over them, nor did it always run fresh as if from a hot spring; and they did not believe that it mattered at all how perfectly pure was the water into which they were to leave their dirt. Ye gods, what a pleasure it was to enter those dim baths, covered with a common sort of roof, knowing that therein your hero Cato, as aedile, or Fabius Maximus, or one of the Cornelii, had tempered the water with his own hand! For this also used to be the duty of the noblest aediles — to enter these places to which the populace resorted, and to demand that they be cleaned and warmed to a heat required by considerations of use and health, not the heat that men have recently made fashionable, as great as a conflagration — so much so, indeed, that a slave condemned for some criminal offense now ought to be *bathed* alive! It seems to me that nowadays there is no difference between 'the bath is on fire,' and 'the bath is warm.'

"How some persons nowadays condemn Scipio as a boor because he did not let daylight into his perspiring-room through wide windows, or because he did not roast in the strong sunlight and dawdle about until he could stew in the hot water! 'Poor fool,' they say, 'he did not know how to live! He did not bathe in filtered water; it was often turbid, and after heavy rains almost muddy!' But it did not matter much to Scipio if he had to bathe in that way; he went there to wash off sweat, not ointment. And how do you suppose certain persons will answer me? They will say: 'I don't envy Scipio; that was truly an exile's life — to put up with baths like those.' Friend, if you were wiser, you would know that Scipio did not bathe every day. It is stated by those who have reported to us the old-time ways of Rome that the Romans washed only their arms and legs daily — because those were the members which gathered dirt in their daily toil — and bathed all over only once a week. Here someone will retort: 'Yes; pretty dirty fellows they evidently were! How they must have smelled.' But they smelled of the camp, the farm, and heroism. Now that spick-and-span bathing establishments have been devised, men are really fouler than of yore. What says Horatius Flaccus, when he wishes to describe a scoundrel, one who is notorious for his extreme luxury? He says, 'Bucillus smells of perfume.'"

XXXII

IN LIGHTER VEIN

We have been acquainting ourselves with what may be called Roman amusements in the grand style. The theater, the circus, the amphitheater, and the baths were four great public institutions involving vast outlay and patronized by the citizenry in masses.

If we were to stop here, we should know less intimately than is desirable the human side of the ancient Roman. While all these amusements represent the use he made of his leisure time, and while the drama and the diversions of the baths did not quite so completely as amphitheater and circus force the surrender of his own self to the self of the crowd, all four were collective or mass amusements, and in all four the individual was absorbed or at least obscured by the multitude. If we are to know the Roman personally, we must follow him away from the excitement of the crowd. We must see what he does in smaller groups, in his family and among his friends, and how he acts and what he enjoys when by himself and choosing for himself. Was he a lively person? Would he have been a pleasant person to meet?

This is a difficult undertaking. The last thing we are able to appreciate in another race than our own, excepting religion, is its play of spirit. The Romans are alien to us not only in race but in space and time. Their painting is almost entirely lost, and their sculpture is in fragments, and art, besides, does not usually deal with life in its common moments. Their literature was not so easily published as

A Restoration of the Lower Campus Martius from the Capitoline Hill

Right to left: Theater of Pompey with Temple of Venus, Circus Flaminius; Theater of Balbus; Portico of Octavia, inclosing two temples; Tiber Island with obelisk and Temple of Aesculapius. Beyond the Tiber is the Janiculum, with the Wall of Aurelian leading to and inclosing it.

ours, and consequently was compressed and almost wholly of the serious type; and time has made it more serious by selection. We shall have to look between the lines, and we shall have to argue back from our own times, remembering that much in human life is constant.

Let us begin by saying that the great formal public amusements were not the only diversions which were patronized. The State theaters, for example, were no more alone in Rome than the first-class theaters are the only places with stage entertainment in a modern capital. Those for whom the stately adaptations of Greek tragedy were a bore, and who found even the comedies of Plautus and Terence demanding an amount of good will, went elsewhere for their dramatics. They went to some nameless place where they were really made to laugh by a farce, or a mime, or perhaps the marionettes, or where they were entertained by a serious play that reflected back to them their own life, and was adapted to their own intelligence, which was none too profound, and to their own taste, which was none too refined. Perhaps they went to an eating or drinking place, to chat over plate or cup as they heard a lively song or looked on at a lively dancer, of course from Greece or at least with a Greek name; or to some variety hall, with acrobats and sword-dancers, mountebanks and sleight-of-hand artists, tight-rope walkers and performing bears.

But these are more or less formal pleasures, and still in the class of public amusements. There were the entirely informal and unbought pleasures also that belong to any city and any age. There were the brilliant porticoes of the rich business section to walk and talk in, resembling somewhat the elegant glass-vaulted galleries of Naples and Milan to-day. There were the many gardens or parks in and on the skirts of the city, landscaped or natural, the gifts and bequests of

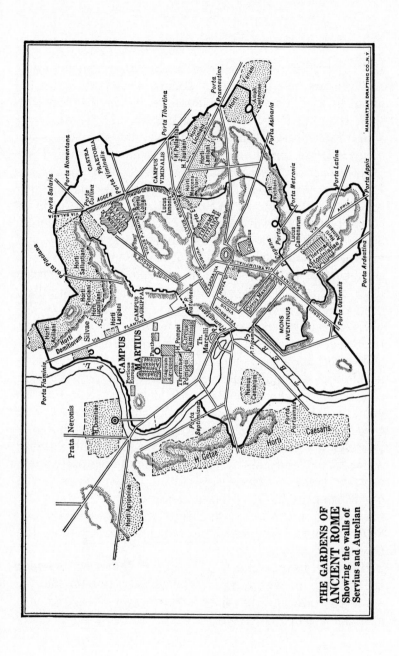

THE GARDENS OF
ANCIENT ROME
Showing the walls of
Servius and Aurelian

wealthy citizen and emperor, with shrubbery and fountains and vendors and refreshment stands, and children darting about in their play while their nurses and mothers sat with their spinning and knitting. There was the Tiber, along whose banks it was pleasant to walk, and there was the promenade on the sunny embankment, *agger*, mentioned by Horace, once the fortification of Servius Tullius crossing the Esquiline. There were the pleasures of eating and drinking, whether on the sidewalk in front of the restaurant, or in its room or little open-air garden, or at home with the family. There was dining in a friend's garden under huge pine and white poplar mingling their branches above the grass and shrubbery and streamlets, or in splendid halls with mosaic floors and painted walls and coffered ceilings and tall pillars of the world's richest marbles. There were visits to the villas or country houses, plain or magnificent according to the owner's fortune or position. There were genial meetings of the accidental sort, and all the pleasant contacts of a people moving in the open air of mild winters and fervid summers. There were window and balcony to lean from as you talked with neighbors across the court or alley. You came upon your friends in the evening sitting at their doors, or walking in the street or public garden, at the running water of the fountain or hydrant, filling the big bronze jars to carry home on their heads, sitting at the games or the play, riding in their carriages, doing their daily shopping, hurrying to the baths, going their way to the office and the day's business. You asked and were asked many times the news.

Here we have come to a striking difference between ancient and modern times. The ancient Roman had no newspaper beyond the scant and scantily circulated *acta diurna*, or daily Government news. He had no printing press, no daily papers, no magazines, no picture news, no comic journals, no comic strips, no advertising worth the mention. Books were published, and published in quantity, but they were not in any large quantity fiction, they were not trifling, and they were not written for and not read by

A MODERN ROMAN PUBLIC GARDEN
The Laghetto of the Villa Borghese. The ancient gardens must be imagined as equally charming.

the common man, and not by many women and girls. There was a cultivated class which read and wrote, and the proportion formed by those who read with real thoroughness and wrote with distinction was probably greater than in our own day of quantitative reading and writing; but outside of these there was no great population reading for news and general information, culture, and entertainment. With the vast majority, the tongue and the ear, and not the page, were the medium of communication with the world of fact, thought, and sentiment. The spoken word was all-important in the average life, as indeed it continued to be until a century ago, when the printed message really began to reach the masses, and as it continues to a great extent to-day in lands too poor, too wise, or too distrustful to attempt the education of the masses.

Let it not be too hastily concluded, however, that the ancient Roman dependence upon tongue and ear was a total disadvantage, either for knowledge or happiness. The Mediterranean lands are open-air countries, invite the contact of man with man, and afford the maximum natural encouragement of speech in public and private; the person who talks and listens much, and hears and expresses again and again, is likely both to accumulate much practical knowledge and to have many definite ideas; and it requires nothing profounder than a little observation to be convinced that the human being is never better entertained than when he is talking. To the eye at least, and probably in reality, the happiest part of Rome to-day is the Trastevere, where the printed page has little to do with life, and all the waking minutes in the glowing Roman summer not given to work are spent in walking and sitting and talking in the streets and squares.

If we inquire next what minor diversions the Roman engaged in, such as our cards and other social games, we find little to note. There were the dice, of ivory, stone, or wood; there were *tali*, originally the knuckle or ankle bones of sheep or goats, but made too of ivory and other material, which served the children as jackstones and were used also like dice; there were flipping and matching of coins; there was gambling by means of these games and others, and there were the usual more or less unsuccessful attempts of law to stop it. There were no card parties, though it seems impossible that there were no card games; there were, so far as can be known, no boy-and-girl or men-and-women parties, no teas, no smokers, no social dancing of our sort. The

CHILDREN'S GAMES IN A SARCOPHAGUS RELIEF

Three games are shown: at the left, a "marble" game with nuts; in the center, two boys strike the holder of a rope until he catches them; at the right, nuts or balls are rolled down an incline.

dancing of antiquity, so far as amusement was concerned, was likely to be either the simple folk-dancing of the villagers or the professional dancing of the stage. In the latter, no citizen could participate without loss of respect. With the richer classes, the formal dinner seems to have occupied the place of all these; with the less wealthy and the poor, less formal dinners and informal family gatherings. With the middle and lower classes in general, there was no doubt frequent exchange of visits. The modern Roman fondness for little dining excursions to simple garden restaurants outside the city gates is not unlikely to have existed in ancient times.

In the realm of physical diversion, the differences are somewhat less pronounced, and are quite as easily explained.

The Roman children indeed seem to have been like other children, though they do not figure largely in Roman literature, and but slightly in the arts of painting and sculpture. They had their pets and played with them, such as dogs, birds, donkeys. The cat seems not to have been common. They played circus racing, and soldiers, and no doubt gladiators. They played with jackstones; they played leapfrog and blindman's buff; they must have played school; they must have had dolls and toys, though not much remains to show it; they rolled the hoop. They probably counted out, and they had their sing-songs, such as the one we suspect that Horace alludes to —

Rex eris si recte facies,
Si non facies non eris.

"King you'll be if you play fair,
Never a king if you don't play fair."

They ran races and wrestled and tumbled and shouted and screamed to gratify their restless, growing little bodies.

The older brothers and the fathers of the little Romans, however, engaged in bodily exercise as the result of reason rather than physical joy or the spirit of sportsmanship. In the times of the citizen-soldier, being fit for the ranks meant all the physical exercise a man needed or had time for. Under the Empire, if he was not of an occupation requiring physical effort, his physical fitness depended much on his pride in being master of the manly and soldierly arts, and, if not on that, on the desire to keep in health. There was the Campus Martius, the soldiers' field and playground through the centuries, there was the Tiber, there were the gardens, and there were the baths. He could swim in the Tiber, and in the Campus he could ride, run and jump, throw the spear and discus, wrestle and box, play handball and three-cornered catch, and bowl. He could do, and probably did, most of these by preference in the baths, where it was more convenient. Possibly some of the gardens were equipped in a small way. Many went hunting or fishing. The wild boar was taken by beating the woods with dogs and driving him into a strong net or killing him with the spear. Rabbits were snared, and birds taken by snares or birdlime. Pliny the Younger writes of taking his tablets with him on a hunt-

WILD BOAR AND DOGS
The boar is attempting the side stroke which the tusk made so effective.

ing excursion, and writing as he sat waiting at the net for the boar to come. Fishhooks are among the interesting finds in Pompeii.

But we hear of no cross-country runs, no ball with bats, no football, no championship teams, no Marathons, no records made or broken, no great meets and glorifications. For rivalry and great excitements, there were the circus and the amphitheater, and the boxers with loaded gloves. Athletics proper were a means to an end. Cicero in the essay *On Old Age* expresses their spirit: "We must have regard for health; we must engage in moderate exercise; we must take enough food and drink to replenish our powers, not to weigh them down. And we must do not only what we can for the body, but much more for the mind and soul." A

BOXERS WITH THE CAESTUS, OR GLOVES

rather sensible ideal, and entertained to-day by many people outside the college atmosphere or beyond the college age.

Yet the difference between ancient Rome and twentieth-century America as regards athletics is accidental, not fundamental. If racing and boxing to-day filled as great a place in our national life as they did in the life of Rome, athletics with us would take the same modest place as it did with them.

One more factor in the diversions of the Roman should be considered. This is the enjoyment he got from his own thoughts as he went about his occupation or moved among his fellows or sat apart in contemplation of them. The man who is not consciously both a spectator and a part of the *comédie humaine*, who never notices the absurdities of men's behavior as they spend themselves in the racing and chasing and milling and perspiration of their little lives, is in a poor way for real diversion. It is this bustling type, without resources in itself and always greatly in the majority, that has for all time made the more brutal sports and the grosser entertainments the paying thing. It has also served as a background to bring into relief the charm of the delicate wit and humor which mark refinement and are its most distinctive quality.

Wit is capacity for the perception of the truth, the power to see accurately and immediately the relationships of things. The fit expression of wit must be brief, rapid, and pleasing. Humor, at least in its most frequent aspect, is that part of wit which is employed in the perception of the incongruous, the droll, the absurd, the surprising. The expression of humor as well as of wit will be neat, but it will be also leisurely and genial. Without further definition or distinction, let us try to appreciate the part they played in the lighter vein of Roman life.

First, it must be noted that the humor of the exaggerated, grotesque, and explosive kind which is known to the world as American has left scant traces in Roman literature and art. The farcical absurdities and boisterous expression of Plautus, in his Braggart Soldier, in the twin Menaechmi, in Amphitruo and Sosia returning home and coming upon themselves in Jove and Mercury disguised as another Amphitruo and Sosia; the social atrocities of the newly rich Trimalchio; the Lilliputian pigmies and monkeys and other grotesqueries on the walls of Pompeii — show that the broad and loud type, as might be expected, was not unknown; but we can hardly believe it thrived as it does with us to-day. It must be remembered that the ancient world was less fluid than ours, that there were no "columns" and that consequently the circulation of the comic and the education of the public in its ways were less pronounced.   It should be noted, too, that the European humor of to-day is less exuberant than the American, and because of conditions which were present also in ancient times.   To have the American willingness to laugh and to start a laugh requires a well-fed body and a mind that is free from apprehension and full of confidence; and these are possible only when there is plenty of space for freedom of movement and expansion, and plenty of this world's goods to win.   Europe has not and never had, even in the times of Roman expansion, so great an abundance and so nearly a universal possession of prosperity.

It is time to illustrate by example the quieter sort of humor to be found here and there in the ancient Roman page. It must be remembered that in transfer from language to language, or culture to culture, or period to period, the flavor of *bon mot* and jest always loses much of the piquancy it had as it left the lips of its inventor.   It is not so much the substance of what is preserved that is important as the indication it affords of the philosophic, witty, and genial strain in character which made life a richer thing.

In a long passage in *De Oratore* on the employment of wit and humor by the orator, Cicero relates the anecdote of Scipio Nasica calling on the poet Ennius.

"Having gone to see the poet Ennius, and being told by the servant girl as he asked for him at the door that he was not in, Nasica saw that she had said so at the bidding of her master, and that he really was in the house.   A few days afterward, when Ennius had come to Nasica's house and was asking for him from the doorway, Nasica called out that he was not at home.   Then said Ennius, 'What! don't I recognize your voice?'   Whereupon Nasica: 'Aren't you the shameless man! When I came asking for you, I took your servant girl's word for your not being in, and won't you take mine when I tell you myself?'"

In his professional life, Cicero was noted for the quickness and sharpness of his tongue, and Plutarch says that "by giving it too free exercise he hurt the feelings of many and gained the reputation of being malicious." His great admirer Quintilian also thinks he jested too easily. The orator himself declares that "in our joking we should suffer only the light of an upright nature to shine forth"; but confesses that "for men who are witty and sharp of tongue it is extremely difficult to hold back the bright sayings that come into their minds." After his death a collection of his witticisms in three books was published.

But Quintilian and Plutarch are thinking of the flashing rapier of Cicero's wit, of his piercing and stinging statements of unpleasant truth, and not of the genial drolleries which abound in his letters. He writes Marius, "So if you have made any appointment with Madame Gout, see that you put it off to another day." He rallies his young lawyer friend Trebatius, who is in the wilds of Gaul, where of course there are no lawyers worth mention: "I gather that our friend Caesar considers you a very fine lawyer. You ought to congratulate yourself on having reached a place where you pass for a man of some capacity. If you had gone to Britain too, there would surely have been in all that big island no one more expert than yourself." He has also his jesting messages for little Attica, his friend's daughter.

To take another type, there is Vespasian, the bluff old soldier born in the Sabine mountains and become emperor.

"Not only at dinner but on all other occasions he was most affable, and he turned off many matters with a jest. When an ex-consul called Florus called his attention to the fact that the proper pronunciation for 'wagons' was *plaustra* rather than *plostra,* he greeted him next day as 'Flaurus.' On the report of a deputation that a colossal statue of great cost had been voted him at public expense, he demanded to have it set up at once, and, holding out his open hand, said that the base was ready. He did not cease his jokes even when in apprehension of death and in extreme danger. And as death drew near, he said: 'Woe's me! Methinks I'm turning into a god.'"

Still another type is to be seen in the Younger Pliny, whose humor is likely to be quite of the self-conscious and artificial type, but whose liking for the country and its solitudes we enjoy.

THE EMPEROR VESPASIAN

The drapery is in colored marble, hardly in keeping with the countenance, which is that of a shrewd and matter-of-fact person.

" You will laugh," he writes, after a hunting trip, "and laugh you may. I, really I myself, your friend, have taken three wild boars and mighty fine ones too. 'Yourself?' you say. Myself; and yet without altogether giving up my inert and inactive ways. The way I did was to sit down near the nets, not with hunting spear or lance at my side, but with pencil and notebook; and to cogitate and write down my thoughts, so that I should bring back full tablets even if empty hands. Really, a manner of study not to be despised. It is wonderful how being bodily active and moving about arouses the mind. In addition, the wood on every side and the solitude and the very silence that must be observed when you engage in the hunt are great stimulations to thought. Hereafter, when you go out, you may use me as a precedent and take a notebook with you the same as knapsack and flask. You will find that Minerva roams the woods quite as much as Diana."

But it is while with Horace that we feel most deeply convinced of the presence in ancient Rome of many a gentle spirit that found in itself and in the company of congenial friends abundant sources of entertainment. He loiters on the Sacred Way, musing on some trifle and all absorbed in it. He goes about among humble folk of the city, and asks them how their business is faring. He sits in the shade of the vines in his garden with his glass of wine. He stands in the door of the Sabine villa and gratefully thinks of his happiness. He mingles with the villagers in their holiday enjoyments. He sits in the shade behind a crumbling rustic sanctuary and writes to a friend that his happiness lacks nothing but the presence of that friend. He likes to look at the landscape, and he likes to look at life. He sees the absurdities and inconsistencies of the struggle for happiness. He sees men enter into real slaveries for the sake of imagined liberties. He enjoys the matchless humor of the simple little stories that have proved their worth and his taste by retaining their charm two thousand years — the country mouse and the town mouse, the weasel and the greedy fox caught in the bin, the rustic sitting and waiting for the river to get by. He knows that worry and fear are futile, and wastes no time in rebellion against the inevitable. He realizes that modest living and liberty are better than the lot of the wealthy who are never alone and never free. His prayer is not for more possessions, but for the sound body and sane mind that will insure the enjoyment of what he has :

> "Son of Latona, hear my vow !
>   Apollo, grant my prayer !
> Health to enjoy the blessings sent
>   From heaven ; a mind unclouded, strong ;
> A cheerful heart ; a wise content ;
>   An honored age ; and song."

There were others as well as Horace who looked on life in this way and found it good. They were a minority, but they not less than the rich who bought their pleasures and the poor in spirit who looked for theirs to noise and excitement should be counted as a part of Living Rome.

XXXIII

SATIRE AND ITS TARGETS

The word *satura*, later written *satira*, is Roman, and satire itself, according to Quintilian, scholar, teacher, critic, and author, was "entirely our own." When it first comes into sight, from the pen of Ennius, "the father of Roman poetry," it was a pleasant medley or entertainment in varied meters, and perhaps not different enough from a similar product by the Greek Menippus to be called original.

Satire at Rome soon began to undergo a development, however. By the time of Lucilius, about 150 B.C., its pleasant medley had changed in tone, and included attack by name on the political enemies of his patrons, the Scipios, and on other persons, high and low, who represented the vices of the city in general; so that Horace says that he

> "Assailed the lords and those of humbler birth,
> Kind to worth only and the friends of worth."

Horace extended the range of satire to society in general, made it more unified and less rambling and crude in both substance and form, and established its character as a criticism of life, penetrating but genial and tolerant. Horace's imitator, Persius, A.D. 34–62, less gentle than his master, increased the sharpness of its tone, and Juvenal, A.D. 60–140, with his bitter and sweeping denunciation of the faults of his time, gave to it finally the character by which it has ever since been known. In its end, if not in its beginning, it was quite truly all Roman.

The development of satire in this manner from mere entertainment and comment on life to scolding condemnation was at the same time the expression of the development of Roman society from the comparative simplicity and homogeneity of an Italian capital to the complexity and sophistication of a world capital. We have been engaged in describing and commenting on the main features of this living capital. It will help our appreciation of its life if we pause to hear what satire had to say in criticism of it, and thus learn what the ancient Romans thought of themselves.

Of Ennius, living through the strenuous times of the Second Punic War and the conquest of the East, it may be said that he felt no call to satire in the usual sense. Even had the temper of the poet been of the caustic sort, the heroisms of Rome and the promise of the expanding State were too great to leave room for the discouragement and pessimism that form the basis for satire. With Lucilius, 180–105 B.C., living to see new perils to the State in the rise of party enmities, it must be suspected that the satirical indignation was due less to moral concern than to the personal feeling of an old soldier loyal to the Scipios against a city growing radical and unappreciative of its men of worth.

In Horace, we have the more universal though the gentler critic. Yet, even in Horace's time, men are living in the light of hope. Rome is now the Eternal, the City of Destiny. "The great round of the ages is beginning anew." The world has crashed into fragments, but the Augustans are gathering them up, and something greater than ever is to be. The poet, looking to the new régime and actively committed to it, has his moments of impatience and even of pessimism, when he feels that "the age of our sires, worse than our grandsires, has begotten us, who will soon bring forth a generation still more vicious"; but on the whole his tone is that of the man who knows the crimes of mankind but can afford to be amused by its follies, and even to plead for lenient judgment on them.   Horace is an essayist rather than a satirist, and rightly calls his satires and epistles *sermones*, "talks," or *causeries*.   The sins he "smilingly tells the truth" about are lack of charity, going to extremes, running too hard in the race for wealth, entertaining false ambitions,

MARBLE PORTRAITS OF ROMANS

inconsistency, dining in bad taste, neglecting philosophy and misjudging values, sacrificing independence, being discontented.   The only heinous immorality he attacks at length and by itself is legacy-hunting, and even here the indignation of the satirist is tempered for both writer and reader by the pleasure of skillful parody.

By the time of Juvenal's writing, however, in the reigns of the Emperors Trajan, A.D. 98–117, and Hadrian, A.D. 117–138, though the eternity and the destiny of Rome were believed in still, belief in the "great round of the ages" and what it would do had suffered severe shocks.   Sane Augustus had been succeeded by gloomy and suspicious Tiberius, mad Caligula and silly Claudius had followed, spoiled and willful Nero had terrorized, three emperors had come and gone by

violent means in the single year of A.D. 68–69, and wholesome
Vespasian and Titus had given place to tyrannical Domitian.
The evils of personal rule and hereditary succession had been
too clearly demonstrated for men longer to have perfect
faith in autocratic government. The growth in population from foreign sources, the dying out of the old families
that had built the State, and the filling of their places
by the newly enriched, the newly free, and the newly
Roman, had changed the blood and lessened the unity of the
olden times. The increase of wealth and the multiplication
of opportunity, together with loss of liberty and removal of
civic obligation, had made easy the growth of selfishness and
vice and slavishness. There were the enormously rich, restrained by no ideal and fearful of only the arrogant above
them. There were the hundreds of thousands of idle or
semi-idle fed and amused by the rich and the court, a
degraded yet arrogant mob whose loyalty waxed or waned
with the coming and going of "bread and games." What
wonder that in this weltering age the satirist was not a
Horace looking on amused and unalarmed, but a Juvenal
seeing red with wrath, and waiting only for the death of the
tyrant to liberate his pen?

But let us look at the targets at which Juvenal aims his
shafts. There is the wealthy and vulgar upstart who was
recently a barber or slave, and now wears Tyrian purple,
"whilst on his sweating finger he airs a ring of gold in summer,
unable to endure the weight of a heavier gem." Wealth is
now a deity. And yet, when was avarice more greedy?
Men gamble now, not from purses, but with whole treasure
chests. They will prostitute themselves to the ugliest vices
for money, sacrificing all self-respect. There are the immoral
and the criminal who owe immunity to the use of bribes.
There are the effeminate and unnatural. There is the

husband who will profit by his wife's disgrace. There are
the gluttons eating and drinking to their ruin. There are the
arrogant indulging in every luxury and every whim, and
the obsequious who sell their liberty for the slightest favor.
There are those who have not only thrown away their
dignity and accept the dole, but will even crowd and cheat at
its distribution. There are those accepting the dinners of
insolent patrons who serve themselves with the best and their
guests with the cheapest. There are the sons of the venerable families of Rome degrading with every meanness the
names they bear. There is the forger boldly trusting the
fruits of his crime to give him respectability. There are the
unterrified poisoners and other plotters against life; in these
days, if one is to be noticed, he must be a criminal in the
grand style. There is the foreigner, above all the hungry
Greek, with his cleverness and hypocritical servility, on
every hand supplanting the natives of Rome.

And there is woman — the woman who spends her husband's money and lives with him as if she were only his
neighbor; the adulterous woman, so bold and so numerous
that there is no such thing as purity in the home; the
woman heartlessly cruel to her slaves, who has them whipped
if a curl of her hair is out of place, and during their bloody
flogging sits and reads the day's news; the woman intoler-
ably wealthy, who never gives a thought to the cost of her
perverted pleasures, as if money were forever welling up
afresh from the exhausted strong-box; the woman fanatical
over Isis or the Great Mother and enriching their sly and
calculating priests; the woman gone crazy over the fortune-
tellers, who will not go for a drive or salve a sore eye without
first consulting the horoscope; the woman who goes in for
music and is forever fingering instruments; the mannish
woman who visits the baths by night, uses the gymnasium,

takes cocktails for her appetite, and eats and drinks herself sick; the intellectual woman, who sits down to dinner and straight begins to discourse on Virgil and Dido, comparing *Homer* and the *Aeneid*, correcting her friends' grammar, and plying her tongue with such speed and loudness that no

PORTRAITS OF ROMAN WOMEN

lawyer or auctioneer, or even another woman, can get in a word; the new woman, who rushes about attending men's meetings and knows what is going on all over the world and tells it to everyone she meets at the street corners; the woman crazy over beautification, with high heels, bedaubed face, and tiers and stories piled one upon another on her head.

"She ridiculously puffs out and disfigures her face with much dough; she reeks of rich Poppaean cosmetics which stick to the lips of her unfortunate husband. It is for her lovers that she buys all the perfumes the slender Indians send to us. In good time she removes the first coatings, discloses her face, and begins to be recognizable. Then she bathes her skin in the famous milk from the she-asses which she would take with her if she were exiled and sent to the North Pole. But a face plastered over and treated with all these beauty preparations, shall we call it a face or a sore?"

It is not only the ways of the Romans that irritate Juvenal, but the ways of the city itself. The famous *Third Satire*, whose imitation in his poem *London* brought Samuel Johnson into prominence at twenty-nine, is one of the most vivid bits of realism in literature. Let us look at parts of it in the attractive old-fashioned translation of William Gifford. The poet's disgusted friend is bidding farewell to him and to Rome.

> "Grieved though I am to see the man depart,
> Who long has shared, and still must share, my heart,
> Yet (when I call my better judgment home)
> I praise his purpose; to retire from Rome,
> And give, on Cumae's solitary coast,
> The Sibyl — one inhabitant to boast!

> "Full on the road to Baiae, Cumae lies,
> And many a sweet retreat her shore supplies —
> Though I prefer ev'n Prochyta's bare strand
> To the Subura: — for, what desert land,
> What wild, uncultured spot, can more affright,
> Than fires, wide blazing through the gloom of night,
> Houses, with ceaseless ruin, thundering down,
> And all the horrors of this hateful town?
> Where poets, while the dog-star glows, rehearse,
> To gasping multitudes, their barbarous verse! . . .

> "Umbritius here his sullen silence broke,
> And turned on Rome, indignant, as he spoke.
> Since virtue droops, he cried, without regard,
> And honest toil scarce hopes a poor reward;
> Since every morrow sees my means decay,
> And still makes less the little of to-day;

I go, where Daedalus, as poets sing,
First checked his flight, and closed his weary wing. . . .

"But why, my friend, should I at Rome remain?
I cannot teach my stubborn lips to feign;
Nor, when I hear a great man's verses, smile,
And beg a copy, if I think them vile. . . .

"The nation, by the great, admired, carest,
And hated, shunned by me, above the rest,
No longer, now, restrained by wounded pride,
I haste to show, (nor thou my warmth deride,)
I cannot rule my spleen, and calmly see,
A Grecian capital, in Italy!
Grecian? O, no! with this vast sewer compared,
The dregs of Greece are scarcely worth regard:
Long since, the stream that wanton Syria laves
Has disembogued its filth in Tiber's waves,
Its language, arts; o'erwhelmed us with the scum
Of Antioch's streets, its minstrel, harp, and drum. . . .
A flattering, cringing, treacherous, artful race,
Of torrent tongue, and never-blushing face;
A Protean tribe, one knows not what to call,
Which shifts to every form, and shines in all:
Grammarian, painter, augur, rhetorician,
Rope-dancer, conjurer, fiddler, and physician,
All trades his own, your hungry Greekling counts;
And bid him mount the sky, — the sky he mounts! . . .
Greece is a theater, where all are players.
For lo! their patron smiles, — they burst with mirth;
He weeps, — they droop, the saddest souls on earth;
He calls for fire, — they court the mantle's heat;
'Tis warm, he cries, — and they dissolve in sweat.
Ill-matched! — secure of victory they start,
Who, taught from youth to play a borrowed part,
Can, with a glance, the rising passion trace,
And mould their own, to suit their patron's face;
At deeds of shame their hands admiring raise,
And mad debauchery's worst excesses praise. . . .

"Who fears the crash of houses, in retreat?
At simple Gabii, bleak Praeneste's seat,
Volsinium's craggy heights, embowered in wood,
Or Tibur, beetling o'er prone Anio's flood?

CRUMBLING ROME

Part of this modern house suddenly fell away. The props may be seen
which support the rest.

While half the city here by shores is staid,
And feeble cramps, that lend a treacherous aid:
For thus the stewards patch the riven wall,
Thus prop the mansion, tottering to its fall;
Then bid the tenant court secure repose,
While the pile nods to every blast that blows.

"O! may I live where no such fears molest,
No midnight fires burst on my hour of rest!

For here 'tis terror all; midst the loud cry
Of 'Water! water!' the scared neighbors fly,
With all their haste can seize — the flames aspire,
And the third floor is wrapt in smoke and fire,
While you, unconscious, doze: Up, ho! and know,
The impetuous blaze which spreads dismay below,
By swift degrees will reach the aerial cell,
Where, crouching, underneath the tiles you dwell,
Where your tame doves their golden couplets rear,
And you could no mischance, but drowning, fear! . . .

"Flushed with a mass of indigested food,
Which clogs the stomach and inflames the blood,
What crowds, with watching wearied and o'erprest,
Curse the slow hours, and die for want of rest!
For who can hope his languid lids to close,
Where brawling taverns banish all repose?
Sleep, to the rich alone, his visits pays:
And hence the seeds of many a dire disease.
The carts loud rumbling through the narrow way,
The drivers' clamors at each casual stay,
From drowsy Drusus would his slumber take,
And keep the calves of Proteus broad awake!

"If business call, obsequious crowds divide,
While o'er their heads the rich securely ride,
By tall Illyrians borne, and read, or write,
Or (should the early hour to rest invite),
Close the soft litter, and enjoy the night.
Yet reach they first the goal; while, by the throng
Elbowed and jostled, scarce we creep along;
Sharp strokes from poles, tubs, rafters doomed to feel;
And plastered o'er with mud, from head to heel:
While the rude soldier gores us as he goes,
Or marks, in blood, his progress on our toes.

"See, from the Dole, a vast tumultuous throng,
Each followed by his kitchen, pours along!

Huge pans, which Corbulo could scarce uprear,
With steady neck a puny slave must bear,
And, lest amid the way the flames expire,
Glide nimbly on, and gliding, fan the fire. . . .

"Pass we these fearful dangers, and survey
What other evils threat our nightly way.
And first, behold the mansion's towering size,
Where floors on floors to the tenth story rise;
Whence heedless garreteers their potsherds throw,
And crush the unwary wretch that walks below!
Clattering the storm descends from heights unknown,
Ploughs up the street, and wounds the flinty stone!
'Tis madness, dire improvidence of ill,
To sup abroad, before you sign your will;
Since fate in ambush lies, and marks his prey,
From every wakeful window in the way:
Pray, then, — and count your humble prayer well sped,
If pots be only — emptied on your head.

"The drunken bully, ere his man be slain,
Frets through the night, and courts repose in vain;
And while the thirst of blood his bosom burns,
From side to side, in restless anguish, turns. . . .
There are, who murder as an opiate take,
And only when no brawls await them wake:
Yet even these heroes, flushed with youth and wine,
All contest with the purple robe decline;
Securely give the lengthened train to pass,
The sun-bright flambeaux, and the lamps of brass.
Me, whom the moon, or candle's paler gleam,
Whose wick I husband to the last extreme,
Guides through the gloom, he braves, devoid of fear.
The prelude to our doughty quarrel hear,
If that be deemed a quarrel, where, heaven knows,
He only gives, and I receive, the blows!
Across my path he strides, and bids me stand!
I bow, obsequious to the dread command;

What else remains, where madness, rage, combine
With youth, and strength superior far to mine?
'Whence come you, rogue?' he cries; ' whose beans to-night
Have stuffed you thus? what cobbler clubbed his mite,
For leeks and sheep's-head porridge? Dumb! quite dumb!
Speak, or be kicked. — Yet, once again! Your home?
Where shall I find you? At what beggar's stand
(Temple, or bridge) whimp'ring with outstretched hand?'

"Whether I strive some humble plea to frame,
Or steal in silence by, 'tis just the same;
I'm beaten first, then dragged in rage away;
Bound to the peace, or punished for the fray! . . .

"Nor this the worst; for when deep midnight reigns,
And bolts secure our doors, and massy chains,
When noisy inns a transient silence keep,
And harassed nature woos the balm of sleep,
Then, thieves and murderers ply their dreadful trade;
With stealthy steps our secret couch invade: —
Roused from the treacherous calm, aghast we start,
And the fleshed sword — is buried in our heart!
Hither from bogs, from rocks, and caves pursued
(The Pontine marsh, and Gallinarian wood,)
The dark assassins flock, as to their home,
And fill with dire alarm the streets of Rome. . . .

"O! happy were our sires, estranged from crimes;
And happy, happy, were the good old times,
Which saw, beneath their kings', their tribunes' reign,
One cell the nation's criminals contain!"

Such are the targets of Juvenal's satire. The attentive
reader will see among the follies and vices and crimes which
aroused his indignation many that are still familiar. Reflecting on their presence among us, knowing how many of
them on closer acquaintance in their setting are found to
be less terrible than they seemed, he will wisely conclude
that in ancient Roman society also the good and evil were
mingled, and that much of the evil was less evil than it looks.

XXXIV

A DINNER WITH THE NEWLY RICH

Juvenal angrily lays the lash on offenders of every kind, and never smiles. The author of the *Satyricon*, perhaps the Petronius whose suicide by order of Nero is described by Tacitus, is a laughing satirist. What remains of its sixteen books is largely composed of the story of an incredibly absurd dinner given at his home in Cumae by Trimalchio, a newly rich and ignorant but self-satisfied freedman.

The whole work was a picaresque novel, or romance of roguery, in which were related the variegated experiences of one Agamemnon, a teacher of rhetoric, Giton, a boy, and two freedmen called Ascyltus and Encolpius, as they went an adventurous way from Marseilles to Croton in southern Italy. The following abridgment contains about one fifth the story of the dinner.

Trimalchio's Dinner

"The third day had come. A good dinner was promised. But we were bruised and sore. Escape was better even than rest. We were making some melancholy plans for avoiding the coming storm, when one of Agamemnon's servants came up as we stood hesitating and said: 'Do you not know at whose house it is to-day? Trimalchio, a very rich man, who has a clock and a uniformed trumpeter in his dining room, to keep telling him how much of his life is lost and gone.' We forgot our troubles and hurried into our clothes, and told Giton, who till now had been waiting on us very willingly, to follow us to the baths. We began to take a stroll

395

in evening dress to pass the time, or rather to joke and mix with the groups of players, when all at once we saw a bald old man in a reddish shirt playing at ball with some long-haired boys. It was not the boys that attracted our notice, though they deserved it, but the old gentleman, who was in his house shoes, busily engaged with a green ball. He never picked it up if it touched the

MARBLE PORTRAITS OF ROMANS

ground. A slave stood by with a bagful and supplied them to the players. . . .

"At last then we sat down, and boys from Alexandria poured water cooled with snow over our hands. Others followed and knelt down at our feet, and proceeded with great skill to pare our hang nails. Even this unpleasant duty did not silence them, but they kept singing at their work. I wanted to find out whether the whole household could sing, so I asked for a drink. A ready slave repeated my order in a chant not less shrill. They all did the same if they were asked to hand anything. It was more like an actor's dance than a gentleman's dining room. But some rich and tasty whets for the appetite were brought on; for everyone had now sat down except Trimalchio, who had the first place kept for him in the new style. A donkey in Corinthian bronze stood on the side-board, with panniers holding olives, white in one side, black in the other. Two dishes hid the donkey; Trimalchio's name and their weight in silver was engraved on their edges. There were also dormice rolled in honey and poppy-seed, and supported on little bridges soldered to the plate. Then there were hot sausages laid on a silver grill, and under the grill damsons and seeds of pomegranate.

"While we were engaged with these delicacies, Trimalchio was conducted in to the sound of music, propped on the tiniest of pillows. A laugh escaped the unwary. His head was shaven and peered out of a scarlet cloak, and over the heavy clothes on his neck he had put on a napkin with a broad stripe and fringes hanging from it all round. On the little finger of his left hand he had an enormous gilt ring, and on the top joint of the next finger a smaller ring which appeared to me to be entirely gold, but was really set all round with iron cut out in little stars. Not content with this display of wealth, he bared his right arm, where a golden bracelet shone, and an ivory bangle clasped with a plate of bright metal. Then he said, as he picked his teeth with a silver quill: 'It was not convenient for me to come to dinner yet, my friends, but I gave up all my own pleasure; I did not like to stay away any longer and keep you waiting. But you will not mind if I finish my game?' A boy followed him with a table of terebinth wood and crystal pieces, and I noticed the prettiest thing possible. Instead of black and white counters they used gold and silver coins. Trimalchio kept passing every kind of remark as he played, and we were still busy with the hors d'oeuvres, when a tray was brought in with a basket on it, in which there was a hen made of wood, spreading out her wings as they do when they are sitting. The music grew loud: two slaves at once came up and began to hunt in the straw. Peahen's eggs were pulled out and handed to the guests. Trimalchio turned his head to look, and said: 'I gave orders, my friends, that peahen's eggs should be put under a common hen. And upon my oath I am afraid they are hard-set by now. But we will try whether they are still fresh enough to suck.' We took our spoons, half-a-pound in weight at least, and hammered at the eggs, which were balls of fine meal. I was on the point of throwing away my portion. I thought a peachick had already formed. But hearing a practised diner say, 'What treasure have we here?' I poked through the shell with my finger, and found a fat becafico rolled up in spiced yolk of egg. . . .

"As we drank and admired each luxury in detail, a slave brought in a silver skeleton, made so that its limbs and spine could be moved and bent in every direction. He put it down once or twice on the table so that the supple joints showed several attitudes, and Trimalchio said appropriately: 'Alas for us poor mortals, all that poor man is is nothing. So we shall all be, after the world below takes us away. Let us live then while it goes well with us.'

"After we had praised this outburst a dish followed, not at all of the size we expected; but its novelty drew every eye to it. There was a round plate with the twelve signs of the Zodiac set in order, and on each one the artist had laid some food fit and proper to the symbol; over the Ram rams'-head pease, a piece of beef on the Bull, kidneys over the Twins, over the Crab a crown, an African fig over the Lion, a barren sow's paunch over Virgo, over Libra a pair of scales with a muffin on one side and a cake on the other, over Scorpio a small sea-fish, over Sagittarius a bull's-eye, over Capricornus a lobster, over Aquarius a goose, over Pisces two mullets. In the middle lay a honeycomb on a sod of turf with the green grass on it. An Egyptian boy took bread round in a silver chafing-dish. . . .

"Trimalchio himself too ground out a tune from the musical comedy *Asafoetida* in a most hideous voice. We came to such an evil entertainment rather depressed. 'Now,' said Trimalchio, 'let us have dinner. This is sauce for the dinner.' As he spoke, four dancers ran up in time with the music and took off the top part of the dish. Then we saw in the well of it fat fowls and sow's bellies, and in the middle a hare got up with wings to look like Pegasus. Four figures of Marsyas at the corners of the dish also caught the eye; they let a spiced sauce run from their wine-skins over the fishes, which swam about in a kind of tide-race. We all took up the clapping which the slaves started, and attacked these delicacies with hearty laughter. Trimalchio was delighted with the trick he had played us, and said, 'Now, Carver.' The man came up at once, and making flourishes in time with the music pulled the dish to pieces; you would have said that a gladiator in a chariot was fighting to the accompaniment of a water-organ. Still Trimalchio kept on in a soft voice, 'Oh, Carver, Carver.' I thought this word over and over again must be part of a joke, and I made bold to ask the man who sat next me this very question. He had seen performances of this kind more often. 'You see the fellow who is carving his way through the meat? Well, his name is Carver. So whenever Trimalchio says the word, you have his name, and he has his orders. . . .'

"But a clerk quite interrupted his passion for the dance by reading as though from the gazette: 'July the 26th. Thirty boys and forty girls were born on Trimalchio's estate at Cumae. Five

THE PERISTYLE OF A POMPEIAN HOUSE

From a painting by Bazzani.

hundred thousand pecks of wheat were taken up from the threshing-floor into the barn.   Five hundred oxen were broken in.   On the same date: the slave Mithridates was led to crucifixion for having damned the soul of our lord Gaius.   On the same date: ten million sesterces which could not be invested were returned to the reserve.   On the same day: there was a fire in our gardens at Pompeii, which broke out in the house of Nasta, the bailiff.' 'Stop,' said Trimalchio, 'when did I buy any gardens at Pompeii?' 'Last year,' said the clerk, 'so that they are not entered in your accounts yet.'   Trimalchio glowed with passion, and said, 'I will not have any property which is bought in my name entered in my accounts unless I hear of it within six months.'   We now had a further recitation of police notices, and some foresters' wills, in which Trimalchio was cut out in a codicil: then the names of bailiffs, and of a freedwoman who had been caught with a bathman and divorced by her husband, a night watchman; the name of a porter who had been banished to Baiae; the name of a steward who was being prosecuted, and details of an action between some valets.

"But at last the acrobats came in.   A very dull fool stood there with a ladder and made a boy dance from rung to rung and on the very top to the music of popular airs, and then made him hop through burning hoops, and pick up a wine jar with his teeth.   No one was excited by this but Trimalchio, who kept saying that it was a thankless profession.   There were only two things in the world that he could watch with real pleasure, acrobats and trumpeters; all other shows were silly nonsense. . . .

"Trimalchio cheered up at this dispute and said: 'Ah, my friends, a slave is a man and drank his mother's milk like ourselves, even if cruel fate has trodden him down.   Yes, and if I live they shall soon taste the water of freedom.   In fact I am setting them all free in my will.   I am leaving a property and his good woman to Philargyrus as well, and to Cario a block of buildings, and his manumission fees, and a bed and bedding.   I am making Fortunata my heir, and I recommend her to all my friends.   I am making all this known so that my slaves may love me now as if I were dead.' They all began to thank their master for his kindness, when he turned serious, and had a copy of the will brought in, which he read aloud from beginning to end, while the slaves moaned and groaned.

Then he looked at Habinnas and said: 'Now tell me, my dear friend: you will erect a monument as I have directed? I beg you earnestly to put up round the feet of my statue my little dog, and some wreaths, and bottles of perfume, and all the fights of Petraites, so that your kindness may bring me a life after death; and I want the monument to have a frontage of one hundred feet and to be two hundred feet in depth. For I should like to have all kinds of fruit growing round my ashes, and plenty of vines. It is quite wrong for a man to decorate his house while he is alive, and not to trouble about the house where he must make a longer stay. So above all things I want added to the inscription, 'This monument is not to descend to my heir.' I shall certainly take care to provide in my will against any injury being done to me when I am dead. I am appointing one of the freedmen to be caretaker of the tomb and prevent the common people from running up and defiling it. I beg you to put ships in full sail on the monument, and me sitting in official robes on my official seat, wearing five gold rings and distributing coin publicly out of a bag; you remember that I gave a free dinner worth two denarii a head. I should like a dining room table put in too, if you can arrange it. And let me have the whole people there enjoying themselves. On my right hand put a statue of dear Fortunata holding a dove, and let her be leading a little dog with a waistband on; and my dear little boy, and big jars sealed with gypsum, so that the wine may not run out. And have a broken urn carved with a boy weeping over it. And a sundial in the middle, so that anyone who looks at the time will read my name whether he likes it or not. And again, please think carefully whether this inscription seems to you quite appropriate: 'Here lieth Caius Pompeius Trimalchio, freedman of Maecenas. The degree of Priest of Augustus was conferred upon him in his absence. He might have been attendant on any magistrate in Rome, but refused it. God-fearing, gallant, constant, he started with very little and left thirty millions. He never listened to a philosopher. Fare thee well, Trimalchio: and thou too, passer-by.'

"After saying this, Trimalchio began to weep floods of tears. Fortunata wept, Habinnas wept, and then all the slaves began as if they had been invited to his funeral, and filled the dining room with lamentation. . . .

"'Well, as I was just saying, self-denial has brought me into this fortune. When I came from Asia I was about as tall as this candle-stick. In fact I used to measure myself by it every day, and grease my lips from the lamp to grow a moustache the quicker. Still, I was my master's favorite for fourteen years. No disgrace in obeying your master's orders. Well, I used to amuse my mistress too. You know what I mean; I say no more, I am not a conceited man. Then, as the Gods willed, I became the real master of the house, and simply had his brains in my pocket. I need only add that I was joint residuary legatee with Caesar, and came into an estate fit for a senator. But no one is satisfied with nothing. I conceived a passion for business. I will not keep you a moment — I built five ships, got a cargo of wine — which was worth its weight in gold at the time — and sent them to Rome. You may think it was a put-up job; every one was wrecked, truth and no fairy-tales. Neptune gulped down thirty million in one day. Do you think I lost heart? Lord! no, I no more tasted my loss than if nothing had happened. I built some more, bigger, better and more expensive, so that no one could say I was not a brave man. You know, a huge ship has a certain security about her. I got another cargo of wine, bacon, beans, perfumes, and slaves. Fortunata did a noble thing at that time; she sold all her jewelry and all her clothes, and put a hundred gold pieces into my hand. They were the leaven of my fortune. What God wishes soon happens. I made a clear ten million on one voyage. I at once bought up all the estates which had belonged to my patron. I built a house, and bought slaves and cattle; whatever I touched grew like a honey-comb. When I came to have more than the whole revenues of my own country, I threw up the game: I retired from active work and began to finance freedmen. I was quite unwilling to go on with my work when I was encouraged by an astrologer who happened to come to our town, a little Greek called Serapa, who knew the secrets of the Gods. He told me things that I had forgotten myself; explained everything from needle and thread upwards; knew my own inside, and only fell short of telling me what I had had for dinner the day before. You would have thought he had always lived with me. You remember, Habinnas? — I believe you were there? ' You fetched your wife from you know where. You are not lucky in your friends. No

one is ever as grateful to you as you deserve.   You are a man of
property.   You are nourishing a viper in your bosom,' and, though
I must not tell you this, that even now I had thirty years, four
months, and two days left to live.   Moreover I shall soon come into
an estate.   My oracle tells me so.   If I could only extend my
boundaries to Apulia I should have gone far enough for my life-
time.   Meanwhile I built this house while Mercury watched over
me.   As you know, it was a tiny place; now it is a palace.   It has
four dining rooms, twenty bedrooms, two marble colonnades, an
upstairs dining room, a bedroom where I sleep myself, this viper's
boudoir, an excellent room for the porter; there is plenty of spare
room for guests.   In fact when Scaurus came he preferred staying
here to anywhere else, and he has a family place by the sea.   There
are plenty of other things which I will show you in a minute.   Take
my word for it; if you have a penny, that is what you are worth;
by what a man hath shall he be reckoned.   So your friend who
was once a worm is now a king.   Meanwhile, Stichus, bring me
the grave-clothes in which I mean to be carried out.   And some
ointment, and a mouthful out of that jar which has to be poured
over my bones.'

"In a moment Stichus had fetched a white winding-sheet and
dress into the dining room and . . . [Trimalchio] asked us to feel
whether they were made of good wool.   Then he gave a little
laugh and said: 'Mind neither mouse nor moth corrupts them,
Stichus; otherwise I will burn you alive.   I want to be carried
out in splendor, so that the whole crowd calls down blessings on
me.'   He immediately opened a flask and anointed us all and said,
'I hope I shall like this as well in the grave as I do on earth.'
Besides this he ordered wine to be poured into a bowl, and said,
'Now you must imagine you have been asked to my funeral.'

"The thing was becoming perfectly sickening, when Trimalchio,
now deep in the most vile drunkenness, had a new set of performers, some trumpeters, brought into the dining room, propped himself on a heap of cushions, and stretched himself on his death-bed,
saying: 'Imagine that I am dead.   Play something pretty.'
The trumpeters broke into a loud funeral march.   One man especially, a slave of the undertaker, who was the most decent man
in the party, blew such a blast that the whole neighborhood was
roused.   The watch, who were patrolling the streets close by,

thought Trimalchio's house was alight, and suddenly burst in the door and began with water and axes to do their duty in creating a disturbance. My friends and I seized this most welcome opportunity, outwitted Agamemnon, and took to our heels as quickly as if there were a real fire.

"There was no guiding torch to show us the way as we wandered; it was now midnight, and the silence gave us no prospect of meeting anyone with a light. Moreover, we were drunk, and our ignorance of the quarter would have puzzled us even in the daytime. So after dragging our bleeding feet nearly a whole hour over the flints and broken pots which lay out in the road, we were at last put straight by Giton's cleverness. The careful child had been afraid of losing his way even in broad daylight, and had marked all the posts and columns with chalk; these lines shone through the blackest night, and their brilliant whiteness directed our lost footsteps. But even when we reached our lodgings our agitation was not relieved. For our friend, the old woman, had had a long night swilling with her lodgers, and would not have noticed if you had set a light to her. We might have had to sleep on the doorstep if Trimalchio's courier had not come up in state with ten carts. After making a noise for a little while he broke down the house door and let us in by it."

XXXV

THE CRIMINAL

Juvenal's sweeping denunciations of the degenerate patrician, the wasteful rich man, the insolent parvenu, the servile and unprincipled common crowd, the greedy, lying foreigner, the unabashed new woman, the groveling courtier, the arrogant and irresponsible ruler, the dangerous characters of the street and the night, are suggestive rather than descriptive of crime. They are the expression of one thoroughly disgusted by the behavior of men not so much because of its violation of law as because of the degradation and indecency it represents. The forger, the poisoner, and the adulterer are the chief and almost only offenders he mentions against the law of the land, and in them he is attacking the arrogant, the covetous, and the impure rather than the offender against the State. In Martial, who saw the same things that Juvenal saw, but as a spectator without indignation and only in search of matter for the epigram, and in the *Satyricon* ascribed to Petronius, there is even less pointing out of actual crime.

If we wish to know what constituted crime in ancient Rome, the degree of disapproval its various forms aroused, and what it meant in the character of the Roman people, we must not depend on the satirists and other literary observers, but upon the laws that have been preserved, especially that part of them providing for the compensation and the punishment of crime. This chapter will be devoted, first, to an enumeration of criminal offenses; second, to an enumeration of the penalties attaching to them; and third, to the courts which had jurisdiction over them.

In the first place, offenses were capital or noncapital as they affected or did not affect the *caput*, the status of citizen. Capital crimes were not only those for which life was forfeited, but all offenses involving punishment by loss of the freeman's status, of the rights of citizenship, or of family rights. The degrees of capital punishment are thus: (1) death; (2) loss of the freeman's status and consequently citizenship and family rights; (3) loss of citizenship with loss of family rights but not of liberty; (4) loss of family rights only.

In the second place, criminal offenses were either violations of absolute duties, or violations of relative duties; that is, crimes in which the State or society and not the individual was the injured party, or crimes in which the State and also the individual were injured. Some of these were capital, some noncapital.

We may now specify the crimes in which the State alone was the injured party.

There were naturally those offenses which affected the safety of the State: bearing arms against it, deserting to its enemy, causing the ambush or surrender of its army, preventing the success of its arms, inciting a friendly state to make war on it, abetting its enemy by any material means or by communication and advice. This whole group of acts, which were against the State's external safety, constituted treason. It was known to imperial times under the name *crimen laesae maiestatis*, and earlier as *perduellio*.

A second group consisting in acts of subversion or usurpation was directed against the State from within, and included plotting against or attacking the emperor or questioning his choice of a successor, attempting the life of any member of the *consilium* or *consistorium*, his intimate advisory body, causing any person to take oath for subversion, raising an army or levying war without the emperor's authority, and conspiring to kill hostages without his authority. This group, like the first, was treason.

Thirdly, there were offenses against the State's tranquillity : any seditious gathering or conspiracy, or an armed

SPARTACUS IN PRISON

From " Spartacus"

assembly seizing any public place. Fourthly, there were offenses against the public force : desertion from the army, and the instigation to riot or sedition. These two groups were also treason.

A fifth group consisted in offenses against the administration of justice : to conspire for the death of a magistrate, to set free one that had pleaded guilty to a criminal charge, to use force in the prevention of a trial or the influencing of a magistrate, to accept a bribe for accusing or not accusing a person of a criminal act, to use false testimony in convicting a person of a crime punishable with death, wrongfully to give or withhold testimony, to corrupt a judge or cause him to be corrupted, maliciously to accuse of crime, to conceal crime or by collusion to secure acquittal of a defendant, to abandon prosecution without sufficient cause. The first and second of these were treason.

Sixthly, there were the offenses against the public funds: exacting taxes without authority, counterfeiting or falsifying in any way the coinage of the State, or refusing to accept it if pure and properly stamped, converting to personal use the State's money or money held in trust.

A seventh group consisted in offenses by servants of the State: to refuse to yield authority to a successor, to use authority in causing the death or scourging or torture of a Roman citizen pending an appeal, to accept money as a magistrate for causing a charge of capital crime, to accept money or other value in violation of public duty, willfully as juror to judge contrary to an enactment, to betray a client.

Eighthly, there were offenses in the matter of weights, measures, and markets. Among these were the selling of bread by false weights, the attempt at artificial raising of the prices of provisions, the withholding of goods from the market to increase their prices.

Ninthly, there were the offenses against decency or morals. These included adultery and incest.

Finally, there were such offenses in respect of religion and witchcraft as to play the prophet, to consult with reference to the emperor's life, to offer sacrifice in the hope of injury to neighbors, to participate in magic or to possess books on the subject of magic, to introduce strange worships likely to cause disturbance.

So much for the crimes in which the State only was the injured party; that is, the violation of absolute duties. Let us now consider those in which the State and also a specified individual were injured; that is, those which were violations of relative duties.

First among these were crimes against the person: parricide, meaning the willful causing of death to ascendant, brother, sister, aunt, uncle, cousin, husband or wife or other relation by affinity, or patron; murder, to kill any person, even a slave, to prepare, sell, or to give poison for the killing of any person, to go armed with weapons for murder and theft, or to conspire for murder; wounds and assaults, alone or in company; restraint of the person by willful imprisonment or shutting up, willful concealment, imprisonment, or purchase of any freeman or freedman against his consent; libel, its origination or dissemination; attempts on the chastity of women, girls, and boys.

Second among the violations of relative duties were crimes against rights involving things. Here are to be classed the theft of animals, housebreaking and stealing by night, sneak thievery, stealing from a burning house or a wrecked vessel; robbery, on the highway, with others in the assault of a house, or by blackmail; forcible ejectment with arms; approval of armed slaves acquiring possession; arson; the theft or conversion to personal use of sacred or public movables; the violation of sepulture by removal or spoliation of the dead or of the tomb in any part.

A third class of offense against relative duties consisted in the making of fraudulent contracts, compelling by force the entrance into contract, forging or altering accounts.

Fourthly, there were the crimes involving status: for a freedman to represent himself as freeborn; to falsify in the matter of a child; for a wife to be unfaithful to the marriage relation ; to tempt a married woman to be unfaithful or to divorce her husband.

Fifthly, there were the offenses in relation to inheritance ; to take from an inheritance before the heir's title was confirmed ; to forge or tamper with a will, or to open it during the maker's life.

We are ready now to enumerate the punishments. They will of course be capital and noncapital.

Capital punishment has already been described as not confined to death, but as including the loss of freedom, the forfeiture of citizenship, and the forfeiture of family rights.

Death, the *summum supplicium* or extreme penalty, was by A.D. 222 the punishment for all but the mildest forms of treason ; under Julius Caesar, framer of the law on treason, the penalty had been the famous Interdiction from Water and Fire, a civic excommunication amounting to exile. Death was the penalty also for the exercise of the magic arts, for parricide, for murder by persons not of rank, for the worst offenses against chastity, for repeated robbery, for serious cases of arson, for violation of the tomb by force and for removing bodies, for bribery, for causing a citizen to be killed, beaten, or tortured pending appeal, if done by persons not of rank, and for cases of forgery by slaves. This discrimination in favor of rank occurs in many cases.

The manner of the death penalty varied. There was burying alive for the unchaste Vestal, throwing from the Tarpeian Rock in early times for false witness, crucifixion, for slaves only, burning, beheading, facing the wild beasts in the arena, entering the gladiatorial lists with a chance of life. Crucifixion and condemnations to the arena were abolished by Constantine, who encouraged sanctity in the marriage relation by making death the punishment for adultery. He also made burning the punishment of counterfeiters not of rank.

The second capital punishment, deprivation of the freeman's status, was the consequence of sentence for life to the mines. The third, forfeiture of citizenship, was the consequence of the water-and-fire interdiction, or outlawry and banishment, under the Republic, and, under the Empire, of deportation for life to an island or condemnation to labor for life on the public works. Forfeiture of property naturally went with both. In the case of the common people, sentence to the mines was the penalty also for embezzlement, for using potions, for fraudulent contract, for sacrilege, for highway robbery, and for ordinary violation of tomb. Sentence for life to the public works might be pronounced against thievery by night or in the baths, housebreakers by day, sneak thieves; deportation to an island, invented by Augustus to prevent banished men in numbers from meeting together, was the sentence for the mildest forms of treason, for false witness and withholding testimony, for armed violence, for extreme cases of libel and extreme crimes against chastity, for cases of forgery by free men, for extreme cases of accepting bribes by public servants, for prophets returning after a first penalty, and for persons of rank convicted of the offenses bringing the death sentence to the common man — for example, false witness resulting in the conviction of a person charged with a crime punishable by death, counterfeiting, introduction of strange and disturbing religion, and conspiring to murder.

The noncapital punishments were: (1) relegation for a time or for life, meaning banishment to or from a definite area, or exile without loss of property or citizenship; (2) corporal punishment, by flogging or beating; (3) imprisonment; (4) fines; (5) loss of rank, as expulsion from the Senate and the senatorial rank in Rome, or from the curia, or local senate, of another city; (6) suspension from the exercise of a calling, as the disbarment of an advocate.

Banishment for life or various periods, *relegatio*, was the sentence for treason before the Empire made it death. It was the sentence also for some cases of accepting bribes, for selling bread with false weights, for artificial raising of prices, for killing by negligence, for willful imprisonment or detention, for sneak thievery, for receiving stolen animals, for stealing from a burning house, for milder cases of robbery on the highway, for armed expulsion of a man from his land, for alteration of accounts and forging signatures. For persons of rank, banishment was the sentence for crimes punishable in the common man by deportation, the mines, public works, or death. These crimes included alloying the State's metals, adultery, using potions, theft of livestock, appropriation of sacred, public, or devoted property, fraudulent contract.

Corporal punishment, in the form of beating with rods, was inflicted for swearing falsely by the emperor's Genius, for adultery at least in Justinian's time, and for sneak thievery. Malicious accusation of crime might be punished with branding of the letter K, until Constantine replaced it with banishment or degradation from rank.

Imprisonment in the usual sense seems to have had little to do with criminal law. "Punishments of this sort," writes Ulpian, a chief contributor to legal science who died A.D. 228, "are forbidden; for the prison must be regarded as a place for the detention of men and not for punishment." If the prison had the effect of punishment, it was by reason of the detention in it, as a result of the law's delays and abuses, of men accused or condemned of crimes and waiting for trial or execution of sentence. Imprisonment for debt, which early took the place of enslavement for debt, and was in its turn abolished by Constantine, was not an act of the State, but an act of the creditor sanctioned by the State, and has nothing to do with criminal law.

Fines could be levied on persons of rank who gave potions, for taking part in ejectment by means not forcible, for causing the torture of another man's slave, and in earlier times for kidnaping. In earlier times also the appropriation of sacred or public property was punished with fourfold restitution. Cato speaks of thieves being penalized twofold and usurers fourfold.

Degradation from rank might follow malicious accusation of crime or fraudulent contract, and was incidental to the major crimes. Suspension from professional practice was of about the same severity as temporary exile.

Before going on to general conclusions regarding the criminal law, a word should be said about places of detention in Rome. The visitor to the Tullianum at the head of the Roman Forum to-day who is familiar with classical letters also can hardly fail to reflect on the scantness of this prison of two chambers and the silence of Roman literature as to any other prison in the city. Rome had a million or more inhabitants, and many criminal offenders. We recall, for example, Juvenal's reference to the robbers who, "every time the Pomptine Marshes are made safe by armed guards, come running into the city for refuge as if to a preserve. At what forge and on what anvil are not heavy chains being made? So great is the amount of iron consumed for shackles that you are afraid the plowshare will fail us and the mattock and hoe give out. Happy the generations of our forefathers, ah, happy the times of old which under the kings and tribunes saw Rome content with a single prison!"

What has been said of imprisonment explains in part. With the prison used only as a place of detention until the next step in law was taken — until a trial was called, or until execution took place, for example; and with deportation, banishment, and hard labor in the mines or public

THE TULLIANUM

Called also the Mamertine Prison, this was the dungeon into which the conspirators were thrown by order of Cicero, in which Jugurtha and Vercingetorix were confined, and which tradition says received Saints Peter and Paul. The column at which it is said that the Apostles were bound is inclosed in an iron frame, the spring from which they baptized their jailors and fellow prisoners is below it, and a commemorative inscription above.

works taking the place of the modern penalty of imprisonment, there could have been no great, long-period, residential prisons like those of to-day. The Tullianum served for the convicted awaiting execution — a Jugurtha, the conspirators of Catiline, a Vercingetorix; and the neighboring prison chambers not visible to-day, with the seven stations and fourteen substations of the seven thousand men of the city watch, for those awaiting less tragic fates, and for the disturbers usual in the streets of a large city.

Such were crime and punishment as reduced to final system under the Empire. No thoughtful person needs to be told that the system was the result of long development. The simple laws of the first kings, when the monarch in person or by delegation heard and decided every case whether civil or criminal, were multiplied and specialized as the State grew and its life became complex, until their written statement in the Twelve Tables was necessary. The long attempt of the Republic to accomplish justice by popular means was full of trouble. The trial of the accused before the assembled people, presided over by the praetor or other magistrate, was inexpert and cumbersome, and its outcome likely to depend on feeling rather than fact. The Special Commissions for criminal cases, sitting in small numbers, knowing more of law, and less the prey of prejudice, were a partial remedy, and soon led to the Standing Commissions, each a court for a special crime and having its own constitution and procedure.

But the defects of democratic justice went deep. Even with these courts, there was much inexpertness, and much opportunity for prejudice. The praetor and the president, who was his substitute on occasion, were not necessarily learned in the law, and the praetor was a politician owing office to the people. The jurors were at first from the senatorial class, then from the equestrian, then from both, then from the senators again under Sulla's domination. Their office throughout the Republic was never free from politics. Trials were at first held in the open air, and then in the basilica, with the public crowding about and likely to let its preferences be known. Worst of all was the right of the people's tribunes to interfere in cases of the death penalty. By the time of Polybius, 150 B.C., the tribune's aid to the capital offender had been exercised so often that exile instead of death was possible for at least all criminals of rank or prominence. This was due to the thoroughly ingrained feeling of the tribune that it was his duty to intercede for the individual against the magistrate.

With the coming of the Caesars, a great change took place. The control of the courts, like every other activity, was centralized in the emperor. Like the king in the beginning, he was in person or by delegation the supreme judge as well as the supreme lawmaker.

To aid the emperor in this function, Augustus in 25 B.C. created the prefect of the city of Rome, with the cohorts as instruments of law and order. In time the prefect's civil jurisdiction extended a hundred miles beyond the city limits, his criminal jurisdiction, of course with the aid of delegates, through all Italy. He had the power to banish, deport, and send to the mines, and heard appeals from all parts of the Empire, his sentences admitting of no appeal except to the emperor. The praetorian prefect, in command of the emperor's life guards, was also important in criminal matters.

Outside Italy, criminal as well as civil jurisdiction was given by Augustus to the twelve legates or presidents in charge of the twelve provinces under Augustus' personal control, and to the twelve proconsuls in charge of the senatorial provinces. Both classes of governors were intrusted with universal and absolute powers, but were responsible to Rome for their proper exercise.

The enumeration of crimes and punishments contained in this chapter depends mostly upon the statements of the law in the legal treatises and compilations of the Empire.

It need not be thought, however, that the laws themselves were greatly different from the laws of the last century of the Republic. The law no doubt kept on with its natural change and natural growth, but laws are conservative. It was in the administration of the laws that the great change took place — in its removal from the sphere of politics, in its concentration in responsible hands, in the expedition of its processes by personal authority, in the freedom of governor and prefect from too strict regard for precedent. The matter of the law remained much the same. The principal laws of the Empire touching crime had been formulated long before they appeared in the Code of Justinian or in the famous legal writers three hundred years before him. The Julian Law on Treason, for example, was passed under Julius Caesar; the Julian Law on Adultery, under Augustus; the Julian Law on Violence either Public or Private, and the Julian Law on Embezzlement, it is uncertain whether under Caesar or Augustus; the Cornelian Law on Assassins, and the Cornelian Law on Forgery, under Sulla; the Pompeian Law on the Murder of Blood Relations, under Pompey the Great. The Fabian Law on Kidnaping was known to Cicero; and there were other Julian laws, on Corrupt Practices in Election, on Extortion by Provincial Governors, on Food Prices, on Incomplete Accounts.

The criminal laws of the Empire were therefore substantially those existing under Augustus at the end of the last century before Christ. Many were the work of Sulla's reforms before that, and many had been in operation in their essentials since the Roman State began.

XXXVI

THE ROMAN DEAD

At a death rate of fifteen in a thousand per year, a moderate average in capital cities to-day, in the Rome of one million inhabitants there would have been fifteen thousand Romans carried to their last resting places in the year, and about forty every day. The fact of death was important in Living Rome.

The fifteen thousand who died each year included the high and the low, the slave and the free, the native and the alien, the old and the young, the woman and the man, the variously employed, the variously worshiping; and the evidence on death and the disposal of the dead in literature, inscriptions, sculpture, tombs, sarcophagi, and bones and ashes embraces many centuries. Care must be taken not to confuse one period with another, or the particular with the general.

Let us begin with the Roman of noble and wealthy family of Augustan times. The members of the family are about his bed as he sinks into the dark unknown and leaves to them only the inert clay so different from his former self. When the first shock is over, one or all bend over him and several times cry out his name. This is the *conclamatio*, the " crying out together." It is at the same time an expression of grief and a formality, and may have begun in primitive times with the attempt to wake the dead back to life. The nearest of kin perhaps also kisses him as if to receive into the family line the last breath, and makes the formal announcement, " *Conclamatum est* — the cry has been raised."

The women of the house, or perhaps the professional from outside with his assistants, now take charge. The eyes that see no more are closed, the body is bathed, perhaps embalmed, then dressed in the toga, the full dress of Roman

A ROMAN LYING IN STATE

The sloping roof shows that the scene is the atrium. Tall funeral torches burn at the four corners of the bier, and there is a lamp on a candelabrum at either end. Mourners and attendants surround the dead person; one plays the pipes, and others beat their breasts and sing the dirge.

times, decorated with all the insignia won in a long and distinguished career, and placed on the stately funeral couch in the darkened atrium, feet toward the vestibule and street, to await the day of carrying forth. Possibly an old custom is observed, and a coin placed in the mouth as passage money

across the Styx. Tall candelabra supporting burning censers
are placed at the corners of the couch. The rising and falling
light plays on the rich, deep-hued draperies of the couch, and
on the round wreaths of palm and flowers and ribbons that lie
on the dead and about him. Attendants are by, with watch-
ers, and perhaps even the paid funeral mourners.

At some time before the lying in state, a wax impression
of the face has been taken, the *imago*. This will occupy its
niche in the family room, one of the two *alae* off the rear
corners of the atrium, with all the similar masks of the ancestral line, and will be accompanied by its inscription, or *titulus*,
placing on record the name, parentage, years, offices, and
deeds of the dead. The right of thus displaying *imagines*
belongs only to those of curule rank. Cicero acquired it on
the day he was elected curule aedile.

Outside, the fact of death is made known by the display
of a branch of cypress or pine at the street door, like the
flowers and ribbons or sprinkled sulphur of to-day. This is
also a safeguard for neighbors and strangers against religious
or social impropriety.

Three to seven days elapse before the funeral. In exceptional cases it is conducted by and paid for by the State or
city. Its coming occurrence is cried through the streets in
an ancient formula. When the hour arrives, the *dissignator*,
or master of ceremonies, is at hand with his lictors and has
given his instructions. The funeral train begins to move.

The musicians with the solemn notes of their brasses are
first, and perhaps the professional chanters of the dirge.
Dancers and pantomimists follow, impersonating the deceased, sometimes even with jests. Then come the chariots,
scores of them, if not the six hundred at the funeral of
Marcellus, in which are men in the official costumes of the
dead man's long line of ancestors, wearing their death masks,

now taken from the niches in the *ala*. The long train of consuls, praetors, and generals thus recalled to life, each preceded by his lictors, is conducting the most recent of the family line to his place with them in the shadowy nether world.

Then come the dead man's memorials, after the manner of a triumph — his horses, his insignia, his trophies, and paintings or tableaux portraying his exploits; and then more lictors, these with down-pointed fasces, and men with torches, a remnant of one-time burial by night; and then, high on the jolting and rumbling funeral car, or on the shoulders of the men of his house, the dead himself, uncovered to the sky, or inclosed but represented by a statue clad in his robes and mask. About him are the favored slaves, now freedmen, emancipated in his will, and, following him, the mourning family, clothed in black, the sons with veiled heads, the daughters with heads uncovered and hair flowing, the women without ornament and the men without insignia showing office or rank, and such of the friends and the public as were prompted to follow.

The funeral is a great spectacle. On both sides, as the solemn parade passes, the Roman populace presses to the line, throngs the steps of the public buildings, and fills every window and balcony.

The procession slowly threads the long street between the lines of the tall houses, and emerges into the Forum. The chariots with their ghostly occupants deploy on its pavement, and the dead is carried through their midst to the Rostra. As he lies on its broad platform in the presence of ancient memorials of the city's greatness, with massive arcaded façades and the tall colonnades of temples looking down from every side and the Capitol rising far above, his nearest survivor's voice is raised in the funeral oration, the *laudatio*, a glorification of the dead and his forefathers which will be preserved in the family archives.

The funeral train forms again, passes through the Arch of Augustus, winds up the Sacred Way between temples and

THE APPIAN WAY ABOUT THREE MILES FROM ROME

The Appia was excavated and cleared by order of Pius IX in 1853. Ruins of tombs and monuments are plentiful. Two carabinieri, or country police, are seen with their mounts.

porticoes, and descends to the street that leads through the city gate to the Appian Way. In one of the long lines of lots that border the Queen of Roads there stands a newly erected funeral pyre, perhaps in the form of an altar. Here the procession halts. The dead is placed upon the pyre, with ornament, arms, or other possessions cherished in life, and tokens brought by friends and relatives.

When all is ready, the nearest of kin, a beloved friend, or some civic dignitary, with averted face applies the torch. The pyre and its burden are speedily enveloped in crackling flames, are consumed, and sink in a glowing mass. The embers are quenched with water or wine, a final farewell is uttered, like another conclamatio, and all return to the city but the immediate relatives. These remain behind to collect the remnants of the cremated body, to bury formally a fragment of the body in order to preserve the form of inhumation, to perform ceremonies in consecration of the ground and in purification of themselves from contact with the dead, and to partake of a funeral communion in the family tomb-chapel.

Nine days of mourning follow, on one of which the now dry ashes are inclosed in an urn of metal or marble and carried by a member of the family, barefooted and ungirdled, to their final place of rest in the tomb chamber. At the end of the nine days, a feast to the dead, called *sacrum novendiale*, is celebrated at the tomb and a funeral banquet held at the home. Mourning continues ten months for husbands, wives, parents, and adult sons and daughters, eight months for other adult relatives, and in the case of children for as many months as their years. Memorial festivals of the nature of a communion are celebrated on February 13–21, the Parentalia or pagan All-Souls', on the birth or burial anniversary, and at the ends of March and May, the Violaria and Rosaria, when violets and roses are profusely distributed, lamps lighted in the tomb, funeral banquets held, and offerings made to the Manes, the spirits of the dead.

The funeral of the grandee thus described was not unfamiliar to the Roman people, but it was the exception and

not the rule. The splendor of its appointments, the dignity
of its participants, the stately progress of the procession, the
magnificent setting of the Forum, the Sacred Way, and the
Appian Way, made it one of the most imposing spectacles
of all time. It is best compared with the funerals of the
princely families of modern Rome, or of Italian royalty,
though its display was probably far greater. Still more imposing were the great imperial funerals, whose trains proceeded from the Forum through the magnificent distances of
the Campus Martius to the Mausoleum of Augustus at its
northern end.

" He was twice eulogized," Suetonius says of Augustus, "in
front of the Temple of Divine Julius by Tiberius and in front
of the Rostra Vetera by Drusus, the son of Tiberius, and was carried on the shoulders of senators to the Campus and there cremated. And a man of praetorian rank came forward to swear
that he had seen the effigy of the cremated rising to the sky. The
remains were gathered up by the ranking men of the equestrian
order, in tunic, ungirdled, and barefoot, and laid away in the
Mausoleum. This building, between the Via Flaminia and the
Tiber bank, he had built in his sixth consulship and at that time
too had opened for the use of the public the groves and walks
lying about it."

Polybius, a century and a half before Augustus' funeral,
writes vividly of the great Roman funerals as an institution
contributing to Roman character:

"Now not only do Italians in general naturally excel Phoenicians and Africans in bodily strength and personal courage, but
by their institutions also they do much to foster a spirit of bravery
in the young men. A single instance will suffice to indicate the
pains taken by the State to turn out men who will be ready to endure everything in order to gain a reputation in their country for
valor.

"Whenever any illustrious man dies, he is carried at his funeral
into the Forum to the so-called Rostra, sometimes conspicuous in

THE FORUM RESTORED AS SEEN FROM THE TEMPLE OF JULIUS CAESAR

From right to left: small shrine of Venus Cloacina, Basilica Aemilia, gable of the Senate House, Arch of Septimius Severus, Rostra, Temples of Concordia, Vespasian, and Saturn, Basilica Julia. Above, on the Capitoline Hill: Temple of Juno, Tabularium, Temple of Jupiter.

an upright posture, and more rarely reclined. Here, with all the people standing round, a grown-up son, if he has left one who happens to be present, or if not, some other relative, mounts the Rostra and discourses on the virtues and successful achievements of the dead. As a consequence the multitude, and not only those who had a part in these achievements but those also who had none, when the facts are recalled to their minds and brought before their eyes, are moved to such sympathy that the loss seems to be not confined to the mourners, but a public one affecting the whole people. Next, after the interment and the performance of the usual ceremonies, they place the image of the departed in the most conspicuous position in the house, enclosed in a wooden shrine. This image is a mask reproducing with remarkable fidelity both the features and complexion of the deceased. On the occasion of public sacrifices they display these images, and decorate them with much care, and when any distinguished member of the family dies they take them to the funeral, putting them on men who seem to them to bear the closest resemblance to the original in stature and carriage. These representatives wear togas, with a purple border if the deceased was a consul or praetor, whole purple if he was a censor, and embroidered with gold if he had celebrated a triumph or achieved anything similar. They all ride in chariots, preceded by the fasces, axes, and other insignia by which the different magistrates are wont to be accompanied, according to the respective dignity of the offices of State held by each during his life; and when they arrive at the Rostra they all seat themselves in a row on ivory chairs. There could not easily be a more ennobling spectacle for a young man who aspires to fame and virtue. For who would not be inspired by the sight of the images of men renowned for their excellence, all together and as if alive and breathing?"

The funerals of middle- and lower-class people, and of most of the upper class, were less pretentious, without the masks and oration. Children, citizens of the lowest class, and slaves were carried to their last rest with few formalities and few followers other than the nearest relatives.

The Roman cemetery was not like our modern burial

grounds, apart and silent, but took the form of a very long and narrow series of private lots along the highways leading from the city gates. The lots began at the lines of the road, and their imposing monuments were almost at its edge. There was probably no road without tombs near the city, and frequently they stood also along the country roads or on estates. The highways most used for cemeteries at Rome were the Via Flaminia and the Via Salaria on the north, the Tiburtina and Praenestina on the east, the Latina and Appia on the south, and the Aurelia and Cornelia on the west. The most famous of all was the much-traveled Appian Way, which is still bordered for many miles with almost continuous tomb ruins.

The two hundred or more larger tomb remains on the Appian Way include most of the types of the Roman sepulcher. There was the mausoleum, round and probably with conical summit, whose name and shape were due to the tomb of Mausolus, the king of Caria, who died about 351 B.C. The tumulus, a conical mound of varying size heaped over the body or ashes, also a reminder of Asia, was another form. There was the tomb built above ground, the tomb excavated in the tufa bed of the Campagna, and the combination of tomb below and family chamber or chapel above. There was the *columbarium*, for ashes of the burial associations or brotherhoods so frequent in Rome; and there were the underground chambers and corridors now called catacombs.

The burial lots of the Appian Way were marked by stones inscribed with dimensions: e.g. *in fronte p. XVI, in agro p. XXII*, " frontage 16 feet, depth 22 feet." On some stones and tombs there were added threats, curses, or legal formulae, to safeguard the area and monuments against violation. A frequent abbreviation, *H M H N S*, meant, *Hoc monumentum heredem non sequetur* — " this monument shall not follow the heir," and was due to the fear that the survivors might appropriate the monument for other purposes.

The more pretentious areas were great family lots, for all the members of a gens, or of the branch of a gens, including its freedmen and slaves, and sometimes other clients, and friends. Such a burial place might include a large plot of ground, with an area for the tomb, a garden behind it, a crematory, *ustrinum*, shrines with statues of the dead, *aediculae*, a room for anniversary communions, pavilion, well, and custodian's quarters.

THE TOMBSTONE OF MINICIA
MARCELLA

"To the departed spirit of Minicia Marcella, daughter of Fundanus. She lived 12 years, 11 months, 7 days."

The eagle between the rosettes may symbolize the flight of the soul.

The Roman tomb inscriptions, cut on slabs let into the front of the monument, or on stones at the graves of individuals, or near the remains inside the vault, are varied in content and expression. Most of them contain the name, parentage, public offices, and an accurate statement of the length of life, without dates of death and birth. An example is afforded by the epitaph of Minicia, daughter of Fundanus, whose death is the subject of a letter by Pliny, who says she was scarce thirteen, and already had all the wisdom of years and the sedateness of a matron, but joined with youthful sweetness. Her tombstone is in the National Museum in Rome: " To the Departed Spirit of Minicia Marcella, Daughter of Fundanus. She lived 12 years, 11 months, and 7 days." A portrait bust sometimes accompanied the epitaph, still a frequent practice in the cemetery at Rome, where photos or paintings of the dead are also seen on tombstones. Sometimes the inscription was an address to the passer-by from the departed, as that of one Marcus Caecilius lying by the Appian Way:

"This monument is erected to Marcus Caecilius.
Stranger, I am pleased that you stop at my resting place.
Good fortune to you, and fare you well; may you sleep
without care."

Such appeals as this, with the use of portrait sculpture and the practice of roadside burial, show how keen was the Roman reluctance to be cut off entirely from the affairs of the living —

"For who, to dumb forgetfulness a prey,
This pleasing anxious being e'er resigned,
Left the warm precincts of the cheerful day,
Nor cast one longing lingering look behind?"

Possibly they show also the instinctive belief in a future existence.

A frequent form of tomb among the humbler classes, especially freedmen and the working part of the population, was the *columbarium*, so named because its walls inside resembled a dove-cote. Long, narrow vaults or chambers were either built above ground or excavated in the tufa, and their walls made into compact rows of niches a foot or so high and wide, large enough to receive an urn holding the ashes of one person, whose name was on the urn or on a little slab below it, sometimes with his bust placed near. One of these columbaria on the Via Appia was for the freedmen of Augustus and Livia, and in it were found three hundred *tituli*, epitaphs. Such tombs were sometimes the gift of some benevolent person, and sometimes represented a business man's investment, but it was more usual for them to be built, or at least managed, by coöperative funeral guilds, which sold stock, assessed regular dues, and paid benefits, thus insuring their members proper entombment. Their administrators divided and assigned the space by lot, and the holders might in turn sell their shares. It is interesting to see the Italian word *colombario* in use to-day, in the cemetery at Rome, applied to the rows of coffin cells built for economy of space.

The lot of the ordinary slave and the poorest class of citizens was less fortunate. Outside the Servian Wall where it crossed the broad and level area of the Esquiline, there existed up to Horace's time an old burial ground which might be called the potter's field of Rome. The poet's patron, Maecenas, transformed it into gardens. Excavations begun in 1872 showed that there was an irregular area of a mile or more, between the present railway terminus and the Lateran Church, which had served from earliest times as a burial ground. One of the poems of Horace quite clearly refers to it.

"Hither, of yore, their fellow slave contracted to carry in their cheap coffins the dead sent forth from their narrow dwellings; here lay the common sepulcher of the wretched plebs. A thousand feet frontage, three hundred feet depth, were the limits the stone gave — the monument not to follow the heirs. To-day you may dwell on a healthful Esquiline, and take walks on the sunny embankment, where but now your sad gaze rested upon a field ugly with whitening bones."

The poet's mention of the cheap coffins and the slave hireling, the contrast between the gloomy Esquiline of former days and the gardens now in its place, and the satiric allusion to the marker as the one monument of a whole city of wretched poor, " not to follow the heirs," speak plainly of the lot of the lowest classes after death. The excavations brought to light pit graves, thirteen to sixteen feet square and of great depth, into which we must suppose the bodies of the criminal and otherwise unfortunate were thrown one above the other, unburned, and with little ceremony.

Throughout the pagan period, cremation and inhumation existed side by side, with cremation increasing until it came to be all but universal. The earliest burial places of Rome — the lowest stratum on the Esquiline, and the prehistoric cemetery discovered on the Sacred Way near the Forum in 1902 — contain both cinerary urns of terra cotta and coffins made of hollowed logs. The later strata in the Esquiline cemetery also contain both. The burial chambers of the Scipios, who were a branch of the Cornelian gens, on the Appian Way outside the walls of their time, but within the later wall of Aurelian, were filled with sarcophagi of stone containing unburned dead. In many large tombs the heads of families were laid away in sarcophagi, with the cremated freedmen and humbler members of the household deposited about them in the same chamber. Burial without burning, because the natural and originally cheaper way, was the basic and popular custom in the early stages of the Roman community. Even in Augustan times, when cremation had almost entirely displaced inhumation, it was customary, as a symbol of earth burial, to inter a small part of the body, the os resectum, usually a joint of the little finger.

We have reviewed the variations in burial practice due to differences in class, wealth, belief, taste, and tradition principally in the first century of the Empire and in the city of Rome. There were naturally also variations according to period. For example, burial by night was a practice of earlier times, and was prescribed again by Julian, A.D. 361, on the ground of inconvenience to the city's traffic caused by daylight funerals. Again, the burials of the earliest times were less distant, by reason of the lesser circumference of the city walls; each successive line of defense carrying the line of tombs farther out because of the law forbidding burial within the city limit. There was less of both display and poverty before the rise of the Empire, though laws forbidding extravagance in funerals were known from the first centuries of the city. The use of chambers and galleries excavated in the soft tufa bed of the Campagna, long known

THE CREMATION AND APOTHEOSIS OF THE EMPRESS SABINA

From the pyre the soul of the Empress is borne aloft by the winged Spirit of the After-life. The grieving Emperor Hadrian looks on, with finger pointed to the sky. At the foot of the pyre is a figure symbolizing the Campus Martius, where the cremation took place. Behind Hadrian is Antoninus, who will succeed him.

on a small scale in the pagan era, grew much more general after the rise of Christian Rome, developing the great communal burying places of the catacombs. Cremation died out because of belief in the resurrection, and perhaps also because it was more expensive.

In other cities of the Empire, especially in the West, burial practices, like most other customs, were essentially the same as at Rome.   In small towns and villages, no doubt there was much conservatism, and some customs were retained long after they had gone out in the capital.   All periods in the history of Roman burial, however, are unified by the belief of all but the few in the continued existence of the dead and in his shadowy presence in the life of the family and community, and by the consequent scrupulous care in proper burial and in the maintenance of right relations with the spirits of dead ancestors.   The communion of the living with the dead is by no means unknown to the belief and feeling of to-day, but to the ancient Roman it was much more real.

PART IV
GREATER ROME

GREATER ROME

Thus far we have been concerned in the main with a Rome on the Seven Hills. We have seen the physical setting of Rome in the Italy of to-day and its capital, modern Rome, and its cultural setting in the language and letters, law and religion, arts and ideals, inherited by modern times from ancient Rome. We have seen the Roman as he looked and moved at home and on the streets in the round of personal affairs. We have seen him as he moved in the larger environment of the varied life of his million neighbors, a part of Living Rome.

This has been to make acquaintance with Rome the City, compact and clearly outlined, warm with the energy of growth and action, distinct in character.

But the Rome we have been describing was not the only Rome; or, rather, it was not the whole of Rome. There was not only Rome the City, *Urbs*, covering the hills and crossing the stream and having its bounds; there was also Rome the Empire, *Orbis*, the vast organism of land and sea reaching out to the oceans and rivers and deserts and barbarian wilderness which nature seemed to have intended as its limits. This Rome is not the City, but a civilization thinking the thoughts and living the life of the City. It may be called Greater Rome.

XXXVII

THE SPREAD OF ROMAN CIVILIZATION

The rise of the Roman State has already been described: the annexation of the neighboring hills and tribes, the leadership in Latium, the conquest of the Volscian, the Etruscan, the Latin, the Samnite, and the Greek of South Italy, the crossing into Sicily, the Carthaginian wars and the winning of Sardinia and Corsica, Spain, and northern Africa, the Macedonian wars and the expansion to the east, the absorption of Greece and Asia Minor and Egypt, the push into Gaul and Britain, the invasion of Dacia, the advance to the Tigris and Euphrates. The world conquered by the citizen-soldier of the Republic, shaped and set in order by Augustus, maintained by Tiberius, extended by Claudius and the Flavians, completed by Trajan, and stabilized by Hadrian, was bounded on the north by the Black Sea, the Danube and the German wall and the Rhine, and the British wall from the Tyne to the Solway, except where it went beyond these lines to include Dacia and the German provinces; on the west it was bounded by the Atlantic; on the south, from Tangiers to the Red Sea, by the line of the Atlas Mountains and the desert; on the east, by the Arabian Desert and the Euphrates.

At its longest and widest, the Empire thus bounded was 3,000 miles from west to east, and 2,000 miles from north to south. It contained 2,500,000 square miles, and a population estimated at 100,000,000. The modern population is about twice that. To reach from Rome the last fort on the

438

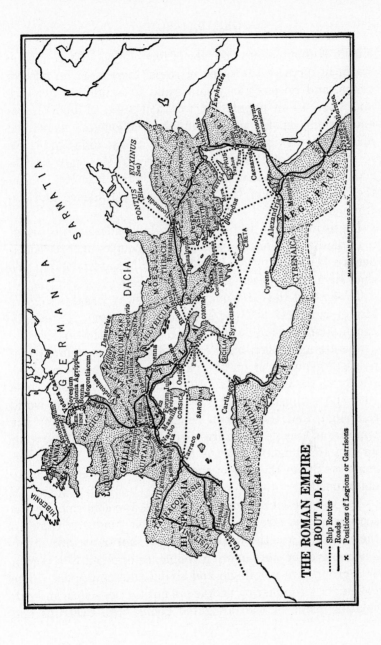

THE ROMAN EMPIRE
ABOUT A.D. 64

······· Ship Routes
——— Roads
x Positions of Legions or Garrisons

MANHATTAN DRAFTING CO. N.Y.

Nile in Nubia meant a journey of forty days. There was no steam to increase the speed of ships, there were no express trains, and no electricity and radio to annihilate distance and time. The population was composed of many races and colors, spoke many different languages, worshiped many different gods, and was at many different levels of culture. Yet the peace and unity of this vast territorial miscellany to-day, compared with the Pax Romana in the best centuries of the Empire, is as turbulence and distraction.

Let us look, first, into the causes that underlay this bringing together into one household of the peoples of three continents and the countless islands of the Mediterranean. We shall then be prepared to appreciate their effects.

To say that the extension of Roman sway was due to mere lust of conquest and the satisfaction of greed, is the easy explanation of shallow minds. These are the motives of deliberate aggression on the part of ambitious military and political geniuses or on the part of calculating oligarchies. No Cyrus the Great or Napoleon inflamed the Roman people with the enthusiasm that sweeps all before it in the world campaign, and the Roman Senate, always harried by the opposition, was never an irresponsible coterie of plotters for its own enrichment. By the time dictator and emperor became the State, the area of the Roman world was practically determined.

The Empire set in order by Augustus and confirmed by his successors was already conquered when Augustus came to the task. It was the work of a people, not of an individual. The motives of a conquering people, as opposed to a person or a group, are not single and simple, but multiplex. The policies of a conquering people are not the conscious and calculating plans of the farsighted genius who overruns and unites a world in one lifetime, but the sum of the uncertainties and inconsistencies of the slow-moving centuries.

The Roman people's advance to the domination of the world was not always the precise and steady march of an army well commanded. The needs of the moment, and even accident, as well as foresight and design, determined its

THE EMPEROR TRAJAN AND HIS LICTORS
The idealized retinue of the Emperor imitate his manner of wearing the hair.

policies. Rome's first growths in territory were due to alliances for safety's sake which soon resulted in union and amalgamation in the common interest. The advance of its borders, due to this natural cause, created the usual friction and the usual problems of security. The student of national expansion to-day does not need to be told that beyond the border there is always a zone whose menaces to safety necessitate its conquest, and whose occupation brings another border and another zone, until the limit of territory or of strength establishes a final boundary. The Roman Republic was not secure in Italy until by alliance, peaceful annexation, conquest provoked by the enemy's threats, and conquest compelled by actual aggression, its borders had reached the sea on three sides and the Alps on the fourth. It was not secure on the sea until it had made the Mediterranean a Roman lake. It was not secure for great distances beyond this until it had reached the Atlantic, the Rhine and the Danube, the Pontus, the Euphrates, the Red Sea, and the Sahara, and had supplemented the work of nature by erecting the English and Scottish walls and the three hundred and forty-five miles of palisade across the gap from Rhine to Danube.

The growth of the Roman power was the growth of a living organism. It was as inevitable as the expansion of a healthy plant or animal. When men of Virgil's time began to talk of Eternal Rome and the Destiny of Rome, they were only expressing in artificial fashion the feeling that Rome had conquered the world and was ruling it, not because of the lust for power or the greed for gain, but because she was the instrument of a power beyond human control and beyond the realm of human comprehension. The reverent poet thought of that power as divine and of another world. Plain-thinking men, without resort to the other world, thought of it as Nature.

To say that Roman expansion was the work of nature, however, and that the Roman people was its instrument, is not to declare that the lust of conquest and the appetite for worldly gain did not exist. The Roman was human and knew temptation, and Nature herself is not kindly toward those who interfere with the growth of her creatures.

From the first, the Roman possessed the vigorous physique, the healthy courage, the ready intelligence, and the feeling for discipline that make the soldier. As he left behind him the ever lengthening line of successes against his enemies in

THE SPREAD OF ROMAN CIVILIZATION

arms, the mastery of the science of war and the consciousness
of power developed his courage into the disciplined confidence
that shrinks at no personal danger and faces odds as a
matter of course. It must not be supposed that this confidence was unaccompanied by pride and that it did not
sometimes impel its possessor to the arrogant and arbitrary
use of arms.

From the beginning, too, the Roman was of a thrifty
nature. The little wars he won in Latium, whether forced
upon him or of his own provoking, brought him his little gains
in land or animals. The wars which made him master of the
Etruscan, Samnite, and Italian Greek opened up to him
the riches of Italy's fields and forests and quarries. With
the control of rich provinces across the mountains and the
sea that soon followed, Roman commerce and Roman investment, already active before the lands were Roman, assumed
much larger proportions. It must not be supposed that the
gains which were at first the accident of war did not at times
become a contributing cause of war. The opportunities
promised by the annexation of a new province or the acquisition of a further sphere of influence were a temptation too
great to be always resisted.

Let us think of interests involved. There was the State
and its need for greater revenues. There was the crowded
capital, welcoming the opportunity to send out colonies and
thus to relieve itself of pressure and reduce the list of parasites
receiving the dole. There was the dictator or military hero
in need of lands with which to reward his veterans. There
were the politician and the demagogue wanting material for
promises. There were the contractors and men of capital
looking for new fields for earning and investment. There was
the party or person in power looking for an issue with which
to win favor or divert disaffection. There was the army man

ambitious for a career or eager for opportunity to test the latest military engine or idea. There were the general and his staff and the rank and file, ready for adventure and not without thought of the spoils of war. Our surprise should be, not that Roman character for a time weakened under the strain of almost unparalleled temptation that came with the avalanche of territory after the Carthaginian and Macedonian wars, but that the Roman State did not make conquest a business for its own sake.

THE EMPEROR MARCUS AURELIUS RECEIVING THE NORTHERN BARBARIANS IN SUBMISSION

As it was, the case of aggression pure and simple and without excuse was rare. If we had the views of Carthaginian and Greek and Gaul and German and Briton at the moment of defeat, no doubt we should be told such cases; but the Roman would be ready to advance his justification. Roman citizens and property at the border, he would have said, had been molested and made to feel unsafe; trader and traveler on Roman ships had been taken by pirates in waters not patrolled by the claimants of jurisdiction over them; the rights of Roman citizens in the offending territory had not been respected; a treaty had been violated; an ally had been aggrieved or attacked and must be quieted; a petty and backward or decadent state was hindering the march of civilization, and Rome was after all performing a service to the world and the conquered state itself. In short, the Roman apologist would have demonstrated that what seemed an arbitrary act of aggression was provoked and inevitable.

The charge of hypocrisy is easily made. When motives are mixed, as we have seen was the case in Roman conquest, it is necessary only to emphasize the unworthy motive to the exclusion of the rest. It is in some respects to the interest of the United States, for example, to hold the Philippine Islands; therefore, it might be argued, the United States is holding them for selfish reasons, and is the enemy of freedom and the friend of tyranny.

Without attempting to justify the abuses of Rome's earlier rule in the provinces, or denying the use at times of arbitrary measures in both administration and conquest, let us make a few observations bearing on Roman expansion in its entirety.

In the first place, the Roman conscience was shocked and aroused by the fact of abuse in provincial government. The earliest special standing court established by the Government at home, in 149 B.C., was the court on extortions. As early as 171 B.C., complaints of insolence and avarice on the part of Roman magistrates in the two Spains were promptly followed by legal action at Rome, and the measures taken were collaborative, not autocratic. If there were scandalous abuses in the provinces, the fact that we know it because of the prosecutions at home in the earnest attempt to correct them is not without significance as to the Roman intent.

In the second place, one of the earliest and one of the most effective of Augustan reforms was in provincial administration. The readiness with which it was accomplished must mean that the previous régime was not so hopelessly corrupt as is sometimes represented. It must be remembered, too, that the witness in the case against Rome for maladministration is Rome itself, and that self-condemnation is not to be taken at face value.

In the third place, as the decades passed after the enormous conquests following the Second Punic War, and the conquerors realized the immensity of their task of governing a world, the feeling of responsibility deepened in them. The governed must be protected against the governor; the weak must be protected against the strong; the barbarian must be taught; the decadent must be recalled to pride; the law must equalize rights and duties; life must be made safe, prosperity increased. No one can read Livy's glowing accounts of Flamininus at the Isthmian Games proclaiming the freedom of the Greeks, and of Aemilius Paullus visiting the cities of Greece after the final defeat of their Macedonian oppressor, and of the Carthaginian envoys declaring that the Romans had increased their sway almost more by sparing the vanquished than by conquering them, or Cicero's orations in behalf of the Sicilians against Verres, the influential politician exploiting a province, or the letters written by Cicero while governor of Cilicia, or the odes of Horace reminding the Roman that he rules the world only because he walks humbly before the gods, or Virgil's noble lines on the mission of Rome, without feeling that through all the incapacities and abuses of the Republic in the provinces there was a conscience at work in the State and an ideal present and growing.

In the fourth place, the Roman gave as well as took. In return for total surrender to authority, the conquered nation

received the civilization of the conqueror.   Let us pause at
this point to ask what Romanization meant.

It meant, first, regularization and protection under Roman
authority.   The Roman law and Roman system followed
Roman conquest.   The lands taken over became the prop-

A ROMAN AQUEDUCT IN SPAIN
This fine construction is a few miles from Tarragona, ancient Tarraco.

erty of the Roman State, and were redistributed to colonists
and former tenants, subject to the land tax which formed the
government's principal source of revenue.   The humbler
members of many a community experienced for the first time
the certainties and the justice of enlightened government.

It meant, second, the benefits of an expert language.   The
language of the law and the ruling class in all their communications, oral and written, was Latin.   The schools that fol-

lowed the Roman standards into the backward lands were Latin schools. In many communities they were the first and the only schools, and Latin the first written language in the community's experience.

Again, Romanization meant the arts. The most distant outposts of the Empire had an architecture like that of the capital. The local market place became a little Roman Forum. The sculpture of provincial towns differed only in excellence from that of the centers of art. Mosaics and paintings, wherever found, reflect the art of the capital and Italy.

Still further, it meant the amusements of the capital. The ruins of circus, theater, amphitheater, and baths, now indicating in deserted spots the former presence of a city, are the signs of luxuries in entertainment reaching, for better and worse, the one-time abodes of barbarism.

It meant, fifth, connection with the world of enterprise. The Roman road traversed the provinces, touching the principal centers of prosperity. The Roman ship made calls. The produce of other lands and the news of the world enriched and enlivened existence where hitherto monotony and stagnation had prevailed. The advent of the Roman military road was like the coming of the railroad and its creativeness into the life of the American West or the heart of Africa.

It meant, again, the stimulation from new religious contacts. As Roman altars and temples rose and the Roman immortal gods in their majestic humanity appeared, comparison with the old went far with many a barbarous tribe to make it a convert to the other features of Romanization as well.

Seventh, and greatest of all, the coming of Rome meant sooner or later the rights of the Roman citizen. The rise of the noncitizen to citizenship, whether from captivity in war, or from slavery by purchase, or other alien condition, was a distinctive feature of Roman society.   Beginning in early times, it increased in ease and frequency until in A.D. 212 all free men in the Empire were citizens.   Roman born or alien, Italian or non-Italian, they were on equal footing.   Rome and Italy identified themselves with the world they had conquered.   Unlike most imperial powers of modern times, Rome was not democratic at home and despotic abroad.   The provincials were gradually Romanized and the Roman and Italian gradually universalized, until the distinction between Italian and provincial disappeared.   All called themselves Roman.   Virgil could thus become the poet of all who dwelt within the line that separated culture from barbarism, and Cicero the model for the written and spoken tongue.   What before was *Urbs*, was now *Orbis*.

Finally, with citizenship, if not before, came the Roman ways of thinking and feeling.   Enjoying local and individual freedom under central authority, and recognizing in Rome the source and guarantee of his freedom, the Roman, wherever he was and of whatever blood, looked to the city by the Tiber with loyalty and affection.   Reflecting on the vastness, the unity, and the solidarity of the Empire of Rome, he felt the pride of participation in world rule.   Remembering the centuries of Rome's existence, he called her the Eternal City without question of her continued sway.   If an emperor misruled, or a series of them, it was for the Roman but an episode.   The emperors were for an age, but Rome for all time — Rome, " Mother of Arms and Justice," " Rome, destined to live as long as men shall be," " the city as everlasting as the Pole," " to whose reign there never shall be an end."

Such were the changes which constituted Romanization. They were more thorough or less according to the status of the subject people, who varied from the free-spirited and cultivated Hellene to the ignorant and despot-ridden Egyptian, from the sophisticated, commercial Carthaginian to the barbarian of the German forests, from the rude Spaniard to the luxurious Greeks of Asia.   There were some who profited

THE ROMAN BRIDGE OVER THE GUADIANA AT MERIDA IN SPAIN
Parts of the bridge, which is half a mile long, are of later periods.   The ancient
name of Merida was Emerita Augusta.

more than others, but there were none who did not benefit by the Roman feeling for organization and unity — and by the Roman law.   They were more thorough or less in the same province or city, according to the status of the individual.   The official and commercial circles, whether Italian or native born, represented Rome completely in language, dress, religion, manner of diversion, and mental habit.

Persons of the lower classes, who had less incentive to imitation, kept on with their own language, dress, and customs, and were welcome to do it if they chose. Roman rule in nonessential matters was wisely elastic. The Roman did not feel impelled, like many conquerors, to impose a uniformity in everything. On obedience, loyalty, and good behavior he did insist, but imposed no galling conformities in language, interfered with religion only in case of actual conflict with the State, and allowed the subject people, whenever possible, the laws and usages to which they were born.

In conclusion, if the Roman treatment of the conquered still is in need of vindication, its result may be indicated in evidence. The tongue of the conquerors became the tongue of all the conquered except the Greeks, who had long possessed superior culture, and the Teutons, far away on the border. Even Dacia spoke Latin, and the Roumanian tongue to-day, surrounded by Hungarian, German, Slavic, and Greek, is a romance tongue, the sister of the French, Italian, and Spanish that cover so much of the New World and the Old. The religion of Rome was accepted by them all, and humanized them into the ready recipients of the Christian faith in later years. The Roman Peace enveloped them. There were five hundred towns in Asia without a garrison. In all Gaul, Lyons was the only military post, with twelve hundred men to serve for all the regions that for ten years had resisted the arms of Caesar. The standing army for the Empire's one hundred millions of population was about three hundred thousand, in city-camps along the circumference, and these mostly on the Rhine and Danube, with but infrequent calls to service as some barbarian foray disturbed the peace. The Roman law had won its way among them. It made life safer and relations more just. So thorough an instrument was it that after its service to the ancient world it descended to the medieval and the modern world, and is now the law of Italy, Spain, France, Belgium, Portugal, and all the Latin-speaking countries elsewhere, Greece and southeastern Europe, Switzerland, Holland, Germany, and the Church; and is rivaled as a world force only by the English law.

The political, visible empire of Rome in the West passed out of existence in the fifth century at the coming of the Northerner. In the East it survived longer in the mingling of Greece and the Orient as the Byzantine Empire. From the first consuls of the Republic to the Code of Justinian more than a thousand years elapsed. The civilization thus enduring and leaving after it an inheritance that is living still was not a civilization based on force and greed alone. Whatever its faults in detail, as a whole it owed its initial success and its permanence to character. The Roman people were not only physically strong and temperamentally resolute, but endowed with the sense of justice and responsibility.

" Empire is retained," according to a maxim quoted by James Bryce, " by the same arts whereby it was won." The Empire of Rome from Augustus on, until causes deep-seated and beyond control had sapped its powers, retained its subjects by the arts of peace. It may not have won its subjects by the arts of peace alone, but it could not have won them permanently, as it did, without the arts of peace.

XXXVIII

THE ARMY

The Roman State was founded upon force, though not upon force alone, and the great instrument that made possible the advance and the permanence of its borders was the army. The Roman army, however, must not be thought of merely as a weapon. Taken throughout the history of Rome, it is seen to have been the means not only of conquest but of civilization. This will be made plainer as its uses and character are described.

First, let us consider the army in its purely military aspect, and at a time when its organization is fully developed and practically fixed; for, like everything else Roman, the army also was a product of evolution. The period of the first emperors will be convenient.

The largest unit of the army was the legion, or division, consisting at full strength of 6,000 men. The legion was divided into 10 cohorts of 600 men each, and the cohort into 6 centuries of 100 men each. All were heavy-armed infantry, except 120 cavalry. After long service in the field, or in times when recruits were scarce, the legion might have a much smaller number, and the cohorts and centuries be correspondingly weak in men. Their commanding officers were the *legatus*, lieutenant general; the *tribunus*, colonel; the *centurio*, captain. The commander-in-chief in the time of the Republic was regularly a consul, the two consuls alternating; or, in case of operations in a province, a proconsul, such as Caesar in Gaul; or a dictator, such as Fabius Maxi-

mus in the Second Punic War or Sulla during his control.
Under the Empire, the commander-in-chief was the emperor,
imperator, who sometimes delegated his powers to the
governor in a province, called *legatus pro praetore*, praetorian legate.

THE EMPEROR AND THE GENIUS OF ROME
The Genius presents him with the Symbol of Universal Power.

The organization
thus described consisted of Roman
citizens, and was
only half the army.
The other half consisted of the auxiliaries, a noncitizen
force of about equal
numbers in the main
under citizen officers,
and so divided that
to the 6,000 of every
legion there were
attached 6,000 auxiliaries, in cohorts of
500 to 1,000, with
500 cavalry. The
two together formed
the regular or standing army as established by Augustus. The chief differences
between them, besides the matter of citizenship, were, first,
that the legionaries were volunteers enlisted in any part of
Roman territory and from any blood, while the auxiliaries
were conscripted from subject races and served in racial or
tribal regiments, thus representing a tribute in men exacted

of the conquered; second, that the auxiliaries contained a greater proportion of cavalry; third, that in ordinary times they performed a great deal of frontier police duty; and, fourth, that for the sake of guarding against revolt they soon came to be assigned to service in parts of the Empire far distant from their native soil. When the army went to war, each legionary commander had under him about equal numbers of legionaries and auxiliaries, but the cohorts of the latter, under tribunes or prefects, had their separate camp.

The regular army of the Augustan reform was the natural culmination of Roman military experience. When the primitive Roman State went to war, it was with an army of able-bodied farmers, cattle men, and villagers led by their king and his retainers, all of them citizens. If they were the aggressors, or had the choice, they went forth in March, the month of Mars, carried on their operations until the rains and cold of late autumn ended the military season, and passed the winter in comparative inactivity so far as the field was concerned. With the spread of Roman authority through Italy, there came the need both of improved military science and of larger armies.

The need of military science was supplied by the development of the legionary system and the strict exclusion from it of the noncitizen; every citizen was bred to expertness in arms and every citizen of able body between 18 and 38 owed the State his service at the call to arms. It was the legion composed solidly of the citizen-soldiers of the Republic that occupied the post of honor and consequently met the brunt of battle.

The need of larger armies, the greater because of this exposure of the citizen to danger, was met by the use of men conscripted from the vanquished. When the business of conquest carried the Roman arms beyond Italy's borders, the need of men for operation and occupation increased so much that not only were more auxiliaries employed, but it was no longer possible to insist on Italian birth, to say nothing of Roman, as a qualification for enrollment in the legion. The citizen from outside Italy was admitted as a private, and in time as an officer. The noncitizen also, in time, was accepted, but by the act itself became a citizen.

Long before Caesar's time, the army had lost the civic and taken on the professional character. Its rank and file served for pay and enlisted for a term, and its officers made the army a career. So far had the original identity of the army and the body of ordinary citizens disappeared that generals like Caesar, Pompey, Marius, and Sulla raised armies and paid them almost without action on the part of the State and employed them sometimes even for private ends. When Augustus unified the military forces of the State and made himself commander-in-chief of the standing army of legionaries and auxiliaries, the act was a completion of the process of making military service professional as well as a beginning of the army's use as a scientific instrument in the employ of the State.

The number of men under arms in the Roman State, as well as their character, varied according to period and conditions. The army that met disaster at Cannae in 216 B.C. numbered about 80,000 infantry and 6,000 cavalry, while Hannibal's forces were 40,000 infantry and 10,000 cavalry. Caesar's forces in the first campaign in Gaul, 58 B.C., consisted of six legions and 20,000 auxiliaries, and are estimated at a total of 40,000 to 50,000 men; in the seventh campaign, 52 B.C., they amounted to about 70,000, consisting of 11 legions and about 30,000 auxiliaries. To the ten existing legions, Caesar added five in the course of the war, all enrolled by himself. The number of legions under his command rose

from 6 out of 12 in the first year to 11 out of 15 in the seventh.
Under the Empire, Tacitus tells us that Tiberius had 25
legions, and we know that by the second century the number
had increased to the maximum of 30. If every legion were at
full strength, this would mean a total of 180,000 legionaries,
which, with an equal number of auxiliaries, makes the total
military establishment amount to 360,000 men. As the
ranks of ancient legion, cohort, and century, however, like
those of the modern division, regiment, and company, were

ROMAN CAVALRY
The plumed helmets, lances, and ensign are to be noted.

not always full, it must be remembered that this is an estimate. The average fighting strength of Caesar's legions
in Gaul, for example, is variously estimated at from 3,000 to
5,000 men.

The soldier of the legion wore a uniform consisting of sandals with thick soles studded with heavy nails, a leather
tunic or corselet covered with metal hoops or plates and
reaching nearly to the knee, coarse breeches if he served in a
cold climate, and close-fitting metal helmet. The auxiliary
might keep to the soldier's dress of his native country, but

usually approximated the legionary in uniform. The officers of both were no doubt equipped with uniforms of superior quality.

The weapons with which the Roman conquered the world were the pike or javelin, *pilum*, a stout wooden shaft with a long iron head, the whole measuring about six feet; the spear, *hasta*, like the pike but lighter; and the sword, *gladius*, about three feet long, two-edged, broad, and straight. He was protected in battle by the helmet; the iron plates or leather of his corselet; the shield, *scutum* or *parma*, of various shapes, made of wood with metal or leather covering; and sometimes greaves, *ocreae*. Some of the auxiliaries had their special, native weapons; the Balearic slingers, for example, and the Syrian bowmen. The cavalry were armed with the spear and sword and shield.

The fighting of the Roman was hand-to-hand. Advancing steadily until a few hundred feet from the enemy, at the signal of horn and trumpet sounding the charge the legion went into the double-quick. Stopping suddenly at a distance of fifty feet or so, the front ranks of the first line of cohorts hurled their javelins into the opposing lines and then with drawn swords followed their missiles with a rush and engaged the enemy in personal combat. If the battle was not soon decisive, the front line of cohorts was relieved by the second line, which advanced through the intervals between the first and engaged the enemy until relieved in its turn. It was in these encounters that the effects of the discipline given by the sixty centurions and six tribunes of the legion were made manifest.

Fighting of this sort was as direct and effective as a duel; in fact, it may be said to have consisted of a great many duels fought simultaneously. Far more than modern battle since the time of gunpowder, it was a trial of the endurance and skill of the individual soldier. If we are inclined to think it simple, we should remember the scientific nature of the Roman attack as compared with the mass onset of the Gauls and Germans, which really was simple, and the elaborate training that prepared the legionary to hurl the pike with sure effect, to thrust and parry with the spear and sword, and to manage the dagger and shield. It was direct fighting, usually soon over, and usually decisive, but it was not simple.

Even in the slower and less direct operations of the siege, there was much more actual contact of enemy with enemy than is true of modern times. The besiegers of camp or town were within easy sight and sound of the besieged. Instead of shelling the walls from miles away, they battered them with a heavy, swinging, iron-headed beam called *aries*, the ram, under cover of a shed or mantlet, *vinea*, which the defenders tried to wreck with fire and stones; or they mined and sapped, sometimes meeting unexpectedly the enemy countermining; or they advanced in the *testudo* or turtle formation, with shields interlocked over their heads to protect them from darts, arrows, and rocks until they could use the ladder or burst through the wall. They built high towers on wheels or rollers from which to throw weapons, stones, and fire among the garrison on the parapets before letting down a bridge and attempting to cross over. They had an artillery service. There was the *ballista*, the ancient cannon, with intensely tightened springs of gut or cord taking the place of explosive, hurling a stone ball of up to fifty and one hundred pounds weight from five hundred to one thousand feet, and mounted on a carriage quickly drawn by horses to any point desired. There was the *onager*, smaller than the ballista, and, like it, a sling in principle; and the *catapulta*, a giant bow which hurled an immense arrow, sometimes wrapped in blazing material.

As measures of defense, there was the wall and parapet, fronted sometimes by river or moat. At Alesia, where Caesar's lines were drawn about the hills on which the city stood, and were in turn surrounded by the Gallic army of relief, the Roman commander's defenses included a double ditch, a rampart and palisade with twenty-three forts at intervals, and lines of rough tree branches, trenches, and small and deep pits set with sharp stakes called *stimuli*,

CAESAR'S DEFENSES AT ALESIA

From right to left: pits containing sharp stakes; tree branches imbedded in the ground, the ancient barbed-wire entanglement; two trenches; palisaded dike with towers for the defenders.

known to the soldiers as " lilies." These devices were the barbed-wire entanglements of ancient warfare.

The thoroughness of Caesar's preparations in the eight miles of Alesia's defenses was hardly exceptional. The Roman commander of his time had the accumulated experience of centuries to draw on, knew what was the right thing to do in any given situation, and took no chances. The army on the march had a special formation as it proceeded through country whose friendship was doubted, and even for a halt of a single night constructed a fortified camp, the selection and laying out of whose site had been done in advance by a party of scouts and surveyors, so that on arrival the work of every soldier was ready for him. The daring of generals in penetrating hostile country and engaging numerically over-

THE STATUE OF VERCINGETORIX AT ALESIA

The ancient town, situated beyond the statue on this height, has been partially excavated, and many interesting finds are to be seen in the museum of the near-by town of Alise-Ste. Reine. The statue was erected by Napoleon the Third.

whelming foes was not the taking of chances, but the confidence of the commander in the superiority of his men and their equipment and in his own mastery of military science.

But the Roman army was not always engaged in marches and battles and conquest. Even in the conquering times of the Republic, it performed many duties by way of consolidation and civilizing, and in the Empire its activities included comparatively little actual warfare.   With the adoption of a nonexpansion policy and the fixing of boundaries, the day of campaigns in the grand style passed.   The legions were stationed far away at the Empire's edge : along the great wall on the Scottish border, along the Rhine and Danube and the wall connecting their headwaters, along the border of the Sahara where the wild tribes surged up from the desert areas, on the always troubled and wavering boundaries by the Arabian desert and the Euphrates and Tigris.   Vigilance was always necessary here, and on the northern European front there were serious problems of defense ; but most of the time on the border it was the foray rather than war that troubled the Roman Peace, and in the great body of the Empire the only wars were those of rival emperors, and even of these, which were mostly the affair of the Praetorian Guards at Rome, there was none worth mentioning from Vespasian to Septimius Severus.   From the middle of the third century there was ever increasing need of the army on the northern front, until the line against the outer world no longer could be held, and the Western Empire came to its end ; but even during these times the service in most places and for most of the time consisted of garrison duty and border policing rather than actual warfare, and the soldier's life was almost that of the civilian.

It was in this semimilitary, semicivil capacity that the Roman soldier made his greatest contribution to civilization. From the first, the Roman procedure with the conquered was a mixture of policy and force, with the army for its instrument.   The garrison on active duty was used for pacific ends as well as for security ; or, rather, was used in measures of pacification for the sake of consolidating conquered territory.   Trade, the language, the customs, and the law of

Rome went with the eagles. The colony composed of veterans became another Rome and a little capital which soon converted its people into Romans. The permanent border camps, at first mere outposts to hold the line of defense, soon became the camp cities whose remains in Britain and at

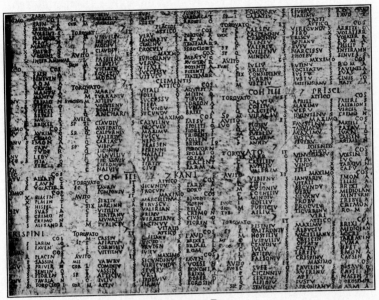

A MILITARY ROLL

The roll shows the names of men and their home towns, and above them the number of the cohort, its officer's name, and the consuls of the year. Thus:

Cohort Third, Century of Kanus
Torquatus and Atticus Consuls
Treasurer (fisci curator) L(ucius) Taurius Secundus Parma

Timgad and Lambaesis in Africa and elsewhere show how much more they were cities than camps.

The soldier in them perhaps never saw important active service. He enlisted for his twenty years, married a woman of the neighborhood, reared a family, kept a garden, perhaps had business connections. Whether a native Roman or Italian, or a Roman citizen from elsewhere, he and his comrades were the great means of naturalizing the surrounding districts as Roman. Their language, their manners, their religion, their law, their ideas, their sentiments, their institutions, were those of the Roman citizen. Their long residence and intimate mingling in the life of the community made Spain, France, England, Roumania, Italy and Sicily, and Africa for the time of its occupation, into Roman countries. The legion, like many a modern regiment, retained its name and in some cases its post for centuries. The Valeria Victrix, the Alauda, the Tenth, the Spanish, and the Emperor's Own went on, the places of their dead supplied by new recruits, their history enriched by gallant incident, until their names stood for the history of the army and the State. The cities of Chester, *castra*, in England, and León, *legio*, in Spain, still testify by the names to their origin in the camp city of Rome. The Greek-speaking culture, in lands already old and established in the arts of war and peace, and more thickly populated, they did not transform to the same extent, but even the East was ruled by Roman law, and it was an Eastern emperor, Justinian, who performed the final and greatest service of the ancient Roman to modern times by reducing Roman law to system in the great Code.

Such in outline was the Roman army and its work. To go more into detail is not possible here. It would halt us too long to be told what the legionary ate and drank and how he was provisioned; to learn of his work as engineer and scout and in the signal service; to follow him on the march with his scientifically ordered columns and baggage train, and to witness the speed and accuracy with which he built a bridge and crossed a river, or converted the rough plot of ground in the wilderness into the camp with every convenience and safety; to share in imagination his battles, sieges, fortunes, and to tell of his disastrous chances,

> "Of moving accidents by flood and field,
> Of hair-breadth 'scapes i' the imminent deadly breach,"

and perhaps even of his " being taken by the insolent foe," and, like Othello, sold to slavery; to participate in the warm comradeship of camp and campaign which gave his adven-

A MODEL OF ANCIENT ROMAN ARTILLERY

Stone balls of one to fifty pounds were hurled by this mechanical sling, called ballista, a distance of 500 to 1000 feet. The arm carrying the sling was drawn down toward the horses, the stone was placed, and the arm released by trigger. The bag of sand received the arm as it spent its energy.

tures a zest and relieved routine of dullness; to feel with him the joys of promotion and the furlough; to learn, less pleasantly, of the coarseness and roughness and cruelties and tyrannies he had to suffer and to inflict in the course of his duties. We are looking at the Roman army in the large as one of the institutions of the Roman State which for a thousand years performed its work successfully, and failed only at the end; and failed then because it had trained in its own ranks the border nations that swept it back in the day of its old age and exhaustion. Let us conclude by asking what were the causes of its thousand years of successful marching and battling, and settling and keeping settled the affairs of Roman civilization.

The answer to this question will not be that the enemies whom the Roman army subdued were its inferiors in physique, or in numbers, or in wealth, or even in experience. It did indeed meet and subdue inferiors in these respects, but it met and subdued also armies that surpassed it in them all. What the Roman army possessed which was not possessed in equal measure by any of its antagonists may be simply expressed. It was what the Roman people in general possessed. It was character as men and discipline as men engaged in the work of a state. Without these and with every other possible advantage, there would have been no onward march of either army or State.

But let us make room for two testimonies from the ancients themselves — one a Roman four hundred years after Christ, and one a Greek who wrote almost six centuries before the Roman.

" In any battle," writes Flavius Vegetius Renatus in a military treatise, "it is not so much numbers and untrained valor as expertness and training that bring victory. It is clear that the Roman people subdued the world simply because of their attention to training in arms, their camp discipline, and their experience in military science. What could the Romans with their small number have done against the Greeks with their multitudes? How could the short-statured Roman have dared to face the gigantic German? It is plain that the Spaniards surpassed our men not only in numbers but in stratagem and money. No one ever doubted that we were inferior to the Greeks in knowledge and wisdom. But where we have had the advantage over all these things has been in the skillful picking of the recruit, the instruction of him, so to speak, in the law of arms, the hardening of him by daily drill, the preparation of him by practice in the field to meet every situation that can arise in the line of battle, the taking of stern measures against the sluggard. For it is knowing the science of war that increases daring in battle. No one is afraid to do what he is confident he has learned well."

The other and older testimony is from Polybius, the Greek historian of Rome and friend of Scipio the Younger, a witness of the destruction of Carthage, and a resident in Rome about 165–148 B.C.

"Owing to the extreme severity and inevitableness of the penalty [bastinado by all members of the camp], the night watches of the Roman army are most scrupulously kept. While the soldiers are subject to the tribunes, the latter are subject to the consuls. A tribune, and in the case of the allies a prefect, has the right of inflicting fines, of demanding sureties, and of punishing by flogging. The bastinado is also inflicted on those who steal anything from the camp; on those who give false evidence; on young men who have abused their persons; and finally on anyone who has been punished thrice for the same fault. Those are the offenses which are punished as crimes, the following being treated as unmanly acts and disgraceful in a soldier: when a man boasts falsely to the tribune of his valor in the field in order to gain distinction; when any men who have been placed in a covering force leave the station assigned to them from fear; likewise when anyone throws away from fear any of his arms in the actual battle. Therefore the men in covering forces often face certain death, refusing to leave their ranks even when vastly outnumbered, owing to dread of the punishment they would meet with; and again in battle men who have lost a shield or sword or any other arm often throw themselves into the midst of the enemy, hoping either to recover the lost object or to escape by death from inevitable disgrace and the taunts of their relations.

"If the same thing ever happens to large bodies, and if entire maniples desert their posts when exceedingly hard pressed, the officers refrain from inflicting the bastinado or the death penalty on all, but find a solution of the difficulty which is both salutary and terror-striking. The tribune assembles the legion, and brings up those guilty of leaving the ranks, reproaches them sharply, and finally chooses by lot sometimes five, sometimes eight, sometimes twenty of the offenders, so adjusting the number thus chosen that they form as near as possible the tenth part of those guilty of cowardice. Those on whom the lot falls are bastinadoed mercilessly in the manner above described; the rest receive rations of barley instead of wheat and are ordered to encamp outside the camp on an unprotected spot.

"They also have an admirable method of encouraging the young soldiers to face danger. After a battle in which some of them have distinguished themselves, the general calls an assembly of the troops, and bringing forward those whom he considers to have displayed conspicuous valor, first of all speaks in laudatory terms of the courageous deeds of each and of anything else in their previous conduct which deserves commendation, and afterwards distributes the following rewards [various decorations like the modern distinguished service medal]. . . . The recipients of such gifts, quite apart from becoming famous in the army and famous too for the time at their homes, are especially distinguished in religious processions after their return, as no one is allowed to wear decorations except those on whom these honors for bravery have been conferred by the consul; and in their houses they hang up the spoils they won in the most conspicuous places, looking upon them as tokens and evidences of their valor. Considering all this attention given to the matter of punishments and rewards in the army and the importance attached to both, no wonder that the wars in which the Romans engage end so successfully and brilliantly."

XXXIX

MARE NOSTRUM

We have said little thus far about the vast inland or "midland" sea called the Mediterranean which is so great a factor in the story of Rome. This is partly because we have been studying mostly the city of Rome and the people within its walls, but it is also partly because our habit of thought regarding this body of water is not quite correct.

We think and speak of the Roman Empire as if it were to be defined as an aggregation of territories bordering on the Mediterranean, and do not realize as we should that the sea itself was a part of the Empire. The Mediterranean united as well as separated the parts of the Roman territory that lay on its shores. Roman subjects dwelt on its few larger islands and its innumerable smaller islands, and made their homes on the craft that went to and fro upon its bosom; it had its population as well as the land.

The sea also had its riches to yield, as well as the land. It furnished, and still furnishes, a great part of the salt used in countries far and near. With its fish, it helped to feed the Roman people. It yielded the shellfish that made the purple dye of the imperial robes. It furnished the sponge.

But these were not the only contributions of the sea. It modified and equalized the climate of all its borders. It tempered the North wind in winter and in summer sent its breezes inland to make the heat more endurable. It sent its evaporations over the land to condense and fall as the gentle rain of heaven.   It ministered to variety and beauty in the landscape.   Its high shores, clothed in orchard and vineyard and interrupted by fruitful valleys, its precipitous mountain borders, its picturesquely smoking marine and coastal volcanoes, its gleaming islands of limestone and marble rising steeply out of fathomless depths, its bluest of waters shimmering in the calm or sparkling with gold or lacy with curling foam in the gale, its white-winged sailing ships and brown-winged fishing fleets, its lazily wheeling gulls and joyously leaping porpoises — what other sea is its equal in the brilliance of its charms?   And what other sea is peopled like it with Naiads and Nereids and rising Proteuses and Tritons blowing their wreathed horns, or conceals in its depth such wonderful caverns and grots and palaces, or has furnished the settings for an *Odyssey* or an *Aeneid?*

The Mediterranean in historic times is but a fraction of the great sea which in remote ages extended far eastward and included the Black and Caspian seas and the plains of Central Asia; yet even in its diminished form its extent is hard to realize.   The area of the United States in North America, exclusive of Alaska, is 3,042,494 square miles; the area of the Mediterranean is 1,145,830 square miles. The Mediterranean is thus a little more than one third the size of our 48 States.   It is a little less than one third of Europe's total area of 3,785,000 square miles.   It is equal to 20 Wisconsins, or 24 New Yorks, or 13 Kansases, or 7 Californias, or 19 Georgias, or 4 Texases, and is 140 times the area of Massachusetts.   It would contain the area of our Great Lakes ten times.   Italy, the largest peninsula indenting it, is one tenth its area, the peninsula of Greece one forty-sixth; Sicily, its largest island, one hundredth.

There are four natural divisions composing the Mediterranean: the Western, bounded by Africa, Spain, France, Italy, and Sicily; the Sicilian-Ionian, bounded by Sicily, the southern extremity of Italy, Greece, and Africa; the Adriatic; the Eastern, bounded by Greece, Tripoli, Egypt, and Asia, and including the numerous Greek archipelagoes. Of these, the Adriatic forms about a twentieth part of the total area, and the other three something less than one third each. The niche in the Eastern basin occupied by the Aegean Sea is four hundred miles from north to south, longer than Lake Michigan and more than twice as wide.

The life of man in the Mediterranean basin began many hundred thousand years ago with the westward migrations from somewhere beyond the eastern end of the sea; perhaps from Egypt, perhaps from some point where Europe and southwestern Asia meet. The routes of the earliest men can only be conjectured. They probably advanced by both the southern shore and the northern, but mostly by the southern, peopling by slow degrees the fertile fringe of Africa between sea and desert, crossing into Spain, and continuing to north and east until they met their fellows advancing by the northern route and thus completed the encircling of the sea. From the time they began to use tools, that is, from the beginning of the Old Stone Age, it is calculated that a hundred and twenty-five thousand years have passed. The last part of this period, about 40,000 B.C. to 12,000 B.C., has been much studied the past half century in the caves of France and Spain. The men who lived in these dwellings could make shapely implements of war and peace, and decorated these and the walls of their caverns with beautiful drawings. Their age was called the Reindeer Period because of its most prominent animal, and came to an end with the fourth retreat of the glaciers, about 14,000 years ago, with which the present climatic era began.

THE ROMAN EMPIRE
AT ITS
GREATEST EXTENT

Scale of Miles

0   100 200   400   600

ABBREVIATIONS
A.P. Alpes Poeninae
A.M. Alpes Maritimae
R.C. Regnum Cottii

KEY

Roman territory at the beginning of the 1st Punic war (264 B.C.)
Acquisitions during the 1st. Punic war (238 B.C.)
      „   up to the end of the 2nd. Punic war (201 B.C.)
      „   „   „ 133 before Christ
      „   „   „ the death of Julius Cæsar (44 B.C.)
      „   „   „   „   „ Augustus (14 A.D.)
      „   „   „   „   „ Marcus Aurelius (180 A.D.)
------ Boundaries of the Roman provinces before Diocletian
——— Imperial provinces   _ _ _ _ _ Senatorial provinces
—·—·— Boundary of the east and west Roman Empire 395 A.D.; shaded
edging means half-dependent; flat shading means incorporated; figures
show the year of acquisition and when marked with an a mean A.D.

Not to attempt a further account of the movements of the earliest men on the Mediterranean shores, let us go on by saying that at the more or less obscure dawning of history there was a double migration by the northern and southern routes. By the northern, from the borders of Europe and Asia not far from the Caspian Sea, advanced the Indo-European stock whose westward movement resulted in the Greeks, the Romans, the Celts, and the Teutons; by the southern, from Phoenicia principally, advanced the Semitic stock which made Carthage a new and richer center of power and spread Semitic culture and commerce along the shores of Africa, across the strait, and up the coast of Spain.

As the north and south shores met at the Pillars of Hercules between Spain and Africa, and as the Mediterranean at Carthage is almost bridged by Sicily, it was hardly possible that the two civilizations should not some day collide. The fact that their peoples were of different bloods and nations was enough to make them hostile, and there was in addition to this a rivalry on the sea.

The rivalry began with the clashing of Greek with Carthaginian. Carthage had inherited and developed the commercial and naval power of her mother country, Phoenicia, and the Greek had become expert on the waters and in the markets of the West as well as the East. The Aegean islands, the west coast of the Adriatic, Corcyra, the South of Italy, the West of Italy as far as Cumae, Marseilles and its neighborhood, composed a Greater Greece of trade and colonization; the north coast of Africa, and southern Spain with New Carthage as its capital, made a Greater Phoenicia or Greater Carthage.

For a long time the ships of Indo-European Greek and Semitic Carthaginian contended in the rivalries of trade without appeal to arms. When they did come finally to the test of arms, it was in the Western sea. When in 600 B.C. the Greeks founded Massilia, the ancient Marseilles, and later, when from Massilia they attempted to extend their colonies and trade control to Spain and Corsica, they came into conflict with the Carthaginians and their allies, the Etruscans, on the sea. In the campaign of Xerxes against the Eastern Greeks which ended at Salamis in 480 B.C., the Carthaginians participated by invading Sicily, whose western part had long been controlled by Carthage as its eastern part had been controlled by Greece. The battle of the Himera, said to have been fought on the very day of Salamis, resulted in the defeat and destruction of the Carthaginian army and fleet. In 474 B.C. the Etruscan sympathizers with Carthage were defeated by the Sicilian Greek fleet off Cumae, which they were besieging. Henceforth, the Carthaginian was definitely halted in Sicily and confined to southern Spain and the coast of Africa.

Meanwhile the Roman power was expanding in Italy. Because its ambitions were compelled to center in the subjugation of the peninsula, it paid little attention to commerce on the sea and less to the maintenance of ships of war. Both the military and the trade problems of Rome up to the opening of the third century B.C. were concerned mostly with its neighbors on Italian soil. This does not mean that it had no interest at all in overseas people or trade, or that it had not felt the need of naval power. From an early time, it had used the Tiber and had bartered with the coastal towns as well as the inland. It had known the imports from the Myceneans and the Greeks and from farther east. It had intimate relations with the Greeks of Massilia. There still survives the substance of a treaty between Rome and Carthage dating perhaps as early as 500 B.C., and certainly

not later than 348 B.C., which indicates at least some sharing
by Rome in the traffic of the sea. In 338 B.C. the defeat of
the Latin allies by Rome in the naval battle of Antium
increased the Roman navy by many captured ships. In
311 B.C. the appointment of *duoviri navales*, two commissioners of the fleet, and in 267 B.C. the institution of four

A BIREME

Note the two rows of oars, the animal figurehead, the rostrum or beak, the forecastle, and the marines, two of whom are ready to leap for the land.

quaestors of the fleet, to be stationed at Ostia, the port of
Rome, at Cales in Campania, at Ariminum on the east coast,
and at a fourth point not known, are further indications of
the growth of naval ambition at Rome.

Yet all this meant little in comparison with Greek or
Carthaginian commercial and naval power. The treaty with
Carthage prohibited Roman trade in the eastern Mediter-
ranean and on the Atlantic, leaving free only the western
Mediterranean, and not even that without restriction. Such

a treaty was possible only because of Roman helplessness. Occupied with Italian affairs of war and peace, possessing a small navy, and having great stretches of coast open to attack by the superior navy of Carthage, the Romans had no choice.

It was only when the Roman set foot across the two miles of water separating Italy and Sicily that Roman naval history began in earnest. This was in 265 B.C., when, in answer to the appeal of the people of Messana, the present Messina, two Roman legions were sent to their aid in defiance of the wishes of Carthage, by that time strong in Sicily. This crossing of the straits brought on the First Punic War, 265–241 B.C. In its fourth year the Romans, adopting the plan to drive the Carthaginians from Sicily, in six weeks created a fleet of a hundred ships on the model of a stranded enemy ship. They lost seventeen of them with their admiral in a first battle, in the second badly defeated the Carthaginian fleet, and in a third established the naval superiority of Rome. These two great victories, at Mylae in 260 B.C. and at Ecnomus in 256 B.C., were equaled by the victory at Aegusa in 241 B.C., which ended the war and made Sicily a Roman island.

From the First Punic War on, the freedom of Rome on the sea could hardly be questioned. When, with the Second and Third Punic wars, and the Macedonian wars, the greater part of the shores also passed under the control of Rome, the Roman supremacy in naval power was almost wholly unchallenged, and the Roman navy was looked to as responsible for order and safety on the sea. It took nearly a hundred years after the destruction of Carthage in 146 B.C. for Rome properly to meet this obligation.

The Mediterranean was infested by piracy of two kinds. There was the ordinary piracy of the robber individual or the robber group or race who stopped a ship and seized its cargo and held its crew or passengers for ransom, and there was the piracy consisting of guerilla warfare on the sea carried on or instigated by the eastern border enemies of Rome. Of the former, the Balearic pirates in the West

MOSAIC AT OSTIA SHOWING A PORT

Above two dolphins symbolic of the sea are two ships under full sail, each with two steering-oars, riding in the gale before a lighthouse.

and the Cilicians in the East were notorious; of the latter, the numerous raiders in the employ of Mithridates of Pontus, in Asia Minor, an able trouble maker for the Romans from 105 B.C. to his death in 63 B.C., whose activities reached as far as Spain, including an attack on Ostia, fifteen miles from Rome.

The Balearic pirates were effectively halted in their career by an expedition in 123 B.C. under Metellus, who occupied the islands and took measures for their Romanization. The Cilicians and Mithridates were not so easily managed. The Cilicians had many ships, conducted a lively trade in slaves, had important commercial connections, were sometimes employed by the scheming rulers of the East, and met with a toleration that made them overbold. The activities of Mithridates, we are told, included the destruction of four hundred towns in the Mediterranean through the employment of pirate ships.

The end of all these troubles, and of disorders more local in origin, came with the Gabinian and Manilian laws of 67 and 66 B.C., conferring on Pompey the supreme command against piracy wherever found, and also against Mithridates in his dominions. Cicero's oration for the Manilian Law, advocating the extension of Pompey's commission to include the war against Mithridates, not only tells us of Pompey's great success in clearing the seas, but indicates the state of the Mediterranean before the expedition.

" Need I tell you that these years the sea has been closed to our allies," the orator asks, " when your own armies have never crossed from Brundisium except in the middle of winter? Am I to complain to you that envoys coming to you from foreign lands have been captured, when envoys of the Roman people have had to be ransomed? . . . What state before has ever been so slight, what island so small, that it could not defend for itself its own harbors and fields and some part of its coast and territory? And yet, by Hercules, for a period of several years before the Gabinian Law, the great Roman people, whose name as far back as our memory goes has never suffered defeat in battles at sea, had lost a great part, yes, by far the greatest part, not only of its trade advantages but of its dignity and authority. We, whose forefathers overcame King Antiochus and Perseus on the sea, and in every naval battle vanquished the Carthaginians, a nation most thoroughly trained and prepared in the use of the sea, had long been unable to meet the freebooters in any single place. We, who before had not only kept Italy safe, but were able by the strength of our authority to guarantee safety to all our allies on the remotest shores . . . we, I say, were kept not only from our provinces and the coasts of Italy and from the use of our ports, but even from the Appian Way; and in times like that the magistrates of the Roman people were not ashamed to come on to this very platform, though our fathers left it to us adorned with naval trophies and the spoils of enemy fleets!

"Immortal gods! Can it be that the unbelievable, the divine abilities of a single human being could in so brief a space of time cause so much light to shine upon our State that you, who but a moment ago looked upon the enemy's fleet before the entrance to the Tiber, now hear that on this side of the entrance to the Ocean not a single ship of the pirates is left? And though you see with what swiftness these things were accomplished, I must nevertheless not pass it by; for what man, either in his eagerness to perform a duty or in the pursuit of gain, could ever have visited so many places and made such long voyages with the rushing speed of this great campaign on the sea under Pompey's leadership? The season for navigation had not yet opened when he sailed for Sicily, reconnoitred Africa, and then came with the fleet to Sardinia. These three grain resources of the State he furnished with the strongest garrisons and with naval forces. Next, after having returned to Italy, he strengthened the two Spains and Gaul with garrisons and ships, sent ships likewise to the coast of Illyricum, to Achaia, and to all Greece, and equipped the two seas of Italy with the greatest sea power and the strongest military protection, while he himself set out from Brundisium and on the forty-ninth day annexed all Cilicia to the territory of the Roman people. All pirates everywhere in part were taken captive and executed, and in part surrendered themselves to the authority and power of this one man. He went on; from the Cretans, in spite of their sending envoys as far as Pamphilia to beg his clemency, he did not take away their hope of being allowed to surrender, and levied hostages. In such wise this great war, lasting so long and diffused so widely and far, a war from which all nations and races were suffering, did Gnaeus Pompeius make ready for at the end of winter, undertake at the beginning of spring, and in midsummer bring to an end."

Pompey's 49 days in the East were preceded by an equally effective 40 days in the West. The record included the capture of 377 ships and the burning of 1,300. This was the last of the Cilician and the Mithridatic marauders, and the first of an orderly Mediterranean.

Before peace on the waters could be permanent, however, the naval movements of the civil war between Pompey and Caesar, between Pompey's son Sextus and Caesar's successor Augustus, and between Antony and Augustus, ending with the battle of Actium in 31 B.C., were necessary. When Augustus emerges from the conflict of thirteen years between Julius Caesar's death and Actium, he makes the harbor at Misenum, west of Naples, and the harbor at Ravenna in the Northeast the stations of the imperial fleet, with guardian ships elsewhere at convenient points. The Mediterranean for the first time ceases to be a sea separating three continents, and is a Roman lake — *mare nostrum*. When Horace writes,

" Pacatum volitant per mare navitae,"

it is the end of one long story and the beginning of another. The navy henceforth is a body of marine police, a convenience for the administrators of the Empire, a transport service, a carrier or escort of the emperor and his high officials, and only on occasion the instrument of actual war ; and then far away in the North Sea, on Rhine and Danube, or in the Black Sea.

It remains to say something of the unit which composed the navy and of the navy as a whole ; the ship of commerce will find mention elsewhere. The Roman warship, *navis longa*, was propelled by wind and oar, and was classified according to its oarage, which was arranged in rows or banks. There were biremes with two banks, triremes with three, quadriremes and quinqueremes with four and five, and ships extraordinary with six, seven, ten, fifteen, and even greater numbers. The oars projected through holes along the hull which were fitted with leather in such a way as to

A TRIREME
The crew are resting on their oars.
(From "Ben Hur")

keep the water out. The rowers, who were allies, freedmen, captives, slaves, criminals, or others constrained to a hard and unpopular service, were seated on benches running the length of the ship's interior and corresponding to the banks of oars, with one bench above another but not directly, and each bench farther removed from the hull than the next, in order to suit the longer leverage of the oars with farther sweep. The arrangement cannot be explained with precision. For speed, six to eight miles an hour was a good average, the higher made possible and easier by one large square sail on the main mast, sometimes aided by a square sail below and a triangular above. The ship was steered in quite simple fashion by means of two large oars, and had cord or chain cables. It was armed at the prow with a metal beak, usually of bronze, for the purpose of ramming the enemy ship, tearing a hole in its side below the water line, and sinking it. On the foredeck was also a tower, from which to throw weapons, the ancient form of the "forecastle." For boarding purposes, there were poles and ladders, a small boat, and tall beams with hooks at the end to let fall on the enemy's deck and hold him.

The warship was probably manned, like the Greek trireme, with about 170 oarsmen, arranged from lowest to highest in rows of 54, 54, and 62, and with about 20 sailors and 10 fighting men, making a total of about 200 men. A quinquereme had 375 men, including 310 at the oars. The trireme was about 24 horsepower, had a tonnage of 75, and under favoring conditions could make 10 miles an hour. With painted figurehead of Mars or Neptune, with officers and men in full uniform and panoply standing at attention, with the imperial ensign flying, it was no doubt a stirring sight as the squadron, gay with decorations and proud with trophies, came up the Tiber from Ostia on the return from distant seas and swept into the city between the cheering crowds to put in at the docks by the Campus Martius.

The size of the navy after the fall of Carthage was determined by the need of the times, and not by rivalry in time of peace with powers expected some day to be active enemies. At Actium, Antony's 500 ships and Cleopatra's 60 were met by Augustus with 250. Pompey's command against the East included 500 ships. At Ecnomus in 256 B.C., the Romans had 330 ships and the Carthaginians 350, each side with a total of about 150,000 men as crews and fighters. In A.D. 16 there were a thousand vessels in the North Sea and on the Rhine, but not on the footing of actual war. The total shipping of the imperial fleets was no doubt very great, yet not so great as might be thought from the number of craft in the North. Like the army, the navy, under the Empire, was on duty chiefly at the border, and the Mediterranean squadrons were comparatively small.

Such was *Mare Nostrum*, and such the naval arm of Rome.

XL

BY LAND AND SEA

In our account of the Roman army and of Roman control over the Mediterranean in the center of the Empire and over the various waters on its borders, we have considered the two great arms by which the Roman State acquired and held its dominion. We have been dealing with movement, but military and navy movement. A better understanding should be had now of movement in times of peace and in the ordinary ways of life; that is, of the travel, commerce, and verbal communication by which the Empire was knit together into a coherent and compact whole. This will involve some attention to Roman roads and their use, to the carrying trade in men and goods by land and sea, and to the sending of letters and other messages.

The great arteries of the Roman Empire were the roads. Their total mileage at the maximum is estimated at 47,000, of which Gaul, or France, had 13,200, and Sicily a thousand. They served the same purposes as those accomplished by the modern railway, and their history resembles that of the railway lines. They followed the lines of communication already existing, and replaced the poorly kept and often indirect dirt roads and paths by solid, straight, durable, stone pavements over which men and goods could reach their destinations with greater convenience, safety, and speed. As a usual thing, their construction followed the extension of the Roman sway, for the double purpose of facilitating commerce with the newly acquired territory and of providing for the rapid movement of the army. The Appian Way, for example, was paved with stone from Rome to Capua in 312 B.C., twenty-six years after Rome's victory over the Latin Confederation, whose various members occupied territories along its line. Later, when the Samnites and South Italy became Roman, the Appia was extended to Beneventum and Brundisium.

The Appian Way was the oldest of the improved Roman roads, and the most celebrated. Its beautiful description as *Regina Viarum*, Queen of Highways, occurs in the poet Statius. It left Rome at a southern gate, traversed the Campagna on a long bed of basalt which served then, and still serves, as a quarry for the street-paving material of the city, to the slopes of the Alban Mount; continued along the base of the Volscian Mountains to the sea at Tarracina; crept around the cliffs and went on through the mountains to Beneventum, reaching the Adriatic at Barium, whence it kept to the coast until its termination at Brundisium.

Another of the great highways was the Via Flaminia, which began in the Via Lata, the modern Corso, inside the gates, crossed the Tiber at the Mulvian Bridge, and terminated at Ariminum on the Adriatic. It was begun by Gaius Flaminius, censor in 220 B.C. and builder also of the Circus Flaminius, and was finished in 187 B.C. The extension of it through the plains of North Italy to what are now Piacenza and Milan was called the Via Aemilia, from M. Aemilius Lepidus, its builder as far as Placentia, the modern Piacenza.

The Via Aurelia, climbing the Janiculum, made for the west coast, which it followed, like the modern railway, to Pisa, Genoa, and the Rhone Valley in Gaul. The Via Salaria was the line of communication between Rome and the Adriatic through the Sabine country and Picenum. The

Tiburtina entered the Apennines at Tibur, modern Tivoli, after eighteen miles through the plain of Latium, and continued as the Via Valeria to the Adriatic, a little south of Adria, the city which gave the sea its name. The Via Latina ran inland parallel to the Appia and joined it in

THE SACRED WAY IN ROME

The heavy basaltic blocks, from the quarries near Rome, are one to three feet thick. This is the Via Sacra on which Horace walked: *Ibam forte Via Sacra sicut meus est mos.*

Campania. The Via Cassia passed the lake of Bolsena and ran through Clusium and Arretium to Florentia and Luca, near which it joined the Via Aurelia.

These were the main-traveled roads in Italy. There were other roads from Rome, and of course there were branches of the main roads, some of them interprovincial, and some only local. Outside of Italy, the chief routes were continued beyond the Alps in France and Britain and in the Rhine and Danube country. Beyond the Mediterranean they continued the paths of the sea into Spain, Africa, Egypt, Asia, the Black Sea country, Greece, and Dalmatia. All roads radiated from Rome the capital, the center and heart of their world, or were feeders to those which did. "All roads lead to Rome" is not an empty expression.

There is no better way to an appreciation of the part played by the Roman road than the comparison of it with the modern railroad.

In the first place, it has already been noticed that the two main purposes of road construction were the facilitation of military movement and the encouragement of trade. Both are purposes familiar in modern times; the Simplon road of Napoleon, the railways of Germany and France at the border, the roads of India, are illustrations. We do not forget, of course, that in the older countries conquered by Rome, the roads were already established, and were only taken over and improved.

In the second place, Rome is to be thought of as a road center just as Paris and London and Chicago are railroad centers. Some sixteen roads came into Rome, seven of which ran to the sea or the Alps, with connections beyond, and were what might be called main lines.

Thirdly, the Roman roads represented routes determined by natural and commercial convenience. They followed the coast, or the straight line in the plain, or the river valleys leading to passes in the mountain country, or connected thriving towns, quite like the modern railroad. Like the railroad, too, their coming created many a town. They were at the same time the effect and the cause of Roman extension.

Fourthly, the construction of the Roman road as an engineering enterprise was comparable to railroad building. The line from point to point was generally straight, and the stretches of the line were as long as physiography permitted. The Appian Way in its first stretch ran from Rome to Tarracina on the coast, seventy-five miles. Cuttings,

THE APPIAN WAY TWO MILES FROM ROME
The stone margins and pavement are still to be seen in many places, and the road is bordered for miles by tomb ruins.

viaducts, gradings, and even tunnels are still to be seen on many of the routes, the evidence of this refusal to deviate.

The roadbed itself was systematically laid. Two parallel trenches were first dug, ten to fifteen feet apart on main lines and less on local or cross lines, and the material between was excavated. In this excavation was laid a triple foundation consisting of a stratum of small broken stones, a stratum of smaller stones mixed with mortar and firmly tamped, and the bed of cement which received the massive blocks of the actual pavement. The blocks were of limestone from the mountains or, more frequently, of silex, or basalt, from some volcanic quarry, and might be either rectangular or polygonal; the basalt usually being the latter, and carefully dressed and accurately fitted into a smooth and beautifully patterned surface. To take care of the drainage, the surface was slightly rounded and there were runnels at the sides, with now and then a main or culvert under the road. At the extreme edges were curbs, and beyond them graveled paths for walkers.

The features thus described were characteristic of the normal main road near Rome and in the richer parts of the Empire. Roads naturally varied with the region traversed and the spirit of the builder. In the mountains, the natural rock would serve partly as foundation; in the marshes, the foundation had to be made of piles. At Rome, there was plenty of basalt, the most durable of stones; in other places, the harder kinds of limestone had to serve, or, in districts of less importance, the leveled earth road or the graveled surface.

In the fifth place, the Roman roads, like many railroad systems, were built, administered, and operated by the State. There are differences to be noted, however.

A first difference is to be seen in the fact that many Roman roads by their names testify to an origin in the special concern of individuals. Appius Claudius, Gaius Flaminius, Aemilius Lepidus, and others after whom main lines or branches were named, were the pioneer organizers in road-building enterprise, and probably were responsible for some part of its cost. Under the Republic, the authority of the State operated in Italy through a censor, a consul, a local magistrate, or the general of an army in the field; in the provinces, through the proconsul or propraetor acting as governor. Under the Empire, the emperor was the source of authority.

A second difference was that the maintenance of the road, and in many cases the original cost, was charged, in part or whole according to period, to the cities or provinces through which it ran. Under the Republic, the burden fell heavily on the subject peoples at first, and afterward on both subjects and allies. Under the Empire, it was shifted to the Government; by the time of Septimius Severus that part of the traffic which was public had been nationalized and was maintained at the imperial expense, but local obligations were still of such weight as to cause bitter complaint. In the late Empire, when, according to Professor Westermann, the transport of supplies was assigned to individual private citizens as a compulsory duty, and "finally became a hereditary obligation upon those engaged in it," the maintenance of the roads also was probably assigned at least in part. The method was not unknown in earlier times; the triumvirs of 43 B.C., Octavius, Antony, and Lepidus, compelled individual senators to repair roads at their own expense.

A third difference to be noted is that the ancient road was not devoted to a single method or means of traffic. It was freely used by pedestrians, riders, and drivers, public and private alike, not limited to paid regular service of one sort. It was a road, and not a track with a fixed gauge. One resting by the roadside an hour might have seen a dozen kinds of vehicles and animals pass. There was the light and nimble, two-wheeled, two-horsed, open *cisium*, with one double seat. There was the *raeda*, a big, heavy four-wheeler drawn by two and four horses, for a larger number of passengers. There were the *carpentum*, two-wheeled, two-horsed, and covered, and the *pilentum*, four-wheeled, heard of as used on

A Mosaic on the Floor of Baths in Ostia

About an ornamental device with four Atlas figures enclosing the center of the chamber floor are four scenes of mules and their drivers. Four of the animals are named Pudens, Podagrosus, Potiscus, Barosus. The last two are unhitched and having their feed. Study the carts, harnesses, drivers, whips, gestures, and the mules' ears and attitudes.

state occasions by the flamens and the Vestals. There were the *plaustra*, dray or work wagons; the *carrus*, a big two-wheeled transport cart; the *petoritum*, a baggage carrier. There was the *carruca*, a four-wheeled traveling carriage *de luxe* in which the passenger could sleep, not heard of before the first century after Christ. There were the war chariots and the farmers' carts, and there was the litter or sedan chair, *lectica*, in use for short distances in town and carried by polemen. The beasts that drew these vehicles were horses, mules, donkeys, and oxen.

Sixthly, to return to comparisons in likeness, the promiscuous use of the ancient highway was accompanied by a government post service. This, like many other features of Roman life, existed in an undeveloped form at the time of the Republic, and was regulated and improved by the emperors.

To insure the rapid transmission of dispatches there were stations called *mutationes* for the change of the horses ridden by the *stratores*, saddlemen, or couriers. For the carrying trade in money and goods of small compass, and for the passenger and freight traffic, there were stations equipped with horses and vehicles for change, and with supplies in general for the road. These places were called *mansiones*, waiting places. The employees in them included riders, drivers, conductors, doctors, and blacksmiths, especially wheelwrights. In a good day's journey, the traveler passed six or eight of these post stations, at each of which there were some forty beasts, with corresponding outfit of rolling stock and other supplies, and probably with conveyances to hire on special demand.

The affairs of the entire post system as developed in the Empire were under the control of a central office whose head, *a vehiculis*, the general manager, was responsible to the emperor, and who had under him a number of inspectors called *curiosi cursus publici*, division superintendents. From the fourth-century legislation on the post, it may be seen that tickets were sold, *diplomata;* that in the case of distinguished persons they might include lodging and meals, *tractoria;* that there were first- and second-class tickets ; that there were sleeping cars, *carrucae;* that there were fast and slow carriages ; that there were stopovers ; that passes were sometimes issued, good for one to five years or for the emperor's life, and that there was a freight service, ordinary and express. There were even the familiar attempts to defraud : by using tickets or passes which had run out, by using tickets belonging to other parties, by misrepresenting the ages of children, by exceeding stopover rights.

One feature of travel is missed by the modern reader interested in ancient movement. The subject of hotels is so rarely referred to that it is clear that the hostelries of antiquity were not the luxurious places of to-day. Men of rank depended on friends or business associates for lodging away from their own towns, this relation being so frequent that tokens of hospitality entitling the bearer to accommodations were used. Ordinary travelers went to the usual inn, which no doubt was not pleasant to persons of taste. Men might also travel with tent arrangements, especially in case of a long journey and a large retinue.

The speed of ancient Roman travel on land may be estimated from Cicero's mention of the *cisium*, the lightest and most rapid carriage, as making 56 miles in 10 hours. Horace's famous journey of 340 miles to Brundisium, about 37 B.C., took 15 days, an average of 22⅔ miles per day, with daily records of 10 to 36 miles ; but this was leisurely travel, part on muleback, part by carriage, and one night by canal, over occasional stretches of bad road at a speed sometimes

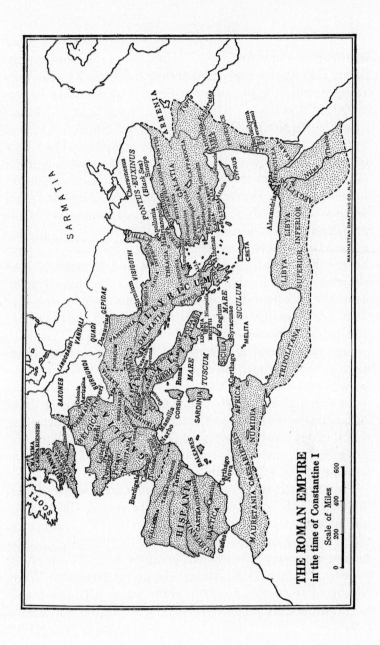

THE ROMAN EMPIRE
in the time of Constantine I

Scale of Miles

0   200   400   600

described as "crawling," and before the Augustan reforms. To say that light travel could accomplish 60 to 75 miles on a spring or autumn twelve-hour day would probably be not far from the truth.

Such were the general features of the Roman road and its life as they are known under the Empire. They were different only in detail under the Republic, and they differ only in detail from the life of the post road in after generations up to the coming of the railroad. Any reader of Dickens will be able to see and hear in imagination on the roads leading to and from Rome much that has not survived in the formal evidence — the drivers and postilions in livery, the cracking of whips and the rattle and thunder of hoof and wheel on the hard and not always smooth basaltic pavement, the gallant courier speeding by and disappearing over the hill, the sun lighting up the bright colors of the coach and glinting on its wheels, the grand arrival at the station, with station master and travelers and crowd of curious idlers waiting for the stage, the alighting of passengers to end the journey or to "stretch their legs," the hostlers unhitching and leading away the steaming horses, the bringing on of fresh animals, the settling of seats and baggage, the slamming of the doors, the mounting of some old Tony Weller and the guard to their high seats, the blare of the horn, the cracking of the whip — and away!

The principal function of the Roman road was in travel movement. It served the army on the march, the emperor and his agents on their administrative errands, the man of affairs on his business missions, the commercial traveler making his rounds, the student going to Athens to finish his training, the rich man making the grand tour, the farmer driving to town, the neighbor going for a visit, the family out on a pleasure jaunt. Something should be said also of

The Emperor and Empress on the Road

its use in the communication of news and messages, and of the transportation of freight upon it.

We have already mentioned the mounted couriers of the post, and may imagine a speed much greater than the five or six miles per hour of the light carriage. The relaying of messages by means of riders, known to us first from the time of Darius the Great, was practiced by the Romans of both Republic and Empire, but with greater system in the later time. Less public and less regular were the *tabellarii*, the letter carriers, either of private citizens engaged in important business or of magistrates who maintained a special service. Tax-gatherers, bankers, money-lenders and money-changers, speculators, contractors, and commercial concerns in general, especially before the imperial régime, used this means of sending messages or papers and valuables to their correspondents in other towns or countries. Such service was more regular or less according to the character and size of the interests concerned. In some cases the carrier was employed at irregular intervals as need arose, and in others made his daily or weekly trip; and there were no doubt messengers depending for employment upon commissions thrown in their way by chance. The letters of Cicero and his friends were delivered by their own slaves, by carriers regularly employed, by carriers in the employ of others but happening to be at hand, and by friends finding it convenient to act as carriers. Letters and packets were carefully sealed.

The time required for transmission of letters may be judged from the evidence of Cicero's correspondence. It shows that a letter from Astura on the sea coast to Rome, 40 miles, required 1 to 2 days; from Arpinum, about 70 miles, 1 to 4 days; from Pompeii, 150 miles, 3 to 5 days; from Puteoli, 125 miles, 4 to 6 days; from Mutina, modern Modena, 300 miles, 5 to 6 days; from Dyrrachium, across the Adriatic, 10 days; from Africa, 20 days; from Britain, 26 days; from Athens, 46. The time from Athens no doubt represents delay of some kind, and the variations in time from other places, as 1 to 4 days in the case of Arpinum, indicate that the means of transmission varied or that accident interfered.

To omit altogether the transportation of goods would be to miss much of the reality in our thought of Roman life. The routes of the Roman Empire by land and sea were alive with commercial movement. The roads that led to Rome from Gaul and Central Europe, or from the ports of Italy, whither came the goods from other distant lands, were thronged with laden carts and wagons and wagon trains. The sea paths that crisscrossed the Mediterranean between cities great and small were crowded by the single ships of traders, the laden argosies of the importer, the great grain fleets of the companies operating under Government, the heavy transport ships that carried cattle and troops, and the fishing fleets. The rivers of the Empire, the Rhine, the Danube, the Nile, the Tiber, were busy in their way. The big ships that in Augustus' time could no longer enter the Tiber because of the silt, anchored off Ostia, where lighters received their cargoes and took them up the river to Rome. In the times of Claudius and Trajan, they made for the near-by harbors built by those emperors. There was not only the trade in grain and cattle and the fisheries; there was the lumber trade, there were the mines in Spain and Central Europe, there were the thousand luxuries of diet and clothing brought from the ends of the earth to Rome and the cities of the West, there was the salt trade, there were the red coral and sponge industries, there were the dyes — and there was the trade in slaves. Nor should the desert routes of Africa and Asia be left out of the picture, with the great caravans bringing the spices and gold and ivory and woven splendors of the tropics and the far-away Orient. Three continents ministered to the needs of the Mediterranean Empire.

The sea seemed all the busier because the ancient ships were small and numerous. The merchant ship, called "round" in distinction from the "long" ship of war, might measure 200 by 50 feet, carry about 250 tons cargo, and be

A ROMAN GALLEY
(From "Ben Hur")

manned by sailors and oarsmen up to 200. The Vatican obelisk, which with its base weighed 500 tons, was brought from Egypt for the Circus of Caligula in a special ship whose ballast consisted of 800 tons of lentils, making a cargo of 1300 tons, or displacement of about 3200 tons. If the entire cargo had been of wheat, there would have been about 500,000 bushels. In Sicilian and South Italian waters, in Greek waters, and off the Nile and the Red Sea passage, where their lines converged, the grain fleets, the fishing fleets, and the navy squadrons must in times of special coincidence have seemed to cover the sea. At Corinth, a device for drawing warships and small freighters across the isthmus was in constant use, and the Nile Canal and Red Sea route, created by Darius and reconstructed by Trajan, was still navigated in A.D. 710.

The ancient ship at best was slow and uncertain. It was sailed without a compass, and "kept to the stars." It was easily swept out of its course by storms, and was the more liable to wreck because its course was preferably from island to island or from point to point not distant from the land. The sailing season began in early spring, and movement on the sea was practically suspended in late autumn when the rough and frequently starless weather arrived. "The clear west winds will bring your Gyges back faithful to you at the first of spring rich with Bithynian merchandise," Horace consoles Asterie. "Forced to put in at Oricum after the raging stars of the Goat, he is passing cold and sleepless nights not without many tears." There were forty days of etesian winds in midsummer. A wind on the route to the Red Sea and India blew six months constantly in either direction. With favoring breeze and the aid of oars, the trader made Crete from Egypt in 3 days, Sicily from Alexandria in 6 or 7, Puteoli from Alexandria in 9, Tauromenium from Puteoli in 3, Rome from Tarraco in 4, Ostia from Gades in 7 to 10, Carthage from Gibraltar in 7, Rome from Carthage in 3.

Compared with twentieth-century conveniences and speed, it was a slow-moving and halting world. Its greatest speed on land was that of the man on a horse; on the sea, the speed of a ship propelled by wind and oars. No man, no news could travel faster than this. There was no telegraph, no wireless; there were no locomotives, no automobiles, no air-planes, no liners making 500 miles a day. The Roman governor traveled a little less than six weeks to reach the last Roman outpost in Nubia; the English civil service man can reach the remotest parts of India from London in less than two weeks by land and sea, by air can almost annihilate the distance, and with the telegraph can communicate his orders in an hour.

Yet it was neither an inexpert nor a backward world. It went as far as it could with the means it possessed, and the world that succeeded it did no better up to the time of our great grandfathers. Says Professor Westermann: "No additional force which was basically new could be evolved by the Roman Empire. Nor was any new force brought in until in recent times when steam, electricity, and gas were applied as motor forces to vehicles in the transport of goods."

It may be added in conclusion that the long distances and the long time required to cover them does not necessarily mean that business was poorly done, or even slowly. All phases of civilization settle to their own natural ways, and have their relative standards. No doubt the ancients talked of being busy and of being hurried, much as the present age of swiftness talks. The streets of the capital and many other cities were crowded, and had their traffic rules restricting use in certain hours and areas. If business was slow, it was at least deliberate, and probably safer than that of a swifter age. If transportation and communication were much less prompt than now, there was a measure of compensation in the lack of the noise and nervous haste which shatter the nerves of men to-day and rob life of its calm.

XLI

THE ROMAN LAW

"Justice is the steadfast and perpetual will to render to every man his right. Jurisprudence is the knowledge of things divine and human, the science of the right and the not-right. The precepts of the law are these: to live honorably, to injure no other man, to render to every man his own."

These are the opening sentences of the *Institutes* of Justinian, a beginners' book for students of law, published on December 30, A.D. 533, as a part of the Emperor's great legal reform. The conclusions expressed by them, at the end of Rome's more than a thousand years of experience in the living and the studying of law, are the base on which all civilization rests. To us they seem commonplaces, and, happily, among enlightened peoples they are commonplaces. That they are, and that the world of ancient Roman times and the world of to-day possessed and possesses the means of translating them into life, is overwhelmingly due to the Roman steadfast and perpetual will to render to every man his right, and to Roman earnestness in pursuit of the science of the right and the not-right.

We have seen the part played in the spread of Roman civilization and in the unification of the ancient world by the Roman road, the Roman army, the Roman navy, and by commerce; but without the working of Roman law in the confirmation of conquest by regulation and reason, the amalgamation and assimilation that "made of one blood all nations" would never have taken place. These facts, especially the fact that large parts of our world to-day are still using the laws of Rome and are thus in that respect living still the life of Rome, are of such importance that if we wish to understand either ancient Rome or modern times we must pay some attention to the subject of Roman experience in the search for justice and the means of justice.

"And so," to use the words of Sextus Pomponius, author of a manual in Hadrian's time, "it seems to us necessary to set forth the beginnings of law itself and the course of its development." There need be no fear in this case that an historical account will be mere facts in chronological order. The life of Roman law was full of movement and adventure.

"Indeed, when our State came into being," continues Pomponius, "the people began at first without law either in writing or in common custom, and everything was done with the king as leader and at his discretion." The historical sketch he then gives extends to the name of Salvius Julianus of his own time, and is the basis of every subsequent account of the rise of Roman law.

We begin the story of the law, then, in prehistoric and even prelegendary times, when the chieftain or king in the Latin land embodies or represents the law, and when the law is unwritten and consists in common custom rather than in what is called legislation. This is hard to imagine, and we advance immediately to the time when the chieftain, with the aid of his councilors, seizes on the habitual acts and inclinations of the community and builds upon them the rules that make his control of the people easier and less unstable. Use and custom are formalized and become the law, though recorded nowhere but in the minds of those who easily remember them because established by their own life and practice.

When the laws begin to be written, the era of statutes has
arrived. This is recorded as already occurring in the time
of the Seven Kings. Romulus and the succeeding rulers,
with the Roman people, are said to have created laws which,
at first inscribed on tablets in the Forum, were finally
gathered together and published by Gaius Papirius, under

A BASILICA INTERIOR

The pagan basilica had an influence on the early Christian church, also called
basilica. This interior, if terminated by a semicircular apse, would have the church
form.

Tarquin the Proud or early in the Republic. The account
of their authorship by various kings belongs to legend, and
the laws themselves were mostly concerned with religious
observances.

With the famous Twelve Tables, Roman law becomes
historical. In 451–450 B.C., sixty years after the Republic
began, a specially appointed Board of Ten, the *Decemviri*,
composed the code of rules which Livy calls the fount of all

public and private law, and which was held in reverence and not repealed until Justinian's code superseded every previous law. The code of the Decemvirs consisted, first, of the approved laws hitherto in force, both those of statute and of custom; second, of contributions of their own to meet the need of the time; and, third, of adaptations from the laws of Greece. The people in assembly voted on the code and it became their statute and was published for their use on twelve tablets of stone or bronze. The reasons for its compilation and publication were that the growth of the State in size and complexity called for a restatement of the laws, and that the common people demanded direct access to the laws in order to protect themselves against abuses by the ruling class. Hitherto, the expert knowledge of the law was confined largely to the board of pontifices at the head of the State religion, and to men of family in political life. So much of the law was involved with religion that the chief priests in the mastering of what concerned their office mastered the law as a whole, and, as long as it remained uncodified and unpublished, possessed it, whether they would or not, as in some sort a trade secret.

But the Twelve Tables, even when published, were but a clumsy and imperfect instrument. They did not contain every detail of law, they were general rather than specific, they needed interpretation, and they left much, especially in the matter of procedure, to the magistrate and other parties to their administration. Most important of all, the society in which they functioned was constantly growing and constantly changing. From the day of their enactment the Twelve Tables were in need of amplification, and the increase in the need of experts for the interpretation and application of the law outstripped by far the people's growth in familiarity with it. Let us consider now the manner in which the body of law was amplified, and the manner in which its use was facilitated.

The sources of new law from the Twelve Tables to the first emperors were as follows. First, there was the *lex* proper, affecting all the people. This was an enactment proposed by a senatorial magistrate, such as the consul or the praetor, with the approval of the Senate, and passed by the people in the centuriate assembly. Second, there was the *plebiscitum*, also called lex, prior to 287 B.C. affecting only plebeians. It was proposed by a plebeian magistrate, usually the tribune, with approval by the Senate, before the tribal assembly. The enactments of the tribal assembly were likely to concern private law, that is, the affairs of citizen with citizen; the centuriate assembly legislated more on governmental and foreign relations. Third, there were the decrees or resolutions of the Senate. In theory, these were advisory only, and had no power to make or unmake a law; in practice, they frequently had the force of law, especially in matters outside control by the law as it stood.

The three foregoing were direct sources. There were also three which were indirect.

First, there were the praetor's edicts. The praetor was created in 366 B.C. to lighten the burden of the consul by assuming control of suits at law. In 242 B.C. a second praetor was created to relieve his colleague of the cases in which one party or both were alien. They were called the *praetor urbanus* and the *praetor peregrinus*, the urban and the foreign. Their number was later multiplied, and their importance always great. The urban praetor especially was important to the growth of the law because of close and varied contact with the life of the citizen in Rome and Italy, and because of the power granted both praetors in 140 B.C.

to correct or amplify the operation of the law in cases where its literal application caused injustice. The chief instrument by which his modifications of the law became a part of the law as a body was the praetor's edict. Any magistrate could issue edicts, and many an uncertain situation was clarified by the act ; but the praetor's *edictum perpetuum,* the edict written on white tablets and posted in the Forum, announcing at the beginning of his year of office the principles or precedents he would observe in decisions during his tenure, what old clauses in the law he would omit or alter, and what new ones he would add, was of greater consequence than others. There are two reasons why this was true. In the first place, it contributed greatly to the certainty and peace of mind of litigants for the year. In the second place, it actually made additions to the law, whose weaknesses it frequently remedied, and whose identity in the course of the years it substantially modified. With good right the praetor's edict was known as the "living voice of the law," *viva vox iuris civilis.*

Second, there were the ópinions delivered by the jurisconsults. In time, the pontifices lost the distinction of being the only masters in the knowledge of the law. As the great public offices, including their own, came within the reach of plebeian candidates, and as the need of experts increased, the number of those who interested themselves in mastery of the law as incidental to career or with purpose to profit also increased. The class of professional jurists, ready to advise the magistrate or the party in a suit, came into being. Some of them published their learning, and became the first in a long line of brilliant writers on the law. Whether oral or written, their learning and their conclusions affected the praetor's thought and action, were manifest in his edicts, and thus with them came to affect the law.

They affected the structure of the trial system as well. Their expertness in special fields was an encouragement to the establishment of the standing courts for special offenses that did so much for criminal law.

Lastly, long-continued and universally approved custom might in the same indirect manner become embodied in the law.

With the revolution that resulted in the Empire and its absolutism, there was added to the statutes, plebiscites, decrees of the Senate, praetor's edicts, and professional jurist's responses, the last of which became now a contribution of greater dimensions than ever, one more very plentiful and important source of law. This was the *constitutiones* of the emperor, constitutions or enactments in various forms, all of which might find a permanent place in the statutes, though many did not. Their importance in the course of the law is realized when we remember that the decline of the republican law-making instrumentalities had gone so far by the third century that the emperor's right to make law was taken for granted, and by the fourth was the only source of legislation. The praetor's edicts had been edited into a final form, and nothing new could appear unless by imperial sanction. The Senate no longer exercised the right to legislate allowed by Augustus and the earlier emperors, and was little more than an ordinary city council. The last statute enacted by the people in assembly dated from the time of Nerva.

The constitutions or enactments took four forms. These were the edict, the decree, the rescript, the mandate.

The edict was issued by the emperor in his capacity of magistrate, and differed from the praetorian edict in being valid for its author's life instead of one year, and for the whole Empire instead of a part. At first corrective and

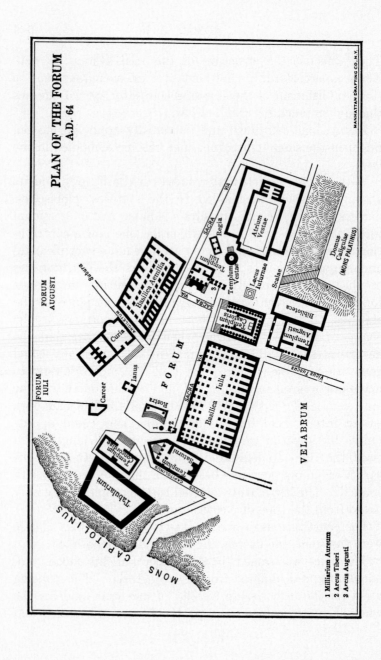

PLAN OF THE FORUM
A.D. 64

1 Milliarium Aureum
2 Arcus Tiberi
3 Arcus Augusti

MANHATTAN DRAFTING CO., N.Y.

supplementary of existing legislation, by Hadrian's time it could be the vehicle for entirely new law.

The decree was a judicial decision of the emperor as magistrate, or as he intervened in a case in answer to appeal or of his own motion. It was usually a decision on some point in existing law, for the purpose of clarification or for the correction of an injustice wrought by literal application of the law. Its use declined as the rescript came into use for the same purpose.

The rescript was a letter to an inquiring official, such as Trajan's answer to Pliny's inquiry regarding the Christians, or an indorsement written on an application or petition and returned with it. At first explanatory of the law, with the praetor's loss of the power to initiate in the edict the rescript came into use as the vehicle of the emperor's sanction, now necessary to new rulings by the praetor.

The mandate was usually an instruction to a provincial administrator, differing besides from the other three enactments as operative in the official's territory for the emperor's life.

As time went on, all four of the *constitutiones* were frequently referred to as *leges*, and distinctions between them were largely lost.

To conclude without further mention of the Roman juristic writers this account of the sources which made the Roman law a living and changing organism constantly growing toward maturity, would be to slight the greatest source of all except Roman living itself. The rise and perfection of juristic literature was a natural movement. The experts of the Republic who aided praetor and suitor and orator not only developed soon into a learned profession, but by reason of the demand for mastery in specific subjects and for clear and accurate statement in writing soon began to produce from their number the specialist and the author. From about the end of the fourth century before Christ, when the responses ceased to be the exclusive privilege of the pontifices and aristocrats, for upwards of four hundred years the history of Roman letters and law is ornamented by important names.

The recital of the chief of these names will in itself be in brief a history of the development both of law and of legal practice. It will show how it progressed not only from the general to the special and from the unsystematic to the organized, but also from the limited to the comprehensive, and from the particular to the universal.

The line begins about 300 B.C. with Appius Claudius the Blind, or possibly his secretary Gnaeus Flavius, and the first publication of a court calendar, with the forms of bringing action. Tiberius Coruncanius, the first plebeian pontifex maximus, about 265 B.C., by offering the first public instruction for parties at law and for students of the law, completed the process of making law a public possession. Aelius Paetus, consul in 198 B.C., wrote commentaries on the Twelve Tables in three parts : text and notes ; interpretation ; forms of action or suit. A Cato, about 160 B.C., composed fifteen books on points of law and special cases. About 150 B.C., Marcus Junius Brutus published commentaries on the civil law, Fabius Pictor an exposition of the pontifical law, and Marcus Manilius a work on actions. Sempronius Tuditanus, consul in 129 B.C., wrote a special work on magistrates, and Marcus Junius Gracchanus, friend of Gaius Gracchus, wrote on constitutional and social history.

The foregoing bring us to the golden age of jurisprudence. Quintus Mucius Scaevola the pontifex maximus, consul in 95 B.C., to whom Cicero attached himself after the death of Scaevola the augur, remaining with him perhaps up to his murder by proscription in 82 B.C., and whom Cicero called first of all ages and countries because of his abilities as administrator, orator, and jurist, published in eighteen books the first systematic presentation of the civil law. Sulla and his advisers, 88–78 B.C., in their criminal-court reforms, produced the first code in book form since the Twelve Tables. Lucius Cincius, of Cicero's time, wrote concerning the calendar, the assemblies, the consular powers, the office of jurisconsult, and war, and made a glossary of ancient words. Servius Sulpicius, consul in 51 B.C., the friend of Cicero and author of the famous letter of consolation on the death of Cicero's daughter Tullia, published works on many special themes, such as dowries, the praetor's edict, and the Twelve Tables, and was a writer and teacher of great distinction. Trebatius Testa, famous as a pupil and correspondent of Cicero and a friend of Horace, wrote works called *De Religionibus* and *De Iure Civili*, and was an adviser to Augustus.

The greater names of the Empire are Salvius Julianus, Sextus Pomponius, Gaius, Aemilius Papinianus, Domitius Ulpianus, Julius Paulus, and Herennius Modestinus. The great work of Julianus, born in Africa and holding office under Hadrian and Antoninus Pius, was his digest of the praetorian edicts, so important that the *Digest* of Justinian quotes it upwards of five hundred times. Pomponius, under Antoninus Pius, wrote the short history of Roman law mentioned at the beginning of this chapter. The contribution of Gaius, living in the times of Hadrian, Antoninus Pius, and Marcus Aurelius, was the *Institutes*, a very human treatise discovered in 1816 in Verona written on a parchment which served afterward for the letters of Jerome and had served previously for a work on theology. Its four books dealt with: law and its sources in the author's own times; the law in relation to persons, slave and free; the law in relation to things, divine and human, corporeal and noncorporeal; heredity; and processes. Papinian, praetorian

THE EMPEROR ANTONINUS PIUS

This was the fourth of the Five Good Emperors — Nerva, Trajan, Hadrian, Antoninus Pius, Marcus Aurelius. Their period was important in the history of the law.

prefect, or supreme judge, under Septimius Severus and murdered in Caracalla's reign, wrote 37 books of *Quaestiones*, or *Cases*, 19 books of responses, 2 books of definitions, and 2 treatises on adultery, was admired for both learning and form, and was quoted by the *Digest* of Justinian in 596 extracts. Ulpian of Tyre, a pupil of Papinian, and meeting the same fate, was praetorian prefect and adviser to Emperor Alexander Severus, and the author of works on the edict and civil law, a collection of *regulae*, or rules, and numerous other treatises. The *Digest* of Justinian owed 2,462 extracts to Ulpian, or one third of its total content in pages. Julius Paulus, of Padua, also a pupil of Papinian, and like him ambitious to cover the whole field of law, wrote 86 works in 319 books, and 2,083 extracts from him compose one sixth of the *Digest*. His most celebrated work was on the edict. Modestinus, the last of the im-

Roman Territory 264 B.C. *Before Punic Wars*
"   "   201 B.C. *After Second Punic War*
"   "   133 B.C.
"   "   44 B.C. *Death of Caesar*
"   "   14 A.D. *Death of Augustus*
"   "   Second Century A.D.

30° 40° 50°

50°

Borysthenes
(Dnieper)

MARE

CASPIUM

CAUCASUS

40°

ACIA

Danuvius Tomi PONTUS EUXINUS
(Black Sea)

ESIA

THRACIA Sinope ARMENIA

Byzantium

Constantinopol PONTUS

Nicomedia BITHYNIA

Thessalonica Troia GALATIA PARTHIA

salus Mytilene ASIA Sardes PHRYGIA CAPPADOCIA MESOPOTAMIA ASSYRIA

Mare Smyrna Colophon Ephesus PAMPHYLIA Euphrates

Athenae ICARIA LYCIA CILICIA

Aegaeum Antiochia Tigris

RHODUS CYPRUS Palmyra Babylon

CRETA PHOENICIA SYRIA

Tyrus Damascus

RRANEUM 30°

PALAESTINA Hierosolyma
(Jerusalem)

Alexandria Pelusium

ARABIA

AEGYPTUS **IMPERIUM ROMANUM**

Nilus Scale of Miles

100 200 300 400 500

Greenwich 30° 40° MANHATTAN DRAFTING CO. N.Y.

portant jurists, was a pupil of Papinian and Ulpian, and a
member of the advisory council of Alexander Severus.
From his works, including one on *Excusationes*, there were
345 excerpts.

Such is a list of the greatest juridical authorities, both the
unofficial under the Republic and the appointees of the
throne in imperial times. Besides their enormous influence
as investigators, interpreters, compilers, editors, teachers,
and practical advisers, from the time of Hadrian, who ruled
that the opinions of authorized jurists, if unanimous, should
have the force of law, they became creators. In the year
426 their power was confirmed, and increased still more by
the Law of Citations, drafted under Theodosius II, which
established the authority of Gaius, Papinian, Ulpian, Paul,
and Modestinus, and ruled that on any point a majority
opinion of the five was to be decisive; that, in case of only
an even number containing opinions on the point at issue
and being tied, the opinion of Papinian was to decide; and
that, in case his opinion was lacking in the tie, the magistrate was to decide for himself in the ancient style. This
law, by making decisions to some degree mechanical, must
have detracted somewhat from the earnestness and originality of the legal profession.

One century later occurred the ultimate and the greatest
usefulness of the jurists, when excerpts from the works of
thirty-nine of them, beginning with Quintus Mucius Scaevola,
consul in 95 B.C., and ending with writers of about A.D. 300
went into the making of the *Pandects* or *Digest* of Justinian, the restatement finished in A.D. 529 and published
with the force of law on December 30, A.D. 533. Twelve
of these thirty-nine sources compose eleven twelfths of the
Digest, the chief of them being Ulpian and Paul, Papinian,
Gaius, and Modestinus; Ulpian and Paul together furnish-

ing three fifths of the whole work.　Justinian's *Institutes*, of
the same date and effect, was a students' treatise containing
large amounts of material from the *Institutes* of Gaius and
from Ulpian and others.

The great legal reform of Justinian consisted of four parts,
viz. : 1.　The *Institutes*, A.D. 533 ; 2.　the *Digest*, 533 ; 3.　the
Codex, a compilation of the code of Theodosius, A.D. 438,
two previous imperial codes, and the imperial laws since
438, published April 16, 529, and in revision on December
29, 534 ; 4.　the *Novellae* or Novels, his more recent, supplementary laws.　The compilation published in 533 and 534
constitutes what is usually called to-day the *Corpus Iuris
Civilis* or *Code of Justinian*, the great body of Roman law
which is still the instrument of civilization in large parts
of the Western world, and consequently our most direct
connection with antiquity.

It will lend reality to Justinian's enterprise and to the
subject of Roman law in general if we listen to an account of
the *Code* by an American lawyer.　Professor William Her-
bert Page, of the University of Wisconsin School of Law and
the American Institute of Law, in an unpublished address
entitled *The Restatement of the Law*, comments as follows on
Justinian's restatement :

"Probably there was no period of history in which there was as
much powerful, fine, constructive juristic work as under the early
Empire.

"The growing despotism of the emperors finally crushed it out.
Juristic writing virtually ceases about the middle of the third
century.　The emperor then was deciding questions of law ; and
his *rescripta principis* took the place of the *responsa* of the great
jurists as far as bureaucratic despotism can take the place of free
individualism.　By the end of the third century, the right of giving official responsa ends.　The natural growth and development
of law is dead.　Only imperial legislation keeps on.

"Almost three hundred years later, a barbarian, perhaps a Slav, came to the throne of the Eastern Empire; a Roman Empire from which Italy and the West had been torn by the barbarians. Perhaps he translated his Slavic name, Uprauda, into the name by which he is known to fame, Justinian. He is somewhat vaguely known to the person of miscellaneous reading as the man who wrote the Roman law. What he did was to make a restatement of it in his own way.

"The problem which confronted him was this. Roman law had ceased to grow. It was decaying; and likely to be lost forever. There were some two thousand volumes of it: the responsa, the commentaries, and the general works on the subject. The lawyers complained of its bulk. No library was anywhere near complete. The sudden eclipse of juristic writing had left unsolved a number of questions; on some of which the ancient authorities were sharply at variance. Was it not possible to get the law into a shape in which it could be used readily? The vigorous barbarian despot, full of plans for a great reconquest and revival of the Empire, had but one answer to this. The job was to be done, and right promptly. First, the *ius novum*, the imperial legislation, was brought together into a sort of *Revised Statutes*. This was the so-called *Code*. Ten commissioners, with plenty of assistance, no doubt, did this in fourteen months, A.D. 529.

"His Majesty then moved on to attack the *ius vetus*, the writings of the great jurists, where the wisdom of the ages lay embalmed, with the doubts of the centuries.

"First for the doubts. Justinian had his experts work out the most serious points in dispute. There happened to be fifty of them. Being an autocrat, he settled these *quinquaginta quaestiones* by his *quinquaginta decisiones*. He then took up the most striking cases in which the law, which had stopped two centuries before, now failed to fit the conditions of his time. Here, too, a series of imperial constitutions brought the law up to date, sharply and promptly, if not always scientifically.

"He then appointed an imperial commission; Tribonian at its head, four law professors, and eleven practitioners, to revise the *ius vetus*, and to do it quickly.

"The result seems queer enough to our eyes, for we expect some kind of outline and system based on the nature of the different legal rights and their relation to one another. This did not seem at all necessary to the Roman lawyer. Long before, each praetor had made his own statement of the law, on taking office, declaring in advance how he would decide cases. He generally followed the statement of his predecessor, adding from time to time as omissions became evident. This was the praetor's edict. The order of topics was thus purely accidental. The Roman lawyers were used to this haphazard arrangement; commentaries were often based upon this edict. What more natural than to use the same traditional, unsystematic, unscientific succession of topics in the new collection of old law?

"But it was worse than that. Working under pressure, the commissioners split up into committees, and worked through their various sources. Then apparently, under each topic, the work of the different committees followed in order, without the least attempt to get together the statements of law in any arrangement based upon the nature of the topic itself.

"The copyists, under instructions, copied extracts from the writings of the earlier jurists. Those extracts were revised in the light of the *quinquaginta decisiones* and of the other imperial constitutions. Over nine thousand of them were selected, and each tagged with the name of its author and a reference to the book from which it was copied; and they were then put together, with the lack of system which I have described; and thus, A.D. 533, was made the great *Digest* or *Pandects*.

"Its acceptance was assured by another imperial edict, which made it the law, repealed all law contrary thereto, forbade any citation of any other writings of the jurists, even by way of illustration, and even forbade any commentaries to be made upon the *Digest* itself.

"A rough enough job, done at high speed, with the Byzantine equivalent for scissors and paste, giving us only pitiful fragments of the work of the great jurists of the classical period; yet saving for us almost all of their writings that have been saved; itself being preserved by the merest chance, rising from its tomb to be the center of the intellectual life of the Western barbarians as they turned to study the culture of the past, and finally to displace the laws of the West, save only where the English law was entrenched in the mingled learning and obstinacy of the Islanders."

Professor Page's words are the more interesting because he is taking part in a repeating of history. Like the Roman law when Justinian came to the throne, American law is becoming unmanageable, and needs a restatement. Not all the great bulk of our law is in the regular statute books. In an age of inventions and innovations, the courts are constantly confronted with new problems, and "law must answer every question that life puts to it. It will not do for the courts to say: 'We do not know. This is a new question. There is no law on it. We can do nothing.' If there are no rules on the subject, the courts must make them up, then and there, and give the best solution they can. That is the way in which law grows; and if it cannot do this, it does not grow. Law, as it grows in this way, is found in the writings of those who technically know the law."

The answer of the court to a new question constitutes a precedent, and precedents in the American courts are of great importance. There are at present some ten thousand volumes containing the reports of perhaps a million adjudicated cases, in which there lies more or less hidden a vast amount of potential law by precedent. The courts are the jurisconsults and praetors of to-day, and their precedents are the jurisconsults' responses and the praetors' edicts of ancient times; only, after the fact and not conveniently posted.

The law these precedents represent must be made accessible. The American Law Institute, composed of 813 judges, lawyers, and professors of law, with 33 members acting as Council, is engaged in the solution of this problem. The result will be the restatement of the law in a series of convenient volumes, one for each special topic, as contracts, agency, torts, which will get their authority from the process of their creation together with the approval of bench and bar as they are used.

Let us conclude with a few observations as to some notable features in Rome's thousand and more years of experience with the making of law.

First, the law-making of Rome was the work of no one man or group of men, but was the product of community life from its beginning in a society of the humblest fashion and on the lowest scale to its end in a highly sophisticated State. The Empire did great things in the law, but, as far as human living was concerned as a factor, the experience was complete before the absolute régime arrived.

Second, the difficulties met by Roman law-making were those belonging to a society in which the people ruled themselves and were their own teachers. They were problems to be solved by experimentation in the laboratory of human life. There was the problem of the disassociation of the divine and human, which are always mingled and confused in primitive society; that is, the secularization of law. There was the problem, always hard and never quite solved in any society, of distinguishing between sin and crime, and between crime and wrong. There was the problem of determining what was really injurious, and the problem of deciding on the punishment that was beneficial. There was the problem of the death penalty. There was the problem of how far to leave the settlement of personal grievance to private retaliation or revenge. There was the problem of separating politics from law. There was the problem of system.

Third, the perfection of the working of Roman law required the autocracy. The principle of autocracy is the unresponsible possession and exercise of authority by one man. If he is a capable man and a conscientious man, the result will be expert government and the welfare of the people in all except the encouragement of the active qualities of citizenship. If he is incapable or bad, the result will be the

A Restoration of the Quirinal Region

The view is from the north end of the Capitoline Hill. From right to left: Forum, Basilica, and Column of Trajan. In the left background, Aurelian's Temple of the Sun.

tyrannies and cruelties of despotism. The principle of autocracy was already present in the courts from the time the praetor perforce assumed the authority and the responsibility of the edict. When the law had fallen behind the times and no longer fitted the needs of life, the praetor's manipulation of it by adding to or subtracting from it, by new interpretation, or by adaptation, was a matter of his own initiative. But the praetor was an elective officer, a part of the many-headed, emotional, uncertain democracy, and was neither a specialist in legal science nor master of himself. The living, thronging, struggling, suffering people furnished the raw material of law; their leaders, working with and for and upon and through them, helped them to express in laws and institutions their ideals; but for the execution of the laws and the working of the institutions there was needed an authority unhindered by the prejudices, passions, shortsightedness, and slowness of the crowd.

Republican Rome was the great mother of men and ideals, but failed in the practical expression of her ideals in the State. Imperial Rome, with all that is charged against her, unified her world and governed it well through the longest period of peace the Western World has ever seen. We are still disputing as to the relative merits of republic and autocracy. The lesson of Rome is that each has its virtues, and each its time.

XLII

ON THE SOUTHERN BORDER

Once the Roman State had reached the limit of its expansion, the border became as nearly a definite and immovable line as nature and man could establish. Desert, mountains, rivers, ocean, and seas were nature's contribution; the contribution of man was the art of defense.

Of the defenses afforded by nature, only the ocean could be regarded as final; beyond it and on it were no foes. But beyond the Rhine and the Danube, beyond the Two Rivers in the remote East, and beyond the North Sea and the Black Sea and the Red, there were ever watchful and sometimes dangerous enemies. The defense afforded by river and sea had to be supplemented by fleet and fort; their waters could invite attack as well as repel it.

The desert was like the sea. Across its uninhabited wastes of sand and rock might come at any time the mobile hordes of nomad barbarians in the South or the armies of ancient kingdoms in the East. As for the mountain barrier, it had its passes to be defended.

Where neither mountain nor desert nor water lent its aid, where the border ran through fertile populated country or through the forest wilderness, no foot of the line was left unguarded, and the Roman wall and ditch marked the legal limit. Where neither nature nor art could be made to suffice, as on the eastern border in Asia, diplomacy and the buffer state supplied the lack.

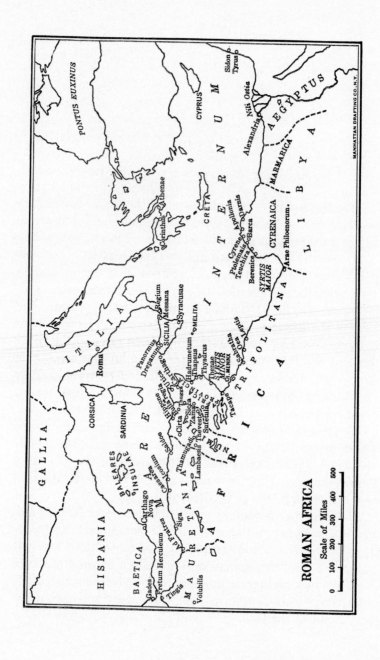

ROMAN AFRICA

Scale of Miles

0   100   200   300   400   500

PONTUS EUXINUS

GALLIA

HISPANIA

BAETICA

Gades
Fretum Herculeum
Tingis
Volubilis

CORSICA

SARDINIA

BALEARES INSULAE

Carthago Nova

Siga

ITALIA

Roma

Panormus
Drepanum
SICILIA
Regium
Messana
Syracusae
MELITA

M A U R E T A N I A

A F R I C A

Thamugadi
Lambaesis
Theveste
Sufetula
Thala
Zama
Sicca
Thusca
Hippo
Tacape
Sabratha
Oea
Leptis
TRIPOLITANA

Cirta

MINOR
Thenae
Thysdrus
Thapsus
Hadrumetum

SYRTIS MAIOR

Berenice
Teuchira
Barca
Ptolemais
Cyrene
Apollonia
Darnis
CYRENAICA
Arae Philoenorum.

M A R E

I N T E R N U M

CRETA

CYPRUS

Corinthus
Athenae

Sidon
Tyrus
Alexandria
Niti Ostia
AEGYPTUS
MARMARICA
L I B Y A

MANHATTAN DRAFTING CO., N.Y.

During the four hundred years that elapsed from Augustus to Alaric, it was only at the periphery of the Empire that the military and naval arms of the Government were actively employed; and actual war even there was but the episode in the long stretches of peace during which the legions in their camp cities wore away the quiet years of semicivic garrison life. The visible presence of power in wall and fort and men and equipment, with its occasional demonstration in prompt and vigorous action, safeguarded the Roman world in the ways of the Pax Romana. In the vast area covered by modern Europe's battling nations, where war and not peace is the normal state, the tread of armies and the wash of the oar were rarely heard save on the errands of peace.

Roman Africa began its history in 146 B.C., with the destruction of Carthage and the annexation of the neighboring regions, but at the end of two hundred years had come to include the entire north coast of the continent from Carthage to the Libyan desert on the east and to the Atlantic Ocean outside Gibraltar on the west. It thus comprised the provinces of the two Mauretanias, with capitals at Tingis and Caesarea, represented to-day by Morocco and its best-known city, Tangier, and Algeria, with the city of Cherchell, a little west of Algiers; the province of Numidia, with its capital, Cirta, equivalent to eastern Algeria to-day and Constantine; the province of Africa, with its capital, Carthage, equivalent to Tunisia and Tunis; and the strip which bordered the Lesser and Greater Syrtes, including Tripolitania and the Cyrenaica of to-day, with the ruined ancient towns of Sabrata, Oëa, Leptis, and Cyrene, and the modern towns of Tripoli, Benghazi, and Cyrene.

In a word, Roman Africa in the time of Claudius was roughly the equivalent of the Barbary States, which to-day as

Italian, French, and Spanish territorial spheres have largely lost their Berber identity; or, still more simply, it was the south shore of the Mediterranean from the Atlantic to the confines of Egypt, a fertile strip or fringe of 2,000 miles between desert and sea, with an average width of little more than 125 miles, the distance from the coast to Timgad at the Sahara's edge.

This far-extended strip occupied by Rome was everywhere backed by the great African desert. From the Pillars of Hercules to Carthage, the formation was much the same: first, a narrow fringe of great fertility at the shore, sometimes, as at Algiers, greatly resembling the European shore; second, the parallel band of the mountains, consisting of the Tell Atlas on the north and the Sahara Atlas on the south, with broad depressions between; third, the descent into the desert levels of the Sahara. From Carthage eastward, the fringe at the shore was narrower, the mountains less prominent, and the desert more immediate. The climate was semitropical, with a two months' rainy season and a long period of dryness and heat. With the aid of elaborate irrigation, the coastal slopes and valleys, especially the exuberant soil near Carthage and in parts of Numidia, were rich in grain and oil and wine, the date, and other fruits. Besides these products of the soil, there were dyes and sponges from the sea, porphyry and onyx from Mauretania, the creamy *giallo antico* and the richly mottled *africano* from the marble mines of Numidia, and, from the desert and the reaches beyond, the camel cargoes of ebony, ivory, and gold, the lions and elephants of the amusement trade, and the negro slave.

Carthage and Numidia, the richer, nearer, more civilized, and more accessible parts of Roman Africa, were the base from which the province was founded, settled, and governed.

A colony of six thousand Italians, sent by Gaius Gracchus in 122 B.C. to replace Carthage as Junonia, soon declined. A second settlement, in 35 B.C., was renewed by Augustus and became in about 16 B.C. a colony with the Roman franchise,

ROMAN TEMPLE AT TEBESSA
This was Roman Theveste. The temple is now a museum.

and the residence of the proconsul of Africa. Cirta, the capital of Numidia, high on its inaccessible thousand-foot rock fifty miles inland, and rich in the memories of Syphax, Masinissa, Micipsa, Jugurtha, and Juba, the native princes who opposed Rome from Scipio Africanus to Marius, in

the second century before Christ, became a colony first
under Julius Caesar, to be firmly established by Augustus.
Caesarea, now Cherchell, 340 miles west of Cirta and 50
west of Algiers, and Tingis, modern Tangier, 500 miles
farther west, were made colonies under Claudius, and became the two capitals of Eastern and Western Mauretania.
The civilization of the four provinces thus formed was less
advanced as the distance from Carthage increased; Mauretania Tingitanis was little removed from barbarism. East
of Carthage, Cyrene, formally added to Roman territory in
46 B.C. after the battle of Thapsus, was a Greek foundation
already six centuries old.

Of the ancient inhabitants of Roman Africa, the basic
stratum was the original prehistoric stock known throughout
history as Berber. The next stratum was brought by the
Phoenician invasion which resulted in the founding of
Carthage and eventually the Punic control of the whole
coast, southern Spain, and a part of Sicily. The third
stratum was the Roman occupation just described.

A traveler in Africa in the time of Trajan or Hadrian
would have found there many thriving cities with Roman
architecture, Roman amusements, Roman religion, and
Roman customs in general predominant but not universal.
In these cities, and in the large villas near them, and on the
large estates or plantations farther removed, he would have
found the Roman ruling class, the Roman bankers, speculators, and traders, and the Roman landowners. He would
have found among these gentry few of the Roman nobility,
but a great many middle-class people either directly come
from Italy or descended from the veterans who formed the
first Italian settlers. Next, the traveler would have noticed
the Punicized character of a great part of the country: the
Punic language and the Punic accent of the Latin; the

Punic dress with its turbans and gowns; the temples to Baal and Astarte and the half Roman and half Punic worship in many temples; the Punic control of a great deal of trade, especially the small trade and the trade of small towns; the scents and colors of the bazaars in which were exposed the

SIDI OKBA

This little oasis town, in the Sahara near its northern border, is kept in order by an agent of the French Republic, as towns in the far corners of civilization were by the administrators of the Roman Empire.

perfumes and spices and rugs of the East and the wares of the Punic handicraftsmen; the Punic shipping in the harbors. In the country districts, he would have found that the small farmers and shepherds and the nonslave portion of the workers on the Roman large estates also were of the Punic stock. The smaller the towns, and the more remote the farms, the fewer Romans he would have found. By this time he would have been conscious of the basic stock of all, the Berber, or African, or Libyan. Rare in the large cities and confined to the poorer quarters, in the villages and in the country these native inhabitants, gowned in rough material and speaking a language separate from both Latin and Punic, formed a larger part of the population; in the remoter, rougher, and desert regions, with their camels and horses and flocks they were the ancient nomads, as shifting, and as eternal, as the shifting desert sands.

The government of Roman Africa was chiefly in the hands of four men: the proconsul at Carthage, appointed by the Roman Senate for one year; the praetorian legate at Cirta, holding command of Numidia as long as the emperor pleased; and the procurators at Caesarea and Tingis, the two capitals of Mauretania. Under them were the various officials and secretaries necessary to the administration of the imperial finances and other provincial business. The management of more purely local interests was left in large measure to the individual town, at whose head were the *duoviri*, or board of two, and the *decuriones*, or council.

All this, which is based on the evidence left from Roman times, to the modern traveler in Africa sounds much as if written of the same lands to-day. In the French protectorate of Tunisia, established 49 years ago, with its population of 2,159,000 in 1926, there are 173,000 Europeans, of whom the French number 71,000, and the Italians, 89,000. If the 173,000 Europeans are thought of as a parallel to the ancient Romans, the remaining 1,986,000, who are composed mostly of Arabs and Bedouins, are to be thought of as the ancient Punic population and the original Berber stock. Further, in the modern capital, Tunis, there are 72,000 French and Italians, and about 114,000 Arabs and Berbers, the last forming but a small part. That is, in Tunisia at large there is about 1 European to 12 Arabs and Berbers; in the capital, there is 1 European to about 1½ Arabs and Berbers, the latter hardly counting. In Algeria at large, now for one century a protectorate, the proportion is 1 to 7; in Algiers, 1 to 4. There is no certainty regarding the proportions in antiquity, but we shall not be far wrong in taking the modern figures as a rough statement of the relative distribution of the ancient Roman, Punic, and native stocks in country and city.

The noting of other details will help still further in the understanding of Roman conditions. In the French resident-general is to be seen the modern form of the proconsul of Africa. The European population is predominantly middle class, and composed of official and commercial groups. The Arab majority is disturbed as little as possible in its laws, religion, and manners. The Berber farmers and nomads away from the cities and out in the semidesert wastes are hardly touched by the culture of Europe. It is interesting to learn that the French highway and railroad are a chief means of development and consolidation, and that the country is held by comparatively small garrisons in few posts. It may be observed that agriculture is the chief industry; that the grain acreage of Algeria and Tunis is about 9,000,000 and that of Italy more than 12,000,000; that the wine product of Algeria and Tunis is 237,500,000 gallons, and that of Italy, 750,000,000; and that the French are taking lessons from the ancient Romans in their conservation of water in tanks and reservoirs for use in the dry season. It is also true that one reason for the development of Tripolitania and Cyrenaica, or Italian Africa, is the crowding and poverty of parts of Italy, just as the crowding and poverty of ancient Rome was a reason for the colonization of Africa.

But both population and products of Roman Africa must have greatly exceeded those of to-day. The indirect evidence of literature alone would warrant this conclusion. The power of Carthage, reduced by Rome in three wars between 265 B.C. and 146 B.C., was based on a well-developed and wealthy civilization. The Africa of the Empire was not

THE BYRSA, OR CITADEL, OF CARTHAGE

The buildings at present on the hill are chiefly the Cathedral of St. Louis, the Seminary of the Pères Blancs, or White Fathers, and the Musée Lavigerie, named from the French cardinal who founded it in 1875. The ruins of Punic, Roman, and Byzantine Carthage are abundant in both museum and landscape.

only a chief granary of Rome and the source of much of the capital's distinction in beautiful building material, but came to have so rich an individuality as to contribute to the Empire in less material ways. Six emperors came out of Africa: Pertinax, Septimius Severus, Alexander Severus, Macrinus, Vibius Gallus, and Volusianus. Fronto, famous as rhetorician, man of letters, and beloved tutor of the young Marcus Aurelius, came from Cirta. Caecilius Natalis, who speaks for paganism in the *Octavius* of Minucius Felix, was probably a triumvir of Cirta. Sicca, a hundred and twenty-five miles southward of Carthage, produced Eutychius Proculus, another teacher of Marcus Aurelius, and a medical writer named Caelius Aurelianus. Symmachus, orator and writer of letters, one of the last defenders of paganism at Rome, came from Carthage. Priscian, the grammarian of the fifth century, came from Caesarea. Perhaps the best known of all the literary Africans is Apuleius of Madaura, not far west of Carthage, author of the *Metamorphoses*, in which is preserved the most delightful of stories, *Cupid and Psyche*.

Of Christian writers, leaders, and martyrs, Africa produced a brilliant galaxy, most of them belonging to the second and third centuries and to Carthage. First to become famous was Tertullian, of Carthage, about A.D. 160–230, the vehement defender of Christianity and assailant of its foes, who finally was himself carried away by heresy. There was Cyprian, bishop of Carthage in 248 or 249, martyred in 258. There were Arnobius, about 300, a converted pagan from Cirta, who like Tertullian took the offensive against paganism, and his pupil Lactantius, about 250–330, sometimes called the Christian Cicero because of his humanism. Greatest of all was Augustine, 354–430, born at Thagaste near Madaura, the home of Apuleius; teacher of rhetoric in Carthage, Rome, and Milan; priest, and bishop of Hippo; author of the famous *Confessions* and *The City of God*.

We need not depend, however, upon the indirect evidence of history and letters. The most eloquent witnesses to the prosperity and even splendor of Roman Africa are its ruins. Their number and importance are always the surprise of the traveler.

The most superficial visit to Roman Africa requires a fortnight. If Tripolitania and the Cyrenaica are included, longer time is necessary. From Naples to Tunis, with stops at Palermo and Trapani, the ancient Drepanum of Virgilian fame, takes about thirty-six hours. The hill of Carthage, the Byrsa or citadel, is on the right as the ship enters the gulf of Tunis. From Tunis, a city of one hundred and seventy-five thousand, the electric train quickly reaches the station of Carthage, ten miles away. Here by the shore, on plain and hill and on the high Byrsa, are the remnants of the Roman town which succeeded to what Polybius called the wealthiest city of the world, the city said by tradition to have been founded by Dido the refugee from Tyre and hostess of Aeneas and the Trojans. They include the ruins of the admiralty and the harbors, gigantic baths, the theater, the amphitheater, in which is a memorial cross of Saints Perpetua and Felicitas, martyred in 203, tombs in great numbers from both Punic and Roman times, reservoirs and roads, temple foundations, and the wonderful collection of Punic and Roman remains in the museum on the Byrsa named after Cardinal Lavigerie, founder of the monastery of the Pères Blancs which contains it. In the environs of Tunis is the Bardo, the greatest of the African museums, in which are to be seen the famous bronzes recovered in 1907 from the bottom of the sea, where a cargo of them sank in ancient times, a great display of the mosaics for which African villas were noted, and the celebrated mosaic portrait of Virgil writing the Aeneid, from Susa, or Hadrumetum. Not far to the south of Tunis are the ruins, 66 feet high, of the 50 miles of aqueduct capable of supplying ancient Carthage with water at the rate of 6,000,000 gallons daily. In 1925, the excavations of Professor F. W. Kelsey of Michigan and Count Khun de Prorok at the west side of the commercial harbor of ancient Carthage revealed 1,100 cinerary urns, 300 altar-shaped and shrine-shaped monuments, and many dedications. All were in the temple area of the goddess Tanit, and Professor Kelsey suspected that the children's ashes contained in most of the urns represented the sacrifice by fire with which the Carthaginians were charged.

THE TEMPLE OF DEA CAELESTIS, OR TANIT, AT DOUGGA

Twenty-one miles to the northwest of Tunis are the ruins of Utica, where Cato took his life after the defeat by Caesar in 46 B.C. at Thapsus. Forty-one miles to the southwest, up the valley of the Medjerda, the ancient Bagrada, are the sightly remains of Dougga, ancient Thugga: theater, temples, Roman and Punic tombs, prehistoric dolmens, on a height 1,970 feet above the sea, and among the best preserved in Africa.

Susa, or Hadrumetum, reached by train ninety-three miles south of Carthage on the coast, with a fine museum of Roman remains, is the port from which Hannibal left his native land after Zama. Beyond it thirty miles are the cisterns, amphitheater, tombs, and quay representing Thapsus. Mehdia, near which the shipload of statuary above referred to was found, is ten miles farther on. At Sbeitla, a hundred and twelve miles from Susa to the southwest, are the beautiful Capitol and the triumphal arch of Constantine preserved from ancient Sufetula. Forty miles south of Susa near the coast is El Djem, once Thysdrus, now a little village rendered inconspicuous by the gigantic Roman amphitheater, among the largest in existence. Near by are extensive ruins of baths, reservoirs, a circus, and a smaller and older amphitheater. Farther south a hundred and thirty miles are Gabes, once Roman Tacape, and the island of Djerba, thought to be Homer's land of the lotus-eaters. From this place, called Meninx, came the Emperors Vibius Gallus and Volusianus, A.D. 251–253.

A voyage of five hundred and forty-four miles by sea from Tunis brings one to Tripoli, the ancient Oëa, where Apuleius met and married the widow and was charged with magic. The name Tripoli is descended from Tripolis, meaning "three cities," the name given by the ancient Sicilian traders to the towns Oëa, Leptis Magna, and Sabratha. They were the means of communication between the riches of the Sudan and the ports of Carthage, Sicily, and Italy. From here came the Emperors Septimius and Alexander Severus, the latter of whom is said to have learned Latin only after going to Rome, and always to have retained an accent. Tripoli contains a grand triumphal arch in honor of Marcus Aurelius and Lucius Verus. Since the Italian occupation of Tripolitania in 1911, the Italian Directorate of Fine Arts has restored this arch, founded an important museum, and carried on the excavation of Sabratha and Leptis Magna. Sabratha was the birthplace of Vespasian's empress, Domitilla, and the scene of Lucius Apuleius' trial before the Proconsul Claudius Maximus in A.D. 157. Among the monuments to be seen now where a few years ago everything was buried in the sands are the amphitheater, the foundations of the Capitolium with a colossal bust of Jupiter, a bathing establishment, and many inscriptions. At Leptis, there have come to light, from the forty feet of sand in which the ages have safely kept them enveloped, numerous excellent triumphal reliefs and statues, baths, a vast basilica, harbor works, and an arch of Septimius Severus. The city was twice the size of Pompeii, and its abundant stone and marble ruins in the grand style have been preserved in a wonderful freshness and splendor.

Cyrene, a long distance east of Tripoli, is another scene of recent Italian achievement. Here, in 1911, a downpour of rain, loosening a bank of earth, disclosed the Venus of Cyrene, now in the National Museum at Rome, the most important sculpture discovery of recent times.

Thus far we have been enumerating sites near Carthage and farther east. The important sites to its west are chiefly Le Kef, ancient Sicca Veneria; Bulla Regia; Tebessa, ancient Theveste; Thibilis; Constantine, ancient Cirta; Lambaesis; Timgad; Cherchell; and Tangier. There are few ancient remains at Le Kef, though it was famed for its worship of Astarte and was of much strategic importance both in Roman antiquity and in the wars of the French occupation and, before that, the wars between the beys of Tunis and Algeria. Bulla Regia, a hundred miles west of Carthage, was the scene of a battle in 203 B.C. between Scipio and the Carthaginians under Syphax and Hasdrubal.

Its deserted site is rich in the ruins of a city equipped with every means of comfort and culture. About fifty miles farther west and a hundred and fifty-four miles from Tunis, at Souk-Ahras, was ancient Thagaste, the birthplace in A.D. 354 of the great churchman, Aurelius Augustinus, Saint Augustine. Like Bulla Regia, it is at about two thousand feet elevation. South of it about seventeen miles is Madaura, the native city of Apuleius, and sixty-three miles farther south is ancient Theveste, marked by a fine arch of Caracalla, an almost perfectly preserved temple of Minerva, now a museum, and an imposing early Christian basilica. Hammam-Meskoutine, sixty-four miles west of Souk-Ahras, is now and was in Roman times a sulphur bath resort. Two or three hours' walk to the southwest, through pleasant, rolling uplands, leads to ancient Thibilis, on a hill at twenty-three hundred feet elevation, an entire town laid bare by excavation in 1905 and following years. A visit to these thoroughly excavated though not especially important ruins is an excursion long to be remembered for archaeological and natural charm.

Constantine, the ancient Numidian and Roman Cirta, whose modern name goes back to the Emperor Constantine, is a city of about 60,000, surpassed in Algeria only by Algiers and Oran. Situated on a rock twenty-one hundred feet high, from the times of Masinissa and Syphax until its capture by the French in 1837 Cirta has been an important stronghold. The present bridge, four hundred and seven feet above the Rhumel gorge, overhangs the ruins of the Roman bridge. There are also remnants of the ancient aqueduct and reservoirs. It was in Cirta that Sophonisba, the sister of Hasdrubal, beloved by the young Masinissa, is said to have taken poison at his bidding when the Roman general Scipio ordered their separation. Philippeville, on the coast fifty-four miles north, has the largest Roman theater in Algeria.

Batna, seventy-three miles south of Constantine, is the station for the motor excursion to Lambaesis and Timgad. Forty-one miles farther south, on the line to Biskra, is the famous Roman bridge, El Kantara. Biskra, thirty-five miles farther and one hundred and forty-nine miles from Constantine, is an oasis town south of the mountains on the desert's edge, and was Roman Bescera.

Lambaesis, to-day Lambessa, is a perfect specimen of the Roman camp city which had so much to do with the Romanization of conquered lands. At an elevation of 3,875 feet at the north side of the Aurès Mountains, which border the Sahara thirty miles away, this post was the key of this part of Africa from the time of Trajan to its decline, when Constantine was made the capital of the region. Abandoned as an active camp, it was probably overwhelmed and destroyed, like Timgad, by the Berbers from the wild Aurès near by in the raids of 535. Both lay deserted and buried until the French occupation in 1830. The Roman camp at Lambaesis is a maze of foundation walls and fragments covering an area of about 1,600 by 1,300 feet, arranged on the regulation axes of the cardo and decumanus, the two long streets which crossed at right angles in the heart of the camp, and dominated by a praetorium 75 by 100 feet and 49 feet high. The post was meant for permanence, and not only possessed offices, club rooms, forum, shrine, baths, and other civic conveniences, but soon came to be surrounded by so many dwellings and places of business and amusement as to assume the dimensions and partake of the character of an ordinary city. More than one veteran, on receiving his discharge and donation, invested his savings in a home and passed the remainder of his life on the outskirts of the camp in which for a score of years he had lived. The African legion, and the only one, was the famous Third Augustan, and it was stationed at Lambaesis upwards of three hundred years.

, "No camp in any part of the world," says Alexander Graham in *Roman Africa*, "has left so many indications of its existence, or so many memorials of military life and administration, as the camp of this Numidian legion. The inscriptions already discovered and interpreted number more than 2500, and continued systematic exploration is constantly bringing others to light. They are in the form of memorials of soldiers of all ranks who have faithfully discharged their duty, of dedications to emperors for just and benevolent rule, and of acts of munificence by residents of wealth and renown. One and all they bear testimony to a long period of tranquil enjoyment of life in a pleasant and fertile country, to the prevalence of respect paid by soldiers to their superiors, and to loyal obedience to imperial authority."

Timgad, fifteen miles from Lambaesis, and excavated from 1880 on, was founded about A.D. 100 as Colonia Marciana Traiana Thamugadi, and its abundant inscriptions prove that the architects and engineers of the Legio Tertia Augusta at Lambaesis were its chief planners and builders. Timgad is the most perfectly excavated city of ancient times, and ranks next to Rome and Pompeii as a document of Roman life. Its ruins include eleven baths, two markets, forum, library, public toilets, basilica, senate, theater, Capitolium and other temples, colonnades, an arch to Trajan, shops, and private houses in great number.

Cherchell, or Zerschell, the ancient Colonia Claudia Caesarea, capital of Mauretania Caesariensis, is sixty miles west of Algiers. High on the coast twenty-four miles before reaching Cherchell is the remarkable tomb, over 100 feet high and 200 feet square at the base, conjectured to be that of Juba II, the enlightened ruler of Caesarea in 25 B.C.–A.D. 22. Fourteen miles farther on, from side to side of a deep valley, is the Roman aqueduct, 100 feet high in three stories. In the town are the remnants of Roman fortifications, a fine bathing establishment, a theater, and a good museum of antiquities. Near by are the naval harbor, the ruins of an

THE RUINS OF TIMGAD

The Arch of Trajan is in the distance. The camp city of Thamugadi was about 400 yards square. Its excavation was begun in 1880 by the French Government.

amphitheater, and the usual reservoirs. The name Cherchell is composed of Caesarea and the earlier Punic name, Iol.

Tangier, ancient Punic Tingis, 563 miles west of Algiers and 1,140 miles from Tunis and Carthage, given the rights of citizenship by Augustus and made a colony by Claudius, was the capital of Mauretania Tingitana. The not very plentiful remains of Tingis are an hour's walk from the modern town.

This is but the briefest indication of the archaeological interest of northern Africa. Lambaesis, Timgad, Tebessa, Constantine, Carthage, and Dougga are the sites most frequently and most easily visited, and even these few are astonishing in their wealth of ancient interest; but in them, and in all the others here mentioned with them, the list is far from complete. Nor have we paused to notice every relic of interest. In the vicinity of Tebessa, one archaeologist knew of more than 260 ruins. In the Mateur neighborhood, 40 miles to the northwest of Carthage, there are as many as 300.

Yet even the imperfect exploration of Africa tells the essential truth of the Roman occupation. The Indo-European and the Semite, in parallel advances to the north and south of the great sea, came into collision where Sicily and Spain made contact unavoidable. The permanent safety of the Roman required the defeat of the African and the occupation of his shores. A decaying civilization along the fertile coast and a benighted barbarism in the inland wastes were lifted back into something like enlightenment. The sea became a means of unity instead of separation. The lifeblood of a universal commerce and a universal culture was let into veins that were nearly emptied, and health and vigor took the place of atrophy. The energy and patience of a hardworking race crisscrossed and dotted the areas of an almost rainless country with aqueducts and conduits and reservoirs and cisterns, and made the desert blossom as the rose. There were cities of thousands and scores of thousands of people where now are villages and towns of hundreds. There were comforts and amusements and luxury in city and country which died with the Roman withdrawal and only now are faintly coming to life again with the French employment of the ancient methods and means.

The Roman Empire in Africa declined, as it declined elsewhere. The Vandals overran it in the fifth century, the
Byzantines recovered and held it in the sixth, and the Arabs
ran through its narrow length like fire in the seventh and

THE AMPHITHEATER AT CARTHAGE

The cross is in memory of Saints Perpetua and Felicitas, martyrs A.D. 203.

were at the gates of Spain by the eighth. The Roman cities
crumbled and sank, the winds and the sands covered them,
and for twelve centuries it was as if Roman Africa had never
been. It was the victory of nature over art. The parching
heat, the desiccating rainlessness, the mountains and rocks,
the wild beasts and desperate men from the barren hills and
the deserts and beyond, and, above all, the broad and deep

substratum of the native Punic and Berber population, were the potent forces, elsewhere not so great, that made the holding of Africa in the Roman tradition too much for human strength. When the Arabs came, it was the taking up of the old Semitic tradition.

Yet it would not be truthful to assume that everything of Roman Africa disappeared. For three active centuries its life was mingled in the life of the Empire and helped to form its character. Not even the material contributions of its planters and traders and builders may be said to have wholly perished from the life of the world. Much less may we say that what its men of letters and saints accomplished is not a part of the heritage which descended through Christian to modern times.

XLIII

ROMAN SPAIN

It has been seen how slight was the force required to protect the border in Roman Africa so long as the Empire continued in the ways of growth and prosperity, and how complete, when the Empire had fallen, was the disappearance of Rome and Europe from African shores. On no other border was the pressure of barbarism so easy to withstand, and in no other land of the Empire was the disappearance so complete and lasting, the effect in the actual area so transient. The truth of this will be clearer if we visit another border land.

When Carthage withdrew from Spain in 206 B.C., and the Romans in 197 B.C. divided it into Hither and Farther Spain with capitals at Nova Carthago and Corduba, they found a country disunited both by physical nature and by race diversity. Sharply divided by rugged and irregular mountain ranges, its parts were isolated, communication was hard, defiance of the pursuer easy. Diversity and division in race were quite as sharp. There were the Tartessians or Turdetani in the south, highly civilized and rich, perhaps a remnant of the Aegean migrants of the age of bronze; the Iberians in east and north and northwest, hardly removed from barbarism except in the coastal regions where they were touched by navigation; the Celtiberi in the high central plains of Castile, a blend of native Iberians with original Celts from Gaul; the ever alien Basques in the Cantabrian valleys at the northern limit; Phoenicians on the coasts at the south; Greeks on the sea in the far northeast; and, earlier than all

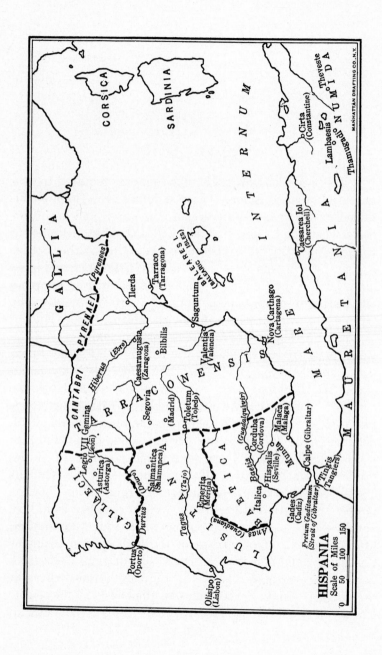

HISPANIA

Scale of Miles

0   50   100   150

Map labels:

CORSICA

SARDINIA

GALLIA

MARE INTERNUM

MAURETANIA

NUMIDA

Theveste

Lambaesis

Thamugadi

Cirta (Constantine)

Caesarea Iol (Cherchell)

CANTABRI

PYRENAEI (Pyrenees)

Ilerda

Tarraco (Tarragona)

BALEARES ISLES (Balearic Isles)

Saguntum

Legio VII Gemina (Leon)

Hiberus (Ebro)

Caesaraugusta (Zaragoza)

Bilbilis

Segovia

(Madrid)

Valentia (Valencia)

TARRACONENSIS

Nova Carthago (Cartagena)

Asturica (Astorga)

GALLAECIA

Durius (Douro)

Portus (Oporto)

Salmantica (Salamanca)

Tagus (Tajo)

Toletum (Toledo)

Emerita (Merida)

LUSITANIA

BAETICA

Baetis (Guadalquivir)

Corduba (Cordova)

Hispalis (Seville)

Munda

Malaca (Malaga)

Calpe (Gibraltar)

Italica

Anas (Guadiana)

Gades (Cadiz)

Fretum Gaditanum (Strait of Gibraltar)

Tingis (Tangiers)

Olisipo (Lisbon)

MANHATTAN DRAFTING CO., N.Y.

the rest, the people who left the dolmens, the groups of up-right stones called *antas*, and the great caves with painted vaults and carvings of stone and bone. The early attempts to subjugate these varied and stubborn peoples, especially the Celtiberians and Lusitanians, cost many a Roman defeat, and it was not until Augustus that the conquest was made complete.

The progress of the Roman conquest during these one hundred and seventy years was marked by notable episodes. Tiberius Gracchus in 179 B.C. inaugurated the policy of conciliation by means of improvements in agriculture and industry, and the leaving of local government to native control. The suppression of the Lusitanians under Viriathus in 140 B.C. was a severe trial to Roman arms. The siege of Numantia in 133 B.C. by Scipio was among the famous military events of the century, and its fall the destruction of Spanish hopes of independence. Sertorius, the able friend of Marius, exiled to Spain, erected a temporary state whose benefits in wealth, culture, and civic instruction were a more effective means of Romanization than all displays of force. Julius Caesar as quaestor of Farther Spain in 69 B.C., as praetor in 61 B.C. in the same province, and in his two campaigns against Afranius and Petreius in Hither Spain, north of the Ebro, in 49 B.C., and against the Pompeians in 45 at Munda near Cordova, acquired a familiarity with Spanish conditions which no doubt had an effect on the relations of Augustus with Spain.

When Augustus addressed himself to the Spanish problem, he found still unsubdued the tribes on the southern slope of the Pyrenees, and the Cantabrians and Asturians in the northwest. Between 36 B.C. and 26 B.C. the vigor of the Roman effort along the Pyrenees was such that six triumphs were claimed by the generals of Augustus. Both sides of the mountains were subdued, and the Roman arms were carried with final results against the Cantabrians and Asturians by Agrippa and Augustus himself.

The Spanish conquests were made permanent by the transfer of hostile tribes to the plains, the creation of garrison towns and forts, and the settlement of veteran soldiers in military colonies. Cities were founded whose names are still to be detected in the Spanish tongue: Asturica in Astorga, Bracara in Braga, Emerita in Merida, Pax Augusta in Badajoz, and Caesaraugusta in Zaragoza. The Farther Province was divided into Baetica, nearly all the south, with Corduba as capital; and Lusitania, the west and much of the north, with Emerita as capital. Hither Spain, with capital at Tarraco, modern Tarragona, instead of New Carthage, was known thenceforth as Hispania Tarraconensis. Three legions were sufficient to hold the country: the Fourth Macedonian, the Sixth Victorious, the Tenth Gemina. Two were in the neighborhood of the present city of León, whose name is descended from the word *Legio*, and one near modern Santander on the north coast. The legions before long were maintained by recruiting from Spain itself.

The government of Spain, like that of Africa and other provinces, was a combination of Roman and native rule. The Roman authority in Baetica was the governor at Corduba, with a quaestor to manage the tax collections and other finances, and a legatus or commissioner residing at Hispalis, the modern Seville. The governor of Lusitania, ruling from Merida, had one legate whose post was probably Olisipo, modern Lisbon. The governor of Hispania Tarraconensis made Tarraco his capital, and had at his service three legates and the three legions allotted to all Spain. Lusitania and Tarraconensis were imperial provinces, and

Baetica a senatorial province, according to the emperor's policy of making the more difficult provinces directly responsible to him. The title of the senatorial governor at Corduba was proconsul; of the imperial governors at Tarraco and Merida, praetorian legate. In either case the

THE AQUEDUCT AT SEGOVIA

The main stretch of this aqueduct is 900 yards long, has 119 arches, and sometimes reaches a height of 94 feet. It was repaired about A.D. 100, and first built much earlier.

rule was autocratic and personal; the governor was immediately responsible to the emperor or the Senate, the commissioners were responsible to the governor, and the numerous underlings who constituted the provincial bureaucracy were answerable to the commissioners.

Roman authority had to do with the keeping of the

country in order, the collection of taxes or tribute, and improvements in public works or administration which affected the general welfare of the province or provinces. Outside this, it was native control that functioned. Matters of local import were left largely to individual communities. These communities might be colonies, municipalities, Latin or federate towns, or tributary villages and areas, according to the measure of privilege granted by the Government at Rome. In the Tarraconensis there were 293 communities, of which 179 possessed constitutions, and the rest some sort of autonomy. The government of the communities was patterned after that of the Italian cities; there were duoviri, senate, and popular assembly, with assessors to manage the tax rates. Once a year, these local senates elected from their number delegates to the provincial assembly which met under the presidency of the provincial priest to hold a cele- bration in honor of the imperial cult, to approve or dis- approve the retiring governor, to elect a patron to represent the province at Rome, to send intercessors to the emperor, and like measures.

The remoteness of Spain in the Roman mind and the perils it offered are suggested by the Ode in which Horace addresses Septimius, who is ready to be the poet's comrade to the world's end and in any danger:

> "Septimius, who with me would brave
> Far Gades, and Cantabrian land
> Untamed by Rome, and Moorish wave
> That whirls the sand."

This was the Spain that still in part resisted. The effect of Augustan conquest and the Roman pacification policy may be seen in what Strabo says in Augustan times of the thirty Spanish tribes near the Tagus:

"Notwithstanding the fertility of the country in corn, cattle, gold, silver, and numerous other similar productions, the majority of its inhabitants, neglecting to gain their subsistence from the ground, passed their lives in pillage and continual warfare, both between themselves and their neighbors. To this the Romans at length put a stop by subduing them and changing many of their cities into villages, besides colonizing some of them better."

Velleius Paterculus, of the next generation wrote, "These provinces, so widely scattered, so numerous, and so fierce, which never knew respite from wars of first-class magnitude, Augustus brought to so peaceful a state that they were free from even acts of brigandage."

More eloquent testimony still is the fact that within a century of the Augustan occupation the number of legions in Spain had been reduced from three to one, that no fleet was maintained, and that no need for it was felt except when the pirates of Mauretania harassed the southern shores. The hundreds of colonies, municipalities, federated Latin towns, and tributary communities, regulating themselves by choice more or less in the Roman way, supplanted the hundreds of petty tribes and chieftaincies. The judicial districts, or *conventus*, of the Republic were reorganized — seven in Hither Spain, four in Baetica, three in Lusitania — and unified their neighborhoods. The old road from the Rhone region down the coast to Tarraco and New Carthage was improved and extended to Corduba and Gades, and other highways, national and local, built by the emperor and the communities. The use of Latin and the toga became widespread, and signified the surrender of the barbarian to Roman ideals. Extortionate governors were held to account, and public spirit began to operate in civic benefactions.

The six millions thought to be the population of Spain in Augustan times became the probable twelve millions of

Hadrian's day when the signs began to indicate that the peak was passed. It was a country rich in material resources. Its metals, minerals, wool, cattle, fish, grain, wine, honey, and oil formed a large part of the imports of Italy and Rome. The gold which was found in its provinces was acquired by the placer and hydraulic methods and by shaft mining. "Nearly the whole of Spain," writes Pliny, "abounds in mines of lead, iron, copper, silver, and gold." "Baetica," he says again, "excels all the other provinces in the richness of its cultivation and the peculiar fertility and beauty of its vegetation." Strabo calls it "marvelously fertile, abounding in every species of produce." It was a country rich in human resources also. Trajan and Hadrian were both natives of Spain. A hundred years of Spanish letters included the two Senecas, Quintilian, Lucan, and Martial. Pliny the Elder was one of its procurators, and Roman administration brought to it many men of ability. We may believe also that it did not lack even then the native independence and charm of character which make it so attractive to the visitor to-day.

The Roman ruins in Spain are not so abundant as those of Roman Africa. They have been despoiled by Vandal, Goth, Moor, and Christian; they have had no desert sands to protect them; wind and rain and frost and heat have crumbled them. Yet Spain is rich in Roman archaeology. At Tarragona and Segovia, it displays two of the mightiest aqueduct ruins outside the Roman Campagna. Tarragona, where Augustus lived in 26 B.C., has also two miles of Roman walls, built by the early commanders in Spain and restored by Augustus on the foundations of the prehistoric Iberian wall; and the city abounds in the more fragmentary remains of theater, baths, temples, villas, tombs, and other buildings. There was a circus five hundred yards long, and near it an

amphitheater, and more than five hundred inscriptions have
been found. At Cartagena, the Spanish capital of the
Carthaginians, the two heights flanking the harbor entrance
were once crowned by a castle of the Barca family and a
temple to Aesculapius. The forum and amphitheater have
been explored, and a monument forty feet high in honor of

THE AMPHITHEATER AT ITALICA

It is about five miles from Seville. Founded in 205 B.C. by Scipio Africanus for
his veterans, Italica was the native city of the Emperors Trajan, Hadrian, and
Theodosius.

the younger Scipio is preserved. New Carthage, the first
Roman capital, was succeeded by Tarraco.

Two of the most interesting sites are Italica and Emerita.
The former is reached by a pleasant walk of five miles from
Seville, the Iberian Hispalis. Both Italica, which was a
veterans' colony of 206 B.C., and Hispalis were on the trade
route from Gades to Emerita and Salmantica, the modern

Salamanca. Trajan and Hadrian were natives of Italica. The foundations of its temples, baths, and forum remain, and its amphitheater is a large and impressive ruin. Emerita, founded by order of Augustus about 25 B.C., is now Merida, on the Guadiana, far inland at the borders of Portugal. The ancient bridge and viaduct across the river, half a mile long, is well preserved and still in use. The aqueduct remains are very imposing, the theater is a ruin in the grand style with fragments of ornament indicating great splendor, there are many temple ruins, and parts of the circus and naumachia remain.

Corduba, the home of the Senecas, Lucan, and the Gallio of *The Acts*, who was the deputy of Achaea when "the Jews made insurrection with one accord against Paul, and brought him to the judgment seat," was made a settlement of veterans in 152 B.C. and figured in the civil wars as the enemy of Caesar. It has a bridge over the Guadalquivir with ancient piers and foundation, the remains of an aqueduct, and other ruins, including some of the many hundreds of columns which make the Great Mosque one of the world's architectural wonders.

Gades the joyous, *Cadiz la Joyosa* of the Spaniards to-day, the *Gades Iocosae* of the epigrammatist Martial, was one of the oldest of the Mediterranean cities and probably the most frequently mentioned Spanish city of ancient letters. Said to have been founded by the Tyrians long before Carthage, it was a city of so much dignity at the time of the Second Punic War that at the close of hostilities the Roman Senate admitted its claim to freedom. Always of great commercial importance, its advantage at the meeting of Mediterranean and Atlantic was increased by the fall of Carthage in 146 B.C. In Augustan times it was reputed to be among the first cities of the Empire in the number of its rich men; its census included five hundred members of the money-making rank in society, the equites, only Rome and Patavium surpassing it. With the multiplication of good land routes leading from new harbors on the east coast through the peninsula to the west, Cadiz gradually sank, to rise again when the Americas came into Spanish affairs and the silver fleets returned from the Spanish Main to anchor in its harbors.

THE HARBOR AT CADIZ, THE ANCIENT GADES

Little of Roman Gades remains. Its famous temple to the Punic-Greek Melcarth-Heracles, in which Hannibal "discharged his vows to Hercules and bound himself by new vows in case the rest of his ventures were prospered," is now under the sea, with most of the city's other buildings. One visits it for the memories of the great Carthaginian leader; of Balbus, the prefect of engineers and useful friend of Caesar and client of Cicero; of Caninius Rufus, the poet friend of Martial and Pliny; of Columella, the agricultural writer; of the merry dancers and singers whose kind survives in the

Cadiz of to-day; and for the delight of the tall houses with balconies commanding the streets and *miradores* looking across the waters, for the freshness of the breezes that blow from the sea on every side, for the flowers and marbles of its patios, and for its clean and silent streets.

With the end of the second century and the beginning of active decline, the Spains partook of the general decay. Taxes and civic burdens increased; freebooters grew bolder; in the reign of Gallienus, A.D. 260–268, the Suevi and Franks came down the eastern coast, and defied authority for a dozen years; the reforms of Diocletian, A.D. 284–306, made still heavier the already unendurable load of citizenship. In the early fifth century the Vandals, Alans, and Suevi lodged in the country, soon to be followed by the Visigoths. By A.D. 484 no Roman garrisons were left in any part of Spain. The authority of the Empire had vanished long before, as far as force was concerned.

Aside from force, however, the Empire did not die in Spain, and is living still. The six hundred years of the Roman domination did not conclude, as in the case of Roman Africa, with the total disappearance of all that was Roman except the ruins of Roman buildings. In Spain, it was only the formal authority of government that disappeared. The Latin language remained, except among the Basques, who have defied the ages and still employ their own tongue. The Roman law survived, and the Roman system of town government was soon adopted by the Goths. The ideals of architecture and the other arts remained. Greatest of all for the preservation of Roman ideals and unity, the Roman Church remained, with her authoritative bishops to restrain their provincials and to keep alive the feeling of kinship with other parts of Spain and with other lands that once had been Roman soil.

XLIV

ON THE NORTHERN BORDER

The line between Rome and barbarism on the south was drawn by the African desert. The line on the north, until Claudius invaded Britain and Trajan carried the eagles into Dacia, was drawn by the Rhine and the Danube. To the west of Dacia, the Danube and the Rhine continued to be the line.

At about the time of Hadrian, the three hundred and forty-five miles between the upper Rhine at Rheinbrohl and the upper Danube at Regensburg, hitherto a narrow protected zone through the forest, became a palisaded defense, to be converted after a hundred years into wall and moat, with a hundred military stations at intervals on the Roman side, with a thousand watch towers, and with military road. In the time of Hadrian also, the tribes in the north of Britain having proved unconquerable, the Roman line in the island was made definite by the great wall between the Solway and the Tyne, along what is now the border between England and Scotland.

Wall and sea and rivers thus marked the limit of Roman rule from the Solway to the Black Sea. The length of the Danube is 1,725 miles, of the Rhine, 700; allowing for the fact that the *limes*, the limit or bound, left the former above Regensburg and joined the latter below Coblentz, and including the distance to the end of the Roman lines in Britain, the entire northern border was over two thousand miles in extent.

To stand on the banks of the rolling Danube, or by the poetic sister stream where

> "The castled crag of Drachenfels
> Frowns o'er the wide and winding Rhine,
> Whose breast of waters broadly swells
> Between the banks which bear the vine,"

and to see in the steady, powerful rush of their currents the line that marked the end of land redeemed from the wilds of tribal barbarism, is an impressive experience; but not until

RESTORED BRIDGE AND GATE OF THE SAALBURG

The Saalburg is the largest known fortress on the walled and palisaded line of defense between Rheinbrohl on the Rhine below Coblentz and Hienheim on the Danube near Regensburg. It is about twenty miles north of Frankfort-on-the-Main.

one visits the barrier that ran through forests and over hills from sea to sea in Britain and from river to river in the heart of Germany does he realize in all acuteness the fact of the Roman Empire as an area set apart — an area one step from which meant the leaving behind of the life of cultivated men;

an area which constituted a unity to be shielded against the rough tribes of the forest and the desert while civilization pursued its experiments in the greatest laboratory the history of human relations has ever known.

In the Germanic Museum in Nuremberg are certain great stakes from the palisade of Hadrian. The railway from Nuremberg to Munich crosses the line of the Limes about thirty miles to the south, and a few miles farther on comes to Weissenburg, on whose western edge are the walls of the military post of Biriciani, one of the hundred stations lying within the boundary at points three or four miles apart. Rising little above the soil of the cultivated fields, they now form a pleasant, sod-covered path between gardens and grain. The station was rectangular, occupied about an acre and a half, had a gate in each of the sides, and contained several buildings of size — including what was probably the prefect's quarters, a grain magazine, a large central structure with a spacious court surrounded by numerous rooms, and perhaps baths, all of them with heating apparatus. Inside the camp, and especially near the gates, were found many spearheads, stone missiles, lances, and human bones. The exploration of the place began in 1889. The field in which the ruins lay had been known as the Kesselfeld, from Kastelfeld, or Castlefield, a name which had lived on long after all trace of the station disappeared.

The station at Weissenburg, like most stations, was five miles or so to the south of the wall defense. The wall may be seen with good effect near Wilburgstetten, a village about thirty miles west of Weissenburg and forty southwest of Nuremberg. A mile from the town, in a thick and rugged evergreen forest, the German Limes Commission has laid bare some hundreds of feet of the stone wall about three feet wide and originally eight feet high, but now little above ground level, which ran east to the Danube seventy miles away at Hienheim, near Regensburg, and west forty miles to Lorch on the Rems, there to meet the earthen rampart which ran over two hundred miles north and west to the

RESTORED TOWER OF THE SAALBURG

Rhine. This was the barrier against which again and again the outer world, covetous of a place in the Roman sun, threw itself in vain, and through which, in the later and weaker days of the Empire, again and again it broke, until at length barbarian and Roman mingled not only within the Limes but south of the Alps and within the walls of Rome, and with the new influx of wild but fresh and vigorous blood the outworn body of the Roman Empire began the new growth which was to result in the Europe and Americas of modern times.

And yet, impressive as are these and other remnants of the German and Raetian lines, they are not to be compared in either size or interest with the wall along the British border from the Solway to the Tyne. Few places outside Italy are so charged with meaning as this for the Briton or American conscious of the Roman heritage of his race.

The British aloofness from the Continent, so often spoken of in modern times, was much more the fact in antiquity. Horace's "Britons, the most remote of the world," "Britons fierce to strangers," and "clouds and dropping rains," reflect the Roman thought. Britain seemed to the Roman imagination more inaccessible than Spain, the African desert, or even the wilds of Scythia. It was not until A.D. 83, when the fleet of Agrippa reached the north end of Scotland, that the country was definitely known to be an island.

With the exception of one Pytheas of Marseilles, who is said to have made an exploratory voyage to Britain in 330 B.C., the first person of historical importance to set foot in the island was Julius Caesar in the two invasions of the summers of 55 and 54 B.C. The people whom he found in South Britain were the Brythons, a Celtic race who had crossed into England about 320 B.C., and were related to the Gaels who settled in Ireland. Preceding the Brythons had been an earlier wave of Celts, and before them a neolithic stock, probably from Spain, and the original palaeolithic race. By Caesar's time, the Celts had pushed their neolithic predecessors out of the South, and the North was occupied by the ruder and more primitive portion of the islanders.

All these peoples left behind them the traces of their cultures: the palaeolithic race, their flints and the skull of the Piltdown man, 100,000 to 300,000 years ago, the first human being whose head-shape and brain-size have been determined; the neolithic men, their stone circles, such as Stonehenge, their places of worship, such as Avebury with its dike, ditch, and circles of monoliths, dating from 2000 B.C. or earlier; the British, their hill camps, such as Old Sarum, near Salisbury, and the frequent barrows representing their burial.

The first invasion of Caesar, with some hundred ships

carrying the infantry and cavalry of the Seventh and Tenth legions, was hardly more than a three weeks' reconnaissance. The second, with five legions in eight hundred transports, lasted four months, but carried the Roman arms hardly beyond the Thames. It was ninety-six years before the next attempt was made. In A.D. 43 the expedition of Claudius, some fifty thousand men, effected a permanent occupation. It was eight years before the British leader, Caractacus, was defeated in Wales, fled to the north, was delivered up by the Brigantes, and was taken to Rome; where, in wonderment as he looked on the glories of the city, he asked how the lords of such palaces could be covetous of the poor huts of his people. Ten years after this, when the Roman army was engaged in an invasion of Mona, the island of Anglesey, the chief religious retreat of the Britons, a general uprising headed by the famous Queen Boadicea, whose capital was Camalodunum, the present Colchester, caused the capture of that city, Verulamium, Londinium, and other smaller places, and the annihilation of the Ninth Legion. The Britons were prevented from driving the Romans from the island only by a fortunate battle at the last moment. In another ten years the Silures, in Wales, the most obstinate in the defense of their native land, were conquered by Frontinus, the general of Vespasian, and in A.D. 78 Agricola subdued the island of Mona. In A.D. 80, Agricola, with the aid of a newly created fleet, reached the Firth of Tay. In A.D. 84, a great battle with all the forces of the highlanders completed the conquest of the island territory so far as it ever was completed.

Three reasons may be given for the halt of the Roman arms without advancing into remote northern Scotland and crossing into Ireland, which Agricola thought should be conquered, "so that Roman arms should be everywhere, and liberty, so to speak, removed from sight." First, the

ROMAN BRITAIN

Scale of Miles

| 0 | 20 | 40 | 60 | 80 |

● Large Fortresses
• Small Forts
⊚ Large Towns
○ Small Towns
— Definite Roads
--- Indefinite Roads
🌲 Forests

Inchtuthill

Strageth
Ardoch
Camelon
Bodotria
WALL OF PIUS
Cramond *Inveresk*
Carstairs
Lyne
Trimontium
Clota
Cappuck
Chew Green
Bremenium
Habitancum
Blatobulgium
HADRIAN'S WALL
South Shields
Corstopitum
Luguvallium *Chester-le-Street*
(Carlisle)
Ituna Aest. *Voreda* *Vinovia* *Huntcliff*
Brocavum *Ravenhill*
Galava *Lavatrae* *Cataractonium*
Hardknott *Scarborough*
MONAPIA *Clanoventa* B R I G A N T E S
Overborrow *Malton*
Lancaster *Isurium* Eboracum (York)
(Alborough)
Bremetennacum *Ilkley*
P A R I S I
Cambodunum *Legiolium*
Coccium *Manchester* *Doncaster*
Warrington *Abus Aest.*
MONA *Canovium* Aquae *Anado* *Lindum*
Segontium *Deva* (Lincoln)
O R D O V I C E S (Chester) C O R I T A N I
Cdergai C O R N O V I I *Branodunum*
Viroconium *Letocetum* *Gariannonum*
(Wroxeter) *Ratae*
Pennal *Caersus* *Venonae* I C E N I
Bravonium *Venta Icenorum*
Castell *Bannaventa* (Caistor St. Edmunds)
Llanio *Collen* *Durobrivae* *Dunwich*
Lactodurum *Godmanchester*
D E M E T A E D O B U N I *Cambridge* T R I N O B A N T E S *Felixstowe*
Maridunum *Glevum* *Durocobrivae* Camulodunum
Isca Silurum (Gloucester) *Verulamium* (Colchester)
S I L U R E S Corinium (St. Albans) *Othona*
Venta (Cirencester) *Dorchester* Londinium
Silurum *Cardiff* *Durobrivae* *Tamesa* TANATUS
Aquae Sulis *Calleva Atrebatum* *Durovernum* Rutupiae
(Bath) B E L G A E *Duroliponte* Dubrae
Ilchester *Sorbiodunum* Venta Belgarum C A N T I U M Portus
D U M N O N I I *Salisbury* (Winchester) *Lemanis*
Clausentum Regnum L I T U S Anderida
D U R O T R I G E S (Southampton) (Chichester)
Isca *Dirnovaria* VECTIS *Gessoriacum*
(Exeter) (Boulogne)
Moridunum

MANHATTAN DRAFTING CO., N.Y.

military capacities of the Empire were already being taxed
by wars along the Rhine and Danube. Second, the occupation of Britain was expensive, and had always been objected
to as an enterprise not worth the effort; and the economic
disadvantage of adding Scotland and Ireland seemed quite

ALTAR FOUND IN
SCOTLAND

The inscription reads:
To Jupiter Optimus
Maximus. Gaius Ar-
rius Domitianus, Cen-
turion of the Twen-
tieth Legion, Valeria
Victrix, willingly and
gladly has discharged
his vow as he should.

clear. "The masters of the fairest and
most wealthy climates of the globe," says
Gibbon, "turned with contempt from
gloomy hills assailed by the winter tempest, from lakes concealed in a blue mist,
and from cold and lonely heaths over
which the deer of the forest were chased
by a troop of naked barbarians." Third,
the Romanization of these two regions
could be attempted with far less hope of
success. The Britons and other Celts in
the South were closely akin to the Gallic
Celts, and easily followed in their footsteps; the Irish and the Scots were Gaelic
Celts, were a wilder race, spoke a language
so different from that of the Britons that
it could not be understood, and were in
general apart from them.

Agricola set up a line of defenses from
the Forth to the Clyde, the headquarters
of the Roman army were maintained at
Eboracum, York, and for thirty-five years
little is heard of British affairs. In the reign of Hadrian, 117–
138, it is generally agreed, the wall defenses from the Solway to
the Tyne were erected. That this was at first not meant as
an actual frontier wall is indicated by the building of a
similar but less elaborate wall by Antoninus Pius, 138–161,
between the Forth and the Clyde, and its strengthening by

Severus, 193–211, who died in the camp at Eboracum, after a vigorous campaign in the land of the Caledonians.

For the next hundred years there is almost no evidence. Then, at the beginning of the fourth century, a view of the border shows that the second or northern wall has been abandoned, and that the line of Hadrian is actively occupied in protecting Romanized Britain south of the Tyne and the Solway from the raids of the Picts and Scots; the Picts being the Caledonians, or "tattooed," and the Scots being the warriors from Ivernia, or Ireland, always then, as now, closely related with northern Scotland both in blood and communication. The details of these exciting forays are little known to us. Hardly more familiar are the details of the last of the three centuries inside the wall that elapsed from Hadrian's death to the end of the Roman occupation.

The end of Roman rule in Britain was due neither to rebellion in Britain itself nor to the assaults of Pict and Scot on the border. The Empire was falling apart. The Northerners had long since made naught of the barrier between the Rhine and the Danube, and Alaric and his Goths in 410 had broken through the gates of Rome itself. The legions were needed in places nearer the center than far-away Britain, and in many places at once. When the need for men became acute, it was the most remote and the least remunerative of the provinces that were first abandoned. Already in the time of Honorius the last legions had been withdrawn, and the British envoys entreating continued protection had brought back the unwelcome news that their native land must shift for itself.

For upwards of forty years it did so shift. The decreasing momentum of Roman government, as represented by the municipal system, the noble families, and the Church, still kept the province in its course. The last useless appeal to

Rome was sent in 446. Unable now to withstand the barbarian pressure from the north, Roman Britain invited, as the lesser evil, the aid of Angle, Saxon, and Jute. The separation from the Empire was complete; the Roman civilization of the island was overwhelmed by the Saxon, and for the time disappeared.

The Roman remains in the British lands are scattered and fragmentary. The Roman arms never crossed to Ireland, and left few signs of their presence north of the barrier erected by Antoninus between Glasgow and Edinburgh. Roman building in Britain was never in the grand style, and the Saxon invaders seem to have burned and pillaged what they found.

The classical traveler in England will visit the ancient remains of pool and chambers and water pipes at Bath, whose waters were used in Roman times as they are to-day, and whose ancient name was Aqua Sulis, the Waters of Sul, in honor of the goddess Sul, the British Minerva. He will find a Roman gate in Lincoln, the Roman camp Lindum; a tower in York, the Roman Eboracum; and city walls at Colchester, the Roman Camalodunum, and at Caerleon and Caerwent, near Newport in Wales, the ancient Isca and Venta, important legionary stations from earliest times. In spots never again built upon after the Saxon invasion, he will find the ruins of Verulamium, near St. Alban's; of Calleva, now Silchester, near Reading; of Viroconium, now Wroxeter, near Shrewsbury. He will find that ten forts on the southeast or Saxon shore have been identified, and that some of them, as Burgh, near Great Yarmouth, Pevensey, near Hastings, and Porchester, near Portsmouth, have left many fragments. He will find many remnants in the heart of London and in smaller cities, and many more, especially the ruins of country houses, here and there in the English fields.

Multitudinous minute objects he will find in the British Museum and in the local collections of numerous towns. He will find many a town interesting for its name or associations: Gloucester, once Glevum; Chester, once Castra, or Camp, and the numerous towns ending in "chester" which once were occupied by soldiers; and the equally numerous towns ending in "wich" which once were *vici* or Roman villages. The ruins usual in less rigorous climes and nearer the Mediterranean — the theater, amphitheater, basilica, monumental baths, aqueducts, and temple — he will find either missing or much less frequent; and he will find most of the ruins of whatever sort either hard to find, or inconvenient, or disappointing in their size and condition.

One monument of Roman Britain in the grand style, however, still remains. The Great Wall of Hadrian, once reaching from sea to sea, a distance of seventy-four miles, with its western end at Carlisle and its eastern at Newcastle-on-Tyne, is still to be seen in remarkable completeness for the middle thirty-five miles of its length, and is traceable for the twenty miles at either end which have in great part disappeared under the assaults of local searchers for stone and freedom for the plow.

The Great Wall was not alone by itself, but was the chief part of a careful zone of defense and aggression. Approached from the south, it consisted of a series of parallel lines: (1) two ramparts or dikes of dirt and stone; (2) a fosse or ditch; (3) a third rampart; (4) a space of open ground varying from 90 feet to half a mile, and averaging 200 feet, threaded by a military road; (5) the *murus*, or Wall itself, 7 to 9 feet thick, of stone and mortar core faced with stones about 9 by 11 inches, and 20 feet high, with battlement, frequent turrets, a small fort or castellum at every mile, and a camp some 5 acres in extent at intervals of about

5 miles; (6) a fosse 40 feet wide and 20 feet deep. The enemy coming from the north thus found himself confronted by a mighty ditch beyond which, rising to 40 feet above its bottom, was the battlemented, turreted, and fortressed wall, in the rear of which were the legionaries dispatched by the

THE ROMAN WALL IN BRITAIN

It went straight across country, taking hills and valleys as they came.

convenient road from the not distant camps that were kept in supplies and men from York over the two divisions of the great highway later known as Watling Street.

The Wall was built, so inscriptions indicate, by the Second, Sixth, and Twentieth legions, and the twenty-three camps manned by troopers from every quarter of the world. Nowhere is it preserved in its ancient height, and nowhere are the moats and dikes at their original depth and height;

but fragments and furrows mark its course in the most unlikely places, and in its middle reaches the lines are perfect, the ditches deep, the wall continuous at four to six or seven feet in height, the mile-castles identifiable, and the outlines of the camp foundations well preserved. At the space where the zone fills the high lands between the head-waters of the Tyne and the Irthing, both country and wall are picturesque. Few excursions in England or Scotland can be so filled with pleasure as a day or two of exploration in this locality. To the charm of its archaeology is added that of nature and romance ; the scenery varies from valley to height, from prairie to woodland, from meadow to crag, from the peaceful English farmstead to the bare, bleak Scottish moorland, and famous names of the Scottish Border are frequent along the way.

At Gilsland, eighteen miles east of Carlisle on the North-eastern Railway, a walk of two miles leads to the hill on which, overlooking the Irthing far below, lie the plentiful ruins of Amboglanna, one of the largest of the camps, a tiny soldier-city of five and a half acres. Here the moss-grown wall is well preserved, running along high ground which, with the Irthing •ċ its base, forms a natural barrier to aid the wall.

Eight miles east of Amboglanna is Borcovicus, a second camp ; and eight miles east again is Cilurnum, a third. The three are beside the modern estates of Birdoswald, House-steads, and Chesters. There was also Procolitia, between the two last, but its remains are less arresting. Borcovicus may be visited from Bardon Mill, ten miles east of Gilsland by rail and four miles from the ruins, and Cilurnum from Chollerford, eleven miles east from Bardon Mill to Hexham, and five miles north on a second line. The full measure of enjoyment and profit, however, is to be had only by walking the entire stretch from Amboglanna to Cilurnum.

"About three and a half miles west of Cilurnum," writes Professor Katharine Allen, "was the station of Procolitia, the outline of whose walls can be traced now only in grass-grown ridges. Beyond Procolitia the wildest and most interesting part of the course of the Wall begins. Between the upper waters of the North Tyne and the Irthing for about ten miles runs a line of high and rugged basaltic cliffs. The ground rises gradually from the south in undulating fells and pastures till it culminates in the broken summits of these heights, then plunges to the moor beyond in a succession of precipices. It has been likened to a gigantic wave or succession of waves of land, petrified just in the act of breaking. The Wall follows this line of crags absolutely, climbing to their highest points and dropping downward into the clefts that divide them. To the boldness of its course here is no doubt due the fact that long stretches of it are still standing in a fair state of preservation, often six or seven feet high."

Such was the Scottish Border in the ancient days when the Scots meant the Irish and the Highlanders were the Picts, and when the Great Wall was the sharp division between the law of civilized men and the lawlessness of the outside world. So long as the Wall stood with the Roman legions behind it, Britain shielded by it continued in the ways of comparative peace. When the legionaries were gone and the Wall was pierced and broken, the southern lands were given over not only to the raids of Pict and Scot but to the ravages of the Saxons invited to rescue the Britons from them. "On this narrow strip of land," says Merivale, "we may read an epitome of the history of the Romans under the Empire. For myself, I feel that all I have read and written on this wide and varied subject is condensed, as it were, in the picture I realize from a few stones and earthworks of their occupation of our northern marches."

The Roman power vanished from Britain as it vanished from Africa. It gave place in Britain to barbarous men from the wilds of the North and across the sea, as in Africa it gave place to barbarous men from the wilds of the South. In Britain as in Africa, it left behind to fall in ruins its characteristic buildings, and it left behind its inscriptions, its coins and pottery, and its instruments of peace and war to be the record of its life for a later age to read.   Yet no more of Britain than of Spain could it be said, as it has been said of Africa, that it was as if the Romans had never been. The mingled Britons and Gaels and Romans and Gauls of Romanized Britain who became the subjects of the Saxon rulers preserved enough of Roman customs, religion, and urban administration to mould the ideas of the invaders. The use of the Roman roads continued, and the cities on them and elsewhere retained much of their Roman character and many of their Roman names.   The forests cleared and ground subdued during the hundreds of years of Roman occupation remained a benefit to the tillers of the soil.

The subsoil of civilization, so to speak, was still Roman. Gaul, well seasoned in Roman ways, was across the Channel. The missionaries of the Roman Church were not without an ally in the deep-laid remainders of Roman culture ; and when the Norman conquerors came, with their Roman tongue and culture, they were not obliged to build on foundations wholly un-Roman.   In time, the language and religion alike, not only of the former Roman Britain, but of the lands of the Pict and the Scot, were Roman.   As in Spain, so in Britain, Imperial Rome had gone and Spiritual Rome had taken its place.

XLV

THE COMING OF CHRISTIANITY

It took centuries for Greater Rome to decay and disintegrate. When the process finally was complete and the framework of the vast organization had fallen apart, it did not mean that the Empire had utterly perished. Within the rotting and weakening substance of pagan life a new life had been growing. When the military and political power of pagan Rome had crumbled, the power of Christian Rome was ready to emerge.

It took centuries for the Christian Empire to attain its growth. The date of the Crucifixion is placed A.D. 31 in the reign of Tiberius and the procuratorship of Pontius Pilatus, the Pilate of the *Gospels*. The reigns of Tiberius and Caligula had passed, and probably most of the reign of Claudius, before the new religion found its way from Palestine to the capital of the Empire under whose procurator its Founder was put to death. That its converts in Rome were banded together by the fourth year of Nero's reign is proved by Paul's *Epistle to the Romans* from Corinth in A.D. 58.

"Paul, a servant of Jesus Christ, called to be an apostle, separated unto the gospel of God," it begins . . . "To all that be in Rome, beloved of God, called to be saints : Grace to you and peace from God our Father and the Lord Jesus Christ. First, I thank my God through Jesus Christ for you all, that your faith is spoken of throughout the whole world. For God is my witness, whom I serve with my spirit in the gospel of his Son, that without ceasing I make mention of you always in my prayers ; making request, if by any means now at length I might have a prosperous journey by the will of God to come unto you.   For I long to see you, that I may impart unto you some spiritual gift, to the end ye may be established. . . .   So, as much as in me is, I am ready to preach the gospel to you that are at Rome also."

CHRISTIAN INSCRIPTIONS FROM THE CATACOMBS OF SAINT CALIXTUS

They show the dove and olive branch, the monogram of Constantine, the epitaph in Greek, and a crudeness in lettering and spelling.   The middle epitaph on the left reads: Ponponiae Proculae Fec[erunt] Aurelius Aper et Ponponia Prima Parentes Benemere[n]ti F[iliae] inconparabili Q[uae] V[ixit] Ann[o] Uno Menses Octo D[eo] V[otum] Ob Merit[a] Eius.   In the lower right corner: Puer Decessit Nomine Dulcisus Qui Vixit Annos V Menses VI.

Paul's letter was carried to Rome by "Phebe our sister, which is a servant of the Church which is at Cenchrea," near Corinth.   Among the persons to whom at its conclusion he sends greetings, the greater number bear Greek names, and the remainder Roman or Hebrew.   Whether or not the names are strictly racial, they show that the Christians at Rome were composed of foreign bloods.

About two years after the *Epistle to the Romans* came Paul himself, landing near Virgil's Lake Avernus, at Puteoli,

" where we found brethren, and were desired to tarry with them seven days: and so we went toward Rome. And from thence, when the brethren heard of us, they came to meet us as far as Appii Forum and The Three Taverns: whom when Paul saw, he thanked God, and took courage. And when we came to Rome, the centurion delivered the prisoners to the captain of the guard; but Paul was suffered to dwell by himself with a soldier that kept him. . . . And when they had appointed him a day, there came many to him into his lodging; to whom he expounded and testified the kingdom of God, persuading them concerning Jesus, both out of the law of Moses and out of the prophets, from morning till evening. And some believed the things which were spoken, and some believed not. . . . And Paul dwelt two whole years in his own hired house, and received all that came in unto him; preaching the kingdom of God, and teaching those things which concern the Lord Jesus Christ, with all confidence, no man forbidding him."

The great fire of Nero in A.D. 64, some three years after Paul's arrival, brought suffering to many of the Christians, who were disliked because of their separateness and supposed "hatred of the human kind." The Emperor, charged by rumor with having caused the fire for the sake of clearing the city for a rebuilding, is said to have tried to divert the charge from himself to the unpopular sect.

" And so, for the purpose of putting an end to rumor," says Tacitus, " Nero charged with the crime and inflicted the most unusual punishments upon those whom the people commonly called *Christiani*, and who were hated for their criminal conduct. The author of this sect, Christus, was put to death in the reign of Tiberius by the procurator Pontius Pilate; and the deadly superstition, repressed for the time being, had broken out not only in all Judea, the original home of the evil, but even in the city of Rome, where all things atrocious and shameful flow from every direction and find favor. And so those were first brought to trial who confessed the charge, and then, as a result of their evidence, an immense number were convicted, not so much because they were charged with being incendiaries as because they were guilty of hatred of the human kind; and as they perished they were made to afford sport for the people by being covered with the skins of wild beasts and torn in pieces by dogs, or by being affixed to crosses to be set on fire, so that when the daylight failed they might furnish light for the night as they were consumed."

It is not until five years after these martyrdoms that we come to the probable date of the Apostle's martyrdom in Rome, more than thirty years since near Damascus "suddenly there shined round about him a light from heaven" and he heard the voice that stopped him as he made havoc of the Church, entering into every house and haling men and women to prison, and breathed out threatenings and slaughter against the disciples of the Lord. It was twenty-five years more before the Christians finally in Domitian's reign became separate in the pagan mind from the Jews, whose origin in Palestine and monotheistic belief at first caused them to be confused with the new sect. In the reign of Trajan they are so well known that the persecutions to which they have been subject do not always appear either legal or in accord with reason. The younger Pliny, governing Bithynia for Trajan in 111–113, is not sure of his ground when confronted by the question as to their treatment. His letter to the Emperor is probably an expression of the state of mind in which most governors of the time found themselves.

"I have asked them whether they were Christians. On their confession of the fact, I have asked them a second and a third time, with threats of punishment. If they have persisted, I have ordered their execution; for I have had no doubt that, whatever they confessed, their pertinacity and their inflexible obstinacy at least ought to bring punishment upon them. There have been some afflicted with the same madness whom, because of their being citizens, I have taken steps to have sent to Rome for trial. Soon, as is usually the case, the offense began to spread because of our very attention to it, and more cases came to my notice. An unsigned letter was sent in, containing many names. When those who have denied that they either were or had been Christians have called upon the gods in my presence, and have gone through the

A Sculptured Christian Sarcophagus

In the upper part : the creation of Adam and Eve, the angel with Adam and Eve in the garden, the occupants of the tomb, the changing of water into wine, the miracle of the loaves, the raising of Lazarus. In the lower : the Holy Family, the Magi bringing presents, the blessing of the children, Daniel in the lion's den, Peter commissioned by Christ, the arrest of Peter (or the anger of Moses), Moses smiting the rock.

forms of worship, with incense and wine, before your likeness, which, with the images of the gods, I have ordered brought in for the purpose, and in addition to this have cursed Christ — none of which acts those who are in real truth Christians can be brought to perform — I have thought them deserving of discharge. Some have said that they were Christian, and then presently denied it, saying that they had been but had ceased to be, certain ones several years ago, some even twenty. These, every one of them, also venerated your image and those of the gods, and cursed Christ. They affirmed, moreover, that the worst crime, or rather mistake, of which they had been guilty, had consisted in their coming together before dawn on stated days to sing together a hymn to Christ, as if to God, and to bind themselves by an oath not to commit theft, robbery, or adultery, and not to deny a deposit when called upon. After this, according to their statement, they had been wont to separate. They had been accustomed to come together again to partake of a meal, common to all, and without blame; but they had discontinued even this after the edict in which, in obedience to your instructions, I had forbidden the existence of secret societies. On this account I thought it the more necessary to search out the truth of the matter from two servants, called ministers, even using torture. I have been able to discover nothing except a distorted and exaggerated superstition, so I dismissed proceedings and with all speed resort to you for counsel. The matter seems to me to demand consultation especially on account of the number of those who are in danger. For many, of every age, of every rank, and of both sexes, are being called into jeopardy, and will continue to be in the future. Not merely cities, but villages, too, and country districts, have been thoroughly infected with the contagion of this wretched superstition, which, it seems to me, can be halted and set right. At any rate one can easily see that temples already almost abandoned have begun to be frequented and holy rites long intermitted to be performed again, and food for the sacrificial animals to be offered for sale, for which hitherto very few purchasers had been found. From this it is easy to draw conclusions as to what a number of people can be set right if a chance for repentance is open to them."

Back of the pagan governor's imperfect understanding in this letter are to be seen the Christian characteristics which so exasperated and puzzled the pagans — their faithfulness to one God and their refusal to bow down to other gods, even to the deity of the State as represented by the emperor its head; their meetings apart at unusual hours in unusual places; their loyalty to the ordinary virtues; their communions; their numbers and the alarming rate at which they grew.

The answer of Trajan shows that the offense of the Christians is the denial of the State gods and therefore a disloyalty to the Empire. Yet even this offense should not make them the subject of active prosecution. "The Christians are not to be sought out," he rules. "If brought before you and found guilty, they are to be punished; but on this condition, that whosoever denies that he is a Christian, and makes good his assertion by performing acts of worship to our gods, is to have full pardon, however greatly suspected in the past." This is as much as to say, prosecute only when there is no escape from it, but, if compelled, uphold the dignity of the law and the State.

With the exception of disturbances in localities here and there, due to specially irritating circumstances, the treatment of the Christians may be said to have been in the fairly humane spirit of Trajan for a hundred years. As their number increased, and with it a confidence that to the pagans seemed aggressiveness, the conviction was gradually confirmed that the Christians were a state within the State and must be either assimilated or crushed. The persecutions which hitherto had been local and occasional became more and more general during the next hundred years until in Diocletian's reign, A.D. 284–305, the Government in the great general persecutions of 303 and 304 gathered all its energies in a supreme attempt to crush the new religion out of existence, and failed. Ten years afterward, the Edict of Constantine in 313 recognized Christianity as of equal rights with paganism, and the old religion entered upon the eighty troubled years of decline which ended with its brief revival by the rebel Emperor Eugenius in 394.

The most impressive relics of Christian Rome are the catacombs. Like the pagan burial places, they were near the great highways; unlike them, they did not stretch out narrowly in stately miles of magnificence beside the road, but were wholly underground and in communities of galleries and corridors and amplified intersections resembling the streets and alleys and squares of the cities of the living. There are forty or more of these communities of the ancient Christian dead within three miles from the heart of Rome. Their galleries, sometimes in stories one below another to the number of six and reaching seventy-five feet into the solid tufa that covers all the region, would measure a total length of more than five hundred miles.   Best known of all are the

A RELIEF FROM A CHRISTIAN SARCOPHAGUS

Jonah is seen as he is cast into the sea, as he is spewed forth on to the land, where a fisherman stands, and as he lies under the vine. Above, at left and right are Lazarus in the tomb and a shepherd with two sheep; in the center, Moses and the water gushing from the rock, and the anger of Moses.

catacombs of Saint Calixtus, beside the Appian Way. Visited through many centuries of ancient and modern times, despoiled of all but fragments by pious and profane alike, they are still one of Rome's most moving monuments.

Christianity and the Church were nearly three centuries in the struggle for toleration, and another century in the ascent to supremacy. Their victory was not a sudden revolution, but a long and persistent striving. The new faith had much to overcome — the natural resistance of the old forms and feelings in a society of pronounced conservatism; the tenacity of custom and sentiment in the great popular amusements which it had to disapprove; the prejudice of the older portion of Roman society against the new, of the noble-born and the rich and the proud against the nameless, the poor, and the humble; the enmity of a Government and its patriotic supporters who saw in its devotion to God a treason to the State; the hatred of a public in whose pleas-

ROME FROM THE PALATINE

The Capitoline, representing the religious center of pagan Rome, and beyond it on the horizon the dome of Saint Peter's, standing for Christian Rome.

ures it could not participate and whose morals it was compelled to condemn; and, in the days of its approach to victory, its own shortcomings in conduct and divisions in doctrine. The fact that in the face of all it nevertheless succeeded was its divine warrant.

Yet it would not be fair to ancient paganism to think of it as in either conduct or ideals entirely the opposite of the

Christian civilization. The passage from the old to the new was not a sudden change of identity, but a growth and an evolution. Pagan religion itself had been changing during the centuries, was dissatisfied with itself, and seeking in its own way after God if haply He might be found. The paganism of three centuries after Christ is declared to have had more in common with Christianity than with the religion of Augustan times. Rome, the Eternal City and Home of the Gods, had been the special seat of pagan sanctity before the new religion also found it a natural capital. Nor was Christianity without allies even in the morals and sentiment of paganism. All the gradually gathering protest of ancient life against the tyrannies, the cruelties, and the injustices of the old régime, all its longing for authority, sympathy, and consolation, all its longing for an escape from the imperfections of a present world to the happiness of an existence in which righteousness should receive the reward denied it on earth, made the new religion its vehicle. Christianity became the spiritual repository of the times.

The philosophic essays and epistles of Seneca were once suspected of inspiration by the Christian faith, perhaps by the teaching of Paul in person. The gentle self-communion of Marcus Aurelius bears few distinguishing marks of paganism. The morality of Cicero *De Officiis* is the morality of the Christian Church. Virgil drew tears from Jerome and Augustine, and appealed to his Christian readers as one of their own. The hymn sung long ago as part of the Mass of Saint Paul at Mantua and later omitted as not historical, records the act and sentiment of many a pious pilgrim to the poet's tomb if not of Paul :

> Ad Maronis mausoleum
> Ductus fudit super eum
> Piae rorem lacrimae.

Quem te, inquit, reddidissem,
Si te vivum invenissem,
  Poetarum maxime!

"When to Maro's tomb they brought him,
Tender grief and pity wrought him
  To bedew the stone with tears.
What a saint I might have crowned thee,
Had I only living found thee,
  Poet first and without peers!"

XLVI

ETERNAL ROME

We have come to the end of our survey and interpretation of Rome and the Romans. We have made the acquaintance of the Roman as a person, observed him in the life of the home and the larger society of which he formed a part, and followed the civilization created by him as it marched into the far parts of the ancient world. We prefaced our study by a visit to the modern city of Rome and its ancient ruins, and by contemplation of the meaning of ancient Rome to our times. Our conclusion shall be a return to the same theme.

For nearly a thousand years after the fall of the Western Empire in A.D. 476, the decay and ruin of the city, which had already been in progress before that date, continued. By 1106, time, fire, flood, earthquake and collapse, and the hand of man had reduced the once magnificent city of a million to so pitiful a condition that Hildebert of Tours on a visit spoke of it as "all but utterly in ruins." To William of Malmesbury, an English pilgrim twenty years later, it seemed, in comparison with its ancient state, "a little town."

The lowest fortunes of the city were reached in the three hundred years intervening between the fires and sacking by Robert Guiscard, the Norman who in 1084 came to the rescue of Pope Gregory the Seventh from his enemies, and the return of the popes in 1377 after their seventy years of absence in Avignon. By this time the population had sunk to at least 50,000, and one estimate places it at 17,000. Even a hundred years later, we are told that "Rome had become like a village of herdsmen ; sheep and cows wandered about in the city."

But the city rose from its ruins and entered into the growth of modern times. It became the splendid capital of the Church in the great days of the Renaissance. It grew to 85,000 in 1500, to 100,000 in 1600, to 166,000 in 1776, to 225,000 in 1870, to 450,000 in 1900, to 660,000 in 1920, and to 902,500 in 1929, and to-day is approaching a million. Thus has the ancient and eternal city recovered from her ruin and given promise of soon being once more peopled as

"In the most high and palmy state of Rome."

If growth and figures were all, if Rome were like other cities which have increased with the increase of modern populations in the new world of science and industries that came with and after the Renaissance, there would be little need of saying more, and the study of Rome or the treading of her streets would be only the seeing and the knowing of one more national center.

But Rome is not merely the national center of Italy and one more European capital. She is the mother of them all, the capital of all the capitals looking westward, and not without her sway in far-Eastern climes. The Greek furnished the art and letters and intellect that leavened the life of the world ; the Roman, the law and institutions with which to govern it. Rome was not only the conqueror of primitive nations to west and north and of decadent and incompetent nations to south and east, but their organizer into an Empire of two languages, one government, and one faith.

The Teutons from the North and the Arabs from the East destroyed that unity, but only outwardly. In spite of the interruption, the Roman Empire still survived in language,

ROME FROM THE AMERICAN ACADEMY

From left to right: Victor Emmanuel Monument, Capitoline Hill, Basilica of Constantine, ruins of the Palatine Hill. The Tiber embankment is in the middle ground.

in law, in architecture and the arts, in religion, in organization, in ideals. In the twelfth century darkly, and clearly in the Renaissance, the workings of the Roman spirit became real in a Europe conquered by it, and European culture, repeating the history of ancient Rome, began in its turn the conquest of the modern world. The Americas and Australia, the rim of Africa, Japan and the shores of Asia, the islands of the great Western Ocean unknown and unsuspected by Rome, the lands "under the car of the too-near sun," the very Poles and their "frozen fields where no tree is refreshed by the breeze of summer," the whole world — has been invaded by Europe's nations and European culture as Europe's tribes were invaded by Rome and Roman culture. Two thousand years after Virgil's birth the Turks are beginning to use the Latin alphabet.

We may not think of England, Spain, France, Belgium, Holland, Italy, and the United States, or of Ancient Rome, as being actuated wholly by unselfish motives, though to think of them as wholly devoid of the spirit of helpfulness, and even of sacrifice, would also be a mistake. Anyone who will, may read in the record of Rome her consciousness of a mission, her sense of responsibility to God and humanity, as clearly as he may read it in the record of the modern colonizing nations; and may likewise trace in both ancient and modern empires the growth of ideals as, in Viscount Bryce's phrase, they "felt their magnificent position." Even should we deny the righteous motive, we may not deny results. Far-away continents have been made a part of civilization, and the civilization is that of Rome. Wherever Spain and France and Belgium and Italy have planted colonies, the language of Rome has gone, and the laws of Rome. The Dutch have carried Roman law to the other side of the globe, if not the Roman speech. The British Empire, the greatest since the Roman and the most resembling it, has spread to the ends of the earth a language half composed of the Roman tongue, a religion descended from the Christian Faith of Rome, and a mode of education based on acquaintance with the Roman tongue and the Roman spirit. The League of Nations and the World Court were conceived and are supported by peoples that confess their intellectual and spiritual descent from Rome.

Our whole Western civilization is thus in origin the civilization of Rome. Rome is the capital of the Western World and all its dependencies — the linguistic capital of all who speak Romance and English; the spiritual capital of all who own allegiance to the Christian ideal; the juristic capital of all who live under Roman law; the cultural capital of all who are bred in the forms of Greek and Italian art and the substance of Greek and Roman letters. It has always been a capital. It ruled with armies and with laws from the Seven Hills, the Rome that conquered and organized; it ruled from the Lateran and the Vatican with religion, the Rome that spiritualized; it ruled from court and palace with the culture of the Renaissance, the Rome that humanized; it rules to-day in the work of the present, the Rome that has made of Italy a united nation, the Rome upon whose Faith the sun forever shines, the farthest-reaching of the world's empires.

Rome is the one city on earth in which both the present and the past are still authoritative. It is the one spot on the earth whither the pilgrim from Europe and the Americas may fare as to the center and the source of the culture in which he is bred, feeling that "its importance in universal history it can never lose. For into it all the life of the ancient world was gathered: out of it all the life of the modern world arose."

CHRONOLOGY

B.C. 1000 Approximate date of arrival of Iron Age invaders of Stone Age Italy.

800 The Etruscan invasion begins.

753 The traditional date of Rome's founding.

753–509 The period of the Kings.

509–49 The Republic.

494 The first tribune of the people.

493 Rome becomes head of the Latin League.

480 The Sicilian Greeks defeat the Carthaginians in the Battle of the Himera.

474 The Greeks defeat the Carthaginians and Etruscans in the Battle of Cumae.

451–449 The Decemvirs and the Twelve Tables.

445 The right to marriage with patricians is won by the plebeians.

443 The censorship is established.

400–200 The Romans conquer and colonize in Italy.

396 The Romans capture Veii and end the Etruscan power.

390 Approximate date of the Gallic capture of Rome.

366 The praetorship is created, and the first plebeian consul elected.

343–290 The Samnite Wars.

340–338 The Romans at war with the Latins.

338 The Latin Confederation defeated at Antium, and the rostra brought to Rome.

272 The capture of Tarentum and submission of Magna Graecia.

265–241 The First Punic War.

264 The beginning of foreign conquest by Rome.

260 The Battle of Mylae.

256 The Battle of Ecnomus.

241 The Battle of Aegusa.

B.C. 234 The birth of Cato the Censor.

218–201 The Second Punic War.

217, 216 The Romans are defeated at Trasimenus and Cannae.

207 The defeat of Hasdrubal at the Metaurus.

197 The Macedonians are defeated at Cynoscephalae, and Greece is liberated.

190 The Romans in the East.

185 The death of Scipio Africanus.

184 The death of Plautus.

168 The Macedonians are defeated at Pydna.

153–133 Wars of conquest in Spain.

149 The death of Cato.

149–146 The Third Punic War.

146 The fall of Carthage and Corinth.

133 The fall of Numantia in Spain.

133, 121 The deaths of Tiberius and Gaius Gracchus.

109–32 The life of Atticus.

106 The births of Cicero and Pompey.

102–101 The victories of Marius and Catulus over the Teutons and Cimbrians.

102 or 100 The birth of Caesar.

102–88 Marius powerful in Rome.

96–55 The life of Lucretius.

90–89 The Italian allies win Roman rights in the Social War.

88–78 Sulla is master in Rome.

84–54 The life of Catullus.

86 The death of Marius.

73–71 The revolt of Spartacus and the slaves.

70–66 The rise of Pompey.

70 The birth of Virgil.

67 Pompey conquers the pirates and clears the Mediterranean.

65 The birth of Horace.

63 Cicero is consul, and Augustus is born.

63–62 The conspiracy and death of Catiline.

59 The First Triumvirate ; the birth of Livy.

58 Cicero is banished

58–50 Caesar conquers Gaul.

48, 46, 45 The battles of Pharsalia, Thapsus, Munda.

B.C. 48 The death of Pompey.

48–44 Caesar rules Rome.

44 The death of Caesar.

43 The Second Triumvirate.

43 The death of Cicero ; birth of Ovid.

42 The Battle of Philippi.

42–28 Augustus overcomes opposition.

31 Antony and Cleopatra defeated at Actium.

27 Death of Varro.

27 B.C–A.D 14 Augustus reigns.

19 The death of Virgil.

8 The death of Horace.

A.D. 14 The death of Augustus.

14–37 The reign of Tiberius.

17 The deaths of Livy and Ovid.

37–41 Caligula.

41–54 Claudius.

54–69 Nero.

64 Nero's persecution of the Christians.

65 The death of Seneca.

66 The death of Petronius.

68–69 Galba, Otho, Vitellius.

69–79 Vespasians.

70 Titus takes Jerusalem.

79–81 Titus.

79 The elder Pliny dies in the eruption of Vesuvius.

81–96 Domitian.

85–102 Martial writes Epigrams.

96–98 Nerva.

96 (?) The death of Quintilian.

98–117 Trajan.

111–113 Pliny the Younger and the Christians in Bithynia.

117–138 Hadrian.

118 (?) The death of Tacitus.

130–180 (?) Aulus Gellius.

138–161 Antonius Pius.

140 (?) The death of Juvenal.

150 (?) Apuleius and Minucius Felix write.

161–180 Marcus Aurelius.

A.D. 180–193 Commodus.

193–211 Septimius Severus.

211–222 Caracalla and others.

217 Calixtus is pope.

222–270 Alexander Severus and others.

270–284 Aurelian and others.

284–305 Diocletian.

306–312 Maxentius.

311–337 Constantine.

313 The Edict of Constantine.

337–361 Constantius II.

354–430 The life of Saint Augustine.

361–393 Julian and others.

393–423 Honorius.

395–408 The poet Claudian writes.

410 Alaric takes Rome.

424–476 Valentinian to the fall of the Western Empire.

476 Romulus Augustulus dethroned by Odoacer.

527–565 Justinian reigns in the East.

533–534 The Code of Justinian.

BOOKS

Those who desire to read more widely on the topics treated in various chapters will find the following books useful. References to them and to special articles and the ancient authors will be found in the annotations in case their use is desired.

Abbott, F. F., *The Common People of Rome*, Scribner, 1913.
  Roman Political Institutions, 3rd ed., Ginn, 1911.
  Roman Politics, Longmans, 1923.
Baedeker, *Central Italy and Rome*, Scribner, 1930.
  Mediterranean, Scribner, 1911.
Bailey, C., *The Legacy of Rome*, Oxford, 1923.
Belloc, H., *Esto Perpetua: Algerian Studies*, McBride, 1925.
Boissier, G., *Roman Africa*, Putnam, 1899.
  Cicero and His Friends, Putnam, 1925.
  The Country of Horace and Virgil, Stechert, 1923.
Bouchier, E. S., *Life and Letters in Roman Africa*, Oxford, 1913.
  Spain under the Roman Empire, Oxford, 1914.
Bryce, James, *The Roman and the British Empires*, Oxford, 1914.
Buckland, W. W., *A Text-book of Roman Law from Augustus to Justinian*, Macmillan, 1921.
Carpenter, Rhys, *The Greeks in Spain*, Longmans, 1925.
Cato and Varro, *Roman Farm Management*, Macmillan, 1913.
Charlesworth, M. P., *Trade Routes and Commerce of the Roman Empire*, Cambridge, 1926.
Conway, R. S., *The Vergilian Age*, Harvard University Press, 1928.
Cumont, Franz, *The Oriental Religions in Roman Paganism*, Open Court, 1911.
  The After Life in Roman Paganism, Yale University Press, 1922.
  The Mysteries of Mithras, translated by McCormack, Open Court, 1910.

Davis, W. S., *The Influence of Wealth in Imperial Rome*, Macmillan, 1910.

Deecke, W., *Italy*, Macmillan, 1904.

De Prorok, B. K., *Digging for Lost African Gods*, Putnam, 1926.

Dill, S., *Roman Society from Nero to Marcus Aurelius*, Macmillan, 1920.

Duff, J. W., *A Literary History of Rome*, Scribner, 1909.

Forestier, A., *The Roman Soldier*, Macmillan, 1928.

Fowler, W. W., *Roman Festivals*, Macmillan, 1899.
   Social Life at Rome in the Age of Cicero, Macmillan, 1915.
   Julius Caesar, Putnam, 1907.
   The Religious Experience of the Roman People, Macmillan, 1911.

Frank, T., *Roman Imperialism*, Macmillan, 1914.
   Vergil, Holt, 1922.

Graham, A., *Roman Africa*, Longmans, 1902.

Grant, C. F., *African Shores of the Mediterranean*, McBride, 1912.

Greenidge, A. H. J., *Roman Public Life*, Macmillan, 1922.

Hallam, G. H., *Horace at Tibur and the Sabine Farm*, Harrow, 1923.

Harper's *Dictionary of Classical Literature and Antiquities*, American Book Company.

Hastings, James, *Encyclopaedia of Religion and Ethics*, Scribner.

Haverfield, F., *The Roman Occupation of Britain*, Oxford, 1924.

Holmes, T. R., *Ancient Britain and the Invasions of Julius Caesar*, Oxford, 1907.
   The Architect of the Roman Empire, Oxford, 1928.

Huelsen, *The Forum and the Palatine*, translated by Helen H. Tanzer, Bruderhausen, 1928.

Hunter, W. A., *A Systematic and Historical Exposition of Roman Law in the Order of a Code*, 2nd ed., London, 1885.

Johnston, H. W., *The Private Life of the Romans*, Scott, Foresman, 1903.

Jones, H. S., *Companion to Roman History*, Oxford, 1912.

Judson, H. P., *Caesar's Army*, Ginn, 1888.

Lanciani, R., *The Destruction of Ancient Rome*, Macmillan, 1899.
   Ancient and Modern Rome, Longmans, 1925.

Lugli, G., *The Classical Monuments of Rome and Vicinity*, vol. 1, Rome, Bardi, 1929.

McCartney, E. S., *Warfare by Land and Sea*, Longmans, 1923.

Mau and Kelsey, *Pompeii, Its Life and Art*, Macmillan, 1899.

Mommsen, *History of Rome*, translated by W. P. Dickson, Scribner, 1900.

Roman Provinces, New York, 1887.

Nardi, B., *The Youth of Virgil*, translated by Belle Rand, Harvard University Press, 1930.

Orsi, *Modern Italy*, Putnam, 1900.

Peet, T. E., *The Stone and Bronze Ages in Italy and Sicily*, Oxford, 1909.

Petersson, T., *Cicero*, University of California Press, 1920.

Platner, S. B., *Topography and Monuments of Ancient Rome*, second edition, Allyn and Bacon, 1911.

Platner, S. B., and Ashby, T., *A Topographical Dictionary of Ancient Rome*, Oxford, 1929.

Rand, E. K., *Founders of the Middle Ages*, Harvard University Press, 1928.

In Quest of Virgil's Birthplace, Harvard University Press, 1930.

A Walk to Horace's Farm, Houghton Mifflin, 1930.

Randall–MacIver, D., *The Etruscans*, Oxford, 1927.

Italy before the Romans, Oxford, 1928.

Robinson, J. J., *Selections from the Public and Private Law of the Romans*, American Book Company, 1905.

Showerman, G., *Eternal Rome*, revised in one volume, Yale University Press, 1924.

Horace and His Influence, Longmans, 1922.

Century Readings in Ancient Classical Literature, Century Company, 1925.

Smith, W., *Smaller Classical Dictionary*, Dutton, 1910.

Dictionary of Greek and Roman Antiquities, 3rd edition, American Book Company, 1926.

Strachan–Davidson, J. L., *Cicero*, Putnam, 1903.

Problems of the Roman Criminal Law, Oxford, 1912.

Strong, E. S., *Art in Ancient Rome*, Scribner, 1928.

Taylor, T. M., *A Constitutional and Political History of Rome*, 5th edition, London, 1923.

Tucker, T. G., *Life in the Roman World of Nero and St. Paul*, Macmillan, 1910.

West, L. C., *Imperial Roman Spain: the Objects of Trade*, Oxford, 1929.

Wilson, L. M., *The Roman Toga*, Johns Hopkins Press, 1924.

Zimmern, H., *Italy of the Italians*, Scribner, 1914.

ANNOTATIONS

PART I

ROME AND ITS MEANING

I

ITALY TO-DAY

Orsi, *Modern Italy.*
Zimmern, *Italy of the Italians.*
Deecke, *Italy.*
Baedeker, *Central Italy and Rome.*

II

ROME TO-DAY

For maps and general information, consult any guide or handbook of
Rome or Central Italy, as Baedeker's *Central Italy and Rome.*
P. 13, l. 17.   Byron, *Childe Harold,* IV 26.

III

THE RISE OF ANCIENT ROME

Showerman, *Eternal Rome,* I–III.
Platner, *Topography and Monuments of Rome,* IV.

IV

THE RISE OF THE ROMAN STATES

Showerman, *Eternal Rome,* III 1, IV 1, V 1.
Frank, *Roman Imperialism.*

V

ANCIENT ROME AND MODERN TIMES

Showerman, *Eternal Rome*, XIII 2.
Bailey, *The Legacy of Rome*.
Our Debt to Greece and Rome Series.

PART II

THE ROMAN

VI

THE CITY IN WHICH HE LIVED

Platner, *Topography and Monuments*, V 45–64, VI–X.
Showerman, *Eternal Rome*, III 2, IV 2, VI 1.
P. 55.   Strabo, V 3, 8, tr. Hamilton.
Fowler, *Social Life at Rome*, I.
Tucker, *Life in the Roman World of Nero and St. Paul*, VII.

VII

HOW HE LOOKED

Johnston, *The Private Life of the Romans*, VII.
Wilson, *The Roman Toga*.

VIII

THE SOCIETY IN WHICH HE MOVED

Fowler, *Social Life at Rome*, IV, II, VII.
Johnston, *Private Life*, V.
Tucker, *Life in the Roman World*, XIV.

IX

THE HOUSE IN WHICH HE LIVED

Johnston, *Private Life*, VI.
Fowler, *Social Life*, VIII.
Mau and Kelsey, *Pompeii*, Part II.
Tucker, *Life in the Roman World*, IX–XI.

X

HIS CHILDHOOD AND EARLY TRAINING

Johnston, *Private Life*, II, IV.
Tucker, *Life in the Roman World*, XVII.
P. 94.   Martial, IX 68, tr. Paul Nixon in *A Roman Wit*.
P. 95, l. 19.   Martial, X 62.
P. 97.   Tacitus, *Dialogus*, 28–29.
P. 98.   Mommsen, *Rome*, tr. Dickson, III 118.

XI

HIS LATER TRAINING

Fowler, *Social Life*, VI.
Johnston, *Private Life*, IV.
P. 103.   Horace, *Epistles*, II 1, 126–131.
P. 104.   Cicero, *Ad Att.*, IX 6, 1; IX 19, 1; V 20, 9.
P. 106.   Juvenal, I 16, X 167, VII 161.
P. 106.   Tacitus, *Dialogus*, 30.
P. 107.   Cicero, *De Amicitia*, 1.
P. 110.   Cicero, *Ad Familiares*, XVI 21.

XII

THE WOMEN OF HIS FAMILY

Johnston, *Private Life*, III.
Fowler, *Social Life*, V.
Tucker, *Life in the Roman World*, XVI.

P. 122, l. 10. Buecheler, F., *Carmina Epigraphica*, 765 (*Anthologia Latina*, II 1).
P. 122, l. 14. *C. I. L.*, VI 1527.
P. 123. Statius, *Silvae*, III 5, tr. Elton; Ausonius, *Epigrams*, XL, tr. Glover; *Parentalia*, IX.

XIII

WHAT HE ATE AND DRANK

Johnston, *Private Life*, VIII.
P. 134, l. 2. Horace, *Odes*, II 14–16.
P. 135. Aulus Gellius, XIII xi.

XIV

HOW HE SPENT THE DAY

Fowler, *Social Life*, IX.
P. 137. Martial, IV 8.
P. 142. Cicero, *Pro Quinctio*, 59.
P. 145. Aquilius in Ribbeck's *Fragmenta*, II, p. 38.

PART III

LIVING ROME

XV

THE ROMAN CAREER

Abbott, *Roman Political Institutions*, VIII, IX.
Greenidge, *Roman Public Life*.
Taylor, *Constitutional Antiquities*.
Fowler, *Social Life*, IV.

XVI

THE SENATOR

Abbott, *Roman Political Institutions*, X, XI.
Smith, *Classical Dictionary*, under *Senatus, Senatus consultum*.
P. 166. Livy, I 8.
P. 173. Livy, IX 17, 14.

XVII

THE VOTER

Smith, *Classical Dictionary*, under *Comitia, Ambitus*, etc.
Platner, *Topography and Monuments*, under *Saepta*.
P. 177. Quintus Cicero, *Commentariolum Petitionis*, 2, 29–31,
54–55.

XVIII

THE LAWYER

Abbott, *Roman Political Institutions*, index, see *Praetor*.
Davidson, *Problems of Roman Criminal Law*.
Greenidge, *The Legal Procedure of Cicero's Time*.
P. 191. Pliny, *Epistles*, V 9, VI 12, IV 16, VI 33.
P. 192. Cicero, *Ad Att.*, I 16.

XIX

THE TEACHER

Johnston, *Private Life*, IV.
Horace, *Satires*, I 6, 72–78; *Epistles*, II 1, 70; *Satires*, I 1, 25.
Juvenal, I 15.
Horace, *Epistles*, II 1, 126–131; *Satires*, I 6, 76–78.
P. 198. Quintilian, tr. Butler, *Loeb Classical Library*, I i 12–13;
I i 15, 18; I i 20; I i 35–36; I ii 1, 2, 4, 9; I iii 8, 10; I iii
13–14; I viii 1–2; II ii 9, 11, 12.

XX

LETTERS AND THE ARTS

Duff, *Literary History of Rome*.
Eugenie Sellers Strong, *Art in Ancient Rome*.
Boyd, *Public Libraries and Literary Culture in Ancient Rome*.

XXI

THE DOCTOR

Johnston, *Private Life*, 306.
Tucker, *Life in the Roman World*, 403.
P. 216. Cicero, *De Officiis*, I, 151; Pliny, *Nat. Hist.*, XXIX 12.
P. 217. Suetonius, *Caesar*, XLII.
P. 219. Pliny, *Nat. Hist.*, XXIX 18; Martial, V 9.
P. 221. E. H. Byrne, *Medicine in the Roman Army*, *Classical Journal*, V (1910), 267.
P. 222. Hippocrates, tr. Jones, *Loeb Classical Library: The Oath; Precepts*, VI; *The Physician*.
P. 223. Martial, I 47.
P. 224. *Ibid.*, VI 53, tr. Paul Nixon.

XXII

THE MONEY-MAKER

Davis, *The Influence of Wealth in Imperial Rome*.
Allen and Greenough, *Latin Grammar*, 632–634.
Fowler, *Social Life*, III.
Mau and Kelsey, *Pompeii*, LVII.
P. 230. Cicero, *Ad Att.*, I 17; Tacitus, *Annals*, XII 43.
P. 231. Livy, XXI 63.

XXIII

THE COMMON MAN

Abbott, *The Common People of Ancient Rome*, pp. 205–234.
Fowler, *Social Life*, II.
Johnston, *Private Life*, XI.

Davis, *Influence of Wealth*, V.
P. 236. Cicero, *Ad Att.*, II 1, 2; XIII 13.
P. 238. Mau and Kelsey, *Pompeii*, Part III.
P. 248. *C. I. L.*, VIII 14683, in Abbott, 224; *C. I. L.*, XIV 2112, in Abbott, 225.
P. 249. Livy, IX 30, 5.

XXIV

THE FARMER

Tucker, *Life in the Roman World*, X.
P. 253. Cicero, *De Senectute*, 56–57; Virgil, *Georgics*, II 516–522.
P. 254. *Georgics*, tr. Dryden, II 143–144; 149–150; Horace, *Epodes*, II.
P. 256. Cato, *De Agri Cultura*, I, III, VI, VII, X, V, CXLIII, LVI, LVIII, LXXI, XCI, CX, LXXV. Cato and Varro may be read pleasantly, with commentary, in *Roman Farm Management*, By a Virginia Farmer, Macmillan.
P. 259. Martial, III 58, tr. Tucker, *Life in the Roman World*, 172.
P. 261. Mau and Kelsey, *Pompeii*, XLIV.
P. 264. The Carducci Sonnet is translated by Dr. Sewall.
P. 265. Lemmi, *Classical Journal*, XXI (1926), 406.

XXV

ROMAN PORTRAITS

Strachan-Davidson, *Cicero*.
Petersson, *Cicero*.
Fowler, *Caesar*.
Showerman, *Horace and His Influence*.
Frank, *Vergil*.
P. 277. Marcus Aurelius, *Letters*, tr. Haines, *Loeb Classical Library*.
P. 278. Marcus Aurelius, *Meditations*, tr. Long, II 17.

XXVI

THE WORSHIPER

Fowler, *The Religious Experience of the Roman People.*
Showerman, *The Ancient Religions in Universal History*, in *American Journal of Philology*, XXIX (1908), 156.
P. 290. Horace, *Odes*, III 6.
P. 291. Symmachus, *Relationes*, III.
P. 292. Suetonius, *Caesar*, LIX.
P. 294. Horace, *Odes*, III 18, tr. Conington; Horace, *Odes*, III 23, tr. Bonnie Blanche Small; the Sophomore Prize Translation, University of Wisconsin, 1928, unpublished.
P. 296. Lucretius, *Century Readings in Ancient Classical Literature*, 374–384.
P. 298. Livy, V 52.

XXVII

ROMAN HOLIDAYS

Fowler, *Social Life*, X.
Tucker, *Life in the Roman World*, XV.
Fowler, *Roman Festivals*.   Introduction and various months.
P. 304. Virgil, *Georgics*, I 268–272.

XXVIII

THE THEATER

Platner, *Topography and Monuments*, under *Theatrum*.
Fowler and Tucker as in Chapter XXVII.
Johnston, *Private Life*, IX.
Duff, *A Literary History of Rome*, 156–234.
P. 314. Cicero, *Ad Familiares*, VII 1.
P. 315. Horace, *Epistles*, II 1, 184–207.
P. 316. Plutarch, *Cicero*, 5; Cicero, *Ad Familiares*, VII 1; Cicero, *De Senectute*, 48; Quintilian, XI iii, 178–180.
P. 317. Mau and Kelsey, *Pompeii*, XX–XXII.

XXIX

THE RACES

Fowler and Tucker as in Chapter XXVII.
Johnston, *Private Life*, IX.
P. 320. Livy, I 35.
P. 321. Platner, *Topography and Monuments*, under *Circus*.
P. 326. Sophocles, *Electra*, tr. Jebb, 741–756.
P. 328. Horace, *Satires*, I 1, 112–116; Pliny, *Letters*, IX 6.
P. 329. Ammianus Marcellinus, tr. Yonge, XXVIII 4.
P. 331. Ovid, *Amores*, III ii.
P. 332. Ovid, *De Arte Amatoria*; I 133–136, 139–140, 143–152, 159–160.

XXX

THE GLADIATORS

Fowler, *Social Life*, X.
Johnston, *Private Life*, IX.
Tucker, *Life in the Roman World*, XV.
Platner, *Topography and Monuments*, under *Amphitheatrum*.
P. 334. Cicero, *Pro Sestio*, 125.
P. 335. Mau and Kelsey, *Pompeii*, XXIX.
P. 340, l. 7. Seneca, *Moral Epistles*, 70, 23.
P. 347. Cicero, *Ad Familiares*, VII 1.
P. 348. Pliny, *Epistles*, VI 34.

XXXI

THE BATHS

Platner, *Topography and Monuments*, under *Thermae, Balnea*.
Mau and Kelsey, *Pompeii*, XXVI–XXVIII.
P. 357. Horace, *Satires*, I 4, 74–76.
P. 362. Seneca, *Moral Epistles*, 56.
P. 363. *Ibid.*, 86, tr. Gummere, *Loeb Classical Library*.

XXXII

IN LIGHTER VEIN

Platner, *Topography and Monuments*, under *Porticus, Hortus*.
P. 370, l. 6.   Horace, *Satires*, I 8, 14 ; *Odes*, II 3.
Suetonius, *Caesar*, 20, on *acta diurna*.
P. 374.   Horace, *Epistles*, I 1, 59–60.
P. 375.   Cicero, *De Senectute*, 35–36.
P. 377.   Mau and Kelsey, *Pompeii*, LVI.
P. 378.   Cicero, *De Oratore*, II 216–271, 276.
P. 379.   Francis W. Kelsey, *Classical Journal*, III (1907), 3.
P. 379, l. 10.   Cicero, *De Oratore*, II 221.
P. 379, l. 17.   Cicero, *Ad Familiares*, VII 4 ; VII 10.
P. 379, l. 30.   Suetonius, *Vespasian*, 22–23, tr. Rolfe, *Loeb Classical Library*.
P. 380.   Pliny, *Epistles*, I 6.
P. 381.   Showerman, *Horace and His Influence*, 1–68.

XXXIII

SATIRE AND ITS TARGETS

P. 383.   Duff, *A Literary History of Rome*, 234–244, 506–518.
P. 384, l. 26.   Virgil, *Eclogues*, IV ; l. 31.   Horace, *Odes*, III 6.
P. 385.   Horace, *Satires*, I 1, 24 ; II 5.
P. 386, l. 26.   Juvenal, I 28–9.   Juvenal I and III should be read.
P. 388.   Juvenal, VI 461 ff., tr. Ramsay.
P. 390, l. 26.   "The sky he mounts."   Samuel Johnson's *London* has :

> "All sciences a fasting monsieur knows,
> And, bid him go to Hell, to Hell he goes !"

P. 393, l. 8.   "Tenth story" : not in the Latin.

XXXIV

A DINNER WITH THE NEWLY RICH

P. 395, l. 3.   Tacitus, *Annals*, XVI 18.
Petronius, *Satyricon*, tr. Michel Heseltine, *Loeb Classical Library*, 26–27, 31–36, 53, 71–72, 75–79.   The selection is to be found in *Century Readings*.

XXXV

THE CRIMINAL

Hunter, *Roman Law*, 1064–1072 in abstract.

XXXVI

THE ROMAN DEAD

Johnston, *Private Life*, XII.
Tucker, *Life in the Roman World*, XXIII.
Mau and Kelsey, *Pompeii*, XLIX, L.
Platner, *Topography and Monuments*, under *Sepulcra*.
Dictionary of Ethics and Religion, under *Disposal of the Dead*.
P. 424. Suetonius, *Augustus*, 100; Polybius, VI 52–53, tr. Paton, *Loeb Classical Library*.
P. 428. Pliny, *Epistles*, V 16.
P. 430. Horace, *Satires*, I 8, 8–16.

PART IV

GREATER ROME

XXXVII

THE SPREAD OF ROMAN CIVILIZATION

Part I, Chapter IV; Showerman, *Eternal Rome*, VI.
Tucker, *Life in the Roman World*, I–III.
P. 442. Virgil, *Aeneid*, VI 851–853.
P. 449. Claudian, *De Consulatu Stilichonis*, II 136, *De Bello Gothico*, 54; Symmachus, *Orations*, III 9.
P. 451. Showerman, *Eternal Rome*, 190–193.
P. 452. Bryce, *The Roman and the British Empires*.

XXXVIII

THE ARMY

Tucker, *Life in the Roman World*, XVIII.
Graham, *Roman Africa*.
Giles, *The Roman Civilization*.
Rice Holmes, *Caesar's Conquest of Gaul*.
P. 466.   Vegetius, *Epitome Rei Militaris*, I 1.
P. 467.   Polybius, VI 37–39, tr. Paton, *Loeb Classical Library*.

XXXIX

MARE NOSTRUM

The expression *mare nostrum* is used by Caesar in *The Gallic War*,
    VI 1, by Sallust in Jugurtha, 17, and others.   *Mare Nostrum*,
    the novel by Blasco Ibañez, has chapters rich in the portrayal
    of the Mediterranean and its life.
For facts, consult Deecke, *Italy; Encyclopaedia Britannica*.
For history up to close of Third Punic War, Mommsen, I 3–8,
    162–187 ; II 131–202, 523–525.
For Mithridates and the pirates, Mommsen, IV 3–55, 400–452.
P. 479.   Cicero, *Manilian Law*, 32, 54–55, 33.
P. 481.   Horace, *Odes*, IV 5, 19.
P. 483.   For the navy, Smith, *Classical Dictionary*, under *Navis*.

XL

BY LAND AND SEA

Tucker, *Life in the Roman World*, II.
Davis, *The Influence of Wealth in Imperial Rome*, 95–105.
Platner, *Topography and Monuments*, 124–128.
Smith, *Classical Dictionary*.
Johnston, *Private Life*, pp. 278–287.
Charlesworth, *Trade Routes and Commerce of the Roman Empire*.
P. 498.   Florence Lentzner, *Letter Writing in Antiquity as Seen in
    Cicero's Correspondence*, B.A. Thesis, University of Wisconsin,
    1910, unpublished.

P. 501. Horace, *Odes*, III 7 ; Davis, 80–95.

P. 502. Westermann, *On Inland Transportation and Communication in Antiquity, Classical Journal*, XXIV (1929), 483.

XLI

THE ROMAN LAW

Robinson, *Selections from Roman Law, Introduction.*
Mommsen, I Ch. XI; II Ch. VIII.
Hunter, *Roman Law*, 2nd edition.
Buckland, *Textbook of Roman Law.*
Greenidge, *Roman Public Life.*
Davidson, *Problems in Criminal Law.*

XLII

ON THE SOUTHERN BORDER

Bouchier, *Life and Letters in Roman Africa.*
Boissier, *Roman Africa.*
Graham, *Roman Africa.*
Belloc, *Esto Perpetua.*
Grant, *African Shores of the Mediterranean.*
Baedeker, *The Mediterranean.*
The World Almanac.
Byron Khun de Prorok, *Digging for Lost African Gods*, IX.
P. 540. Graham, 165.

XLIII

SPAIN

Bouchier, *Roman Spain.*
Louis C. West, *Imperial Roman Spain — the Objects of Trade.*
Carpenter, *The Greeks in Spain.*
P. 550. Horace, *Odes*, II 6.
P. 551. Strabo, III 3, 5, tr. Hamilton; Velleius Paterculus, III 90, 4.
P. 552. Pliny, *Natural History*, III 30 ; 7.

XLIV

ON THE NORTHERN BORDER

Katharine Allen, *Some Glimpses of the Raetian Limes, Classical Journal*, XI (1915), 95.

Mommsen, *Roman Provinces*, I, 185–211.

Haverfield, *Roman Britain*.

P. 558. Byron, *Childe Harold*, III 55.

P. 562. Tacitus, *Agricola*, 24.

P. 564. Gibbon, I, Ch. I.

P. 570. Katharine Allen, *Some Glimpses of Roman Britain, Classical Journal*, XXIV (1929), 254. *The Roman Wall in England, Ibid.*, VIII 2.

XLV

THE COMING OF CHRISTIANITY

Showerman, *Eternal Rome*, VIII.

Rand, *Founders of the Middle Ages*, I, II.

P. 574. *The Acts of the Apostles*, XXVIII; Tacitus, *Ann.*, XV 44.

P. 575. *The Acts*, VIII 3, IX 1–3; Pliny, *Epistolae ad Traianum*, 96, 97.

P. 582. The translation is by John Addington Symonds, *The Revival of Learning*, 1877, p. 63.

XLVI

ETERNAL ROME

Showerman, *Eternal Rome*, XIII.

INDEX

ABACUS, 93.
Abascantus, 242.
abolla, 59.
absolvo, 188.
Academica, 236.
Acceptor, 328.
Accius, 204, 310, 315.
Achaea, 182, 480, 554.
Achilles, 333.
acolyte, 116, 284.
acrobat, 314, 368, 400.
acta diurna, 370.
Actium, 481, 483.
actors, 316.
—— reputation, 319.
Acts, The, 554.
Aculeo, 268.
Adam and Eve, 576.
Adige, 6.
adlectio, 168.
ad meridiem, 145.
adoption, 67, 91.
Adria, 487.
Adriatic, 7, 9, 47, 104, 499.
adultery, 408, 412.
advocate, disbarment, 412.
advocati, 186.
aediculae, 428.
aedile, at games, 304.
—— and plays, 308.
aedileship, 158.
Aegean Islands, 474.
—— migrants, 545.
Aegusa, 477.
Aelius Paetus, 512.
Aemilian gens, 91.
Aemilianus, 91.
Aemilius Celer, billposter, 336.
—— Lepidus, 490.
—— Papinianus, 513 ff.
—— Paulus, 446.
Aeneas, 67, 218, 534.
—— wounded, 218.
Aeneid, 206, 209, 388, 470, 534.

Aequians, 23.
Aesculapius, 216.
Aesopus, 316.
Afranius, 314, 547.
Africa, 7, 26, 207, 230, 448, 463 f., 474 f.,
    499, 525 ff., 545, 552, 556, 571 ff.,
    586.
—— archaeology, 542.
—— colonies, 527.
—— government, 530 f.
—— and Italians, 531, 536.
—— map, 524.
—— modern spheres, 526.
—— products, 526, 531.
—— Punic, 528 ff.
—— races, 531.
—— Romanization, 528, 542.
—— ruins, 533 ff.
African desert, 557, 561.
africano, 241, 526.
Agamemnon, 395, 404.
agger of Servius, 370.
Agricola in Britain, 562.
Agrippa in Britain, 561.
Agrippa in Spain, 548.
alae, 77, 420.
Alans, 556.
Alaric, 20, 291, 525, 565.
Alauda, 464.
Alban Hills, 258, 263.
—— Mount, 11, 49, 295, 330, 486.
—— Mountains, 14.
albi greges, 264.
album, 185.
Alesia, 4, 460.
Alexander, 25, 80.
—— and Darius, 213.
Algeria, Algiers, 525, 528, 531, 537 f.,
    540.
Algidus, 295.
Alise-Ste. Reine, 461.
Allen, Katharine, 570.
alloying, 412.
All-Souls', 423.

611